Sartre and Adorno

SUNY series in Contemporary Continental Philosophy

Dennis J. Schmidt, editor

Sartre and Adorno

The Dialectics of Subjectivity

David Sherman

State University of New York Press

Published by
State University of New York Press, Albany

Printed in the United States of America

For information, contact State University of New York Press, Albany, NY
www.sunypress.edu

Production by Michael Haggett
Marketing by Fran Keneston

Library of Congress Cataloging-in-Publication Data

Sherman, David
Sartre and Adorno : the dialectics of subjectivity / David Sherman.
p. cm. — (SUNY series in contemporary continental philosophy)
Includes bibliographical references and index.
ISBN-13: 978-0-7914-7115-9 (hardcover : alk. paper)
ISBN-13: 978-0-7914-7116-6 (pbk. : alk. paper)
1. Sartre, Jean-Paul, 1905–1980. 2. Adorno, Theodor W., 1903–1969. 3. Kierkegaard, Søren, 1813–1855. 4. Subjectivity. 5. Dialectic. 6. Phenomenology. I. Title.
B2430.S34S52 2007
142'.7—dc22

2006021545

10 9 8 7 6 5 4 3 2 1

For Nancy

Contents

Acknowledgments

As with any significant undertaking, there are many people whose support, whether intellectual or emotional, warrants an expression of appreciation, and it is my pleasure to discharge this debt here. Earlier drafts of this book were reviewed by Kathy Higgins, Kelly Oliver, Harry Cleaver, and the late Louis Mackey, all of whom I learned from. Most helpful of all, however, have been Bob Solomon and Doug Kellner: both personally and professionally their support has meant a great deal to me. Both colleagues and administrators connected with the philosophy department at the University of Montana have been uniformly supportive of my efforts, and I owe a debt of gratitude to Albert Borgmann, Christa Countryman, Fred McGlynn, Ron Perrin, Jami Sindelar, Deborah Slicer, Dick Walton, and, most of all, to Burke Townsend and Tom Huff. So, too, I would like to express my appreciation to Jane Bunker, my editor at SUNY Press, and Dennis Schmidt, the Editor of the SUNY Series in Contemporary Continental Philosophy.

It is also my pleasure to thank the many supportive members of my family—in particular, my mother and late father, Lenore and Jerrold Sherman; my late grandparents, Helen and Sam Rodney; my uncle and late aunt, Bud and Jane Rodney; my sister, brother-in-law, and niece, Ilene, Rich, and Jeri Patasnik; and two cousins who are more like brothers, Jeff and Jim Rodney, their wives, Michele and Susie, and their children (collectively), A. J., Samantha, Alexandra, Emma, Sophie, and Jacob. Most of all, however, it is my pleasure to thank my wife Nancy, to whom this book is dedicated, for it is her love and support that made it possible in the first place.

Finally, I would like to acknowledge the following journals for kindly permitting me to reprint copyrighted portions of my previously published research:

Chapter 1 contains substantial portions of "Adorno's Kierkegaardian Debt," which was originally published in *Philosophy & Social Criticism*, Vol. 27, No. 1 (Winter 2001), pp. 77–106.

Chapters 4 and 6 contain sizable portions of "Sartre, Critical Theory, and the Paradox of Freedom," which was originally published in *Philosophy Today*, Vol. 50, No. 2 (Summer 2006), pp. 198–212.

Abbreviations Used in the Text and Notes

Theodor W. Adorno

AE *Against Epistemology: A Metacritique: Studies in Husserl and the Phenomenological Antinomies*, tr. Willis Domingo (Oxford: Blackwell Publishers, 1982).

AP *The Authoritarian Personality* (New York: W. W. Norton & Co., 1982).

DOE *Dialectic of Enlightenment* (with Max Horkheimer), tr. John Cumming (New York: Continuum, 1991).

JOA *Jargon of Authenticity*, tr. Knut Tarnowski and Frederic Will (Evanston: Northwestern University Press, 1973).

K *Kierkegaard: Construction of the Aesthetic*, tr. Robert Hullot-Kentor (Minneapolis: University of Minnesota Press, 1989).

MM *Minima Moralia*, tr. E. F. N. Jephcott (London: Verso Books, 1974).

ND *Negative Dialectics*, tr. E. B. Ashton (New York: Continuum Publishing Co., 1992).

Jean-Paul Sartre

AS&J *Anti-Semite and Jew*, tr. George J. Becker (New York: Schocken Books, 1974).

B&N *Being and Nothingness: An Essay in Phenomenological Ontology*, tr. Hazel E. Barnes (New York: Washington Square Press, 1956).

SM *Search for a Method*, tr. Hazel E. Barnes (New York: Random House, 1968).

TE *Transcendence of the Ego*, tr. Forest Williams and Robert Kirkpatrick (New York: Hill and Wang, 1990).

Introduction

Since the late 1960s, during which time various strains of poststructuralism and critical theory's linguistic turn have largely demarcated the field in continental philosophy, there has really been only one point of agreement among the preponderance of continental philosophers—namely, that any philosophical approach beginning with "the subject" is utterly flawed. In *The Philosophical Discourse of Modernity*, for instance, Habermas roundly attacks Heidegger, Bataille, Foucault, and Derrida on a variety of grounds, but not once does he attack their rejection of the subject, which he, too, simply takes for granted. Peter Dews thus rightly declares:

> One of the least noted features of the strife between Habermas and his postmodern opponents over the "philosophical discourse of modernity" is the number of assumptions which both sides share in common, despite the energy of the arguments between them. Habermas and his critics coincide in the view—*ultimately derived from Heidegger*—that the history of philosophy is susceptible to an epochal analysis, and that the era of the philosophy of the subject, which is also the culminating era of metaphysical thinking, is currently drawing to a close. Indeed, it is remarkable that *The Philosophical Discourse of Modernity* gives the celebrated account of the "death of man" in Foucault's *The Order of Things*, viewed as a post-mortem on the monological subject, almost unqualified endorsement.[1]

As early as the 1980s, however, there were indications, albeit not explicitly thematized, that continental philosophy could not purge itself of the subject quite so easily. The third volume of Foucault's series on human sexuality, *The Care of the Self*, raised more than a few eyebrows because of its emphasis on aesthetic self-constitution, which, on the face of it, seems to sharply conflict not only with the "death of man" in *The Order of Things* but also with the conclusions of *The History of Sexuality*, the first volume of the series. It is by no means clear that Foucault's rejection of the "repressive hypothesis" in *The History of Sexuality*—that is, Foucault's rejection of the view that social power relations (however abhorrent their constitution) repress rather than productively constitute the subject—can be reconciled with his later turn toward what certain Foucault scholars call "practical subjectivity."[2] So, too, in "Force of Law," Derrida declares that "it goes without saying" that deconstruction has always been "through and through, at least obliquely [a] discourse on justice," and he then proceeds to ground this discourse by speaking of "freedom," "a sense of responsibility without limits," "an epoche of the rule," and the inexorable but hopelessly opaque nature of "the decision,"[3] all of which are associated with the subject. This is a far cry from Derrida's influential essay, "The Ends of Man," in which such notions are, by all appearances, summarily rejected. Finally, even as he continued to reject "the philosophy of the subject" in its diverse incarnations, Habermas turned to Kierkegaard, whose philosophy is perhaps the epitome of the "monological" subjectivity that Habermas rejects, for the purpose of enlisting his existential recalcitrance in opposition to identity formations engendered by flawed forms of communicative interaction. It would seem, then, that if the subject is only the residuum of a washed out metaphysical tradition, it is nevertheless a residuum in which, at least in some sense, its detractors continue to believe.[4]

For good reason, then, in recent years the question of the subject has been explicitly raised anew. As Slavoj Zizek aptly puts it in the opening sentence of *The Ticklish Subject: The Absent Centre of Political Ontology*, "a specter is haunting Western Academia . . . the spectre of the Cartesian subject."[5] As the book's subtitle appropriately suggests, the subject is an ineliminable component of all political projects, or at least, I would argue, political projects that are motivated by the aim of ameliorating the existing state of affairs for human beings. Without a commitment to efficacious subjects—a commitment whose very possibility is being progressively undermined by a polity that is ever more constructed in the circuits of contemporary "postmodern" capitalist globalization processes—there can be no basis for change, and this only plays into the hands of those groups that most profit from the prevailing order of things. Spurred by this insight, there have been, in addition to Zizek, a number of philosophers who have sought to revivify the notion of the subject, but while philosophically elegant, these various endeavors all share one fatal flaw: they theorize the notion of the subject by presupposing theoretical frameworks that cannot bear the weight of their endeavors.[6] As Dews states, the poststructuralists and Habermas share a view of the subject "ultimately derived from Heidegger," whose philosophy is virtually defined by its antipathy toward the notion of the subject. At the risk of being accused of confusing genesis and validity, I would argue that from such quintessentially antagonistic beginnings, there can be no basis for any project that would seek to revivify the subject.

Zizek's book is itself a case in point. To be sure, as he uncontroversially declares, the aim in returning to the Cartesian subject "is not to return to the *cogito* in the guise in which this notion has dominated thought (the self-transparent thinking subject)," and, at least in some sense, he is also right to say that the aim is rather "to bring to light its forgotten obverse, the excessive, unacknowledged kernel of the *cogito*, which is far from the pacifying image of the transparent Self."[7] For Zizek, whose return to the subject also derives from Heidegger, albeit by way of Lacan, this unacknowledged kernel resides in "the pure negativity of the death drive prior to its reversal into the identification with some new Master-Signifer."[8] But this purely negative death drive, "the excessive moment of madness inherent to the *cogito*" that "stands in for the rational subject," is not as opposed to (subjectless) *Dasein's* wholesale collapse into a profane "being-in-the-world" as Zizek thinks.[9] Hypostatized in its utter difference, the pure negativity of Zizek's vaunted death drive, by virtue of its lack of determinacy, has a tendency to unwittingly manifest itself in terms of the very "reality principle" to which it is supposed to function as a counterpose. As is the case with Heidegger's purportedly individuating insight that we are beings-unto-death, which is at the core of a theory that Kristeva rightly calls a "regressive mythological travesty,"[10] Zizek's variation on the poststructuralist preoccupation with death as wholly "other" ends up perpetuating the very sort of social madness that Zizek would have done with.

Even if there is, in principle, some unrecuperable other—indeed, even if the recognition of the unrecuperability of this other is the condition of the possibility for bringing about a state of affairs in which we might more modestly strive toward a genuine ethical comportment—

we must still try to mediate our relation to what substantively constitutes this unrecuperable other at any point in time lest we do violence to the motivating ethical impulse. It is for this reason that my own philosophical orientation remains largely Hegelian in nature. By rejecting all philosophical foundations, Hegel catapulted both reason and the subject into the movement of history, and thus he did no less to "deconstruct" the overblown subjectivity of Cartesianism than his contemporary critics. On Hegel's dialectical account, in which subject and object interpenetrate one another, the historical movement of reason and subjectivity finally leads to the modest recognition that all thought is context-bound, but that as free, self-determining beings we are the ones who construct the historical context, and, therefore, the categories that mediate our relation to the world. So understood, Hegel's "Absolute Spirit," of which this modest recognition is emblematic, stands in sharp contrast to existing caricatures of it, many of which tend to see it either as an ontologically discrete entity altogether,[11] or, at least, some extraordinary human "macro-subject" that runs roughshod over human beings in a "monological self-positing" that "swallows up everything finite within itself."[12]

Yet, by cryptically talking in terms of "Absolute Spirit," which, I have just suggested, is much more modest for Hegel than the phrase actually implies, Hegel does invite such criticism. Indeed, when Hegel infamously declares in the concluding paragraph of the Preface to the *Phenomenology of Spirit* that with the ascendance of Spirit "the individual must all the more forget himself, as the nature of Science implies and requires,"[13] the criticism certainly seems that much more justified. An essential distinction needs to be made here, however. If there is an overemphasis on Spirit in Hegel's philosophy, it pertains to Spirit as universal (human) subject, not as some ontologically discrete entity. Hegel is more than clear throughout his works that his phenomenological approach deals solely with the realm of human thought and action—indeed, according to its most basic tenets, it could deal with nothing else. But this is not inconsistent with the claim that Hegel gives short shrift to the individual (as opposed to universal) subject. Even if Hegel was just appeasing the censors when he made the *Prussian* state into the highest form of ethical life, it is clear that the political embodiment of Absolute Spirit is the state, and that "this final end has supreme right against the individual, whose supreme duty is to be a member of the state."[14] Thus, although he emphasizes the mediation of universal and particular, Hegel ultimately privileges the universal, and although motivated by the desire to truly reconcile the individual to both himself and his social world, the contrived reconciliation that Hegel feels historically compelled to posit ultimately takes place at the expense of this individual. By failing to carry through his dialectic, which is grounded in the notion of determinate negativity,[15] Hegel fails to give the existing individual subject its due, as both the spirit and letter of his dialectic otherwise requires. In this way, he "actualizes" the merely existing, which is the paradoxical element of truth in what is otherwise the opportunistic Right Hegelian reading of Hegel's famous *Doppelsatz* ("What is rational is actual and what is actual is rational").

Giving the existing individual subject its due does not, of course, augur a return to the transcendental subject, which for philosophers such as Kant, Fichte, and Husserl performs the epistemic task of constituting the world of our experience. The abstract, universal structures that compose this kind of individual subject are as incompatible with the notion of a vibrant individual subject as is Hegel's domineering universal subject. And, of course, even from a strictly epistemological standpoint, such a move would be regressive, for it does not have the merit of Hegel's dialectical rejoinder to classical epistemology. In this sense, I am in agreement with poststructuralists, hermeneuticists, and Habermas-inspired critical theorists. Conversely, the existing individual subject is also not to be collapsed into, or otherwise seen as coterminous with, "the self" (or what Anglo-American philosophers might refer to as the ordinary, common sense concept of "a person"), as many of these continental philosophers are inclined to do. Even Heidegger tried to make sense of authentic *Dasein*, but by virtue of its undialectical relation to the world of everyday social practices, which it awkwardly straddles, such a notion was easy enough for his successors to bury. The postmodern "self," understood as wholly determined by the overarching structures of language or power, is still as "fallen" as Heidegger ambivalently understood inauthentic *Dasein* to be, but now without even so much as an impoverished concept against which the recognition of this phenomenon might arise. To use Zizek's terms, but without confining the claim to "Western academia" and "political ontology," the nature of the present individual's experience of both himself and his world is increasingly becoming the absent center of the sociopolitical world.

In opposition to the various schools of thought that continue to hold sway in continental philosophy, most of which reject what Habermas alternately calls "philosophies of the subject" or "philosophies of consciousness," it is my view that it is a mistake to reduce the standpoint of embodied, intentional consciousness, which obliges us to recognize ourselves as free, efficacious agents in the world, to the sociohistorical standpoint. Although subjectivity is plainly mediated by the existing sociohistorical structures, it also has the capacity to affect these very structures in turn, and therefore the self-identities that they engender. Thus, subjectivity is not just passively mediated, which is how it invariably appears when one's philosophical perspective is limited to the third-person standpoint. Due to the continuing historical existence of the subject—that is, the first-person standpoint, which, by virtue of its historical legacy, continues, however tenuously, to presuppose the freedom of its choices in the face of the political totality—subjectivity is also active or *mediating*. And, ethically speaking, the notion that we are mediating subjects is basic to our self-constitution, both collectively and individually. The notion of a mediating subject conceives of subjectivity formation as the product of a dialectical interplay between the first- and third-person standpoints. In contrast to Kant's philosophy, it does not insulate these standpoints from one another, and, in contrast to Hegel's philosophy, it does not collapse the difference in a higher-order synthesis. In sum, without the corrective of sociohistorical theories, consciousness mistakenly sees human social constructs in ontological terms when it reflects on its experience of the world, and without the idea of an embodied consciousness that freely strives to make the world its own, sociohistorical theories do not come to grips with the normative impulse that almost invariably lies at the heart of the critical stance they adopt. Or, to transfigure Kant's well-known expression, critical social theory without the first-person, phenomenological standpoint is empty, while phenomenology without a third-person, critical social theoretic standpoint is blind.

In this book, I aim to mediate these two standpoints by way of the philosophies of Sartre and Adorno. Although beginning from these conflicting standpoints, Sartre's phenomenology and Adorno's critical theory are both committed to the subject-object paradigm, the dialectical privileging of the individual over the collective (or the particular over the universal), and, indeed, the notion of a mediating subjectivity itself. Moreover, by rejecting the idea of a transcendental subject, Sartre and Adorno were in no small part responsible for bringing about the shift that has taken place since the late 1960s in continental philosophy. After all, it was Sartre who asserted that the self is not in consciousness but is "out in the world," and it was Adorno who cautioned that inherent in the very process by which the self is formed is a regressive moment that tends to propel the self toward absolute self-identity—a self-identity that, by closing itself off to its other, makes itself absolutely coercive of both self and other. In contrast to most current philosophers, however, neither Sartre nor Adorno held that the subject is merely a harmful fiction, and both tenaciously defended the moment of agency inherent in the first-person standpoint. Adorno's claim that we must "use the strength of the subject to break through the fallacy of constitutive subjectivity" equally applies to Sartre's claim that we must break through that ubiquitous form of bad faith in which the subject freezes its self-identity into a thing (ND, p. xx). Finally, although Sartre's philosophy starts from the standpoint of consciousness and Adorno's sociohistorical approach starts from the standpoint of the historical dialectic, both implicitly incorporate not only the opposite standpoint into the very core of their thought but actually build toward that standpoint in their later works. In Sartre's case, this is evidenced in the movement from *Being and Nothingness* through *Search for a Method*, the *Critique of Dialectical Reason*, and, finally, *The Family Idiot* (in which he tries to discern the dialectical movement of the two standpoints within a particular life). And, in Adorno's case, this is evidenced in the movement from his philosophical critiques to *Aesthetic Theory*, in which he seeks to unlock the modern promise of rich individual experience by way of the modern work of art. However, because I am interested in investigating the relation between Sartre's first-person standpoint and Adorno's third-person standpoint, I will not engage the latest works of each, and will remain content with identifying the potential of the later movement within the earlier works.

Accordingly, although Sartre's primary focus is on the freedom of consciousness in his earlier works, he does not take this freedom to be historically unencumbered. Instead, because consciousness is nothing other than the objects of which it is "positionally" aware—that is, it is purely "intentional"—a person's freedom is always-already embedded within a "situation." (It is the "nonpositional" consciousness of this positional consciousness, which Sartre heuristically ascribes to the prereflective cogitio, that provides the latitude for our phenomenological freedom, and thus the grounds for a mediating subject.) The situation not only limits the ways in which a person can act on his phenomenological freedom, but also fundamentally circumscribes the very nature of his selfhood. This characterization of "the situation" comports with the description of Fredric Jameson, who declares: "It would not be doing violence to Sartre's thought, meanwhile, to suggest that for him the situation (in the multidimensional class and psychoanalytic senses that he gave to that term) stood as the infrastructure to which the act of 'free' choice brought a superstructural response and solution."[16] When Sartre speaks of selfhood as being formed within the dynamic interaction between consciousness, other persons, and the natural world, therefore, he is already laying the foundation for his subsequent encounter with history. Indeed, Sartre's early notion of the subject thrusts that subject into history, in which he seeks a world that would furnish a level of practical freedom that does justice to our intrinsic phenomenological freedom, which, for Sartre, can be constrained but never terminated:

> For the idea which I have never ceased to develop is that in the end one is always responsible for what is made of one. Even if one can do nothing else besides assume this responsibility. For I believe that a man can always make something out of what is made of him. This is the limit I would today accord to freedom: the small movement which makes of a totally conditioned social being someone who does not render back completely what his conditioning has given him.[17]

Contrary to Sartre, Adorno refuses to consider the subject in abstraction from its concrete sociohistorical situation. Still, he unremittingly attacks those who would conceive of the free self-determining subject as merely a deceptive notion emanating from the metaphysical tradition. These attacks extend to his own mentor, Walter Benjamin, who, according to Adorno, calls into question not just the "over-inflated subjectivism" of the philosophical tradition, "but rather the notion of a subjective dimension itself," which causes the subject to "evaporate," and turns "man into the stage on which an objective process unfolds."[18] Thus, Adorno's numerous attacks on the "Culture Industry," which pointedly contrast with postmodernism's sweeping celebration of pop culture, are spurred by his belief that contemporary capitalist culture manipulates consciousness for the very purpose of undermining the prospect of what I call a mediating subject, which, for Adorno, shares nothing in common with the overinflated, but critically impotent, subjectivism that the Culture Industry fosters. Indeed, Adorno's "negative dialectic," which, crudely, differs from Hegel's dialectic in that it privileges the particular rather than the universal, is impelled by the desire to open up theoretical spaces for individual experience that is undistorted by prevailing concepts, much as phenomenology tries to do. Adorno thus asserts that consciousness and social history are irreducible elements of subjectivity, and that they mutually constitute one another:

> The antinomy between the determination of the individual and the social responsibility that contradicts this determination is not due to a misuse of concepts. It is a reality, the moral indication that the universal and particular are unreconciled. . . . There is no available model of freedom save one: that consciousness, as it intervenes in the total social constitution, will through that constitution intervene in the complexion of the individual. (ND, pp. 264–265)

As these passages from "The Itinerary of a Thought" and *Negative Dialectics* suggest, although they theorize from different standpoints, Sartre and Adorno share similar underlying notions of the subject. What I propose to do in this book is bring about a dialectical movement between these two standpoints so as to highlight this similarity and enrich both in the process. I shall proceed as follows: In part I, I consider Adorno's critiques of three key influences on Sartre in the existential and phenomenological traditions—namely, Kierkegaard (chapter 1), Heidegger (chapter 2), and Husserl (chapter 3)—who reflect the different ways in which the subject-object paradigm can go astray. According to Adorno, Kierkegaard has a notion of subjectivity in which all meaning devolves onto the subject, thus causing the loss of the world; Heidegger devolves all meaning onto the being of the world, thus causing the loss of the subject; and, finally, Husserl seeks to preserve both the subject and the world, but in an unmediated way. Ultimately, Adorno contends, because Husserl seeks to preserve the integrity of both subject and object (although statically), his thought is the high point of the phenomenological and existential traditions.

Because Sartre seeks to preserve the integrity of both subject and object in an existential framework, it is my view that it is his thought that is the high point of the phenomenological and existential traditions, and this is what I try to show in two of the three chapters that constitute part II, which deals with subjectivity in Sartre's early philosophy. Thus, in the initial chapter of this part (chapter 4), I consider Critical Theory's rather attenuated response to Sartre's thought. After looking at Adorno's brief comments on Sartre's notion of freedom, I consider Marcuse's "Existentialism: Remarks on Jean-Paul Sartre's *L'Être et le néant*," which was Critical Theory's most detailed response to Sartre. While sympathetic to some criticisms, I disagree with the basic one, which is that Sartre's emphasis on the ineluctability of freedom is an ugly parody of human beings in an unfree world, for the very concept of human liberation presupposes a free agent. In the following chapter (chapter 5), I deepen my analysis of the ways in which Sartre differs from his phenomenological and existential predecessors, emphasizing the mediated relation between subject and object in his thought. Moreover, I try to show how poststructuralists have seized on certain aspects of Sartre's philosophy, but that in attempting to go past it by rejecting the subject outright, they regress to pre-Sartrean thought, and thus fall prey to the antinomies that plague the philosophies of Kierkegaard, Heidegger, and Husserl. Finally, in the last chapter of part II (chapter 6), I amplify Sartre's notion of a mediating subject by considering such Sartrean staples as freedom, the situation, being-for-others, and the fundamental project. This chapter ends by pointing to the need to augment Sartre's phenomenological approach with a sociohistorical one.

This leads into part III, which considers Adorno's dialectic of subjectivity from diverse perspectives. In the initial chapter (chapter 7), I look at Adorno's notion of the subject in terms of both its formation and deformation. Focusing mostly on *Dialectic of Enlightenment*, I argue that Adorno's take on the enlightenment subject is not as incriminating as some poststructuralists contend, and that Habermas's contention that Adorno wholly abandons enlightenment rationality is wrong—in fact, Habermas himself falls prey to the very dialectic of enlightenment he rejects. I then compare Adorno's analysis of anti-Semitism with Sartre's *Anti-Semite and Jew*, seeking to support the claim in *The Authoritarian Personality* that there are "remarkable similarities" in their depictions of this deformed subject, and I end the chapter by probing Adorno's (qualified) appropriation of Freud's ego theory. In the final chapter (chapter 8), I investigate Adorno's own juxtaposition of the first-person and third-person standpoints, which occurs in his analysis of the freedom (Kant) and history (Hegel) models in *Negative Dialectics*. I then wrap up by examining Adorno's model of "negative dialectics," which, I shall argue, presupposes a subject that can have the sorts of qualitative individual experiences that resonate with Sartre's early brand of phenomenology.

PART I

Adorno's Relation to the Existential and Phenomenological Traditions

Adorno's engagement with the existential and phenomenological traditions was deep and long running. From his 1924 doctoral dissertation ("The Transcendence of the Material and Noematic in Husserl's Phenomenology") and 1931 *Habilitationsschrift* ("The Construction of the Aesthetic in Kierkegaard") through two major works published in the mid-1960s, *Jargon of Authenticity* and *Negative Dialectics* (which deal, in whole and part, respectively, with Heidegger), Adorno's criticisms of these intertwined traditions were as unremitting as they were trenchant. Unlike the so-called orthodox Marxists, who offhandedly dismissed existentialism and phenomenology as bourgeois ideology, however, Adorno was not unsympathetic to the concerns that motivated these philosophical movements. Kierkegaard's desire to preserve the integrity of the individual in the face of Hegel's *Geist*, Husserl's attempt to get back to "the things themselves," and Heidegger's opposition to scientism all resonated with Adorno's own philosophical agenda. Like Adorno himself, all three, in their distinctive ways, tried to break with idealism's penchant for crafting systems in which the concept of a constituting metasubject (either transcendental or historical) dominates human beings and the objects of their experience.[1] Where Adorno does part company with these philosophers, however, is on the question of method, for he believes that each one, by virtue of an undialectical approach that privileges some "first," inadvertently ends up "deconstructing" his philosophy from within:

> Of those modern philosophies in which the self-imprisoned consciousness of idealism is aware of its own imprisonment and attempts to escape from immanence, each develops an exclusive category, an undeviating intention, a distinguishing trait that, under the rule of totality acknowledged by all these philosophies, is intended to mollify the imprisonment. Ultimately, however, this category dissolves the idealist construction itself, which then disintegrates into its antinomies. (K, p. 106)

In this complicated passage, Adorno is actually referring to two types of idealism—one type, made up of "those modern philosophies" that, through the use of an "exclusive category," seek to "escape from immanence" (or, at least, "mollify their imprisonment"), and the other type, the idealism from which these modern philosophies are trying to "escape" (or, at least, whose imprisonment they are trying to "mollify"), but whose "rule of totality" each one endorses all the same. The second type of idealism is Hegel's, while the first type, comprised of "those modern philosophies," includes Kierkegaard's existentialism, Heidegger's fundamental ontology, and Husserl's phenomenology. It is Adorno's view that by trying to break out of Hegel's totalizing system with the use of an exclusive category, which by its very nature is unmediated (and dimly is expected to accomplish the hard work of transcendence precisely because it is unmediated), the modern philosophy that engenders this exclusive category cannot reconcile it with its socially mediated remainder, and thus the philosophy collapses of its own weight: it "dissolves" and then "disintegrates into its antinomies." Finally, contributing its own normative gloss, the philosophy tends to reproduce the very state of affairs that it was bent on superseding. Why is this so?

As an initial matter, because it is designed to act as a first principle or Archimedean point that grounds transcendence, an exclusive category abstracts from the sociohistorical conditions that are the impetus for its formulation, and therefore the philosophy of which it is a central part is, notwithstanding its own self-understanding, no less an "idealist construction" than the idealist construction (Hegel's) that it seeks to supplant. More importantly, however, by abstracting from the existing sociohistorical context, this exclusive category, which purports to surmount the drive for identity (i.e., "the rule of totality") that exists in Hegel's idealism, ultimately reveals itself as an "identity theory" that is far more troubling. In sharp contrast to Hegel's dialectics, in which the subject's drive to conceptually identify the object once and for all occurs within the context of an evolving subject-object relation that is not predicated on transcendental first principles, an exclusive category is ultimately an undialectical positing of transcendence that circumvents the "negative" labor which drives Hegel's dialectic. And by striving for indeterminate truths beyond the profane mediations of the dialectic, this self-identical first principle unavoidably—although unwittingly—makes itself determinate by importing the empirical stuff of its own sociohistorical context. In this way, the profane existence from which the exclusive category seeks to extricate the philosophy uncritically becomes a part of the philosophy itself. Ironically, then, philosophers such as Kierkegaard, Heidegger, and Husserl, who use their first principles to pursue existential or epistemological truths that transcend the mere existing,[2] not only end up replicating idealism's drive toward identity at the very point at which they are intent on facilitating a break with it, but fall behind Hegel's idealism in the process:

> Hegel, the most extreme exponent of the idea of totality and to all appearances anything but a critic of idealism, developed a dialectical process that employed the claim to totality so dynamically that particular phenomena never result from the systematic subordinating concept; instead the system—from which reality truly results—is to be synonymous with the quintessence of fulfilled actuality. (K, p. 106)

To avoid the antinomies that arise from using an "exclusive category" (i.e., "systematic subordinating concept"), which breaks off the subject-object dialectic and therefore leads to the assortment of false reconciliations that are the hallmark of what Adorno calls "identity thinking," one must work through Hegel's "idealist construction," and it is for this reason that Adorno largely conforms to Hegel's dialectical method, while simultaneously rejecting his assumption of an ultimate reconciliation. This is not to say, however, that Adorno believes that we should stop trying to reconcile subject and object (or universal and particular).[3] Although our concepts can never be up to the task of "identifying" objects once and for all, even (indeed, especially) if they were the product of a just society, since subject and object are truly nonidentical, breaking off the subject-object dialectic in recognition of this fact would only hypostatize the terms in their present difference (i.e., as they differ in the present sociohistorical context). This would lead to the same sort of "identity" problem that results from false reconciliations, and would be no less troubling in its practical implications.[4] Thus, Adorno thinks that subject and object must be kept in a dialectical tension, a dialectical tension from which Kierkegaard, Husserl, and Heidegger all philosophically flee.

In the three chapters that constitute part I, I shall critically recapitulate Adorno's analyses of Kierkegaard, Heidegger, and Husserl in order to show that, notwithstanding their relentless nature, there are underlying concerns that link Adorno with each of these philosophers. I shall break with a chronological approach by considering Husserl last because Adorno took Husserl's thought to be the high point of bourgeois idealism: "Husserl purified idealism from every excess of speculation and brought it up to the standard of the highest reality within its reach. But he didn't burst it open."[5] More to the point, I shall begin this work with Adorno's critique of these philosophers in the existential and phenomenological traditions in order to begin to lay the basis for my claim that Sartre's brand of phenomenological existentialism is a necessary complement to Adorno's thought.[6] Unlike his predecessors in the tradition, Sartre's philosophy is inherently dialectical, which means that he can engage the concrete phenomena of everyday existence in a way that does not violate Adorno's methodological strictures. Indeed, Sartre's *Transcendence of the Ego*, which will be considered in part II, is, in some sense, Adorno's "burst[ing] open" of Husserl's transcendental idealism.

1

Adorno and Kierkegaard

Kierkegaard: Construction of the Aesthetic, first published in 1933,[1] is a modified version of Adorno's *Habilitationsschrift*, which had been written a few years earlier. The book, which is critical of Kierkegaard, was at odds with the sentiment of the time, for Kierkegaard's thought was experiencing a renaissance in Germany due to the writings of Tillich, Barth, Jaspers, and Heidegger. Yet, as Susan Buck-Morss states, although he was nominally attacking Kierkegaard, Adorno actually had his sights on the entire existential tradition, and, at least with respect to Heidegger, who was his secondary target, Kierkegaard compared rather favorably:[2] "Heidegger 'falls behind' Kierkegaard, by Adorno's criteria, since the latter's critical perception of social reality led him at least to pose the ontological question negatively."[3] Going one step further, I would argue that a good deal of Adorno's hostility toward existentialism arises from his distaste for its particular German manifestation, and that his "negative dialectics, [which] kept alive an insistence on undefined experience," has strong affinities with many elements of Kierkegaard's "negative" existential philosophy.[4]

After first examining *Kierkegaard*, which anticipates a good deal of Adorno's later work, I shall try to show that Buck-Morss actually tends to understate the allure that Kierkegaard holds for Adorno. Although Adorno uses Hegel's dialectic to expose the ways in which Kierkegaard's thought collapses into the kind of idealism that it purports to leave behind by rejecting Hegel, he is also extremely sympathetic to

Kierkegaard's attack on Hegel's "identity thinking." Of course, for Adorno, Kierkegaard's ultimately undialectical approach backfires, which leaves him open to attack on the precise grounds that he attacks Hegel: Kierkegaard, despite his intentions, makes individual existence abstract. Still, confronted with what he refers to as the "totally administered society," whose levelling drive progressively extirpates individual subjectivity, Adorno embraces certain aspects of Kierkegaard's philosophy, as well as a number of Kierkegaard's techniques for reviving individual subjectivity in mass society—albeit, of course, in a dialectical framework that is more mediative and materialistic.

ADORNO'S CRITIQUE OF KIERKEGAARD

After beginning *Kierkegaard: Construction of the Aesthetic* with a crucial discussion of the need to avoid interpreting philosophy as poetry, which "tear[s] philosophy away from the standard of the real," and thus "deprives it of the possibility of adequate criticism" (K, p. 3),[5] Adorno points out that Kierkegaard equivocates with respect to his own status. Although usually adopting the poet's stance of "speaking without authority," and often stating, in various ways, that he is "a kind of poet," Kierkegaard also sees himself as a philosopher, maintaining in *Fear and Trembling*, for example, that "I am no poet and I go at things only dialectically."[6] Still, certain distinctive attributes of poetry do resonate within Kierkegaard's philosophy, and nowhere is this phenomenon in greater evidence than in his exposition of "the aesthetic," which, in addition to art and art theory, can refer to immediacy, or subjective communication. In all three of these cases, however, Kierkegaard "was not involved with giving form to the contents of experience," which, for Adorno, is the hallmark of aesthetics, "but [merely] with the reflection of the aesthetic process and of the artistic individual himself" (K, p. 8). This leads to what will be the essence of Adorno's attack: "He who as a philosopher steadfastly challenged the identity of thought and being, casually lets existence be governed by thought in the aesthetic object" (K, p. 6). Thus, in response to Kierkegaard's brand of dialectics, in which both the concrete subject and the concrete object are lost, Adorno contends that to understand Kierkegaard philosophically rather than poetically (as Kierkegaard himself demands), we must pierce his poetic pseudonyms, those "altogether abstract representational figures" through whom he presents his philosophy, which is only in keeping with his own requirements: "Kierkegaard the person cannot simply be banished from his work in the style of an objective philosophy, which Kierkegaard unrelentingly, and not without good cause, fought" (K, p. 13).

The intangibility of Kierkegaard's pseudonymous authors is symptomatic of his deeper perspective on the nature of subjectivity itself, which, Adorno states, can be correctly interpreted only by considering the relation between the flesh-and-blood Kierkegaard and the sociohistorical conditions in which he lived, and from which he was largely estranged. As an early nineteenth-century *rentier* involved in neither economic production nor capital accumulation, Kierkegaard lived off a fixed sum of invested money, and was thus highly subject to the market fluctuations of his age (such as the economic downturn caused by the worker revolts of 1848). He was a member of a declining economic class, and, as such, was externally powerless. Under these circumstances, his philosophy "adapts":

> In Kierkegaard the "I" is thrown back on itself by the superior power of otherness. He is not a philosopher of identity; nor does he recognize any positive being that transcends consciousness. The world of things is for him neither part of the subject nor independent of it. Rather, this world is omitted. It supplies the subject with the mere "occasion" for the deed, with mere resistance to the act of faith. In itself, this world remains random and totally indeterminate. (K, p. 29)[7]

As evidenced by the "immanent dialectic" that he proffers within the framework of his explication of the three "spheres of existence," Kierkegaard purports to operate in a dialectical way. Yet, this estrangement from the world leads him to take undialectical stances on the internal relations between subject and object, internal and external history, and history and nature. As to the subject-object relation, Adorno tells us:

> What Kierkegaard describes as "being quit with everything fundamental to human existence" was called, in the philosophical language of his age, the alienation of subject and object. Any critical interpretation of Kierkegaard must take this alienation as

> its starting point. Not that such interpretation would want to conceive the structure of existence as one of "subject" and "object" within the framework of an ontological "project." The categories of subject and object originate historically. . . . If subject and object are historical concepts, they constitute at the same time the concrete conditions of Kierkegaard's description of human existence. This description conceals an antinomy in his thought that becomes evident in the subject-object relation, to which "being quit" may be traced. This is an antinomy in the conception of the relation to ontological "meaning." Kierkegaard conceives of such meaning, contradictorily, as radically devolved upon the "I," as purely immanent to the subject and, at the same time, as renounced and unreachable transcendence.—Free, active subjectivity is for Kierkegaard the bearer of all reality. (K, p. 27)

By breaking off the subject-object dialectic, Kierkegaard hopes to open up spaces within which, come what may, one's personal "meaning" can be preserved. (Indeed, one's personal meaning does not even have to be "positive," as is the case with Kierkegaard's negative theology.) But this tactic—namely, the attempt to protectively isolate subjectivity by casting out everything that is not subjectivity—is fundamentally misguided: "The harder subjectivity rebounds back into itself from the heteronomous, indeterminate, or simply mean world, the more clearly the external world expresses itself, mediatedly, in subjectivity" (K, p. 38). When internalized, therefore, the melancholy that is engendered by an alienated existence becomes an "existential condition." Kierkegaard's melancholy "does not mourn vanished happiness. It knows that it is unreachable" (K, p. 126).

Just as Kierkegaard aims to exclude the external world from subjectivity, he aims to exclude external history from one's "personal" history, which is marked totally by interiority. Nevertheless, external history again comes crashing through the perimeter. Language, ostensibly the form of the communication of pure subjectivity, is itself sedimented by the historical dialectic that Kierkegaard refuses to recognize, and, therefore, drags external history's meanings into the core of inwardness (K, pp. 34–35), thus leading Kierkegaard all the more to fall prey to the objective historical situation that he would just as soon escape. For Adorno, Kierkegaard's objectless "I" and its immanent history is spatiotemporally symbolized by the historical image of the *intérieur* of Kierkegaard's childhood apartment. Drawing on Kierkegaard's own works, Adorno recounts how father and son would stroll within the parlor, all the while pretending that they were passing exciting places. In this way, the external world is subordinated to the *intérieur*, but the very nature of existence in the *intérieur* is simultaneously delimited by the unseen world. (The only semblance of the external world that manages to work its way into the *intérieur* does so through the hall mirror, and what is reflected—the endless row of apartment buildings off which the *rentier* makes his living—is the very historical situation that imprisons its inhabitants.) The *intérieur* is thus analogous to the role of subjectivity in Kierkegaard's philosophy.

Finally, in characterizing the Kierkegaardian *intérieur*, which contains images of the sea, flowers, and other things from nature, Adorno maintains that Kierkegaard fails to differentiate history and nature. In attempting to hold onto a world that has already effectively receded into the past, the *intérieur*, which is designed to preserve that past, would make of it something that transcends the merely historical. It would make this bygone period into something eternal and natural—in other words, into a thing of unchanging nature. In the apartment, then, eternity and history merge together: "In semblance . . . the historical world presents itself as nature" (K, p. 44). Of course, this consolidation of history and nature in the *intérieur* is a counterfeit one, and the artificial representations of nature are symbolic of Kierkegaard's desire to dominate nature, which, according to Adorno, all but precludes an existentially meaningful reconciliation.

Adorno goes on to explicate this relation between history and nature in the penultimate section of the book ("Reason and Sacrifice") in a manner that clearly anticipates the themes of *Dialectic of Enlightenment*.[8] Accordingly, he states that objectless, self-identical consciousness, which is Kierkegaard's "exclusive category" for breaking out of systematic idealism, is actually "the archimedian point of systematic idealism itself: the prerogative of thought, as its own law, to found reality" (K, p. 107). But, paradoxically, while conciousness is posited as an empirically pure foundation on which self-liberation hinges, its sacrifice is ultimately the price of ontological reconciliation, for a meaningful personal existence demands a spiritually inspired leap of faith that requires consciousness to disavow itself in the process of submitting to God. Adorno thus asserts:

> The category that dialectically unfolds here is that of paradoxical sacrifice. Nowhere is the prerogative of consciousness pushed further, nowhere more completely denied, than in the sacrifice of consciousness as the fulfillment of ontological reconciliation. With a truly Pascalian expanse, Kierkegaard's dialectic swings between the negation of consciousness and its unchallenged authority. . . . The category of sacrifice, by means of which the system transcends itself, at the same time and fully contrary to expectation, holds Kierkegaard's philosophy systematically together as its encompassing unity through the sacrificial abstraction of all encountered phenomena. (K, p. 107)

Kierkegaard's trumpeting of consciousness sacrificing itself in order to achieve reconciliation is mythical in character, as is the broader project of idealism itself, because the commitment to reconciliation cannot be immanently fulfilled. By placing nature out of bounds in favor of a spiritual comportment, Kierkegaard's brand of idealism more firmly entangles itself in the very nature that it attempts to escape: "By annihilating nature, hope enters the vicious circle of nature; originating in nature itself, hope is only able to truly overcome it by maintaining the trace of nature" (K, pp. 109–110).

According to Adorno, then, much like his nemesis Hegel, Kierkegaard relies on reason to bring about a mythic reconciliation. But in contrast to Hegel's use of reason, which "produces actuality out of itself" to bring about "universal sovereignty," Kierkegaard's use of reason, which results in "the negation of all finite knowledge," suggests "universal annihilation" (K, p. 119). Adorno contends that the mythic quality of these philosophers arises from a depreciation of aesthetic considerations, and, furthermore, that it is only by returning to "the aesthetic" as a methodological principle that the concrete social reality that is the driving force behind these conflicting philosophies can be revealed. These would seem to be the two impulses that hang behind Adorno's phrase "construction of the aesthetic," which is the book's subtitle, as well as the name of its final chapter.[9]

At the outset of Adorno's book, we saw that while Kierkegaard equivocates with respect to "the aesthetic," every one of its articulations failed to make contact with the concrete contents of experience. To the extent that the aesthetic deals with the nonspiritual—that is to say, the object, sensuous matter, or nature—Kierkegaard depreciates it. (While referring to the later Kierkegaard's aversion to art, Adorno states: "His antipathy for art expresses the longing for an imageless presence . . . an imageless self-presentation of truth" [K, p. 136]). The Kierkegaardian aesthetic is thus wholly rarefied—devoid of a trace of nature. But by virtue of this denial of nature, as we saw, Kierkegaard's thought becomes blindly entangled within it. Adorno asserts, to the contrary, that the aesthetic "sphere of existence," which is the first step in Kierkegaard's "existential dialectic" (and before both religion and philosophy in Hegel's dialectic), is where the greatest truth lies: "Where his philosophy, in the self-consciousness of its mythical semblance, encounters aesthetic characteristics, it comes closest to reality" (K, p. 66). According to Adorno, there can be no impetus for reconciling with reality without first coming to grips with both history and nature, which dialectically "interweave" but can be neither reduced nor sublated.[10] Kierkegaard, however, simply avoids the dialectical problem altogether by fleeing both.

Adorno's "construction of the aesthetic" also reveals his Benjamin-inspired methodology. According to Adorno, for whom, roughly speaking, "the aesthetic" pertains to the "object" side of the subject-object dialectic, "the category of the aesthetic is, in contrast to the position of [Kierkegaard's] aesthete, one of knowledge" (K, p. 14). And in *Kierkegaard*, which employs the same method that he delineated in "The Actuality of Philosophy," Adorno indicates how such knowledge is to be acquired. In "The Actuality of Philosophy," Adorno had maintained that "philosophy is interpretation,"[11] and that philosophical interpretation involves a process akin to "riddle-solving":

> Authentic philosophic interpretation does not meet up with a fixed meaning which already lies behind the question, but lights it up suddenly and momentarily, and consumes it at the same time. Just as riddle-solving is constituted, in that the singular and dispersed elements of the question are brought into various groupings long enough for them to close together in a figure out of which the solution springs forth, while the question disappears—so philosophy has to bring its elements . . . into changing trial combinations [constellations], until they fall into a figure which can be read as an answer.[12]

In *Kierkegaard*, Adorno arranges the miscellaneous elements of Kierkegaard's *ouevre* into a constellation of images that metaphorically illuminates the historical truth that was the impulse for his philosophy. As previously discussed, from the petrified reproductions of nature to the threatening social reality reflected in the hallway mirror, it was the image of Kierkegaard's childhood apartment, the bourgeois *intérieur*, that symbolized Kierkegaard's philosophy of inwardness. And while Kierkegaard could no more escape the reality from which he sought refuge in "inwardness" than in his childhood apartment, the attempt itself, Adorno states, reflects the social truth of his time (i.e., the increasingly perilous fate of "the individual" in industrial society). For Adorno, the appropriate response to this levelling reality is to move toward "the aesthetic," not away from it, as Kierkegaard does. This means adopting a dialectically informed materialist aesthetics that might induce the recognition that, historically, both external and internal nature had been sacrificed in the name of self-preservation, but that the perpetuation of this sacrifice had outlasted any of the objective demands that might have precipitated it.

Yet, in moving away from Hegel's dialectically informed idealistic aesthetics toward what he mistakenly takes to be a "materialist" aesthetics based on "sense perception" (in which "the aesthetic in a man is that by which he immediately is what he is"[13]), Kierkegaard falls into the very idealism that he sought to escape. According to Adorno, this is invariably the result when the dualism of form and content is rigidly maintained, as is the case with Kierkegaard, who attempts to master the breach with the primacy of a subjectively engendered form that "cancels the specific substance of the contents" while simultaneously purporting to give the contents their due: "Through selection, subjectivity becomes the dominant factor by its prerogative over the material, and those contents are omitted that would challenge the rule" (K, p. 18). By managing "the material" in such a way as to exclude the treatment of social experience, Adorno contends, Kierkegaard falls behind Hegel, who mediates the relation between form and content (as well as subject and object, external history and personal history, and history and nature), but veers into idealism by producing the entire process—which from the contrived standpoint of the Absolute is "meaningful" and "rational" throughout—out of his own thought determinations. Thus, although Hegel precipitously brings this concrete dialectical process to completion, Kierkegaard, by stripping "meaning" from existence, never even embarks on it—that is, he fails to attain historical concretion in the first place, a failure that sets a precedent the German existentialists of the twentieth century would emulate.

Accordingly, as was indicated at the start of this chapter, Adorno's attack on Kierkegaard also implicitly functions as an attack on Heidegger. In concluding this review of *Kierkegaard: Construction of the Aesthetic*, therefore, I shall briefly examine Adorno's analysis of the relation between Kierkegaard and Heidegger, which is cursorily set forth in section four ("The Concept of Existence") of the book. Because it is my view that the grounds for seeking a *rapprochement* between Adorno and Kierkegaard are more ample, not to mention more productive, than for seeking one between Adorno and Heidegger, which, nonetheless, has been the far more dominant trend, it is necessary to clarify the basic differences, as Adorno sees them, between Kierkegaard and Heidegger.

According to Adorno, Heidegger erroneously reads the question of the "meaning of existence" out of Kierkegaard because, for Kierkegaard, "existence" is not to be seen as some "manner of being"; rather, the question for Kierkegaard is what gives existence meaning. In other words, unlike Heidegger's "fundamental ontology," which holds that there is a meaning to which existence must correspond, the meaning that Kierkegaard would find is generated entirely out of the domain of existence itself. Without a contribution from the subject, existence itself is meaningless. Consequently, Kierkegaard would have found Heidegger's fundamental ontology as intolerable as Hegel's system, for it fosters the kind of objectifying attitude toward existence that Kierkegaard so thoroughly denounced.

> [Kierkegaard] critiques not only the scientific comprehension of the objective world, but equally the "objectifying" interpretation of subjectivity and, therefore, a priori, the possibility of an "existential analytic of existence." Fichte's "I am I" and Hegel's "subject-object" are for Kierkegaard hypostatizations under the sign of identity and are rejected precisely to the extent that they set up a pure being of existence in opposition to the existing "particular individual." . . . Because the existing takes the place of existence, ontology is removed from existence the more that the question of the existing is directed toward the existing particular person. Individual existence is for Kierkegaard the arena of ontology only

> because it itself is not ontological. Hence the existence of the person is for Kierkegaard a process that mocks any objectivation. (K, pp. 70–71)

More broadly, as this passage suggests, what ultimately differentiates Kierkegaard and Heidegger is that Kierkegaard is a philosopher of nonidentity, while Heidegger is a philosopher of identity. Because, for Kierkegaard, there is no transcendent meaning that is at a distance from the individual's interpetation of his own particular existence, and because the move toward his "ultimate sphere of existence," the religious sphere, necessitates a "leap of faith" into "absolute difference," Kierkegaard's thought is negative. (Conversely, Heidegger's ontology, despite the so-called ontological difference, is positive, as I shall discuss in the next chapter.) Of course, given its objectless inwardness, Kierkegaard's "infinitely negative" subject arguably becomes something positive due to its indeterminate nature, which would suggest that, like Heidegger, Kierkegaard's thought ultimately collapses into an identity theory. Still, due to Kierkegaard's refusal to equate the attainment of what he would deem a truly Christian comportment with a state of reconciliation in either a spiritual or secular sense, it seems to me that he fundamentally remains, like Adorno, a philosopher of nonidentity and negativity. Like Adorno, Kierkegaard longs for a reconciliation that cannot be spoken and is a keen critic of mass society who seeks to revivify individual subjectivity within it.

ADORNO'S KIERKEGAARDIAN DEBT

Given Kierkegaard's unremitting attacks on the pretensions of Hegelian reason, with its supposed ability to sublate "otherness," his embrace of irony, and his use of pseudonyms (which presages the idea of a decentered subject), deconstructionists frequently take Kierkegaard to be a harbinger of many of their own positions.[14] And, in certain respects, they might be right. Still, the "Kierkegaard as proto-deconstructionist" line can be pushed too strongly, for every one of the aforementioned theoretical commitments is in the service of that which deconstruction cannot abide, namely, an efficacious subject who is far more than just a function of language. Indeed, although it goes without saying that deconstruction is heavily influenced by Heidegger's thought, what it disagrees with most in it is Heidegger's idea of existential authenticity, which is the very point at which he draws most heavily on Kierkegaard.

Given Habermas's rejection of every "philosophy of the subject," which is a position that he shares with deconstructionists, it is ironic that it is exactly Kierkegaard's defense of individual subjectivity that prompts him to assert that elements of Kierkegaard's thought are indispensable to his own enterprise, which is based on the idea of "communicative rationality."[15] But while the appeal that Kierkegaard holds for Habermas is, in some sense, understandable—in the absence of robust personal subjectivities the uncoerced consensus of Habermas's "ideal speech community" rings a bit hollow—it is hard to conclude that Habermas's attempt to incorporate Kierkegaard into his own project is anything but misconceived. If, as Kierkegaard contends, only subjective thought can be meaningfully communicated, and then just "indirectly" so as to only provide an occasion for the listener to come to his own subjective truth, how can meaningful intersubjective agreement be reached within the rationalistic confines of Habermas's ideal speech community? Such agreement smacks of the very objectivity that renders "direct" communication superfluous. That is to say, if intersubjective agreement can be reached, then both the speaker and the listener were already in possession of the truth, which is the case with what Kierkegaard describes as that unmeaningful "objective thinking [that] is indifferent to the thinking subject and his existence."[16] Under these conditions, however, the very notion of subjective truth goes by the wayside, and therefore so does the robust individualism with which Habermas would energize his system. Consequently, to fit within Habermas's architectonic, Kierkegaard's thought would have to be domesticated to the point that it would fail to meet the very needs for which it was imported.

Unlike deconstructionists and Habermas, Adorno never explicitly sought to connect with Kierkegaard's philosophy, and his basic criticisms in *Kierkegaard: Construction of the Aesthetic* were never explicitly renounced. Still, a comparison of the works of Kierkegaard and Adorno suggests that various Kierkegaardian themes were assimilated by Adorno—albeit, of course, in a considerably different framework. This was not by accident. As a very young man, Adorno was engrossed in Kierkegaard's thought,[17] and it might well be the case that as Adorno increasingly came to focus on the fate of the individual in "the totally administered society," his earlier work on Kierkegaard came to be increasingly salient.

Along these lines, it should be recognized that *Kierkegaard* was unlike most of Adorno's other works in that it was written before Hitler seized power in Germany. And although, in one sense, Adorno's work was relatively unified over his lifetime—one cannot clearly distinguish between an early and a late period in his works as is often the case with other philosophers—it is, in another sense, undoubtedly the case that his war experiences led him to stress different aspects of his thought. In *Kierkegaard*, Adorno attacks Kierkegaard for breaking off the subject-object dialectic by positing an "abstract self" whose "abstractness is the counterpole to the abstractness of the universal" (K, p. 75)—in other words, his attack on Kierkegaard's "abstract self" comes from the viewpoint of the universal, which dialectically shapes the individual's existence. But, during the war years, when it became increasingly clear that "the abstract universal" (namely, advanced capitalist society, both in its fascist and liberal forms) was tending to wholly assimilate individuality with its homogenizing impulse, Adorno turns his attention toward the individual's viewpoint so as to revivify his subjectivity—albeit, of course, without sacrificing his earlier criticisms of abstract subjectivity, which are the flip-side of the dialectical coin. "World history is for Hegel what the individual is for Kierkegaard" (K, p. 74), and in *Dialectic of Enlightenment* and *Minima Moralia*, which were written around the time of the war, Adorno no longer feels compelled to show that the individual cannot escape world history. To the contrary, he seeks to expose world history so that he might at least open up spaces for critical thought to think against it. Accordingly, during this time period, Adorno also advances a more favorable analysis of Kierkegaard in "On Kierkegaard's Doctrine of Love," which will briefly be considered below.

In the opening paragraphs of *Minima Moralia*, for instance, Adorno declares that Hegel ultimately denies his own thought by failing to carry through the dialectic, and that this failure, which arises from his system's claim to totality, leads him to give short shrift to the individual:

> The dismissive gesture which Hegel, in contradiction to his own insight, constantly accords the individual, derives paradoxically enough from his entanglement in liberal thinking.

> The conception of a totality harmonious through all its contradictions compels him to assign to individuation, however much he may designate it as a driving moment in the process, an inferior status in the construction of the whole. The knowledge that in pre-history the objective tendency asserts itself over the heads of human beings, indeed by annihilating individual qualities, without the reconciliation of general and particular—constructed in thought—ever yet being accomplished in history, is distorted in Hegel: with serene indifference he opts once again for the liquidation of the particular. . . . The individual as such he for the most part considers, naively, as an irreducible datum—just what in his theory of knowledge he decomposes. (MM, pp. 16–17)

Although Hegel's "method schooled that of *Minima Moralia*" (MM, p. 16), his "large historical categories" not only reflect history's "objective tendency" to destroy individuality but also help facilitate the process, and are thus "no longer above suspicion of fraud" (MM, p. 17). Therefore, Adorno states, it may have become necessary for resistance to revert back to the individual:

> In the period of his decay, the individual's experience of himself and what he encounters contributes to knowledge, which he had merely obscured as long as he continued unshaken to construe himself positively as the dominant category. In face of the totalitarian unison with which the eradication of difference is proclaimed as a purpose in itself, even part of the social force of liberation may have temporarily withdrawn to the individual sphere. If critical theory lingers there, it is not only with a bad conscience. (MM, pp. 17–18)

It is clear from these statements that Adorno stands in an ambivalent relation to Hegel, and that the source of this ambivalence arises from concerns that are similar to those of Kierkegaard. At the very least, it would seem that the way in which Adorno would deal with these concerns—that is, "a withdrawal to the individual sphere"—puts him in closer proximity to Kierkegaard than one might have initially suspected given his critique in *Kierkegaard.* In what follows, I shall try to put Adorno's interpretation of Kierkegaard in a somewhat broader perspective.

In *Kierkegaard*, Adorno rails against Kierkegaard because he, like Hegel, fails to carry through the dialectic. But in legitimately attempting to recuperate the individual in the face of Hegel's idea of world history, Kierkegaard catapults to the other extreme. In order to vindicate the individual's existence in the face of objective history, he does away with the object, external history, and nature, thereby leaving the individual in objectless inwardness. As a result, Adorno contends, existence is actually no less abstract for Kierkegaard than Kierkegaard claims it is for Hegel: "Kierkegaard's doctrine of existence could be called realism without reality" (K, p. 86). Jettisoning both the social and the natural world, Kierkegaard's idea of individuality is based on an infinitely negative "vertical" relation to God. Conversely, as we just saw, Adorno is no less troubled by Hegel's individual, who is concretized—indeed, in a real sense, all too concretized. Hegel's concept of *sittlichkeit* is based on a view of "horizontal" relations among people. The community is the ethical substance of the individual, and if it is "rational," Hegel declares, the individual should be reconciled to it. According to Adorno, however, Hegel's ethical community achieves its harmony by crushing the particularities of individuality. Thus, harmony—or at least what has historically passed for harmony—is the "totalitarian unison" to which Adorno refers.

Adorno thus buys into neither Kierkegaard's "vertical" model nor Hegel's "horizontal" one. Indeed, since both ultimately succumb to idealism's siren song, he thinks that neither one gives "the other" its due. Nevertheless, both have an undeniably strong influence on his thought. Of course, this influence has always been much clearer in the case of Hegel, for there can be no question that Adorno embraces the moving impulse in Hegel's dialectic, determinate negativity, if not the ends with which he precipitately brings the process to a conclusion.[18] (And, of course, it is just as clear that he rejects the indeterminate negativity of Kierkegaard's wholly inward dialectic.) But in terms of Adorno's attack on the unrelenting drive toward systematic totality in Hegel's philosophy, Kierkegaard's influence has been underappreciated. In trying to resuscitate the subject in the face of a society that has left him with few resources with which to resist it, Kierkegaard and Adorno share a number of theoretical and stylistic commitments.

Above all, Kierkegaard and Adorno are averse to Hegel's "metaphysics," which both take to be a system that purports to reconcile thought and being at the latter's expense. By rejecting the notion that this is a relation of identity, they converge in their aim to open up spaces for "the other," which is just what Hegel's "system" closes off. By "the other," however, they mean very different things. In Kierkegaard's *Philosophical Fragments*, which is the exact title that Adorno and Horkheimer first selected for what would become *Dialectic of Enlightenment*,[19] Johannes Climacus offers up the "absolute paradox" to confound all attempts to identify "the absolutely different" (which he calls "the god"), of which there is not even a distinguishing mark.[20] This "absolutely different" is designed to escape thought, and the price of reconciliation, as we saw, is intellectual suicide. For Adorno, who still defends a self-conscious form of enlightened thought, "the paradox" itself is an illicit resort to metaphysics, "the other" is not "absolute" because everything is mediated,[21] and the job of philosophy is to try to "unlock" the ephemeral other from the petrified sociohistorical forms within which it has not been permitted to express itself.

Despite their differing theoretical conceptions of "otherness," both also play Kant and Hegel off one another—although, for Kierkegaard, this methodological approach is less self-conscious than it is for Adorno. According to Adorno,

> Kierkegaard's project is the precise antithesis of the Kantian thesis and the Hegelian synthesis. Against Kant, he pursues the plan of concrete ontology; against Hegel, he pursues the plan of an ontology that does not succumb to the existent by absorbing it into itself. He therefore revises the process of post-Kantian idealism; he surrenders the claim of identity. (K, p. 74)

As an initial matter, it should be noted that if we substituted "dialectics" for "ontology" in this passage, it could refer to Adorno himself. Moreover, as antitheses to the "Kantian thesis" and the "Hegelian synthesis," Adorno and Kierkegaard could not help but draw on the thought of both. On the one hand, Adorno's debt to Hegel is clear enough. And although Kierkegaard's "existential dialectic" culminates not in a Hegelian synthesis but rather in a final either/or, it is impossible for even the staunchest anti-Hegelian to deny that "the existential dialectic" bears strong similarities to Hegel's characterization of consciousness formation in the *Phenomenology of Spirit*. Despite its cheapening of individuality, then, Hegel's dialectic furnishes a level of concretion that is missing in, say, the Kantian subject, the transcendental unity of apperception.

On the other hand, while Adorno's debt to Kant's aesthetics is also clear enough, less clear is the fact that both Adorno and Kierkegaard draw sustenance from the *Critique of Pure Reason*. Thus, although the critical philosophy proffers the kind of "constitutive subjectivity" that Adorno so ardently rejects in the Introduction to *Negative Dialectics*, Adorno claims that Kant's notion of the thing-in-itself at least acknowledges the ultimate impossibility of obtaining a conceptual stranglehold on reality—although, clearly, Adorno does not want to buy into its deeper metaphysical implications. Instead, for Adorno, the thing-in-itself is the phenomenon grasped from the standpoint of a sociohistorical reconciliation. Of course, such sociohistorical reconciliations do not attract Kierkegaard—or, at least, not in the same way as Adorno—but, despite Kant's emphasis on reason, Kierkegaard also adverts to him so as to protect "otherness" from being conceptually hypostatized. It is Kant, after all, who limits the pretensions of reason in order to make room for faith, which includes rejecting those proofs of God's existence that Kierkegaard perceives as an affront to Christianity. Furthermore, while neither Adorno nor Kierkegaard buys into Kant's *Critique of Practical Reason*, both of them avail themselves of the space that it affords to critical thought. Despite his rejection of Kant's transcendental subject on the basis of its abstractness, Kierkegaard sees in irony the ability of subjectivity to detach itself from all determinations, which is precisely why Adorno claims that the Kierkegaardian subject is in no way less abstract than the Kantian one (see K, pp. 74–75). Still, Adorno, too, "presupposes a standpoint removed, even though by a hair's breadth, from the scope of existence" (MM, p. 247)—although, to be more precise, Adorno would argue that this "hair's breadth," which runs against the grain of existence, is actually to be accounted for by drawing on that which is already in the realm of existence but has not yet been conceptualized due to identity-thinking. Implicitly referring to Hegel's claim in the *Philosophy of Right* that "philosophy paints its grey in grey," which means that "philosophy succumbs to the existent," Adorno declares that "grayness could not fill us with despair if our minds did not harbor the concept of different colors, scattered traces of which are not absent from the negative whole. The traces always come from the past" (ND, pp. 377–378). Thus, although Kierkegaard and Adorno have differing theoretical commitments, the form of their thought is more than superficially similar.[22]

This similarity in form is principally due to the fact that both Kierkegaard and Adorno passionately embrace "the negative" and both hold fast to the idea of a "negative utopia," albeit for one this idea is theological, while, for the other, it is sociohistorical. Thus, in the Preface to the *Concluding Unscientific Postscript*, Kierkegaard declares that "dialectically understood, the negative is not an intervention, but only the positive."[23] And, in the chapter titled "Possible and Actual Theses by Lessing," he states:

> The negative thinkers therefore always have the advantage that they have something positive, namely this, that they are aware of the negative; the positive thinkers have nothing whatever, for they are deluded. Precisely because the negative is present in existence and present everywhere (because being there, existence is continually in the process of becoming) the only deliverance from it is to become continually aware of it. By being positively secured, the subject is indeed fooled.[24]

As this passage suggests, the negative has a number of connotations for Kierkegaard. It is the source of our freedom; as was suggested above with respect to irony, the individual is always in a position to detach himself from "what is" and try to reconstruct it through his own actions. The negative also reflects our essential existential position in the world; there is no resting place, no end point at which we can just "be done with it." It is only through the wholly negative phenomenon of death that this can come about. (The will to metaphysics is thus a will to death.) In life, however, we who actually "exist" are trapped in a negative relation between the rock of being and the hard place of thought,[25] and thus must bear an interminable deferral of truth. Yet, Kierkegaard says, we must strive toward this deferred truth in passion—that is, we must keep the negative tension alive—lest we become "deluded" and "fooled" persons that fail "to exist." For Adorno, in contrast, the negative does not refer to metaphysical inquiries, but, instead, to the dialectical relation that constitutes such linked dualities as subject and object, individual and society, and nature and history. The fluid tension that is supposed to internally characterize these dualities, however, is fractured by the prevalence of identity thinking, which, in the pursuit of control and, ultimately, self-preservation, eradicates not only the other, but the self as well. (Kierkegaard would see identity thinking as the result of the subject's confused desire to be "positively secured.") Nevertheless, these dualities must be viewed from the standpoint of their potential reconciliation, just as Kierkegaard's existing person must constantly embrace the Absurd with an eye toward his metaphysical reconciliation—regardless of whether the price of this metaphysical reconciliation is "the Absurd," or it is absurd to believe in this metaphysical reconciliation. And, indeed, more like Kierkegaard than one would expect given his atheism, Adorno speaks of a utopian social reconciliation (while questioning its prospect) in theological terms:

> The only philosophy which can be responsibly practised in face of despair is the attempt to contemplate all things as they would present themselves from the standpoint of redemption. Knowledge has no light but that shed on the world by redemption: all else is reconstruction, mere technique. Perspectives must be fashioned that displace and estrange the world, reveal it to be, with its rifts and crevices, as indigent and distorted as it will appear one day in the messianic light. To gain such perspectives without velleity or violence, entirely from felt contact with its objects—this alone is the task of thought. . . . Beside the demand thus placed on thought, the question of the reality or unreality of redemption itself hardly matters. (MM, p. 247)

It is from this "standpoint of redemption" that Adorno advances a rather more favorable interpretation of Kierkegaard in "On Kierkegaard's Doctrine of Love,"[26] which was written in 1939, the same year that Adorno and Horkheimer began their collaboration on *Dialectic of Enlightenment*. This article begins with an examination of Kierkegaard's *Works of Love*, in which Kierkegaard upholds the universality of a Christian love that is ultimately based on pure subjective inwardness. But this love is like the Kantian ethics of duty. Concerned more with its own status than the other, the inward self must abstract from all natural preferences that its empirical self may harbor regarding the particularities of others in order to meet the requirement of universality. Such an undiscriminating love, however, can easily turn into its opposite, a universal hatred of other human beings, and, according to Adorno, this is what happens in the case of Kierkegaard. To this point, Adorno's critique of Kierkegaard's doctrine of love reflects his prior critique in *Kierkegaard*. The demand that the purely inward self love the universalized other reflects an expulsion of nature, and, in turn, nature revenges itself on this abstract self in the form of a mythical taboo against the preferences of natural love, which ultimately transforms into a universal hatred. Yet, Adorno goes beyond this analysis:

> Kierkegaard's misanthropy, the paradoxical callousness of his doctrine of love, enables him, like few other writers, to perceive decisive character features of the typical individual of modern society. Even if one goes so far as to admit that Kierkegaard's love is actually demonic hatred, one may well imagine certain situations where hatred contains more of love than the latter's immediate manifestations. All Kierkegaard's gloomy motives have good critical sense as soon as they are interpreted in terms of social critique. Many of his positive assertions gain the concrete significance they otherwise lack as soon as one translates them into concepts of a right society.[27]

Kierkegaard's hostility toward the masses, in other words, implicitly incorporates in it a hostility toward the dominating mechanisms of a society that turns human beings into a mass. And, in contrast to a positivistic outlook, this hostility can arise only because it is opposed to the ever-present moment of "possibility" in Kierkegaard's thought, the possibility of a transfigured world. (Moreover, Adorno says, "as a critic, he actually grasped the instant, that is to say, his own historical situation . . . Kierkegaard was Hegelian enough to have a clean-cut idea of history."[28])

Finally, despite the differing nature of their substantive commitments to "the other"—that is, the difference between seeing "the other" in theological-metaphysical terms (which raises questions of "immediacy" and "self-presence") and seeing "the other" in sociohistorical terms (which, among other things, raises questions about "the good life")—Kierkegaard and Adorno converge in the tactics that they use to facilitate their ends. (For instance, Kierkegaard would have us "believe against the understanding,"[29] while Adorno, who emphasizes the need to retain conceptuality, would have us understand against the existing understanding.) In particular, they share remarkably similar perspectives on the nature of communication. There is no reason to find this surprising, of course, since both are preoccupied with resurrecting the individual in the face of an intransigent social context that would do its best to wipe out all particularity. Under these circumstances, to spoon-feed a doctrine—even an "antidoctrine"—would just reinstantiate the type of passive individuality that is being mass-produced. Consequently, the very form of the communication must also be its content to perform its therapeutic task, and this is indeed the case for both Kierkegaard and Adorno.

In the first of his four "Possible and Actual Theses by Lessing," which deals with the "paradox" of communication, Kierkegaard says that there are really two types of communication. The first type, which is not of particular interest, is that "direct" form of communication that "is completely indifferent to subjectivity and thereby to inwardness and appropriation."[30] It has no "secrets," but simply seeks to impart objective knowledge that is already possessed by all parties to the communication. It is only the second type of communication, the "indirect" type, that is meaningful. Instead of conveying "objective" truths, it respects the freedom of all parties to the communication by only providing the occasion for the recipients to come to their own subjective truths. For Adorno, too, the objective is to communicate in a fashion that forces the recipients to contribute something to their assimilation of the communication (which is precisely what mass society tends to discourage), and it is this objective that motivates the complex and fragmentary nature of his works. Even Adorno's most "systematic" works, such as *Negative Dialectics* and *Aesthetic Theory*, appear to be little more than a constellation of essays structured around a loose organizing principle, while other central works, such as *Dialectic of Enlightenment* and *Minima Moralia*, are comprised (in part and whole, respectively) of aphorisms. Accordingly, in contrast to Hegel's systematic "dialectical theory, [which] abhorring anything isolated cannot admit aphorisms as such," Adorno's antisystematic style seeks to open up spaces for late capitalism's overdetermined subject: "If today the subject is vanishing, aphorisms take upon themselves the duty to consider the evanescent as essential" (MM, p. 16).

Ultimately, of course, Adorno, in contrast to Kierkegaard and the later Heidegger, will not identify his philosophical form with poetry, for in trying to break through language's reified form, Adorno still relies on "the labor of the concept" to illuminate sociohistorical truths. Still, by virtue of Kierkegaard's attempt to resurrect the subject through language, he stands in much closer proximity to Adorno than does Heidegger, who believes that a proper understanding of language will lead to the elimination of that very notion of subjectivity to which the works of Kierkgaard and Adorno are ultimately geared.

2

Adorno and Heidegger

While Adorno deals most extensively with Heidegger in *The Jargon of Authenticity* and *Negative Dialectics*, which were both written in the 1960s,[1] his engagement with Heidegger's philosophy traversed his entire career. As is evidenced by "The Actuality of Philosophy" and "The Idea of Natural History," the rudiments of Adorno's critique of Heidegger were already largely in place by the early 1930s. Of course, it is no doubt the case that in light of the revelations concerning Heidegger's collusion with the Nazis, Adorno's criticisms took on a more strident tone in his later works—*The Jargon of Authenticity*, in particular, stands out in this regard.[2] But it does not then follow that Adorno's opposition to Heidegger's philosophy was primarily motivated by the latter's disgraceful politics, which is what certain theorists who seek to promote a *rapprochement* between the two philosophers suggest.[3] Accordingly, after explicating Adorno's basic critique of Heidegger, which will be culled from *The Jargon of Authenticity* and *Negative Dialectics*, I shall look at some of the claims of these "*rapprochement* theorists," who argue that despite their distinctive philosophical frameworks, Adorno and Heidegger had "common concerns and shared agonies" that run beneath "open denials or rejections."[4] I shall argue, conversely, that despite superficial similarities, the differences between these two thinkers are deep and irreconcilable.

ADORNO'S CRITIQUE OF HEIDEGGER

As the title *Jargon of Authenticity* suggests, Adorno is not only concerned with the basic categories of Heidegger's "fundamental ontology" but also the language that he uses to articulate them, for Heidegger's philosophy of language is a function of his "fundamental ontology," a fact that Adorno emphasizes throughout the book. Of course, Adorno's recognition that Heidegger's account of language directly follows from his philosophical commitments is, in and of itself, not particularly interesting, for it is well known that Heidegger sought to use language in a way that would allow him to speak in terms that might evade the presuppositions of Western metaphysics, which had supplanted "the question of the meaning of Being" with an instrumentalizing, subject-centered epistemological framework. The significance of Adorno's analysis lies, instead, in his recognition that Heidegger's idiosyncratic language, as well as the ontology that it expresses, effectively operates as a cover for the existing ideology, the "untruth" of the times, and is thus at odds with its own initial impulse: "What is aesthetically perceived in the bad form of language, and interpreted sociologically, is deduced from the untruth of the content which is posited with it: its implicit philosophy" (JOA, p. xx). Although, for Adorno, the "bad content" of the times surely finds direct expression in Heidegger's language—his "existentials," for instance, have a penchant for reflecting existing social deficits—it is the "bad form of language," by virtue of its seemingly transcendent nature, that is especially "ideological." The way that declarations are made, which includes the use not only of the right terminology but also the proper concernful intonation (heavily laden with theological overtones), gives the declaration an "aura" that seems to leave the mundaneness of empirical claims behind. Yet, despite its pretenses, the terms that comprise the declaration cannot be divorced from their sociohistorically engendered meanings, which are dragged unawares into the declaration itself. Consequently, these sociohistorically engendered meanings do not just bar the way to the recovery of some "original meaning," but, far more problematically, tend to become identified with it. The existing sociohistorical reality is, in effect, ontologized.

Adorno's attack on what is ostensibly the transcendent moment in Heidegger's thought should not be interpreted as an embrace of a more positivistic view of language, for Adorno does not want to deny that language contains a transcendent moment. Ideally, according to Adorno, "philosophical language transcends dialectically in that the contradiction between truth and thought becomes self-conscious and thus overcomes itself" (JOA, p. 12). But by fraudulently making transcendence part and parcel of its own petrified dogma, Heidegger's jargon effectively frustrates language's transcendent impulse:

> The jargon takes over this transcendence destructively and consigns it to its own chatter. Whatever more of meaning there is in the words than what they say has been secured for them once and for all as expression. *The dialectic is broken off*: the dialectic between word and thing as well as the dialectic, within language, between the individual words and their relations. Without judgment, without having been thought, the word is to leave its meaning behind. . . . The jargon obliterates the difference between the "more" for which language gropes, and the in-itself of this more. Hypocrisy thus becomes an a priori, and everyday language is spoken here and now as if it were the sacred one. . . . When [the jargon] dresses empirical words with aura, it exaggerates general concepts and ideas of philosophy—for instance the concept of being—so grossly that their conceptual essence, *the mediation through the thinking subject*, disappears completely under the varnish. (JOA, p. 12; emphasis added)

Thus, although Heidegger views the positivistic use of language as a manifestation of a misguided (if inevitable) Cartesian-inspired worldview, because he "breaks off" the dialectic and attacks not only Cartesian subjectivism but subjectivity altogether, Heidegger's philosophy is itself ultimately positivistic. Both fundamental ontology and positivism ahistorically neglect the self-conscious moments in language when it reflectively pushes beyond its existing stock of meanings in order to close the gap between these meanings and the world to which they refer. Instead, by virtue of their respective strictures, fundamental ontology and positivism would just establish an identity between language and that to which language putatively refers. Both seek an absolute language, and in so doing both fall prey to mythological thinking—in other words, thinking that does not reflect on its own sociohistorical determination—the only difference being that at least fundamental ontology acknowledges that "one cannot speak absolutely without speaking archaically" (JOA, p. 43). For Adorno, in contrast to both fundamental ontology and positivism, language can never purport to have identified the truth once and for all. As he puts it in the passage above, there is an "in-itselfness" to the "more" toward "which language gropes." Or, as he puts it in *Negative Dialectics*, "the test of the power of language is that the expression and the thing will separate in reflection. Language becomes a measure of truth only when we are conscious of the nonidentity of an expression with that which we mean. Heidegger does not engage in that reflection" (ND, p. 111). Understood in these terms, Heidegger's philosophical stand against reflection does not result in a dialectical separation always straining toward a fleeting identity between expression and thing. Instead, language tends to lose the thing to which it purportedly refers, for it no longer flows from its subject matter but rather "seems to fly above its correlative, thereby establish[ing] itself as something higher" (JOA, p. 87).

Perhaps the best example of this tendency in Heidegger's language, and the one that is most profoundly intertwined with his "fundamental ontology," is his use of the term "Being" itself. In an important passage in *Negative Dialectics* titled "Copula," Adorno says that in a very real sense Heidegger's philosophy is built on the misuse of "is." "By definition," Adorno states, the copula is "fulfilled only in the relation between subject and predicate. It is not independent" (ND, p. 101). Comprehended in this way, the copula smacks of what Heidegger would call "the ontical." But in taking the general term "is" by itself, devoid of both the subject and predicate, Heidegger transforms this essentially ontical term, whose "generality is a promissory note on particularization" (ND, p. 101), into one that is ontological, and therefore hypostatizes it in its generality. Contrary to Heidegger's aims, then, Being becomes an object, when, in fact, the "is" of Being is no more independent of the "is" in a judgment than the state of facts that ordinarily comprise a judgment (ND, p. 102). In other words, it is not the case that Being "is" if this means that it transcends the subject-object relation by virtue of the "ontological difference," for Being is always-already entangled in this dialectical relation. Thus, while Heidegger revives the question of the meaning of Being in reaction to the drive for identity that is inherent in positivism, his notion of Being falls into the same type of identity thinking:

> Heidegger gets as far as the borderline of dialectical insight into the nonidentity in identity. But he does not carry through the contradiction in the concept of Being. He suppresses it. What can somehow be conceived as Being mocks the notion of an identity between the concept and that which it means; but Heidegger treats it as identity, as pure Being itself, devoid of its otherness. (ND, p. 104)

By placing Being safely beyond the punishing mediations of the subject-object dialectic, Heidegger's thought nonetheless expresses a social psychological need, and it is here, as Adorno says, that the "truth content" of his philosophy lies.[5] The assorted expressions that constitute Heidegger's jargon, such as "the need for shelteredness" and "angst," which are vouchsafed by Being and thus have deep existential meaning, are actually melancholy expressions of the sociohistorical circumstances in which Heidegger and his compatriots found themselves. Those who live in dire economic circumstances, such as the Germans did in the 1920s, have good reason to be anxious about their shelter. With both capital concentration and technological development accelerating (not to mention the severe economic repercussions of World War I), it becomes increasingly clear that the ground of one's sustenance—if, in fact, one is being sustained at all—is not only beyond one's control but is also beyond one's conceptualization. This is what produces that feeling of "meaninglessness," which is actually nothing more than the expression of real need. By explaining this situation in existential terms, however, fundamental ontology not only serves the palliating function of religion but also the concomitant need to be able to make sense of a senseless situation: what "consciousness dreads it turns in such a way that the threat seems to be an innate part of it, and thus it weakens that element of the threat which can no longer be grasped in human terms" (JOA, p. 36).

To accomplish this task, fundamental ontology draws on prior ways of "being" that are able to make sense of existence in a reassuring way: "past forms of societalization, prior to the division of labor, are surreptitiously adopted as if they were eternal" (JOA, p. 59). Small farmers and artisans, in particular, are glorified by Heidegger for reflecting the "splendor of the simple" (JOA, p. 50). But, of course, ontologizing a past form of economic life does not actually make it so, and the supposedly "immediate" relation that had once existed between the farmer and his land, as well as the artisan and his handicrafts, exists no longer. The conditions of the former's increasingly tenuous existence are tied to finance capital, while the latter, who is fighting a losing battle against the mass production of his product, is circumscribed by his calculated opposition to that inexorable process. Heidegger's famed tool room, in which he distinguishes between the phenomena of a hammer that is ready-to-hand and one that is merely present-to-hand, is not insulated against the economic tide. And, indeed, under rapidly changing capitalist production processes it is unclear whether it is the technology or human beings themselves that are ready- or present-to-hand.

Thus, according to Adorno, by ontologizing what are transitory historical circumstances, Heidegger's jargon—despite its various consolations and compensations—actually degrades the very notion of what a human being is. In contrast to thinkers such as Kant, Hegel, Marx, and Kierkegaard, who believed that a state of affairs worthy of human beings must be produced through the force of antagonisms, Heidegger's thought offers up such a state on an ontological platter. Such a move, however, "simply deflects us from seeing how little it is here a question of man, who has been condemned to the status of an appendage" (JOA, p. 60). As the humble "shepherds of Being," all human beings are equal in their "powerlessness and nothingness" (JOA, p. 65), but this degrading equality, which itself is raised to the sublime, hides from flesh-and-blood human beings the fact that their powerlessness and nothingness are the result of social institutions that were thrust on them by particular human beings in a particular relation to nature. In any event, Heidegger's unmediated approach leads to an equally unmediated notion of what a human being is, for, on the one hand, as the shepherd of Being he is privileged in a general and empty fashion, while, on the other hand, he is actually being degraded into a bundle of functions.

This wholly unmediated conception of humanity is formalized in Heidegger's renowned distinction between the "authentic self" and the self that is dispersed into "the they." Although not well articulated by Heidegger, for whom "the they is a cloudy mixture of elements which are merely ideological products of the exchange relationship" (JOA, p. 151), the "they-self," Adorno argues, is actually the self that was initially disowned in the sphere of large-scale production and then dispersed in the culture of mass consumption. And the attributes of this "they self"—"idle talk," "curiosity," and "ambiguity"—are manifestations of the same underlying process. Thus, "idle talk" is not to be understood ontologically but as the type of communication engendered by an economic system that perpetuates itself through expenditures on advertising. "Curiosity," which Heidegger dismisses as a manifestation of consciousness seeking to tear loose from Being, is a much more complicated phenomenon: it is a positive force to the extent that it permits the subject to open himself up to experience, thus circumventing a dull repetition-compulsion, but to the extent that it motivates the subject to inquire into that which does not concern him, it evinces a deprivation resulting from a world that has promised more than it has delivered. And, finally, "ambiguity," or the leveling of understanding, reflects the subjection of production for the sake of use to production for the sake of exchange (or, more simply, the subjection of use value to exchange value), and, as a manifestation of the sort of leveling process discussed by Marx in the *Economic and Philosophic Manuscripts*, has the effect of facilitating identity thinking: what are complex and variegated phenomena are invariably reduced to a number of basic conceptual categories (see, generally, JOA, pp. 101–112).[6]

On Heidegger's account, it is only when the self takes hold of itself in its own way that it becomes an "authentic self." But, according to Adorno, by reformulating the self as "Dasein" ("being-there") to avoid the reifying subject-object dialectic, and then (in some qualified sense) withdrawing this self from the world or "there" of the "they-self," Heidegger's "authentic self" actually signals "a retreat from the empirical content of subjectivity" (JOA, p. 74). In this way, the "authentic self" becomes identical with itself:

> The fact that Dasein belongs to itself, that it is "in each case mine," is picked out from individuation as the only general definition that is left over after the dismantling of the transcendental subject and its metaphysics. The *principium individuationis* stands as a principle over and against any particular individual element. At the same time it is that essence. . . . It is given the rank and rights of the philosophical apriori. (JOA, p. 114)

In other words, Heidegger's "authentic self," formulated in reaction to the reified subjectivity of the "they-self" engendered by "the they," itself becomes the embodiment of reification because that which allegedly individuates it is its own purely formal self-possession. Yet, into this ontological vacuum that distinguishes the "authentic self" from its appropriated selfness flows the bad empirical aspects of "the they," which are then grasped ontologically, not historically. The existing social relations that actually beget subjectivity are thus made into an "in-itself," which brings the metaphysical tradition to an untoward conclusion. Thus, the problem with Heidegger's thought is not that it is composed by aspects of an empirical reality that it wants to transcend, "but that it transforms a bad empirical reality into transcendence" (JOA, p. 116).[7] Indeed, since there is neither an objective determination for what actually constitutes authenticity nor even a subjectivity that could reflect on the question without thereby losing its claim to being authentic, the question as to whether a given subjectivity is authentic is ultimately determined by the arbitrariness of the subject, who—regardless of how substantively warped—is authentic to himself (JOA, p. 126).

Moreover, according to Adorno, the vacuousness of Heidegger's notion of authenticity is foreshadowed by his reliance on the anticipation of one's death ("one's ownmost possibility") as that which carries out the task of separating the "authentic self" from the "theyness" of factical selfness. In viewing human beings as fundamentally "beings-unto-death," Heidegger depends on the nonrepresentability of death to carry out the function of individuation, but in using death in this way it becomes the very stuff of authenticity:

> Death becomes the essence of the realm of mortality. This occurs in opposition to the immediate, which is characterized by the fact that it is there. Death thus becomes something that is artificially beyond the existent. Saved from the They it becomes the latter's sublime counterpart; it becomes the authentic. Authenticity is death. The loneliness of the individual in death, the fact that his "non-relatedness singles out Dasein unto itself," becomes the substratum of selfness. This attitude of total self-sufficiency becomes the extreme confirmation of the self; it becomes an Ur-image of defiance in self-abnegation. (JOA, pp. 151–152)

As that which is purportedly beyond the universal exchange relation (but, in actuality, manifests its culmination in the social world from which it flees), death is posited by Heidegger in opposition to the various "identity theories" that inhere in classical idealism. But by taking death, which is absolutely alien to the subject, and positing it as the ground of transcendence, Heidegger's philosophy ends up as a model of reification. Much like Hegel's famous description of subjectivity during the time of the French Terror, in which subjectivity would not tolerate the limits imposed on it by that which would concretize it, Heidegger's notion of the "authentic self" turns into its own negation and thus resembles the very death that would utterly individuate it. Practically, Heidegger's attitude toward death "robs the subject of its moment of freedom and spontaneity: it completely freezes, like the Heideggerian states of mind, into something like an attribute of the substance 'existence.' Hatred toward reifying psychology removes from the living that which would make them other than reified. Authenticity . . . is made into an object" (JOA, p. 127). Thus, Heidegger's "fundamental ontology" becomes a more invidious identity theory than those against which it rebels. And, despite its nostalgic yearnings for that which precedes the modern, as well as its hostility toward the subject, at its root this philosophy manifests what Adorno and Horkheimer call the "dialectic of enlightenment," for Heidegger's subject-less *Dasein* ends up destroying itself in the name of its own self-preservation. In other words, in the very process of trying to preserve the idea of an authentic self from the they-self of the they, Heidegger requires the bracketing of the they-self through the acknowledgment of one's impending death, but this winnows down the authentic self that he seeks to absolutely nothing. "It is as though self-preservation and selfhood defined themselves qualitatively through their antithesis, death, which is intertwined with the meaning of self-preservation" (JOA, p. 136).

Ultimately, then, the primary categories of Heidegger's philosophy, such as "Being," "Authenticity," and "Death," are self-consciously crafted by thought in opposition to thought, and then put in a safe haven outside thought's reach, as if this could insulate them against the bad empirical reality that inspired their formulation. What Heidegger fails to see is that "otherness" must be dialectically worked toward, and that all attempts to get it on the cheap by evading this process betray the impulse that led us to strive toward it in the first place. Thus, Adorno states:

> What [Heidegger] dislikes in dealing with culture, to which, incidentally, his own philosophical divagations belong, is the business of starting with the experience of something derived. But this cannot be avoided and has to be taken into consciousness. In the universally mediated world everything experienced in primary terms is culturally preformed. Whoever wants the other has to start with the immanence of culture, in order to break out through it. But fundamental ontology gladly spares itself that, by pretending it has a starting point somewhere outside. In that way such ontology succumbs to cultural mediations all the more; they recur as social aspects of that ontology's own purity. Philosophy involves itself all the more deeply in society as it more eagerly—reflecting upon itself—pushes off from society and its objective spirit. It claws itself firmly into its blindly social fate, which—in Heidegger's terminology—has thrown one into this and no other place. This was according to the taste of fascism. (JOA, pp. 99–100)

Adorno and Heidegger Are Irreconcilable

Although Adorno once remarked that Heidegger's thought "is fascist to its innermost cells," over the past twenty years different groups of scholars have stated that their philosophical positions can be reconciled. These groups of Heideggerians, poststructuralists, and second-generation critical theorists have divergent reasons for wanting to bring Adorno and Heidegger together,[8] but the procedure through which they would justify this reconciliation is basically the same: what are real philosophical differences between the two are glossed over as subtleties that belie more basic affinities, a contention that is then substantiated by opportunistically seizing on random sentences located throughout Adorno's large body of work. Adorno and Heidegger, we are ultimately supposed to realize, were motivated by similar interests and concerns, a fact that has been obfuscated by their personal and political antagonisms. It seems to me, in contrast, that these scholars should remember Nietzsche's contention that those who try to conflate seminal thinkers have bad eyesight, for, at least in this particular case, one thing is clear: Adorno and Heidegger are irreconcilable.

Before considering some of the areas in which the substantive interests of Adorno and Heidegger allegedly converge, it is worth briefly considering some of the Adornian texts that are commandeered as an entry point into this infelicitous argument. Fred Dallmayr, whose work (which is inspired by Hermann Mörchen's tome *Adorno und Heidegger*) will serve as the major point of reference, states that aside from Heidegger's ties to the Nazis and sheer competitiveness, "the desire for intellectual differentiation" was a critical motive underlying Adorno's attacks on Heidegger. For support, Dallmayr adverts to Adorno's claim in "Portrait of Walter Benjamin" that "the decisive differences between philosophers have always consisted in nuances," and that "what is most bitterly reconcilable is that which is similar but thrives on different centres."[9] Immediately after making this claim, however, Adorno, who is contrasting *Benjamin* with the existentialists, says that Benjamin "saw through them as the mere mask of conceptual thinking at its wits end, just as he also rejected the existential-ontological concept of history as the mere distillate left after the substance of the historical dialectic had been boiled away."[10] If Benjamin sharply differs from the German existentialists, as this passage indicates, the differences between the German existentialists and Adorno are even more profound, since Adorno attacks Benjamin on the very grounds that he attacks Heidegger, Benjamin's objectivistic rejection of the subject: "His target is not an allegedly over-inflated subjectivism but rather the notion of a subjective dimension itself. Between myth and reconciliation, the poles of his philosophy, the subject evaporates. Before his Medusan glance, man turns into the stage on which an objective process unfolds."[11] Thus, at least with regard to the critical issue of subjectivity, which will be discussed in greater detail shortly, it is clear that Adorno and Heidegger differ by far more than "nuances."

Another scholar, Simon Jarvis, supports his claim that there are "deep convergences between [Adorno's] thought and Heidegger's" by stressing the title of the first part of *Negative Dialectics*, "Relation to Ontology," as well as a 1949 letter to Horkheimer, in which Adorno says that Heidegger was "in favor of false trails in a way that's not very different from our own."[12] With respect to the title "Relation to Ontology," it must be remembered that *Negative Dialectics* also deals extensively with Kant and Hegel, and it should come as no surprise that Adorno—a deeply historical philosopher—would feel the need to place the other major philosophy of his day into the philosophical "constellation" that constitutes the book. But this can hardly be deemed a recognition of an underlying affinity. On numerous occasions, Adorno explicitly lays out his enormous debts to Hegel, and—speaking of nuances—it might be claimed with more than a fair degree of justification that Adorno and Hegel closely converge once we reformulate Hegel's "identity of identity and non-identity" as Adorno's "non-identity of identity and non-identity." This would be stretching the point, however. So, too, as Fredric Jameson rightly points out, from Adorno's preoccupation with the legitimate and illegitimate functions of the dialectic to the basic structure of the book, *Negative Dialectics* imitates the plan of the *Critique of Pure Reason*.[13] Here, too, there is a deep convergence, but Adorno is not a Kantian. Yet, it is a failure to appreciate the Kantian approach in *Negative Dialectics* that leads one to overestimate the similarities between Adorno and Heidegger. Clearly, Heidegger, like Adorno, fought against positivism, but Heidegger's dogmatic approach, which in privileging Being grounds itself on a theologically inspired transcendental entity, ultimately collapses into a reified form of thought that is no less troubling than positivism. The point, however, is that much as Kant played off the empiricists and rationalists in the First *Critique*, Adorno plays off the positivists and Heidegger.

In turning to the substantive philosophical positions on which Adorno and Heidegger supposedly converge, I shall begin with Habermas's influential claim that "as opposed as the intentions behind their respective philosophies of history are, Adorno is in the end very similar to Heidegger as regards his position on the theoretical claims of objectivating thought and of reflection: The mindfulness of nature comes shockingly close to the recollection of being."[14] As an initial matter, it must be pointed out that Habermas's claim erroneously implies that reflection and "objectivating" or "instrumental" thought are one and the same thing for Adorno. (This is not surprising, since Habermas has a tendency to play fast and loose with Adorno's complicated relation to reason.) But, unlike Heidegger, who categorically rejects subject-centered reason as a deformation wrought by western metaphysics, Adorno believes in a recursive or self-conscious form of subjective reflection, which is to be distinguished from "objectivating" or "instrumental" reason. Accordingly, in addition to playing off Heidegger against the positivists in a fashion that recollects Kant's treatment of the rationalists and empiricists, Adorno is engaged in yet another essentially Kantian task: he is critiquing reason by reason.[15]

It is precisely because of Adorno's refusal to jettison self-conscious reason that he can both criticize Heidegger's "recollection of being" and differentiate his own approach to nature or the "non-identical" from it. As we saw earlier, it is Adorno's belief that Heidegger's notion of Being results from an abuse of the copula "is," which leads Heidegger to objectify Being as that unconceptualizable "something more" that exists beyond mere empirical entities, and to which they obliquely refer. But rather than just acknowledge that all things point beyond themselves, which would then make it incumbent on reason to attempt to mediate the difference, Heidegger ends up objectifying the "something more" as "Being," thereby putting it beyond the ontical sphere, as well as the boundaries of reason: "The ontological difference is removed by means of a conceptualization of the nonconceptual into nonconceptuality" (ND, p. 117). Thus, according to Adorno, "in the end, human reason, which cannot conceive Being, is itself disparaged—as if there were any way to separate thought from reason" (ND, p. 105). In the place of reason, Heidegger's account substitutes intuition.

As this critique suggests, Adorno thinks that our relation to nature must be conceptually mediated. And, as early as "The Idea of Natural History,"[16] he states that the antithesis between nature and human history must be overcome dialectically, for the two poles form a unity in which each can only be understood in terms of its opposite. Nature, paradoxically, is both the very stuff of history and that which on principle escapes it. It is the stuff of history because it materially constitutes both us and that toward which social history has been geared to this point, namely, those things that enable us to materially reproduce ourselves; yet, nature escapes history because it precedes thought and can never be completely captured by it. History, conversely, is understood both in unnatural and natural terms. It is unnatural because it is characterized by discontinuities that allow the appearance of what is strikingly new; yet, reified (albeit transitory) sociohistorical arrangements also come to be seen as "natural," a fact that Adorno (following Lukács) refers to as "second nature." According to Adorno, Heidegger had actually attempted to mediate this difference by rejecting, for example, Plato's ahistorical Idea of Being in favor of his own project of viewing "being as historicity." But Heidegger's project ultimately fails because "the problem of historical contingency cannot be mastered by the [purely formal] category of historicity."[17] Phenomena, which are leveled to conform to Heidegger's ontological project, cannot be grasped in their full facticity: what conforms is abstracted from and transposed directly into ontology, in which it is absolutized, while what does not conform is set aside. Both history and nature are assimilated by what is taken to be transcendent Being, which must be "intuited."

In contrast to Heidegger, then, Adorno's project of facilitating a mindfulness of nature is inextricably bound up with facilitating a mindfulness of concrete social history. What's more, the technique that he uses to revive this mindfulness is diametrically opposed to Heidegger's ontological approach. While Heidegger abstracts from phenomena and then subsumes them under the classificatory concept of Being, Adorno attempts to unveil the concrete particularity in phenomena by taking combinations of concepts, which represent these phenomena, and bringing them into nonhierarchical patterns or "constellations" for the purpose of illuminating that which was previously obscured by the reified patterns of "second nature." In the same way that playing around with the components of a puzzle or riddle can suddenly reveal previously concealed answers, constellations can suddenly unlock the pure particularity that was previously concealed in the phenomena, as well as the higher order principles that link them. Moreover, these insights, which are as fleeting as they are sudden because they manifest an ever-changing sociohistorical situation, are not to be understood as intuitions of essences, but instead must then be interpreted by the subject, who conceptually mediates the moment of insight with the sociohistorical context that gives rise to them.[18]

Thus, Habermas's assertion that Adorno's "mindfulness of nature" comes "shockingly close" to Heidegger's "recollection of being" is without merit. To be sure, Adorno does not use reason in Habermas's systematizing way, but neither does he collapse into the intuitionism of Heidegger. Instead, reason is ceaselessly brought to bear on the existing material conditions to open up new ways of seeing and understanding. But even with respect to the otherness of nature, the concept must never be jettisoned, as Adorno makes exceptionally clear: "The more anxiously a philosophy resists [the impulse to articulate the inexpressible], which is its peculiarity, the greater the temptation to tackle the inexpressible directly, without the labor of Sisyphus—which, by the way, would not be the worst definition of philosophy" (ND, p. 108).

This response to Habermas, moreover, anticipatorily rebuts Dallmayr's claim that Adorno and Heidegger shared an "aversion to 'representation' or 'representational' thought, according to which the world is nothing but a construct or conception of mind or else an external imprint on sense organs."[19] Of course, Adorno does reject both the constituting subject of classical idealism and the passive subject of empiricism. But by continuing to rely on concepts (which, of course, should neither be absolutized [Kant] nor understood to overdetermine experience [Hegel][20]), and attacking Heidegger for refusing to do so, Adorno also rejects, in terms that are no less certain, the intuitionism that underlies Heidegger's phenomenological ontology. Analogously, when Dallmayr contends that Adorno and Heidegger shared a concern with positivism's "progressive instrumentalization and corruption of language,"[21] he is once again telling only half the story, for, as we have already seen, Heidegger's ontologically driven approach to language, which pursues an archaic language that precedes its dialectical corruption, ultimately cashes out as the mirror image of positivism.

Ultimately, the blind spot of the *rapprochement* theorists, which stands behind all of the "convergences" that they mistakenly apprehend, is that Heidegger's fundamental ontology itself is beset by precisely those problems against which the philosophies of Heidegger and Adorno are supposedly aligned. This is because Heidegger's rejection of the metaphysical tradition causes him to ahistorically collapse the assorted binary oppositions that this tradition has bequeathed, which then enables his philosophy, albeit on the cheap, to bypass the moment in which critical thought should be brought to bear on concrete socio-historical conditions. Adorno's unremitting dialectical approach, in contrast, discerns that these troubling binary oppositions reflect troubling truths about our antagonistic social situation, which, of course, cannot be discarded as easily. All philosophical attempts to circumvent the metaphysical tradition to begin anew—notwithstanding the tradition's complicity in the antagonistic social situation—are thus essentially misconceived. Susan Buck-Morss eloquently emphasizes the importance of this approach for Adorno:

> Whatever the axis of the analysis, the critical procedure remained the same: dialectically opposed concepts were used as tools to demythologize the world and open it up to critical understanding. . . . To understand this procedure is to grasp the essential mechanism of Adorno's method of criticism as a process of dialectics without identity. It will be recalled that he accepted Lukács's argument that the antinomies of bourgeois

> thought reflected a reality in itself contradictory; they could not be reconciled in theory so long as social reality remained unchanged. Given the premise of an essentially antagonistic, contradictory reality, it is clear why Adorno felt the knowledge of the present demanded the juxtaposition of contradictory concepts whose mutually negating tension could not be dissolved. . . . Only if thought remained fluid and avoided dogma could it be the ally of history as it ought to unfold.[22]

For Adorno, then, there is always the flip side of the dialectical coin, and, depending on the threats posed by a particular set of circumstances, he is liable to invert the character of his criticisms. When attacking positivism, he might seem close to Heidegger, but when attacking, say, Heidegger's empty category of Being, he might begin to sound like a positivist. Shall we seek a *rapprochement* between Adorno and the positivists? In short, Adorno's critical approach cannot be distilled from his deeply contextual philosophical positions, and as the driving force behind these positions, it renders superficial apparent convergences between his philosophy and Heidegger's. This is even true with respect to Dallmayr's seemingly uncontroversial contention that "both thinkers took as their point of departure the dilemmas of late modernity, that is, the predicaments engendered by the sway of modern science and technology."[23] Although, as far as it goes, this is true, the strong strain of nostalgic longing in Heidegger's philosophy arguably leads him to oppose science as a matter of philosophical principle, while for Adorno the matter is significantly more complicated.[24] Thus, despite Adorno's unyielding attacks on "instrumental reason," which is intrinsic to the scientific and technological approach, it could well be argued that these attacks must be understood within the existing sociohistorical context, and that in a different context, in which science did not serve as the basic model for interaction among human beings and between human beings and nature, the scientific approach could be reconciled.[25]

Finally (and most importantly for present purposes), the *rapprochement* theorists' failure to fully understand Adorno's "critical procedure" is most flagrantly demonstrated in their claim that Adorno and Heidegger share similar perspectives on the nature of individual subjectivity. Thus, Dallmayr recounts, "in Mörchen's view one of the deepest and most pervasive affinities between Heidegger and Adorno resides in their departure (or turning away) from metaphysical foundationalism, particularly from modern metaphysics rooted in the category of subjectivity."[26] Mörchen, quoted by Dallmayr, then goes one step further: "both concur tacitly or implicitly in refusing to acknowledge the primacy of the individual and treating it instead as a 'historical category.'"[27] The first claim is exceedingly problematic; the second one is a distortion.

Although Adorno and Heidegger both reject what Adorno refers to as the "constituting subjectivity" of metaphysics, after this initial accord they rigorously part company. With respect to the metaphysical tradition, for example, Heidegger declares in "Letter on Humanism," written as a rejoinder to Sartre's "Existentialism as a Humanism," that metaphysics must be abandoned: "Thinking does not overcome metaphysics by climbing still higher, surmounting it, transcending it somehow or other; thinking overcomes metaphysics by climbing back down into the nearness of the nearest. The descent, particularly where man has strayed into subjectivity, is more arduous and more dangerous than the ascent."[28] Momentarily bracketing Heidegger's reference to subjectivity (as well as the question of the relation between metaphysics and subjectivity), it should now be clear that Adorno rejects any abandonment of metaphysics. As was suggested by the earlier discussion, striving to transcend metaphysics, which entails striving to transcend the antagonistic social conditions that nourish it, is precisely where Adorno's commitment lies. In fact, as Peter Hohendahl states (with admirable concision), "the legitimacy of philosophy [itself], which Adorno treats as questionable but not hopeless, depends on the possibility of refunctioning elements of the metaphysical tradition, without, however, buying into its dogmatic side."[29] The truth of this statement is reflected in the closing section of the final part of *Negative Dialectics*, "Meditations on Metaphysics," in which Adorno worries that our "metaphysical faculty," which is as indispensable as it is problematical, might have been paralyzed in the aftermath of Hitler's gas chambers (ND, p. 362).

With respect to Dallmayr's claim that both Adorno and Heidegger reject the "category of subjectivity," and Mörchen's further claim that both refuse to "acknowledge the primacy of the individual," seeing it instead as a mere "historical category," a number of things need to be said. As to subjectivity, in general, it should be abundantly clear from both the discussion of *Jargon of Authenticity* and, especially, the discussion of Adorno's relation to Kierkegaard that Adorno does not just hold on to a notion of subjectivity in his philosophy, but that the notion of subjectivity is, arguably, at the heart of his philosophy. First, Adorno tenaciously holds on to the subject-object paradigm (which Dallymayr and Mörchen nonchalantly explain away as a "nuance"). And while Adorno rejects the notion of a "constituting subjectivity" because it cannot open itself up to the object, which he privileges, Adorno is, for the most part, motivated in this regard by the desire to free up subjectivity itself. By extirpating spontaneity and imagination, a constituting subjectivity extirpates subjectivity itself: it is "the subject as the subject's foe" (ND, p. 12). Second, much of Adorno's critique of Heidegger in *Negative Dialectics* is principally directed against Heidegger's rejection of subjectivity, or what Adorno calls a "subjective share" that escapes determination (which, as we shall see, is, in some sense, exactly what Sartre's phenomenology offers): "For in the needs of even the people who are covered, who are administered, there reacts something in regard to which they are not fully covered—a surplus of their subjective share, which the system has not wholly mastered" (ND, p. 92). It is Heidegger's desire to extirpate whatever remains of this "subjective share" that actually spells disaster:

> The truth that expels man from the center of creation and reminds him of his impotence—this same truth will, as a subjective mode of conduct, confirm the sense of impotence, cause men to identify with it, and thus reinforce the spell of the second nature. Faith in Being, a dim weltanschauung derived from critical premonitions, really degenerates into a bondage to Being, as Heidegger incautiously defined it once. . . . The subject's readiness to cringe before the calamity that springs from the subjective context itself is the punishment for their futile wish to fly the prison of their subjectivity. (ND, p. 68)

Third, Adorno (qualifiedly) hangs on to a number of enlightenment concepts that are tied up with subjectivity, including "humanism" ("The current talk of humanism is awful enough, but one may well ask whether Heidegger would not end the talk solely because his doctrine would end the matter" [ND, p. 89])[30] and "responsibility" ("Heidegger believes that under the domination of the They nobody needs to take responsibility for anything" [JOA, pp. 102–103]).[31]

As to seeing "the primacy of the individual" as a "historical category," Mörchen is surely right, but the point is that Heidegger and Adorno value this "historical category" in diametrically opposed ways. While for Heidegger the primacy of the individual arises from the philosophical tradition's wrong turn into metaphysics, for Adorno the primacy of the individual is the promise of the enlightenment, a promise to which Adorno remains firmly committed. When he indicates that Hegel hypostatizes "both bourgeois society and its fundamental category, the individual," Adorno is criticizing Hegel for giving short shrift to the individual (that is, for seeing the individual as a mere function of history), not for hanging on to him. It is not just that "in an individualistic society, the general . . . realizes itself through the interplay of particulars, [as] society is essentially the substance of the individual," but also that, since Hegel's time, "the individual has gained as much in richness, differentiation and vigour as the socialization of society has enfeebled and undermined him" (MM, p. 17). In other words, since all of the categories out of which we conceptualize the world are sociohistorically generated, there is nothing especially interesting (or, for that matter, pejorative) about the charge that "the primacy of the individual" is a "historical category." What *is* interesting is that Adorno continues to privilege this category despite the fact that its objective socioeconomic supports are falling by the historical wayside.

In light of the foregoing, the important question about Adorno's relation to Heidegger is ultimately a sociological one—namely, why is it that a fair number of continental philosophers are trying to facilitate this *rapprochement*. Although I am not prepared to argue for the claim in any elaborate way here, my suspicion is that this move toward *rapprochement* is a sign of the political times. J. M. Bernstein's recent work on Adorno, *Adorno: Disenchantment and Ethics*, is suggestive in this regard. Although Bernstein does not argue for a *rapprochement* between Adorno and Heidegger, and although his analysis of Adorno's ethical thought is as penetrating as one is likely to find in the English language, it broadly presupposes the sort of "end of history" thesis that makes all talk of such a *rapprochement* possible.

Accordingly, in the Introduction to *Adorno: Disenchantment and Ethics*, Bernstein states straightaway that

> while the institutional forms of liberal democracy and a market economy have thus far not secured what they apparently

> promised, there is now no viable or available alternative to them, nor is there a sufficient reason to believe that present failure is intrinsic to the character of those forms. And even if it could be shown, as I intend to do, that these institutional forms cannot, in principle, deliver what was promised and hoped, in the absence of a rationally plausible and practically possible alternative, there is no reason for not adhering to them, ameliorating their deficiencies as best we can.[32]

Bernstein's willingness to ditch the notion of an ultimate sociohistorical reconciliation—which, as we have seen, is for Adorno a "demand placed on thought" irrespective of "the question of the reality or unreality of redemption" (MM, p. 247)—has a significant impact on the way in which Adorno's thought is understood. To be sure, Bernstein is way too good an Adorno scholar not to perceive that "Adorno's deepest discovery about the modal status of ethical ideals and norms" is that we must "live our relation to present and future in the mode of a *promise*,"[33] but his seeming willingness to write off anything that remotely relates to emancipatory political practices, which might actually make good this promise, does violence to the spirit of Adorno's thought even as it conforms to the letter. Of course, in contrast to Marcuse (who does not get so much as a mention in *Adorno*), Adorno was tormented by the question of praxis, and, some would argue, lapsed into quietism, but even if this is so, the very torment that constituted his relation to praxis profoundly impacted the nature of his thought. Adorno stood in a relation of interiority to the (im)possibility of political practice and redemption, while Bernstein's Adorno stands in a wholly exterior one, which is just what enables him to reconstruct Adorno's thought in terms of analytic philosophy. And, what's more, the very presupposition that makes good the possibility of "analyticizing" Adorno—namely, the notion that the dialectic has come to a standstill (i.e., that history is at an end and we are now confronted with an eternal present whose conceptual apparatus needs to be refined)—also makes good the possibility of an ontology, whether "critical" (as Dallmayr puts it) or otherwise. In this way, just as for Adorno fundamental ontology and positivism are two sides of the same coin, so are the current attempts to effectuate a *rapprochement* between Adorno and Heidegger, on the one hand, and Adorno and analytic philosophy, on the other.

In any case, in the final analysis, according to Adorno, Heidegger's undialectical thought, which is characterized by Being's premature harmonization of the tensions that inhere within the superseded subject-object paradigm, antinomically manifests both objectivistic and subjectivistic tendencies. The objectivistic aspect of Heidegger's thought, as we have seen, is clear enough: What allegedly comes prior to "the Fall of both subjectifying and objectifying metaphysics will turn *contre coeur* into a stark 'in itself.' A self-denying subjectivity recoils into objectivism" (ND, p. 70). Conversely, Heidegger's thought is also subjectivistic in that it arrogates to its own *ratio*, which is free of any empirical determinations, the power to intuit the nature of Being itself. According to Adorno, this smacks of Husserl's doctrine of essence perception, but, in contrast to Heidegger, Husserl, as we shall see, "wished to have his cake and eat it too" by attempting to bridge the subject-object breach without sacrificing either subject or object (ND, p. 69).

3

Adorno and Husserl

Kierkegaard and Heidegger both flee from the subject-object dialectic, albeit in diametrically opposed ways: Kierkegaard withdraws from the profane world into subjective inwardness so as to preserve his "personal meaning," while Heidegger rejects subjectivity in his quest to recover the "meaning of Being." Moreover, by rejecting one of the two poles in the subject-object relation, and therefore the determinacy that can only arise by maintaining the dialectical tension between them, Kierkegaard and Heidegger both end up advancing an identity theory (although, at least for Kierkegaard, identity theories, such as the alleged identity of thought and being in Hegel's dialectic, are ostensibly an anathema). Husserl, in contrast, holds on to both the subject and object poles, both reason and reality. As a result, although Heidegger builds on Husserl's phenomenology, it is actually Husserl, according to Adorno, who represents the high point of modern idealism. Echoing his position in "The Actuality of Philosophy," in which he had stated that "Husserl purified idealism from every excess of speculation and brought it up to the standard of the highest reality within its reach,"[1] Adorno states in "Husserl and the Problem of Idealism," which was written nine years later (while living in the United States), that

> the value of [Husserl's] whole procedure may consist in its turning against the idealist presupposition of the ultimate identity of subject and object. It appears to me that Husserl's

> philosophy was precisely an attempt to destroy idealism from within, and attempt with the means of consciousness to break through the wall of transcendental analysis, while at the same time trying to carry such an analysis as far as possible.[2]

Although the point should not be pressed too strongly, there are a number of similarities between the philosophical programs of Husserl and Adorno. Husserl's desire to get "back to the things themselves" anticipates Adorno's desire to give the object its due, and thus Husserl, like Adorno, rejects the "constitutive subjectivity" of classical idealism, as well as all other forms of dogmatic rationalism. Despite this rejection, however, neither Husserl nor Adorno give up on idealism's reliance on reason (although, of course, by "reason" they intend very different things). Conversely, both Husserl and Adorno also reject the positivistic implications of the empiricist tradition, which indiscriminately assents to "the facts" as the only imaginable truth. And, in fact, according to Adorno, it is Husserl's attack on psychologistic positivism's "naive and uncritical religion of facts" that constitutes the element of truth in his philosophy.[3] Thus, as this excerpt from "Husserl and the Problem of Idealism" suggests, Husserl, like Adorno, believed that it was necessary to reason through the problems of idealism, to "burst it open" from the standpoint of its deepest contradictions, as opposed to just setting it aside. Yet, ultimately, Adorno thinks that Husserl failed in this aim, for while "he rebels against idealist thinking," he "attempts to break through the walls of idealism with purely idealist instruments—namely, by an exclusive analysis of the structure of thought and of consciousness."[4] For this reason, in *Against Epistemology: A Metacritique—Studies in Husserl and the Phenomenological Antinomies*, Adorno contends that, notwithstanding his intentions, Husserl ultimately falls behind classical idealist philosophers like Kant and Hegel.

Although structured around Husserl's philosophy, *Against Epistemology* considers the far broader question of "the possibility and truth of epistemology in principle" (AE, p. 1). And it is Adorno's view that all epistemological endeavors, including, as we will see, Husserl's, start with a privileged category, an originary concept or absolute foundation, on which firm knowledge, as opposed to mere belief, can be built. But this approach, which Adorno generally calls *prima philosophia*, is fundamentally misguided, for "the absolutely first," which is necessarily held to be immediate, is itself, as a concept, mediated, and thus not "the absolutely first." As a result, all attempts to justify knowledge by way of this privileged category become entangled in antinomy, for the subject himself, who comes into play when the first is made into the ground of certainty, does not stand in a relation of identity to the purported grounds of his knowledge:

> Philosophy of origins took shape scientifically as epistemology. The latter wished to raise the absolutely first to the absolutely certain by reflecting on the subject—not to be excluded from any concept of the first. But the drive to identity is also strengthened in the course of such reflection. Thoughts—which are no longer, in Husserl's words, "straightforwardly" executed, but rather turned back on themselves—seal themselves off more and more from whatever does not emanate from them and their jurisdiction, the immanence of the subject. . . . Epistemology falls into arbitrariness by its own process. The qualification of the absolutely first in subjective immanence founders because immanence can never completely disentangle the moments of non-identity within itself, and because subjectivity, the organ of reflection, clashes with the idea of an absolutely first as pure immediacy. Though the idea of philosophy of origins aims monistically at pure identity, subjective immanence, in which the absolutely first wishes to remain with itself undisturbed, will not let itself be reduced to that pure identity within itself. What Husserl calls the "original foundation" of transcendental subjectivity is also an original lie. (AE, pp. 22–23)

In comparison with Husserl and all other classical epistemologists,[5] Hegel's "system," which itself ultimately drags the subject-object relation back into the subject (AE, p. 21), is far superior, for in recognizing that all knowledge is mediated, it rejects on principle the notion of "the absolutely first." Notwithstanding the fact that Hegel ostensibly attributes an identity to the overarching process, it is actually the nonidentical, antagonistic moments within his dialectic that enable it to unfold in a concrete fashion, and it is from this standpoint that Adorno critiques Husserl's philosophy. Thus, in concluding the largest of the book's four chapters, which is titled "Epistemological Concepts in Dialectic," Adorno asserts that compared with Hegel's attempt to reconcile the subject-object dualism, "Husserl's attempt is so timid and weak that his desired reconciliation slips away" (AE, p. 182). Unlike Hegel's "concrete totality," which is impelled forward by the spirit of contradiction, "Husserl acquiesces to [the safe haven] of pure structures of consciousness connected to the *eidos* ego" (AE, p. 182). Moreover, Adorno asserts, in certain key ways Husserl's thought also falls behind Kant's philosophy. Both sought, in some sense, to synthesize rationalism and empiricism, but while Kant's formalism honored the nonidentical by admitting that there are essential aspects of the object that necessarily escape the subject's constituting concepts, Husserl thinks, precritically, that the object can be essentially grasped in its givenness: "It is just this being-in-itself which the given may not have. Consciousness which claims to have it, knows of it only what is mediated through consciousness" (AE, p. 140).

The impetus for Husserl's brand of phenomenology, and what causes him to contradict his stated desire to return to "the things themselves," is his commitment to the scientific method, and, more specifically, to the truths of logic and mathematics. As an initial matter, Adorno thinks that Husserl's use of the scientific method in his philosophical approach is contradictory. Husserl's project, with which Adorno concurs, is to transcend the positivity of the sciences, but by utilizing the sciences as an archetype for his phenomenological method, he undermines this objective and collapses into the positivity against which he fought (AE, pp. 41–42). By referring all objects back to the immanence of consciousness, Husserl's analysis is supposed to precede science, yet what is encountered in pure consciousness is supposed to be dealt with as a scientific object (AE, p. 53). In this manner, philosophy itself is incapacitated, for "by becoming truer [in the non-dogmatic, positivistic sense] it renounces truth" (AE, p. 42).

Referring to the *Logical Investigations*, Adorno indicates that "Husserl's philosophy was motivated scientifically as a 'philosophical clarification' of pure mathematics and logic" (AE, p. 51), and, indeed, Husserl's conception of truth ultimately flows from what he takes to be the pure validity of mathematical and (especially) logical laws. It should be pointed out, however, that Adorno himself deals with mathematics and logic in different ways, and in reality his attack on the use of the mathematical method as a model for philosophy is much less equivocal than his more nuanced attack on Husserl's logical absolutism. When used as a model for philosophy, according to Adorno, the mathematical method inherently divorces itself from any relation to empirical entities, as its initial use by the Eleatics, Pythagoreans, and Plato demonstrates, and a rarefied epistemology grounded in this method has the tendency to suppress the nonidentical. "Numbers are an arrangement for making the non-identical . . . commensurable with the subject, the model of unity. They bring the manifold of experience to its abstraction. . . . Just in order to enforce continuity and completeness, it must eliminate everything which does not fit from whatever it judges" (AE, p. 10). Logic, however, is different than mathematics, for as Hegel's *Science of Logic* evidences, the objectivity of logic need not on principle sacrifice the subjective moment, as well as the determinacy that results from the subject-object dialectic. Thus, Adorno asserts, Husserl correctly attacks the psychologistic position that the laws of logic can be derived from the laws of nature, for, as we have already seen, Adorno also believes in the "objectivity of truth." So, too, Adorno agrees with Husserl's claim in the *Logical Investigations* that logical psychologism confuses the psychological origins of logical judgments with their justification (AE, p. 72). But because Husserl goes to the other extreme by embracing logical absolutism, which holds that truth is static and timeless, Adorno thinks that he actually renounces truth. By absolutizing the dichotomy between the genesis of logic and its validity to preclude logic from being contaminated by empirical realities, Husserl improperly severs the connection between logic and history. For Adorno, who understands the relation between the genesis of logic and its validity in a dialectical way, truth is neither in history, as psychologistic logicians contend, nor wholly distinct from it, as Husserl contends, but instead "history [is] in truth" (AE, p. 135).

More specifically, because truth includes history, and history consists of both objective and subjective moments, the expulsion of empirical subjectivity from the foundation of Husserl's logico-philosophical approach ultimately runs afoul of the "objectivity of truth" no less than the approach of the psychologistic logicians against whom Husserl himself (properly) levels this accusation. In actuality, the laws of pure logic are themselves nothing more than the product of human thought,[6] and even the most rarefied form of human thought cannot be disentangled from its sociohistorical context. As an initial matter, a subject conceived apart from its sociohistorical context is purely indeterminate: "What Husserl takes as the highest objectivity, 'logic elevated above everything empirical,' would in such elevation be condemned to sheer subjectivity" (AE, p. 71). Moreover, the impulse to understand the subject in this way itself both emanates from and reaffirms the sociohistorical context that has ostensibly been left behind:

> The power of logical absolutism over the psychological grounding of logic is borrowed from the objectivity of the social process which subjects individuals to compulsion while remaining opaque to them. Husserl's scientific reflection unreflectively takes the position of the individual within this social situation. . . . The social process which he never understood was just the truth for him. Its objectivity was spiritualized into the ideal being of propositions in themselves. (AE, pp. 76–77)

Logical abstraction elevated to philosophical method is therefore the projection of self-alienated thought onto truth (AE, p. 63). And when it is elevated to this status within advanced capitalist society, as Marx had indicated, it "takes its cue from the form of commodities whose identity consists in the 'equivalence' of exchange values. By the same token, however, it also looks to a societal relation unperceptive about itself, false consciousness, the subject" (AE, pp. 69–70).

Because Husserl's account cannot tolerate the possibility of a reduction of logical truths to historically engendered human psyches, and because these logical truths are supposedly the foundation for human psyches to essentially intuit objects, Husserl must dichotomize not only the objects of perception but also the subjects that are doing the perceiving. Accordingly, objects are to be understood in terms of being both "real" and "ideal." The "real," which is the essential characteristic of what Husserl calls the "natural attitude," are the facts concerning objects as they are understood by thought in a nonphilosophical fashion: it subsumes both sociohistorically determined and scientific perspectives. The "ideal," in contrast, are logical objectivities: they are concerned with types rather than tokens—for instance, the triangle as such and not any particular illustration of a triangle.[7] The question, of course, is how thought could possibly come to know objects in their pure ideality—or, in other words, how Husserl can make the transition from logical absolutism to epistemology—and what Husserl famously offers to stretch across the chasm are his related doctrines of "intentionality" and "categorial (or essential) intuition."

"Intentionality," in its most general meaning, refers to the directionality of consciousness, which is always about some object. When Husserl uses the term, however, he usually uses it in a more rarefied fashion. To become aware of objects in their ideality, Husserl's phenomenological method first requires that the natural attitude be suspended or bracketed, and by employing this process, the renowned Husserlian epoché, the subject shifts from a psychological perception of "real" objects to a philosophical act that intends the object "as meant." The subject's act of intending the object is "noesis," while the intentional object to which noesis refers is "noema." Thus, on Husserl's account, it is through noesis, which allows the subject to overcome mundane, psychological perceptions, that one can come to know the object in its ideality. According to Adorno, in contrast, what is crucial about the noesis-noema relation is that it is a purely static one "which conceals the idealism of the procedure. . . . The noema [is] a reification of the noesis, which mistakes itself as an in-itself" (AE, p. 161). As a result, although Husserl does, in some sense, hold on to both subject and object, he does so in only the most attenuated way. Stripped of anything empirical, which might lead to the kinds of contradictions that are truly experienced in the world, the theoretical correspondence between egos engaging in noesis and noemata tends to hypostatize the *actual* differences between subjects and objects.

In other words, although it is Husserl's objective to get "back to the things themselves," through the use of the phenomenological reduction he inadvertently projects the perceptions of the empirical subject onto the object being perceived, which is then absolutized as noema and taken to be simply "given" to consciousness. Indeed, despite his attack on idealism's affinity for seeing objects as subjectively constituted, Husserl's philosophy collapses into idealism in this way not because he overemphasizes the subject but because he does not emphasize it enough:

> The "absolutely other," which should arise within the phenomenological epoché, is, under the heel of the epoché, nothing other than the reified performance of the subject radically alienated from its own origin. Thinking the other is, for the sake of its omnipotence, taboo in authentic phenomenology. All the methodological foreplay of phenomenology ends up in the acquisition of an ostensibly "pure" subjective region, but

> the subject itself is not named. Rather that region appears, as the name suggests, to be relatively thingly and objective. . . . The phenomenological reduction to subjectivity believes to begin with that it can at all events manage without a concept of the subject. The representation of the subject and its activity may only pass muster in a rudimentary way, e.g., in the phrase "ray of vision of the pure ego." (AE, pp. 163–164)

Correspondingly, the noematic core, the "essence" that is the in-itself of Husserl's epistemology, turns out to be nothing more than the pure function of thinking. It is merely "an abstract identity of the something," and "says no more and has no more content than the Kantian 'I think,' out of which the noema is supposed to have 'realistically' escaped, though in truth the two just collapse together" (AE, p. 167).[8] What the subject mistakenly takes to be the thing itself, therefore, is only its own sociohistorically determined projections onto the object, which as noema takes on the appearance of timelessness. As such, the noema becomes what we have already seen Adorno refer to as "second nature"—namely, a historical object that by dint of ideology is understood as if it was something natural. Bourgeois thought thus reproduces its own reality.

Husserl's doctrine of "categorial intuition," which involves the perception of the noema's essentiality in unmediated form, and is thus the apparent pay off of Husserl's phenomenological approach, obviously cannot fare any better than the doctrine of intentionality, for it flows from it. Indeed, since it must reconcile the irreconcilable—namely, "the positivistic motif of intuitability and the rationalistic core of being-in-itself of ideal states-of-affairs"—Adorno calls categorial intuition the "paradoxical apex" of Husserl's thought (AE, p. 201). Thus, although categorial intuition is, in some sense, supposed to be a rarefied analogue of sense perception (i.e., the sense perception of a subject operating within the confines of Husserl's logical absolutism[9]) it is really the furthest thing from it. For what Husserl takes to be the most immediate is actually the most mediate—the reciprocal histories of the subject and object, which disappear from "categorial" sight. As a result, "categorial intuition is no 'seeing' of essentialities, but rather a blind spot in the process of cognition" (AE, p. 207).

Finally, in the concluding pages of *Against Epistemology*, Adorno briefly deals with the relation between the transcendental and empirical egos in Husserl's thought, which will serve as an excellent springboard to our discussion of Sartre. According to Adorno, Husserl equivocates about the nature of this relation. On the one hand, the transcendental ego is seen as a variant of the empirical ego, the "I, myself," for unlike the transcendental ego of Kant, which only stands behind experience and makes it possible, Husserl's transcendental ego actually experiences. And, in fact, Husserl concedes that the two egos share the "same content" (AE, p. 225). On the other hand, Husserl also sees the need to make the transcendental (*eidos*) ego totally independent of the empirical ego, because only untarnished by the facticity that attaches to the empirical ego can it obtain the absoluteness that is needed to grasp essentialities. But then the question arises as to how, in the absence of facticity, this ego is able to objectify itself at all. Either way, then, Husserl runs into trouble:

> Both at peak and base the transcendental structure finds itself endangered. At the peak because it remains so long in relation to facts that it reduces to sheer identity. At the base because, aside from the relation to "contents," it cannot be brought to transcendental "experience," however construed. As soon as Husserl's theory ultimately examines the contents themselves, it openly concedes their contingency. (AE, p. 231)

Like all other philosophies that are based on the idea of an "absolutely first," Husserl's phenomenology thus falls under the weight of its own contradictions. Crucially, the idea of an "absolutely first"—including, but not limited to, Husserl's transcendental ego—goes by the wayside in Sartre's brand of phenomenology, and it is to Sartre's notion of subjectivity that I now turn.

PART II

Subjectivity in Sartre's Existential Phenomenology

Sartre's earliest works build mostly on the philosophy of Husserl, but unlike Husserl, who holds on to the notion of a transcendental ego that categorially intuits the object in its essence, Sartre rejects the notion of a transcendental ego altogether. In this way, as we shall see, Sartre's brand of phenomenology is able to avoid the basic charge that we saw Adorno level against Husserl's phenomenology—namely, that it perpetrates a static subject-object relation in which both the empirical subject and the empirical object are lost. According to Sartre, consciousness is always immersed in the empirical world, and it is for this reason that Sartre, like Adorno, reproaches Husserl for the idealistic character of his thought. With the advent of *Being and Nothingness*, which is usually taken to be the culmination of his "early philosophy," Sartre moves beyond his earlier works in at least two crucial ways, one explicit and one implicit. Explicitly, Sartre brings Heidegger's ontology into a productive tension with his own unique appropriation of Husserl's phenomenology—that is, Sartre relies on Heidegger to bring his own notion of a "consciousness in the world" into an existential relation with a world that is peopled (although emphatically not as Heidegger's "being-with"). In this way, Sartre does not fall prey to what Adorno finds most disconcerting about Heidegger's ontology—namely, his "taboo concerning subjective reflection" (JOA, p. 126)—which evidences his rejection of the individual subject in favor of Dasein, whose self-identity is ultimately a mere function of "the they." Implicitly, Sartre appropriates certain crucial features of Hegel's model of subjectivity formation—that is, Sartre relies on Hegel's notion that consciousness is characterized by negativity, which, for Sartre, tends to drive the individual subject past every existing self-identity. In this way, Sartre does not fall prey to what Adorno arguably finds most disconcerting about Hegel's dialectic—namely, the drive toward a "glorified totality," in which the individual is absorbed with "serene indifference" (MM, p. 17).

With respect to the status of other people, which is implicated in these various moves, Sartre's philosophy undergoes a continuous evolution from his earliest works through *Being and Nothingness*, the *Critique of Dialectical Reason*, and, finally, *The Family Idiot*, his five-volume biography of Flaubert. Yet, drawing on Sartre's own words in *Being and Nothingness*—in which he says that his portrayal of interpersonal relations as basically contentious does not preclude the possibility of a "radical conversion" that would produce "an ethics of deliverance and salvation" (B&N, p. 534)—many critics claim that there is a "radical conversion" in Sartre's own thought between *Being and Nothingness* and *Search for a Method*, the introductory essay to the *Critique of Dialectical Reason*. It seems to me that this claim, which is better understood in terms of what Althusser calls an "epistemological break," is wrong, and Sartre himself denies the notion that there is a "conversion" or "break" in his thought. In a 1975 interview with Michel Rybalka and Oreste Pucciano (hereinafter "the Schilpp interview"), he states:

> There is an evolution [in my thought], but I don't think there is a break. The great change in my thinking was the war: 1939–1940, the Occupation, the Resistance, the liberation of Paris. All that made me move beyond traditional philosophical thinking to thinking in which philosophy and action are connected, in which theory and practice are joined. . . . I underwent a continuous evolution beginning with *La Nausée* all the way up to the *Critique de la raison dialectique*. My great discovery was that of the sociality during the war. . . . The sociality is not in *La Nausée*, but there are glimpses of it.[1]

So, too, in a 1976 interview with Leo Fretz, Sartre emphasizes the fact that there is a continuity in his thought:

> I think that there is more continuity in thought. I do not believe that there is a break. There are naturally changes in one's thinking; one can deviate; one can go from the one extreme to the other; but the idea of a break, an idea from Althusser, seems to me to be mistaken. For example, I do not think that there is a break between the early writing of Marx and *Capital*. Naturally there are changes, but a change is not yet a break. . . . BN is a general point of view, a fundamental point of view. And CDR is a point of view that on the contrary is social and concrete. The one is abstract, studies general truths, and the other is not so concerned with that and places itself upon the plane of the concrete.[2]

Yet, when further pressed on the question of a "break" by Fretz, who asks whether "one can say that there is an epistemological break between TE and BN," Sartre responds "yes, absolutely."[3]

It is my view that there is no break in Sartre's thought (or, for that matter, Marx's either), but that if a break does actually exist, Sartre is absolutely correct in situating it between *Being and Nothingness* and his prior works. For example, in *Transcendence of the Ego*, published in 1936, others do not actually come into play, and in *The Emotions: Outline of a Theory*, published in 1939, almost the entire analysis deals with a virtually solipsistic responsibility for one's emotions. It is only at the end of *The Emotions*, when Sartre precipitously introduces a "grinning face [that] appears flattened against the window pane,"[4] that others even remotely come into play. This "grinning face," which Sartre concedes his previous theory of emotion "does not explain,"[5] arguably signifies one of the first encroachments of sociality into his phenomenology. And Sartre's assertion that I am not fully responsible for my "magical transformations of the world" in the face of the other's "magical tranformations of the world" is a crude harbinger of the phenomenon of "the look" in *Being and Nothingness*, as well as the larger claim that others pose an actual (as opposed to imagined or bad faith) limit to my freedom. What this "grinning face" does not presage, however, is that "the Other" might play a basic role in the constitution of my own self-identity, which is precisely what Sartre will assert in *Being and Nothingness*.

In the meantime, however, it is important to emphasize that we must take Sartre at his word when he declares that the war years—during which time he read Heidegger—are what defined his later philosophy. To be sure, as Sartre himself states in the excerpt set forth above, *Being and Nothingness* is more "abstract" in its delineation of a "fundamental point of view," while the *Critique of Dialectical Reason* "places itself upon the plane of the concrete," but for our purposes the key point is that "the other" (or "sociality") has been entirely assimilated by Sartre's phenomenological framework in *Being and Nothingness*. This is not to suggest that Sartre's rather one-sided depiction of the concrete content of social relations is correct—indeed, Sartre's notion that we are basically *for*-others seems to have been affected by the sociohistorical conditions that existed in France at the time[6]—but it is to suggest that Sartre's phenomenological framework in *Being and Nothingness* is up to the task of theoretically supporting the social turn of his later philosophical commitments. To give just one example, Sartre's discussion of the necessity of appropriating existing collective techniques, which is just one small part of his rich examination of the diverse factors that constitute "the situation" within which my freedom is expressed, testifies to his awareness not only that we are socially situated but that, in large part, we are also socially constituted:

> On the level of techniques of appropriating the world, the very fact of the Other's existence results in the fact of the collective ownership of techniques. Therefore facticity is expressed on this level by the fact of my appearance in a world which is revealed to me only by collective and already constituted techniques which aim at making me apprehend the world in a form whose meaning has been defined outside of me. . . . The only positive way which I have to exist my factual belonging to these collectivities is the use which I constantly make of the techniques which arise from them. (B&N, p. 657)

Yet, these techniques—to use another one of Althusser's expressions—do not "overdetermine" us, and, in fact, they are themselves abstract until that point at which they are concretely used by an individual, who employs them in the service of his own freely chosen ends.[7] Referring to one such technique, language, which would come to preoccupy many of those French thinkers that would come after him, Sartre declares that "freedom is the only possible foundation of the laws of language" (B&N, p. 663).[8]

I have opened this part with the question of whether there is an "epistemological break" between *Being and Nothingness* and Sartre's later works because it is my view that these later works presuppose the sort of free but intersubjectively constituted subjectivity that Sartre offers in his phenomenological ontology. Of course, as Sartre puts it, these later works must concretely build on the "general truths" that are contained in *Being and Nothingness*, but the point is that if there actually were such a break, it would indicate that Sartre's doctrine of phenomenological freedom has no place in his subsequent sociohistorical analyses and prescriptions (which is the very charge that Althusser incorrectly levels against the humanistic components in Marx's earlier works). But to view Sartre's phenomenology of freedom as nothing more than a function of the French Resistance, which is then dropped in his move to Marxism, is to fail to appreciate that the notion of a free subject, which is the impetus for *all* projects of social resistance, depends on the phenomenological, or first-person, standpoint, which is the condition of its possibility. There is no question but that Sartre continues to adhere to this position in his later works, and, indeed, it is this adherence to the phenomenological standpoint that fundamentally separates his theory of history from Foucault's.[9]

My focus in this part shall therefore be on *Being and Nothingness*, and, to a lesser degree, the works that led up to it, because these are the works that offer the most comprehensive view of Sartre's notion of subjectivity. In chapter 4, I shall discuss the Frankfurt School's critique of Sartre to lay the foundation for showing that this critique is misplaced. In chapter 5, I shall continue this line of inquiry by showing that Sartre does not run afoul of the strictures set forth by Adorno with respect to those philosophers in the phenomenological and existential traditions whom he actually did consider with some degree of thoroughness (i.e., Kierkegaard, Heidegger, and Husserl). And, finally, in chapter 6, I shall consider Sartre's theory of subjectivity in *Being and Nothingness* so as to show that it is not only compatible with a theory of subjectivity that would correspond to the demands of Critical Theory but is actually an indispensable element of both Critical Theory's program and objectives. For, in the final analysis, if Critical Theory did not both presuppose that human beings are free and that they have their practical freedom as an objective (which is precisely the case with Sartre), they would surrender the standpoint of their critique and their normative thrust, and would simply talk, like Foucault, in terms of "systems of thought."

4

The Frankfurt School's Critique of Sartre

Although Horkheimer had wanted the Frankfurt School to undertake a comprehensive analysis of Sartre's philosophy,[1] the only consideration of it that was anything more than superficial was Marcuse's 1948 article "Existentialism: Remarks on Jean-Paul Sartre's *L'Être et le Néant*."[2] Before I proceed to consider this article, however, I shall briefly piece together Adorno's critique of Sartre by culling from Adorno's various works some of the isolated comments that he makes about Sartre, for Adorno's comments lay bare certain basic aspects of the conceptual scaffolding that underlies Marcuse's more expansive critique.

Adorno on Sartre

Besides the essay "Commitment," in which Adorno attacks Sartre's argument for the committed writer in *What Is Literature?*,[3] his most sustained treatment of Sartre's philosophy is a three-page subsection in *Negative Dialectics* titled "Existentialism." Adorno contends here that Sartre's philosophy dishonors his own literature, for unlike his plays (such as *The Flies* and *The Respectful Prostitute*), which shed light on the cruelty of an unfree reality, Sartre's philosophy honors an unreal freedom: it "raises the inevitable, the sheer existence of men, to the status of a mentality in which the individual is to choose, without his choice being determined by any reason, and without there really being another choice" (ND, p. 51). Despite its pretenses, therefore, Sartre's existentialism collapses into the idealistic view that subjectivity is "the sole substantial being," and that social conditions hardly do more than provide it with an occasion for the exercise of its putative autonomy (ND, p. 50).

Adorno's attack on Sartre is virtually a replay of his prior attack on Kierkegaard, and the words that he uses are often the same as the ones that he uses in *Kierkegaard: Construction of the Aesthetic* (see, e.g., K, p. 29). Elsewhere in *Negative Dialectics*, Adorno not only brings this comparison home, but he also suggests that Sartre (and, indeed, Heidegger) falls behind Kierkegaard because Kierkegaard's existentialism had a closer relation to the social truths of the nineteenth century than Sartre's existentialism has to the social truths of the twentieth century:

> What is true in the concept of existence is the protest against a condition of society and scientific thought that would expel unregimented experience—a condition that would virtually expel the subject as a moment of cognition. Kierkegaard's protest against philosophy was also one against the reified consciousness in which, as he puts it, subjectivity has been extinguished: he opposed philosophy for philosophy's own sake. In the French existentialist schools this is anachronistically repeated. The subjectivity that has been really incapacitated and internally weakened in the meantime is isolated and—complementing Heidegger's hypostasis of its counter-pole, Being—hypostatized. Unmistakably in the Sartre of *Being and Nothingness*, the severance of the subject amounts, like that of Being, to the illusion that transmission is immediacy. As Being is transmitted by the concept, and thus by the subject, so is the subject transmitted by the world it lives in, and so powerless and merely inward in its decision. Such impotence helps the reified mischief to triumph over the subject. (ND, p. 123)

Like Kierkegaard and Sartre, Adorno is troubled by the condition of modern subjectivity, and his attack on Sartre here, undertaken on subjectivity's behalf, is really one that is of a piece with the sorts of attacks that he makes against Kierkegaard in *Kierkegaard: Construction of the Aesthetic*. Crucially, however, Adorno wrongly conflates Kierkegaard and Sartre, and, in fact, his attack on Sartre here is one with which Sartre would fully agree if it was directed against Kierkegaard. In

"Kierkegaard: The Singular Universal," Sartre declares that Kierkegaard's "particular failure" is that he "demonstrated his historicity but failed to find History. . . . He neglected *praxis*, which is rationality. . . . He denatured knowledge, forgetting that the world we know is the world we make."[4] Although this critique of Kierkegaard takes place after Sartre's embrace of Marxism, Adorno's characterization of the "Sartre of *Being and Nothingness*" in Kierkegaardian terms is still way off base: there is absolutely nothing in Sartre's critique that cannot be reconciled with his previous work.

As an initial matter, there is no "severance of the subject," according to the teachings of *Being and Nothingness*, because the subject is inextricably a part of the world. As we shall come to see in greater detail, Sartre's concept of "being-for-itself," which refers to the subject, and is characterized by the intentional nature of translucent consciousness, is surely distinguished from the empirical self, which is "out in the world." But, as Sartre plainly states, the subject, although not the empirical self, must nevertheless live this self "in the mode of not being it." Far from being "hypostatized," as Adorno states, the subject's inexorable freedom, the consequense of its ability "to put its past out of play by secreting its own nothingness" (B&N, p. 64)—that is, its ability to thematize the empirical self and thus transcend it—is "characterized by a constantly renewed obligation to remake the self," which with its "historical content is the essence of man" (B&N, p. 72). And, indeed, properly understood, Sartre's (phenomenological) concept of the subject is structurally analogous to Adorno's. In *Minima Moralia*, Adorno declares that "the morality of thought lies in a procedure that is neither entrenched nor detached. . . . Nothing less is asked of the thinker today than that he should be at every moment both within things and outside them—Münchhausen pulling himself out of the bog by his pig-tail becomes the pattern of knowledge which wishes to be more than either verification or speculation" (MM, p. 74). What constitutes the ideal distance that yields the ability to be "at every moment both within things and outside them," and therefore pull ourselves "out of the bog by our own pig-tails," if not, to use Sartre's terms, the "transphenomenal" nature of consciousness, which, although always already engaged, has the ability to "nihilate" the world within which it finds itself?

Furthermore, as we shall again come to see in greater detail, Sartre does not labor under the illusion that "transmission is immediacy," as Adorno claims. At the beginning of *Being and Nothingness*, Sartre, after reviewing the then prevailing status of phenomenology, argues against the idea that objects can be immediately known. He asserts that the "being of the phenomenon" (i.e., the brute existent) necessarily overflows what consciousness perceives, which implies that the being of what we perceive is not reducible to the meanings that we ordinarily attribute to it. That is to say, the brute existent—the most primordial aspect of Sartre's concept of "being-in-itself" (which, more broadly, refers to facticity)—is also "transphenomenal." This is due to the fact that "the existent cannot be reduced to a finite series of manifestations since each one of them is a relation to a subject constantly changing," which, in turn, "implies the possibility of infinitely multiplying the points of view on that *Abschattung*" (B&N, p. 5). According to Sartre, then, we are, in principle, incapable of getting a conceptual stranglehold on the object—an idea that is in conformity with Adorno's own privileging of the object. And, for this reason, as is the case with Adorno, it is Sartre's view that "philosophy is interpretation."

In sum, then, although I cannot argue for it more extensively at this point, because of his insufficiently appreciated notion of "transphenomenality," which applies to both the subject and the object, Sartre not only retains the subject and object poles but maintains a dialectical tension between them—a feat that his predecessors could not pull off, as Adorno himself aptly shows.

MARCUSE'S CRITIQUE OF *BEING AND NOTHINGNESS*

Marcuse's critique of Sartre's philosophy in "Existentialism: Remarks on Jean-Paul Sartre's *L'Être et le Néant*" fleshes out the criticisms that are implicit in Adorno's epigrammatic comments. Moreover, in numerous respects, Marcuse's analysis builds on Adorno's critique of Marcuse's own previous work, which was based on his commitment to mediating Heidegger's phenomenological ontology and Hegelian-Marxism. In a short review of Marcuse's *Hegel's Ontology and the Theory of Historicity*, for example, Adorno states that Marcuse

> tends from the "meaning of Being" toward the disclosure of Beings; from fundamental ontology toward the philosophy of history; from historicity toward history. This is what makes the work significant as well as vulnerable to criticism. If Marcuse

> goes so far as not only to give an ontological exposition of the possibility of factual being but deduces the possibility of the exposition of factual being from the ontological structure itself, it would have been consistent to ask: why indeed should the "ontological" question precede that of the interpretation of real, historical facts, since Marcuse himself would like to bridge the gap between ontology and facticity?[5]

Judging from Marcuse's analysis of *Being and Nothingness*, it would seem that he took Adorno's criticism to heart, for at the beginning of his article, Marcuse condemns Sartre on the very same grounds: "Sartre's existential analysis is a strictly philosophical one in the sense that it abstracts from the historical factors which constitute the empirical consciousness. . . . It hypostatizes specific historical conditions of human existence into ontological and metaphysical characteristics."[6] It is, nevertheless, my objective in this chapter to demonstrate that Adorno's criticism of Marcuse's attempt to mediate Heidegger's phenomenological *ontology* and Hegelian-Marxism, which I take to be right, is not apt with respect to Sartre's *phenomenological* ontology. Unlike Heidegger, who uses phenomenology to gain access to a fundamental ontology, Sartre's phenomenology, as Marcuse himself accurately suggests, opens up on to nothing less than history itself.

After clarifying the relation between French existentialism and the Cartesian tradition,[7] as well as explicating the fundamental concepts of *Being and Nothingness*, Marcuse considers what he takes to be two conflicting elements in Sartre's philosophy. On the one hand, according to Marcuse, by emphasizing that humans beings are "free even in the hands of the executioner," Sartre recapitulates "the innermost tendencies of bourgeois culture," while, on the other hand, as evidenced by his 1946 essay "Materialism and Revolution," Sartre also "explicitly link[s] up his philosophy with the theory of the proletarian revolution."[8] Despite this seeming inconsistency, which is based on the allegedly regressive tendencies of *Being and Nothingness*, Marcuse claims that the book nevertheless harbors within it the seed of a revolutionary theory—albeit one that runs against Sartre's initial intentions, and is, ultimately, thwarted by them. With his analysis of the body and sexuality, Marcuse argues, Sartre moves in the direction of a revolutionary theory that would turn his principal thesis of absolute freedom on its head: "At the end of the road, the original position is reversed: the realization of human freedom appears, not in the *res cogitans*, the 'Pour-soi,' but in the *res extensa*, in the body as thing. Here, Existentialism reaches the point where philosophical ideology would turn into revolutionary theory."[9] Notwithstanding certain valuable insights, Marcuse's emphasis on the body here is as perilously one-sided as he wrongly takes Sartre's supposedly exclusive emphasis on the "for-itself" to be.

As an initial matter, however, in probing Sartre's claim that the absolutely free for-itself is bound up with the contingency of a concrete "situation," which frustrates every attempt by the for-itself to make its freedom the ground of the self's existence, Marcuse offers a crucial insight:

> For Sartre, the justification [of the absolutely free for-itself] cannot be that which is traditionally featured in idealistic philosophy, namely, the distinction between transcendental and empirical freedom. This solution cannot suffice for him because his analysis of the Ego does not remain within the transcendental-ontological dimension. Ever since his Ego, in the Third Part of his book, had to acknowledge the existence of the Other as a plain "nécessité de fait," his philosophy had left the realm of pure ontology and moved within the ontico-empirical world. Sartre thus cannot claim that his philosophy of freedom is a transcendental-ontological one and therefore neither committed nor equipped to go into the (empirical) actuality of human freedom. Quite in contrast to Heidegger (whose existential analysis claims to remain within the limits of pure ontology), Sartre's philosophy . . . involves a definite attitude toward life, a definite morality, "une doctrine d'action."[10]

According to Marcuse, however, in the final part of *Being and Nothingness* Sartre repudiates the consequences of his earlier insight by attempting to rehabilitate the autonomy of the for-itself. Sartre tries to show that while human beings find themselves in what seem to be overdetermining sociohistorical situations, they still remain absolutely free from an individual standpoint. This is because each person freely chooses his own projects, and it is only from the perspective of these freely chosen projects that he can be said to be "unfree" in any particular situation. By making the unfreedom of a particular situation that which is essentially posited by the oppressed person himself through his freely chosen project, however, Sartre's notion of human freedom, Marcuse says, reaches the point of self-abnegation: "free choice between death and enslavement is neither freedom nor choice because both alternatives destroy the 'realité humaine' which is supposed to be freedom."[11] Thus, Marcuse concludes, Sartre's idea of freedom is the essence of bourgeois ideology: through free competition and free choice each person is responsible for whether he has transcended his situation. And, unlike Hegel's dialectic, in which self-consciousness becomes progressively enriched in a historical movement toward social reconciliation, Sartre's concept of being-for-others, which is itself sociohistorically engendered, ends up being ontologized, thereby ruling out even the theoretical possibility of reconciliation: "Sartre's concepts are, in spite of his dialectical style and the pervasive role of negation, decidedly undialectical. In his philosophy, the negation is no force of its own but is a priori absorbed into the affirmation. . . . The subject moves in a circle."[12]

Marcuse is absolutely right when he says that Sartre's concept of being-for-others (and, it should be added, his concept of being-in-itself, which includes the body and thus our biological needs) pushes the subject out of the realm of "pure ontology" and into the empirical world. And, indeed, it is because Heidegger "remained within the limits of pure ontology" that Marcuse's own misguided attempt to mediate Heidegger and Hegelian-Marxism does not necessarily augur poorly for my own undertaking with respect to Sartre and Adorno. Still, Marcuse takes this insight to be the foundation of his attack on Sartre's philosophy, for it is his view that Sartre's notion of freedom is not up to the task of encountering the empirical world, and that it is really nothing more than an ontological notion with empirical pretenses. This is incorrect. As we shall increasingly come to see, although it is true that Sartre's *phenomenological* notion of freedom should not be confused with social freedom, it does not follow that it is just another internalized view of freedom. Instead, as part of the necessary self-understanding of any efficacious agent, Sartre's phenomenological notion of freedom is the necessary precondition of social freedom. So, too, Marcuse is incorrect when he says that in Sartre's philosophy "the essential contingency of human existence coagulates in the fact that man is and remains his past, and that this past prevents him once and for all from freely creating his being."[13] Basing this conclusion on a misinterpretation of Sartre's example of the waiter in bad faith—Marcuse thinks it is meant to show that the waiter is somehow enjoined to play the part of "the waiter"—he fails to see that the past is just one constituent of a person's "being," which is no less a function of his future goals and projects than his facticity. In any case, Marcuse contends that the way out of this existential impasse, in which an abstract freedom succumbs to a reified social situation, is through sexual desire: "sexuality becomes the force which cancels the entire apparatus of existential freedom, activity, and morality."[14] Anticipating *Eros and Civilization*,[15] Marcuse states that through the process of objectification that is inherent in sexuality, the reified for-itself is itself negated and the ego sees itself in its Other: "Reification no longer serves to perpetuate exploitation and toil but is in its entirety determined by the 'pleasure principle.'"[16]

For reasons that also apply to more contemporary philosophies of the body, this position is troubling. While Marcuse says that "sexual desire accomplishes this negation of the negation not as a mere relapse into animal nature, but as a free and liberating human relation,"[17] there is no reason to think that sexual relations would not just mirror the societal relations of domination and subordination that Marcuse aims to overthrow. This is not to say that some recourse to the body is not theoretically meaningful but rather that the obliteration of subjectivity that Marcuse values in this article reinstantiates instead of transforms a bad social reality. And, indeed, it is for this very reason that it is arguably Marcuse, not to mention more contemporary philosophers such as Deleuze and Guattari, who would unwittingly ontologize the present sociohistorical situation. If there is any part of *Being and Nothingness* that is open to Marcuse's charge that a bad sociohistorical situation is being ontologized, it is Sartre's analysis of the sadomasochistic relations that are intrinsic to being-*for*-others, but by displacing subjectivity with the "fascination of being an object,"[18] Marcuse would again only facilitate these attitudes. Absent a subjectivity that would try to change the existing social structures of domination and subordination, sexuality reconciles itself not with nature but rather with "second nature" (i.e., the existing sociohistorical reality, which, like a force of nature, appears to be an ahistorical absolute). Moreover, Marcuse himself will later recognize the ability of advanced capitalist society to both integrate and blunt the subversiveness of erotic impulses with his concept of "repressive desublimation" in *One-Dimensional Man*.[19]

Along similar lines, Marcuse also briefly considers "Materialism and Revolution," which constitutes Sartre's repudiation of the then prevailing view that only the principles of materialism are compatible with a revolutionary perspective. It is Marcuse's opinion, however, that the essay simply evidences Sartre's misguided attempt to wrest a revolutionary politics from his existential philosophy. Although Marcuse acknowledges that Sartre himself attacks various conceptions of freedom for being nothing more than "idealistic mystifications" (e.g., Stoicism, Christianity, and Bergsonism), he claims that Sartre's own notion of freedom ultimately amounts to the same:

> Isolated from the specific historical context in which alone the "transcendence" of the subject may become a precondition of freedom, and hypostatized into the ontological form of the subject as such, this transcendental liberty becomes the very token of enslavement. . . . Human freedom is the very negation of that transcendental liberty in which Sartre sees its realization. In *L'Être et le Néant* this negation appeared only in the "*attitude désirante*": it was the loss of the "Pour-soi," its reification in the "corps vécu comme chair" which suggested a new idea of freedom and happiness.[20]

Marcuse raises two issues that must be unraveled. First, even if "the body lived as flesh" is the heart of freedom and happiness, Marcuse's ensuing "repressive desublimation" hypothesis, as just discussed, reveals that such an existence can be authentically lived only in an emancipated social context, and, moreover, that an unqualified submission to the bodily drives is not the way to bring this context about. For this reason, Marcuse offers transcendence on the cheap. Even worse, because he admits that sexuality can be assimilated and exploited by the existing powers, Marcuse turns "the desiring attitude," which ideally functions as a negative measure of freedom and happiness denied (as is the case with certain kinds of sublimation), into the positive measure of those social forces that would deny freedom and happiness, particularly when "the desiring attitude" collapses into the "fascination of being an object." As a result, fascinated by being an object, the subjectless "body lived as flesh" bears the unalloyed imprint of the only remaining subject, the oppressive sociopolitical institutions that mediate its libidinal activities, and thus "becomes the very token of enslavement." Second, Marcuse is right to say that isolated from a sociohistorical context in which the transcendence of the subject might genuinely be imagined, "transcendental liberty becomes the very token of enslavement." By virtue of its loss of the object, *transcendental* liberty is, perhaps, invariably the token of enslavement. However, as already suggested (and as shall be discussed in much greater detail in chapter 6), Sartre's notion of phenomenological freedom is not transcendental. When Sartre says that "we are condemned to be free," or, more colloquially, that "we are up to our elbows in it," he is actually saying that we do not have the transcendental posture at our disposal, and that it is for this very reason that we must determinately choose. Moreover (and, again, as shall be discussed in greater detail in chapter 6), Sartre never conflates our phenomenological freedom (the freedom to choose) and out practical freedom (the freedom to obtain). Responding to the mechanistic determinism of the neo-Stalinists of his day,[21] Sartre is simply saying in "Materialism and Revolution" that if human beings are to reappropriate their alientated practical freedom under capitalism, they must be free prior to the actions that they undertake to liberate themselves:

> But, say the Marxists, if you teach man that he is free, you betray him; for he no longer needs to become free; can you conceive of a man free from birth who demands to be liberated? To this I reply that if man is not originally free, but determined once and for all, we cannot even conceive what his liberation might be. . . . No opposition really exists between these two necessities of action, namely that the agent be free and that the world in which he acts be determined. For these two things are not both necessary from the same point of view or in relation to the same realities. Freedom is a structure of human action and appears only in commitment; determinism is the law of the world. . . . It is not true that a free man cannot hope to be liberated. For he is not free and bound with respect to the same things.[22]

Sartre's perspectivism here adroitly sidesteps the metaphysical pitfalls of idealism and materialism. Countering all forms of idealism—"free will" metaphysics, the stoical freedom of inner thought, and the transcendental constitution of the world of our knowledge—Sartre freely admits that phenomenological freedom is always already theoretically and practically limited by the concrete social situation. As he goes on to say, his own "perspective of freedom" is one that only knows and acts in a particular situation: "the possibility of rising above a situation in order to get a perspective on it (a perspective which is not pure knowledge, but an indissoluble linking of understanding and action) is precisely that which we call freedom."[23] This perspective, which involves a particular sort of self-understanding, is a necessary condition of human emancipation. Countering the mechanistic determinism of orthodox Marxist materialism, Sartre tacitly argues that by virtue of the fact that it has a conception of praxis that lacks this perspective, materialism tends to antinomically pull in two different directions. On the one hand, by reducing mind to matter, the Marxist materialist makes subjectivity into a mere function of the existing material conditions, which then "deprives his own statements of any foundation." On the other hand, since the Marxist materialist actually tends to "make of himself an *objective beholder* and claims to contemplate nature as it is, in the absolute," he ends up careening back to the other extreme, namely, to idealism.[24]

Ultimately, Sartre contends, "idealism and materialism cause the real to disappear in like manner, the one because it eliminates the object, the other because it eliminates subjectivity."[25] This view, which Sartre unambiguously reaffirms well after his turn toward Marxism (see SM, p. 33n), is quite close to Adorno's, and it is one with which Marcuse should agree. Nevertheless, Marcuse defends a variant of the very materialism that Sartre justifiably attacks here when he asserts that "Historical Materialism has recognized [the value of] freedom in the important role of the maturity of the revolutionary consciousness. Marx's constant emphasis on the material determination of consciousness in all its manifestations points up the relationships between the subject and his world as they actually prevail in the capitalist society."[26] To be sure, as Marx contends (and Sartre agrees), consciousness does not fashion itself *ex nihilio*. But this does not mean, as Marcuse claims, that consciousness is materially determined in all its manifestations, and that absent a certain confluence of historical factors nothing emancipatory can be conceived, much less done, because the material conditions are inauspicious. As Marx concisely puts it in "Introduction to the Critique of Hegel's *Philosophy of Right*": "Theory itself becomes a material force once it seizes the masses. Theory is capable of seizing the masses once it demonstrates *ad hominem*, and it demonstrates *ad hominem* as soon as it becomes radical. To be radical is to grasp things by the root. But for man the root is man himself."[27] Even Marx's great (allegedly post-humanistic) empirical works, such as *Capital* itself, presuppose a subject that has Sartre's "freedom in situation," a subject that can both make out possibilities beyond the given situation and act in order to politically facilitate them. And, indeed, without presupposing such a subject, accounting for the movement of history itself becomes exceedingly problematical, as it is for Marcuse here (and, to my mind, Foucault roughly thirty years later). In any case, the impetus for Marcuse's view is unclear, for in *Reason and Revolution* he had rejected the older Hegel's claim that philosophy is only able to "paint its grey in grey" in favor of the Left Hegelian position that critical reason can obtain a perspective on the existing material conditions so as to put them into question and ultimately change them.

Years later, when "Existentialism: Remarks on Jean-Paul Sartre's *L'Être et le Néant*" was republished, Marcuse attached a Postscript to the piece in which he says that Sartre's embrace of Marxism constituted the "radical conversion" that he had mentioned in *Being and Nothingness*: Sartre's phenomenology, Marcuse states, "recedes before the invasion of real history, the dispute with Marxism, and the adoption of the dialectic."[28] This severely overstates matters, however. As Sartre himself asks in *Search for a Method*, "what are we to call this situated negativity [that constitutes the dialectic], as a moment of praxis and as a pure relation to things themselves, if not exactly 'consciousness'?" (SM, p. 33n).

5

Sartre's Relation to His Predecessors in the Phenomenological and Existential Traditions

Classic philosophical questions concerning the nature of "Being," "Knowing," and "Death" tend to preoccupy Sartre's predecessors in the phenomenological and existential traditions, and these questions also find their way into Sartre's work. In this chapter, I shall consider Sartre's relation to these perennial questions with the ultimate aim of showing that he avoids many—although not all—of the problems that these questions can engender, and that provide the basis for Adorno's criticisms of his predecessors. This is particularly important, I believe, because, as Adorno's critiques show, a philosopher's position on these questions tends to influence his conception of subjectivity. This chapter will thus clear the ground for an analysis of Sartre's overall notion of subjectivity, which I shall consider in the following chapter.

Being

The beginning of *Being and Nothingness*—roughly, The Introduction ("The Pursuit of Being") and first four sections of part I, chapter 1 ("The Origin of Nothingness"), which conclude with Sartre's claim that "nothingness lies coiled in the heart of being—like a worm" (B&N, p. 56)—is arguably the most ignored segment of *Being and Nothingness*. Because this segment is also the hardest one in the book and, moreover, is seemingly unrelated to Sartre's celebrated discussion of "bad faith," which follows shortly thereafter, this is understandable. Nevertheless, in much the same way that Hegel's master-slave encounter seems to be unrelated to the three "epistemological" chapters that precede it, but is in fact the *aufhebung* of the prior theories with which these chapters deal, Sartre's discussion of bad faith and his ensuing analyses of being-for-itself, being-for-others, "the situation," freedom and responsibility, and existential psychoanalysis are all based on the ways that he sublates the phenomenological and ontological theories of Husserl and Heidegger. This alone provides ample reason for examining the initial segment's treatment of the ontological and epistemological problems that have arisen in the "pursuit of Being." Moreover, for the purposes of this book, there is another reason to consider this segment. In Part I, we saw how Adorno brought to light the theoretical traps into which the "first philosophies" of Kierkegaard, Heidegger, and Husserl fell. In my attempt to mediate the theories of Sartre and Adorno with respect to the question of subjectivity, it is important to show that Sartre himself does not fall into the same traps. An understanding of these prefatory pages, which have given rise to innumerable misconceptions, is essential to this task.

As Arthur Danto discusses in *Sartre*, misconceptions about *Being and Nothingness* arise even before this first segment is examined—indeed, even before the book is opened. For many commentators, the subtitle of the book, "A Phenomenological Essay in Ontology," manifests a contradiction, for phenomenology deals with the way the world appears to consciousness, while ontology deals with the way the world "really is." According to Danto, however, this conclusion is a shallow one. On the one hand, phenomenology does not just seek to record our experiences of the world, as its more hostile critics suppose, but rather attempts to comprehend phenomena in terms of the functions they perform with respect to the structuring of our experiences. Much as was the case with Kant, the phenomenologist's inquiries into the nature of the world begin with the way that our experience is structured by it. On the other hand, ontology does not just seek to catalog the furniture of the world in a way that is divorced from our experience of it, for it knows that all such inquiries invariably take place within the horizon of language, meaning, and truth.[1] Thus, according to Danto:

> Phenomenology is concerned with the structures of consciousness, and ontology with the sorts of being that such structures

> must commit us to on the assumption that consciousness is "true." So the question again is not what there is, but what we are constrained to suppose there is with reference to the structures we have determined as belonging to consciousness. Sartre believes, in a way, that there is no difference to be marked here at all, that the world is just the way it is revealed through the structures of consciousness to be; and a kind of argument can be mounted in support of this view, which will imply that we cannot intelligibly raise questions about reality save as it is given to us, since consciousness's limits are just the limits of intelligibility.[2]

With a couple of qualifications, which shall be progressively fleshed out, I would agree with Danto's analysis of what Sartre means by "phenomenological ontology," and I would argue that Sartre does greater justice to what is ultimately the phenomenological impulse that is the impetus for a *phenomenological* ontology than either Husserl or Heidegger, his immediate predecessors in the tradition.

Despite its pretenses, Husserl's phenomenological reduction does not comport with the underlying phenomenological impulse to "get back to the things themselves" because it rejects the contingent facticity of the world, the way that the world actually appears to consciousness, in favor of an approach that abstracts from consciousness's experience of the world so as to support a (logically inspired) static concept of truth—for example, although natural objects in the world can be destroyed, their noematic correlates remain unaltered. In other words, the concrete things themselves, which appear in the natural attitude, give way to the "essence" of things, and it is this wholly abstract essence that constitutes the thing's "meaning." So, too, although Heidegger understands the phenomenon as that which shows itself, and starts his philosophical inquiry from the perspective of a hermeneutic phenomenology that largely comports with Danto's description, his ultimate recourse to fundamental ontology runs afoul of the phenomenology that is ostensibly its point of ingress. In other words, from a concern with the way that the world concretely shows by way of the structures of experience, Heidegger's motivating concern becomes ascertaining the way that Dasein should comport itself with respect to the destinings of Being, whose primordial "meaning" (some privileged transcendental opening of unconcealment) is distinct from every contingent factical way of being in the world. Notwithstanding the basic structural differences in their philosophies, then, both Husserl and Heidegger offer a two-leveled approach in which the abstract transcendental commitment rather than the concrete phenomenon, the genuine object of phenomenology, drives the analysis. And, yet, according to Sartre, in one crucial respect, both Husserl and Heidegger tend to collapse this distinction: they wrongly view the passage from the phenomenon to being as "a passage from homogeneous to homogeneous" (B&N, p. 7)—that is, they wrongly view both the phenomenon and being as having a "meaning." Or, put differently, both Husserl and Heidegger (despite the latter's nominal aversion to subjectivity) "subjectively constitute" being itself, and thus confuse it with the phenomenon.

On Sartre's account, while there is no "ontological difference" between the "being of the phenomenon" (i.e., the ground of the phenomenon's very possibility, the brute existent, or, more simply, being) and the "phenomenon of being" (i.e., the appearance of being to consciousness, or, more simply, the phenomenon), the being of the phenomenon does not neatly reduce into the phenomenon of being without a remainder—there is, in principle, more to being than can be known by consciousness. Thus, after starting *Being and Nothingness* with the claim that such embarrassing traditional dualisms as interior and exterior, potency and act, and essence and appearance have been theoretically overcome, Sartre claims that a new dualism, the dualism of finite and infinite, "or better, the infinite in the finite" (B&N, p. 6), has taken their place. In this way, Sartre rules out the phenomenalism that his prior discussion seemed to augur: "Having justifiably reduced the object to the connected series of its appearances, [the phenomenalists] believed that they had reduced its being to the succession of its modes of being," but because the object's being is only manifested over the infinite series of its appearances, "being has not been given its due" (B&N, p. 21). This is one of the ways that Danto's characterization of Sartre's phenomenological ontology—namely, that Sartre sees no difference between the way that the world really is and the way that it is revealed through the structures of consciousness—needs to be qualified. Of course, Sartre does not think that being hangs back behind any phenomenon, but he does think that it overflows all phenomena. As Sartre says, there is a "transphenomenality of being": "The being of the phenomenon, although coextensive with the phenomenon, can not be subject to the phenomenal condition—which is to exist only in so far as it reveals itself—and that consequently it surpasses the knowledge which we have of it and provides the basis for such knowledge" (B&N, p. 9). Crucially, then, Sartre's phenomenology tarries with the phenomenon rather than move past it toward essences or being. As to the latter, Sartre states, in opposition to Heidegger, that "being is simply the condition of all revelation. It is being-for-revealing and not revealed being" (B&N, p. 8).

Accordingly, as indicated above, being does not have a "meaning" that is waiting to be "revealed," but this does not mean that there is no "meaning of being" for Sartre: the "meaning of being is valid for the being of every phenomenon" (B&N, p. 25). Although this sounds more than a bit confused, given Sartre's rejection of the notion that being has a meaning, his point here is vital: from the standpoint of "the phenomenon of being" (the phenomenon), the "being of the phenomenon" (being) does have a meaning. A basic part of what it is to be a human being is to attribute meaning to the world. But this attribution of meaning—indeed, the "being of meaning" itself, as Sartre rather unhelpfully puts it—is a product of consciousness: "Consciousness is the revealed-revelation of existents," even if "the primary characteristic of the being of an existent is never to reveal itself completely to consciousness" (B&N, p. 24). In sharp contrast to Heidegger, then, Sartre has no interest in conferring a meaning on (or otherwise deifying) being at the expense of the meaning conferring subject, for he believes (and not without good reason) that the individual's conscious experience of the world is at the heart of the phenomenological impulse. Accordingly, Heideggerians such as Hubert Dreyfus, who believe that the "theory of consciousness" offered in *Being and Nothingness* is only a "misguided reformulation of *Being and Time*,"[3] miss the point. Sartre does not aim to reformulate *Being and Time* any more than Heidegger aimed to reformulate Husserl's phenomenology. Like all philosophers, he only aims to take from his predecessors what is useful for his own project, which, in Sartre's case, revolves around the phenomenological freedom of the subject. Yet, while Sartre's understanding of being in *Being and Nothingness* is largely consistent with his subsequent claim that "existentialism is a humanism" (which precipitated Heidegger's renowned "Letter on Humanism"), in one important respect the book contains an antihumanistic element that harks back to an earlier work.

In "The Ends of Man," Derrida discerns this antihumanistic element in *Nausea*, although he fails to see that it is also exhibited in *Being and Nothingness*. Thus, in the process of rebuking Sartre for the principal role that the "unity of human reality" plays in such works as *Being and Nothingness* and *The Emotions: Outline of a Theory*, Derrida declares:

> The humanism which marks Sartre's philosophical discourse in its depths, however, is very surely and very ironically taken apart in *Nausea*: in the caricature of the Autodidact, for example, the same figure reassembles the theological project of absolute knowledge and the humanistic ethic, in the form of the encyclopedic epistemophilia which leads the Autodidact to undertake the reading of the world library in areas where he is able to love Man in the representation of men. . . . It is in the dialogue with the Autodidact that Roquentin levels the worst charges against humanism, against all humanistic styles; and at the moment when nausea is slowly rising in him, he says to himself, for example: "I don't want to be integrated, I don't want my good red blood to go and fatten this lymphatic beast: I will not be fool enough to call myself an 'anti-humanist.' I am not a humanist, that's all there is to it."[4]

Derrida has not put his best argument forward here, for in Sartre's famous explication of Roquentin's encounter with the chestnut tree, he seems to foreshadow Derrida's own twist on Heidegger's antihumanism. While sitting on a park bench, Roquentin is suddenly seized by the presentation of a chestnut tree: "The roots of the chestnut tree were sunk in the ground just under my bench. I couldn't remember it was a root anymore. The words had vanished and with them the significance of things, their methods of use, and the feeble points of reference which men have traced on their surface."[5] In contrast to his earlier belief that the words of his novel "would be above existence"[6]—or, for that matter, Sartre's youthful belief (as recounted in *The Words*) that language is up to the task of mastering the world—Roquentin is now saying that we do not constitute the world through our words. Rather, the Schopenhauerian epiphany that Roquentin's prereflective nausea manifests is his recognition that we do not live in a human world (or what Derrida pejoratively calls a "human-reality") but rather a world that is totally alien to us. Indeed, Roquentin declares, it is not just the chestnut tree or the Velleda that is "In the way": "I, too, was *In the way*. . . . I dreamed vaguely of killing myself to wipe out at least one of these superfluous lives. But even my death would have been *In the Way*."[7] Roquentin's nausea is the nausea of one whose ability to control the world through words is exceeded by the superfluity of the world, which overflows our ability to grasp it.[8]

Albeit in different ways, this breach between thought and Being—this utter lack of "self-presencing"—is, of course, the abiding focal point for Heidegger and Derrida, and Heidegger's later ruminations on the matter, in particular, anticipate a fair bit of Derrida's philosophy. Thus, while in *Being and Time* Heidegger's fundamental ontology, with its concept of "authenticity," holds open the possibility that this breach can be repaired (which, in "The Ends of Man," Derrida diagnoses as the humanism that is still implicit in Heidegger's thought), in his later works, after the "Turning," Heidegger emphasizes the role of language in attempting to presence the being of things, all the while acknowledging that Being reveals and conceals itself in its difference from such beings. Derrida, in turn, radicalizes this position, emphasizing that the breach cannot be repaired because linguistically structured self-consciousness is always-already at a distance from Being, thus precluding the possibility of "self-presencing." For Derrida, whose early works trade on exposing other thinkers' attempts to collapse this distance into what he calls a "metaphysics of presence," there can be no *rapprochement* between reference and referent: "Being" (now in parentheses)—or, indeed, whatever other referent is put into the central, structuring place that is occupied by "Being"—is nonrecuperable. Yet, Derrida, who like Heidegger is ultimately spurred by onto-theological considerations, tries to give a foundation for his own rejection of foundations through his recourse to *différance*, which, like Heidegger and Husserl before him, evidences his ultimate embrace of *prima philosophia*, the very approach to philosophy that Adorno attacks.

In any case, long before Derrida, Sartre articulates the problematic nature of Heidegger's fundamental ontology in *Being and Time* and, in particular, the possibility of self-presence that it presupposes. In the fourth section of part I, chapter 1 ("The Phenomenological Concept of Nothingness"), which constitutes the last section of what I have called the first segment of *Being and Nothingness*, Sartre attacks the notion of self-presence by criticizing Heidegger's underlying understanding of nothingness. According to Sartre, despite the fact that Heidegger characterizes nothingness as a "concrete phenomenon" that is exhibited in emotions such as anguish, which Sartre takes to be an advance over

Hegel's more "abstract" characterization of nothingness in the *Logic*, he contends that "the characteristic of Heidegger's philosophy is to describe Dasein by using positive terms which hide the implicit negations" (B&N, p. 52). In other words, Heidegger mistakenly understands nothingness as something that is distinct from Being—or, as Sartre puts it, Heidegger sees nothingness in an "extra-mundane" sense. Presumably, it is for this reason that Heidegger believes that a rapprochement between Dasein and Being remains an ontological possibility. For Sartre, however, nothingness is much more basic than Heidegger presupposes:

> We will willingly admit with Heidegger that "human reality" is "remote-from-itself"; that is, that it rises in the world as that which creates distances and at the same time causes them to be removed. But this remoteness-from-self, even if it is the necessary condition in order for there to be remoteness in general, envelops remoteness in itself as the negative structure which must be surmounted. (B&N, p. 55)

Sartre is saying that although human beings strive to overcome their "remoteness-from-self" (which is the condition of "remoteness-in-general"), this condition cannot be eradicated because it is a "necessary condition of their existence" (B&N, p. 55). And the nothingness that is brought to the world by the consciousnesses of human beings, which distances them from the world, does not arise outside of being but rather on the very foundation of being.[9] On Sartre's account, then, nothingness is both remote from being, which explains the distance that is the condition of self-consciousness, and is part of being. Or, to put it in Sartre's terms, being-for-itself is remote from being-in-itself, but both being-for-itself and being-in-itself are a part of being.

Derrida's characterization of Sartre's philosophy as just another "humanism" is therefore a gross distortion, for understood from the standpoint of classical humanism one can justifiably make the claim that Heidegger's concept of self-presencing in *Being and Time* is much more of a piece with it than Sartre's hopelessly riven subject in *Being and Nothingness*. And, indeed, when Sartre asserts that "existentialism is a humanism" he takes great pains to distance his own notion of humanism from the classical type, which he takes to be represented by his critics, and which directly anticipates and dispatches Derrida's attack in "The Ends of Man":

> I've been reproached for asking whether existentialism is humanistic. It's been said. "But you said in Nausea that the humanists were all wrong. You made fun of a certain kind of humanist. Why come back to it now?" Actually, the word humanism has two very different meanings. By humanism one can mean a theory which takes man as an end and as a higher value. . . . This humanism is absurd. . . . But there is another meaning of humanism. Fundamentally it is this: man is constantly outside of himself; in projecting himself, in losing himself outside of himself, he makes for man's existing; and, on the other hand, it is by pursuing transcendent goals that he is able to exist; man, being the state of passing-beyond, and seizing upon things only as they bear upon this passing-beyond, is at the heart, at the center of this passing-beyond. There is no universe other than a human universe, the universe of human subjectivity.[10]

What neither Derrida nor Sartre indicate, moreover, is that by virtue of this characterization of humanism, which in no way participates in classical humanism, Roquentin's antihumanistic nausea is still able to find expression in *Being and Nothingness*, albeit in a somewhat different fashion. According to Sartre, as shall be discussed in greater detail in the next section, although we cannot immediately "know" being, given that our knowledge is mediated through concepts, we can, in some sense, immediately intuit it: "boredom, nausea, *etc.*, and ontology will be the description of the phenomenon of being as it manifests itself" (B&N, p. 7). This indicates that, despite his humanism, Sartre implicitly buys into some notion of being in *Being and Nothingness* that is structurally akin to Heidegger's—that is, some notion of being that is different than the being of concrete beings and things. In other words, although it might be the case that boredom or nausea could be the upshot of particular beings and things, as is the case with Roquentin and his chestnut tree, Sartre gives the rather distinct impression that boredom and nausea are not the upshot of particular beings and things here but rather "being" itself, even if he does not exactly express it with the same grandeur as Heidegger expresses "Being." I think that Sartre's qualified adherence to some notion of being that is different than concrete beings and things is a mistake, and it is a mistake to which I shall return. In any event, this is the other way in which Danto's characterization of Sartre's phenomenological ontology (i.e., that it sees no difference between the way that the world really is and the way that the world is revealed through the structures of consciousness) needs to be qualified.

In the final analysis, then, both Sartre's notion of "nothingness," which "lies coiled in the heart of being—like a worm" (B&N, p. 56) and thus precludes the possibility of self-presence, and Derrida's notion of "*différance*," which is a more primordial difference than the difference between identity and difference and thus precludes the possibility of self-presence, stand in much closer proximity than Derrida admits. Theoretically and practically speaking, then, is it the case that the two terms are structurally analogous? The answer, emphatically, is no. Derrida's early deconstructionism, which, for the most part, is concerned with deconstructing the metaphysics of presence in the works of others, can only aporetically circle around lost Being when it thematizes itself, at which point Derrida moves "upstream" toward the "non-foundational foundation" of *différance*.[11] This move is problematic enough in terms of his previously absolute rejection of transcendental foundations, but it becomes even more strained when he then uses *différance* as a (non)foundation for ethical and political interventions. Perusing such works as "Force of Law" (not to mention *Specters of Marx*), which use the vocabulary of phenomenology, one gets the sense that Derrida's practical works stand in an entirely unmediated relation to his theoretical works. This problem does not arise for Sartre. Nothingness is not a transcendental foundation but rather arises within being itself, thus giving him a theoretical basis for moving "downstream" toward an account of subjectivity in both the natural and historical world: we stand in an interior relation to being and are thus just as much a part of it as we are remote from it. From this point forward, Sartre will deal with the negative relation between being and nothingness *within* being. Or, to be more exact, "being," which has a variety of meanings for Sartre, will come to deal more or less exclusively with the being-in-itself of the natural and historical world that consciousness encounters (i.e., "being" in the first sense) and not the abstract philosophical concept of Being that concerns Heidegger and more current French thinkers (i.e., "being" in the second sense).

In short, for Sartre, the problematic that will be embraced by Heidegger in his late works and Derrida in his early works is anticipated and left behind. With respect to his being-in-itself, which Sartre alternately describes as "solid" or "full positivity," there is really nothing to say: "Being is. Being is in-itself. Being is what it is" (B&N, pp. 28–29). Thus, while the nothingness of consciousness, which is the forerunner of *différance*, "lies coiled in the heart of Being—like a worm" (B&N, p. 56), it is not Sartre's intent to dwell interminably on the fact that nothingness is always-already at a remove from the heart of Being. To the contrary, Sartre goes on to cut the Gordian knot so that he can address himself to more socially relevant existential concerns. This does not mean, of course, that Sartre will arbitrarily institute philosophical closure, for such a move would be no less of an anathema to him than Derrida (or, for that matter, Adorno). Rather, as we shall see in the following chapter, Sartre will reinstantiate this aporia within the context of subjectivity itself—that is, in the inability of consciousness (being-for-itself) to reconcile itself with being-in-itself (alternatively, the human and natural world, which includes the facts about your self), which is manifested in the unavoidability of "bad faith." Before proceeding to the following chapter, however, I will briefly consider Sartre's theory of knowledge (to the extent that he has one), as well as his rejection of any philosophical use of death, which, again, puts him in sharp contrast to Heidegger and his poststructuralist followers.

Knowing

"Sartre is scarcely troubled by epistemology," according to Raymond Aron,[12] and Sartre himself endorses the claim. Thus, when questioned by Michel Rybalka, who tells Sartre that he has "often been criticized for not being interested in scientific thought and epistemology," Sartre replies: "But after all, I never found them terribly absorbing."[13] Nevertheless, although he does not take himself to be dealing with epistemology, as both *Transcendence of the Ego* and *Being and Nothingness* suggest, Sartre does have a theory of knowledge in his earlier works.

In *Transcendence of the Ego*, Sartre contends that Husserl's reliance on a transcendental ego that stands behind consciousness's activities interferes with the fundamental objective of the phenomenological project, "getting back to the things themselves," because the transcendental ego needs to have its relation to the objects of consciousness's intuition mediated. To grasp the object, then, we would first have to grasp the "content" of the transcendental ego, which does not get us back to the things themselves but rather to what Adorno derisively calls the "constituting subjectivity" of classical idealism. Yet, this option, which is no less palatable to Sartre than to Adorno, does not move Sartre to accept Heidegger's rendition of phenomenology, which throws the baby out with the bath water by discarding not only the transcendental ego but the subject in total. As is the case with Adorno, Sartre rejects Heidegger's purge of the subject side of the subject-object dialectic. Instead, he retains the subject-object paradigm of knowledge by carving up the world into pure consciousness and its objects, neither of which is reducible to the other:

> The transcendental *I* is the death of consciousness. Indeed, the existence of consciousness is an absolute because consciousness is consciousness of itself. This is to say that the type of existence of consciousness is to be consciousness of itself. And consciousness is aware of itself *in so far as it is consciousness of a transcendent object*. All is therefore clear and lucid in consciousness: the object with its characteristic opacity is before consciousness, but consciousness is purely and simply consciousness of being conscious of that object. This is the law of its existence. We should add that this consciousness of consciousness . . . is not *positional*, which is to say that consciousness is not for itself its own object. Its object by nature is outside of it. . . . Consciousness knows itself only as absolute inwardness. We shall call such a consciousness: consciousness in the first degree, or *unreflected* consciousness. (TE, pp. 40–41; Sartre's emphasis)

Crucially, for Sartre, this approach, which is fleshed out but still essentially followed in *Being and Nothingness*, produces metaphysical, epistemological, and ethical advantages. The metaphysical advantage is that it saves Sartre from idealism. Because consciousness is "clear and lucid"—that is, it is nothing more than the immediate awareness of some transcendent object that is not itself consciousness—Sartre is in a position to proffer what he calls an "ontological proof" for the existence of the external world: "consciousness is born supported by a being which is not itself. . . . To say that consciousness is consciousness of something is to say that it must produce itself as a revealed-revelation of a being which is not it and which gives itself as already existing when consciousness reveals it" (B&N, p. 24). In other words, from the fact that consciousness is itself nothing other than its awareness, it necessarily follows that the objects of which it is aware are independent of it. The epistemological benefit, which shall be fleshed out momentarily, is that it purges consciousness's "transcendental field" of all egological structures, thus enabling consciousness to apprehend objects in their transparency (TE, p. 93). And, finally, the ethical benefit, which will be fleshed out in chapter 6, is that it sets up the phenomenological-ontological foundation for Sartre's claim in *Being and Nothingness* that we are "absolutely free." Emptied of all "contents," consciousness is determined by neither an inherent self nor the objects of the empirical world.

The "consciousness in the first degree, or unreflected consciousness" to which Sartre refers in this passage is the forerunner of what he calls the prereflective cogito in *Being and Nothingness*, and it indicates both our positional consciousness of objects (i.e., our immediate awareness of the world) and our nonpositional consciousness (of) this consciousness (i.e., our immediate awareness of this awareness), which Sartre takes to be a necessary condition of all awareness. The parentheses around "of"—first used by Sartre in *Being and Nothingness*—are intended to indicate that this foundational nonpositional consciousness is not one that "knows" the positional consciousness of the object in some detached fashion (i.e., as an object in its own right), but rather is one with this positional consciousness: there is "an immediate, noncognitive relation of the self to itself" (B&N, p. 12). This is critical not only because it prevents a situation in which the nonpositional consciousness would need to be an object of another nonpositional consciousness to be grounded, which would occasion an infinite regress, but also because it gives rise to the possibility that this consciousness (of) consciousness can stand in a nonobjectifying relation to its positional consciousness of objects. By avoiding this objectifying relation, which would merely reproduce within a bifurcated consciousness the classic epistemological question as to whether our representations truly correspond to reality,[14] Sartre hopes to avoid the impasse to which this question leads. Accordingly, Sartre's embrace of Husserl's phenomenology, shorn of the transcendental ego, provides the basis for "getting back to the things themselves" because consciousnesness's direct relation to the objects of its awareness yields an immediate, intuitive knowing that, for Sartre, is the privileged form in which we can come to know the thing: "it puts us in the presence of the thing" (TE, p. 35). When Sartre states that "the necessary and sufficient condition for a knowing consciousness to be knowledge of its object is that it be consciousness of itself as being that knowledge" (B&N, p. 11), then, it must be emphasized that the knowledge to which he refers is not conceptual knowledge but rather intuitive "knowledge."[15]

Indeed, the importance of intuitive knowledge for Sartre is implicit in his claim that the prereflective cogito's nonpositional consciousness (of) positional consciousness is a unitary phenomenon, for this suggests that dichotomous reflection is only a secondary phenomenon that presupposes unreflective consciousness: "it is the non-reflective consciousness which renders reflection possible" (B&N, p. 13). This evidences an essential break with Descartes, who, Sartre claims, wrongly conflates the reflective consciousness that says "I think" with the prereflective consciousness that truly thinks (TE, p. 45). Because Sartre's consciousness (of) consciousness merely establishes the foundation on which all consciousness is made possible, this function of the prereflective cogito actually has a much greater affinity with Kant's transcendental unity of apperception than with Descartes cogito. It is not by accident, therefore, that *Transcendence of the Ego* begins with neither Husserl nor Descartes but rather with Kant, and, in particular, his contention that the "I think must be able to accompany all our representations" (TE, p. 32). Like Kant's transcendental unity of apperception, which Sartre characterizes as "nothing but the set of conditions which are necessary for the existence of an empirical consciousness" (TE, p. 33), in Sartre's own thought, the prereflective cogito is the condition that is necessary for the existence of an empirical consciousness. Of course, I do not mean to suggest that Sartre buys into Kant's transcendental unity of apperception (much less his transcendental ego *writ large*, which, with its categories, burdens consciousness far more than Husserl's transcendental ego, and leads to the conclusion that the things themselves are off limits). For Sartre, in contrast to Kant, for whom the "I" is intrinsic to the transcendental unity of apperception, the "I" is neither intrinsic to the prereflective cogito, in particular, nor consciousness, more generally, but is reflectively ascribed by consciousness to itself retroactively: "It is consciousness which unifies itself, concretely, by a play of transversal intentionalities which are concrete and real retentions of past consciousnesses. Thus consciousness refers perpetually to itself" (TE, p. 39). Crucially, then, not only is the ego (i.e., the "me" or empirical self) "outside, in the world" (TE, p. 31), as it is for Kant, but so is the "I." And this is the case whether the "I" is understood materially, "as an infinite contraction of the material *me*" (TE, p. 54), or formally, as the "unity of [my] actions" (TE, p. 60), for even in this way, it neither inhabits consciousness nor effects the synthesis of our experience.

The key epistemological distinction that Sartre draws is between intuitions and concepts, both of which, he states, are rooted in the "phenomenon of being." (Due to the transphenomenal nature of being, it will be remembered, there is no basis for either intuiting or conceptualizing the "being of the phenomenon" itself, which is simply the condition of the appearances that can be intuited or conceptualized instead of the appearances themselves.) While, as a phenomenologist, Sartre privileges the immediate seeing or direct apprehension of things that comes through "the revealing intuition of the phenomenon of being" (B&N, p. 9), he is also concerned with concept formation, and, in particular, concept formation that properly manifests the insights of intuition. Although, in contrast to intuitive truths, conceptual truths are only probable by virtue of the fact that they are mediated—that is to say, they result from a subject-object paradigm in which the content of experience is objectified as a result of being reflected on—they are as necessary as they are fallible. A detailed answer as to why this is so must await chapter 6 (and, what's more, the nature of this answer changes somewhat in the movement from *The Transcendence of the Ego* to *Being and Nothingness*). The short answer for present purposes, however, is that the "I" or "me"—the empirical self that is "out in the world"—is the product of reflection, and therefore from "consciousness in the first degree, or unreflected consciousness," there is an inexorable movement to a "consciousness in the second degree, or reflected consciousness," which then reflects on the things of the world with the aim of making good its own egological commitments.

Thus, although Sartre says that "by not considering being as the condition of revelation but rather being as an appearance which can be determined in concepts, we have understood first of all that knowledge can not by itself give an account of being" (B&N, p. 9), he is not saying that concepts should simply be discarded but rather that as an explanatory tool they should be grasped in a somewhat more modest fashion. Being might outstrip our ability to conceptualize it, but this does not mean that the concept itself is rendered superfluous, for it remains incumbent on us to try to bridge this unbridgeable difference (just as it shall remain incumbent on us to try to bridge the unbridgeable difference between "bad faith" and "good faith"). On this point, it seems to me, Sartre's phenomenology and Adorno's negative dialectic approach one another. It will be remembered that Adorno also attacks both the classic use of concepts, which invariably fails to give the phenomenon its due, and the discarding of concepts altogether, which would merely result in the replication of the prevailing sociohistorical conditions. Along these lines, Adorno states:

> We fail to do justice to the concept of Being, however, until we also grasp the genuine experience that effects its instauration: the philosophical urge to express the inexpressible. The more anxiously a philosophy resists that urge, which is its peculiarity, the greater the temptation to tackle the inexpressible directly, without the labor of Sisyphus—which, by the way, would not be the worst definition of philosophy. (ND, p. 108)

For both Sartre and Adorno (and, for that matter, Derrida), then, there is a recognition of both the inadequacy and unavoidability of concepts.

Moreover, unlike his immediate predecessors in the phenomenological tradition, Sartre's account of conceptual knowledge progresses, albeit implicitly, toward a dialectical theory of knowledge, which is also in keeping with Adorno's position. After introducing what he refers to as the "new dualism" of finite and infinite, Sartre declares that the existent "can not be reduced to a finite series of manifestations since each one of them is a relation to a subject constantly changing. Although an object may disclose itself only through a single *Abschattung*, the sole fact of there being a subject implies the possibility of multiplying [to infinity] the points of view on that *Abschattung*" (B&N, p. 5). Although Sartre's discussion is admittedly cryptic, I believe that his emphasis on a subject that is "constantly changing" has far reaching implications. To be sure, unlike Husserl's transcendental ego, which statically intuits essences from a privileged point of view, Sartre's prereflective cogito, by virtue of its unity with positional consciousness, is inescapably in a changing world. As Thomas Flynn eloquently puts it, "the prereflective cogito considered as transcendence breaks through Husserl's 'pointillism of essence' to the reality of concrete, individual beings in their temporal flow."[16] Moreover, because "concrete, individual beings in their temporal flow" are "constantly changing" due to sociohistorical conditions that are constantly changing, conceptual knowledge is based on an intuitive knowledge that arises from the historically changing nature of immediate experience. I shall elaborate on this shortly.

In the meantime, Sartre's claims concerning an intuitive knowledge of the "phenomenon of being" are somewhat more problematical—largely because Sartre is less than clear on exactly what "being" means in this context. To be sure, an intuitive knowledge of "the phenomenon of being, like every primary phenomenon, is immediately disclosed to consciousness. We have at each instant what Heidegger calls a pre-ontological comprehension of it; that is, one which is not accompanied by a fixing in concepts and elucidation" (B&N, p. 25). And, to be sure, in contrast to Heidegger, although Sartre also believes that we can have a "meaning of being," that meaning applies *only* to the phenomenon of being rather than to being itself—in other words, there can be no intuitive knowledge of the being of the phenomenon that would yield such a meaning. Yet, in another respect, as was mentioned in the last section, Sartre flirts with a position of Heidegger's that he would be much better off rejecting. When Sartre speaks of an immediate apprehension of being, he means not only "concrete, individual beings in their temporal flow" but being itself, more generally, which smacks of Heidegger's distinction between the being of beings and Being. These two senses of being must be clearly differentiated.

Sartre's assertion that we can have an intuitive knowledge of the "phenomenon of being" qua "being" itself is the most flawed aspect of *Being and Nothingness*. For it is here, and not in his explication of phenomenological freedom, that Sartre is most guilty of the charge that is leveled by Adorno and Marcuse—namely, that he has ontologized a bad reality. Therefore, when Sartre asserts in *Being and Nothingness* that "being will be disclosed to us by some kind of immediate access—boredom, nausea, etc., and ontology will be the description of the phenomenon of being as it manifests itself . . . without intermediary" (B&N, p. 7), he is mistaken. Boredom and nausea reveal absolutely nothing about the "phenomenon of being" (understood as "being," more generally) and "ontology" is not a description of its manifestation. What boredom and nausea reveal, rather, are a profound alienation from one's personal (empirical) existence, and it is a psychosocial analysis—not ontology—that more accurately describes this manifestation. Yet, I am not suggesting here that we should drop Sartre's reliance on intuitions, for I think that they are deeply revealing—in fact, as I shall argue, they may be truer than conceptual knowledge in terms of revealing to us the degree to which we are "self-actualized." I am just suggesting that they must be understood dialectically, not ontologically.

Sartre himself begins to recognize this necessity in 1948, which was not only a mere five years after *Being and Nothingness* was published, but was a time when he was still theorizing out of the categories advanced in the book's phenomenological ontology. In *Truth and Existence* (a manuscript that was published nine years after Sartre's death), Sartre continues to maintain that "the criterion of truth" is "Being as presence."[17] Yet, although, unfortunately, he can sometimes lapse into claims about the nature of Being in a more general sense, such as when he claims that anguish "is an absolute revelation and absolutely transmits Being,"[18] he begins to understand the way that Being is "revealed" by intuition in a more dialectical fashion: "Man must seek Being, but through historialization." (Historiality differs from historicity in that it is the perspective of the subject that must actively make itself in history rather than the perspective of a subject that is wholly made by history.) Thus, according to Sartre:

> We can explain the portion of truth that I have grasped in the world through my *Einstellung*, my complexes and my historical surroundings. Thus revelation itself has an outside, as a free operation of my mind, which escapes me at the very time I freely carry out this revelation. I am paralyzed by an objectivity I do not know. This explains the temptation towards pessimism which should be rejected: what I see appears to me as pure, relative *relationship* to my history, my character, my education, etc. In fact, we must hold on firmly to the evidence as absolute evidence that no one can take from us, all the while recognizing that this evidence is paralyzed in its core by the look of others, which defines it but cannot suppress it. . . . It would be a mistake to believe that it is *relative* to th[e] situation, in other words, that it is nonrevelatory and purely subjective epiphenomenon.[19]

Sartre's position here, it seems to me, moves in the direction of fleshing out the notion that "the existent can not be reduced to a finite series of manifestations since each one of them is a relation to a subject constantly changing." He plunges this subject into its "complexes" and "historical surrounding," but without jettisoning the kernel of objective truth—or, as Sartre now puts it, "the *portion* of truth"—that each individual subject is in a position to glean. When Adorno declares that "the splinter in your eye is the best magnifying glass" (MM, p. 50), he is saying much the same thing: the limitations of one's *Einstellung* are also the perspective from which an objective truth can be wrested—that is, one that is "revelatory" and not just a "subjective epiphenomenon."

What I am suggesting, in the final analysis, is that Sartre begins to move in the direction of what I take to be most valuable in his phenomenology—namely, the revealing intuitions of an unabashed first-person perspective, which struggles to do justice to objective truths that might help break up the conceptual stranglehold of a sociohistorically engendered situation that tends to close off alternative ways of seeing and knowing. And, crucially, it is through an unremitting attention to the particulars of the situation—"the reality of concrete, individual beings in their temporal flow"—that this can come about. For Sartre, these revealing intuitions are unique in that they transcend "consciousness in the first degree, or unreflected consciousness" by, in some sense, being reflective, as phenomenological evidence must be, but they are not reflective in the detached, subject-object fashion of conceptual knowledge, as is the case with "consciousness in the second degree, or reflected consciousness." Thus, this consciousness, which addresses the need for reflection without sacrificing the phenomenological imperative for immediacy, is, as Flynn puts it, a kind of "reflective immediacy."[20] So far so good. Yet, this consciousness, which Sartre calls "pure reflection," is, as he acknowledges, limited: "Pure reflection (which, however, is not necessarily phenomenological reduction) keeps to the given without setting up claims for the future. . . . [It is] merely descriptive, which disarms the unreflected consciousness by granting its instantaneousness" (TE, pp. 64–65).[21] This means that phenomenological insights *must* be conceptually mediated, lest they perpetually arise and disappear in the instant (which assumes a consciousness without an empirical self, which Sartre surely denies) or become fetishized (which assumes a conceptual hypostatization that would also hypostatize the empirical self, which is the gist of the ubiquitous Sartrean phenomenon of "bad faith"). And, with the conceptual mediation of these phenomenological insights, phenomenology opens on to historialization, and, ultimately, history, which would incorporate these insights.

DEATH

The nothingness of death figures prominently in the thought of Heidegger and his French followers. According to Heidegger, a person's anxiety in the face of the recognition that one is a "being-towards-death," which frees one from the tranquilizing fashion in which "the they" has conditioned the perception of death, performs an individuating function: a person's recognition that death is actually one's "ownmost potentiality-for-Being, which is non-relational and not to be outstripped,"[22] opens up the possibility that one can assume an authentic stance toward existence, and is therefore the condition of opening up all other possibilities. This foundational approach towards death is rejected by French thinkers such as Levinas and Blanchot, who do not buy into the possibility of self-presence that it implies. But, in rejecting Heidegger's approach to death, they do not reject the theoretical centrality of death. To the contrary, death becomes for them the non-foundational foundation of their theoretical moves.[23]

Sartre will have no truck with this fetishization of death,[24] and in *Being and Nothingness* he offers a number of arguments that deprive death of any foundational status in philosophy. He begins his discussion of death by stating that before Heidegger had raised the idea that death was an event in human life, which required that it be examined from a completely "different point of view," "death had appeared to us as pre-eminently non-human since it was what there was on the other side of the 'wall'" (B&N, p. 680). Sartre's allusion to "the wall" here refers to his short story by the same name, which involves two captured loyalists in the Spanish Civil War who are awaiting execution by the fascists. One of the prisoners, Tom, tries to imagine his impending death, but he cannot do so:

> It's like a nightmare. You want to think something, you always have the impression that it's all right, that you're going to understand and then it slips, it escapes you and fades away. I tell myself there will be nothing afterwards. But I don't understand what it means. Sometimes I almost can . . . and then it fades away and I start thinking about the pains again, bullets, explosions. I'm a materialist, I swear it to you; I'm not going crazy. But something's the matter. I see my corpse; that's not hard but I'm the one who sees it, with my eyes. I've got to

think . . . think that I won't see anything any more and the world will go on for the others. We aren't made to think that, Pablo. Believe me: I've already stayed up a whole night waiting for something. But this isn't the same: this will creep up behind us, Pablo, and we won't be able to prepare for it."[25]

Although Sartre proceeds to examine Heidegger's philosophical appropriation of death "from the beginning" (B&N, p. 682), in the final analysis he will return to an understanding of death that is consistent with Tom's intuition that it is beyond the pale of human significance.

Sartre thus declares that death can be neither one's ultimate possibility nor the thing that gives one's life its meaning. Although it is a factual possibility that can take place at any time, death "can not be apprehended as *my* possibility but, on the contrary, as the nihilation of all my possibilities, a nihilation which itself is no longer a part of my possibilities" (B&N, p. 687). In other words, for death to be *my* possibility, *my* subjectivity would have to be capable of realizing it, but, of course, this presupposes that I will not actually be dead. (In contrast to Tom in "The Wall," the retention of subjectivity by the three protagonists in Sartre's play "No Exit" presents just such a situation. But even in this situation, death could not have been "*my* possibility" for Garcin, Inez, or Estelle because they could not know that their consciousnesses would survive it.) Thus, "since death is always beyond my subjectivity, [and] there is no place for it in my subjectivity" (B&N, p. 700), it is axiomatic that death cannot be my possibility. The factual possibility of my death simply means "that I am biologically only a relatively closed, relatively isolated system" (B&N, p. 685). Similarly, death cannot be that which gives my life its meaning. As an initial matter, since we do not freely choose the time at which we die, it is the arbitrariness of death's timing and not its inevitability that would seem to give life its final meaning. Whether or not I have had the time to realize my projects will determine the meaning of my life. More importantly, as this suggests, since the meaning of my life is determined by the free positings of *my* subjectivity, and since my subjectivity is eclipsed by death, death does not give meaning to life but rather "removes all meaning from life" (B&N, p. 689).

Just because death "removes all meaning from life," however, it does not follow that my life can have no meaning or that it can have no meaning after my death. To the contrary, by rejecting the idea that death can give life its meaning, death just becomes an "unrealizable to be realized" (B&N, p. 700) that ceases to concern us. From this standpoint, our freedom remains untrammeled, and we are forced to confront the fact that we are wholly responsible for giving a determinate meaning to our lives through our choices. So, too, although my death removes all meaning from life *for me*, I continue to have a meaning for those who survive me, just as those who have died before me have a meaning for me. Indeed, for Sartre, this is unavoidable: the for-itself must assume a position in relation to the dead. But, unlike Marx, who emphasizes how the the dead weigh on the brains of the living, Sartre also emphasizes how the living "weigh" on the dead: "Of course the dead choose us, but it is necessary first that we have chosen them" (B&N, p. 694). Through death, which obliterates the for-itself, the dead become an in-itself whose very meaning is crafted to conform with the freely chosen projects of the living. Consequently, "the one who tries to grasp the meaning of his future death must discover himself as the future prey of others" (B&N, p. 695).

In sum, then, as was the case with his positions on being and knowing, Sartre's position on death sharply breaks with both his predecessors and his followers in the phenomenological and existential traditions. As we shall see in chapter 6, the same can also be said for his theory of subjectivity.

6

Sartre's Mediating Subjectivity

Sartre's phenomenological ontology implies that as agents in the world we must, practically speaking, experience ourselves as free and responsible, but this does not mean that it is Sartre's claim that we are "absolutely" free, as so many critics in addition to Adorno and Marcuse have maintained. Matters are far more complicated, for right after Sartre posits the notion that we are free in the final section of chapter one of *Being and Nothingness* ("The Origin of Nothingness"), he proceeds to qualify this position—indeed, in a very real sense, much of the book's remainder is a qualification of this central thesis. In the very next chapter, Sartre deals with the ubiquitous phenomenon of "bad faith," which involves what is by all appearances our inevitable attempt to deceive ourselves about the nature of our freedom. And, after dealing with the general structures of the for-itself in part II, Sartre deals with the problem of being-for-others, which involves the limits that are placed on our freedom by the freedom of "the Other." Thus, when Sartre squarely returns to the issue of freedom in the last part of *Being and Nothingness*, which deals with our freedom *in situation*, as well as the practical limits that are imposed by what he terms "the fundamental project" (the apparently universal human impulse to be a "for-itself-in-itself"), his notion of freedom has been fully developed (if not overwhelmed) and is no longer subject to the charge that it involves understanding ourselves as "absolutely" free. In the final analysis, Sartre does not deny the contextually limited nature of all of our choices but only the notion that any particular choice, regardless of the circumstances, is ever actually determined. As I shall argue in this chapter, this is due to the *phenomenological* space afforded by Sartre's particular conception of consciousness, which puts us beyond determinism and provides the thin margin for the notion of a *mediating* subjectivity.

In the first section, I shall consider the basic constituents of Sartre's decentered subject, which is the product of his synthesis of the philosophies of Husserl and Heidegger. In particular, I shall focus on the prereflective cogito, which is the structure within Sartre's phenomenological ontology that testifies to our experience of freedom. In the second and third sections, I shall then consider the limits to human freedom that are established by our being-for-others and bad faith, respectively. I have broken with Sartre's ordering of these phenomena in *Being and Nothingness* (in which his exposition of bad faith comes before his exposition of being-for-others) because it is my view that our relations with others are an inextricable part of bad faith. Indeed, virtually every example of bad faith given by Sartre revolves around one's own self-conception, which on Sartre's account (like Hegel's before him) is engendered by one's relations with others. Finally, in the fourth section, I shall probe the boundaries of freedom in Sartre's thought, with particular emphasis on the prospects for a "purifying reflection," which is the only way that consciousness frees itself and becomes, in a strong sense, a mediating subjectivity.

SARTRE'S DECENTERED SUBJECT AND FREEDOM

One of the defining ideas in Sartre's philosophy is that human beings are fundamentally decentered—or, to put it in Sartre's words, "divided"—which makes it all the more ironic that he has been virtually ignored by the poststructuralists, who have preferred Husserl and, of course, Heidegger. Still, in contrast to Husserl, whose transcendental ego is "self-present" (in that it coincides with both itself and the objects whose essences it intuits), and Heidegger, whose "authentic" Dasein is present to being, it is ultimately only Sartre who posits the irreparability of our decenteredness. Thus, although Sartre does speak in terms of "self-presence" in *Being and Nothingness*, he uses this term to refer to the unbridgeable rupture that exists between reflecting consciousness and consciousness reflected-on:

> The self represents an ideal distance within the immanence of the subject in relation to himself, a way of not being his own coincidence, of escaping identity while positing it as a unity—in short, of being a perpetually unstable equilibrium between identity as absolute cohesion without a trace of diversity and unity as a synthesis of multplicity. This is what we shall call presence to itself. (B&N, pp. 123–124)

This "ideal distance within the immanence of the subject," which precludes him from becoming self-identical in the very same process through which he *must* posit himself as a unity,[1] not only precludes the subject from becoming his own foundation but also splits him off from the world of which he is nevertheless an inextricable part. It is for this reason that Sartre refers to human beings as "a useless passion" (B&N, p. 784).[2]

Perhaps even more ironic is the fact that the poststructuralists continued to ignore Sartre even after they began searching for the grounds on which to found an ethics for *their* decentered subjects, since in the wake of poststructuralism's earlier theoretical commitments, these thinkers have been dispossessed of the resources that are necessary for such an undertaking. For despite his decidedly one-sided account of human relations (which, at any rate, can largely be balanced without altering the remainder of his thought), as well as his inability to formulate an ethics to his own satisfaction, Sartre provides a powerful theory of agency, and such a theory, which the poststructuralists lack, is indispensable to any ethical project. Thus, according to Sartre, whose exposition of the subject's constitution supports the claim, "each person is an absolute choice of self from the standpoint of a world of knowledges and of techniques which this choice both assumes and illumines" (B&N, p. 709). In other words, each person is not just a function of "a world of knowledges and of techniques," but, just as importantly, surpasses and reformulates these knowledges and techniques in the pursuit of his freely chosen ends. This position sharply contrasts with the position of the poststructuralists, whose subjectless subject is nothing more than a function of these existing knowledges and techniques but is still somehow also supposed to be a vigorous moral agent.

In this section, I shall focus on the prereflective cogito, which is not only the ground of our knowledge, as was briefly discussed in the previous chapter's section on knowledge, but is also the ground of

Sartrean agency. It is, in other words, the active or "mediating" constituent of human subjectivity. Before converging on the prereflective cogito, however, I shall summarily discuss the basic constituents of Sartre's "decentered subject" in *Being and Nothingness*. This general outline will be progressively fleshed out over the following sections.

Human beings, according to Sartre, are dispersed across what he takes to be the three essential structures of being—being-in-itself, being-for-itself, and being-for-others—and the three temporal dimensions (past, present, and future). As we saw in the previous chapter, being-in-itself is that aspect of being that is self-identical, and it is alternatively described by Sartre as "solid," "a synthesis of itself with itself," or "full positivity" (B&N, pp. 28–29).[3] Beyond just referring to the material world, which constitutes his first paradigm of being-in-itself, however, being-in-itself refers to "facticity," more generally, which includes, among other things, the past. Thus, Sartre asserts that the past, "like Facticity, is the invulnerable contingency of the in-itself which I have to be, without any possibility of not being it. It is the inevitability of the necessity of fact, not by virtue of necessity but by virtue of fact" (B&N, p. 173).

Sartre emphasizes fact in opposition to necessity here because being-for-itself, which, quite literally, is nothing other than consciousness, is not determined by "the facts"—although consciousness *must* nevertheless exist its factual context. More specifically, as I previously discussed, because consciousness does not contain the ego or any other substance that would cause it to be determined by the laws of nature, but rather is characterized by intentionality (i.e., it is always about the objects of which it is positionally aware),[4] it is "nothing," or, to be precise, a "nothingness" that perpetually transcends itself. And, in the process of transcending itself, consciousness is a "nihilating nothingness" that gives rise to "negatités." In other words, this "nothingness" is active, and, in accordance with its specific project, it nihilates—that is to say, negates—various aspects of the solidity that is being-in-itself. Thus, on entering a crowded café in search of my friend, I nihilate the fullness of being that is this crowded café, which now constitutes the undifferentiated ground on which my friend will arise. But if my friend does not appear, I will experience the café as being haunted by a negation or a negatité—namely, the absence of my friend, which is an "objective fact." Of course, my project can change at any time, in which case, despite the relative constancy of my factual situation, the undifferentiated ground of my experience will change. Indeed, more basically, as I shall discuss in detail later, the for-itself is *essentially* a project, and therefore it is necessarily always beyond itself. Unlike being-in-itself, then, which refers to the past, being-for-itself refers to the future: "There is in my consciousness no moment which is not defined by an internal relation to the future. . . . The meaning of my conscious states is always at a distance" (B&N, p. 181).

In sum, evidenced here is the first half of Sartre's principal formulation concerning the nonidentical nature of the subject—namely, that consciousness "is what it is not and is not what it is" (B&N, p. 112).[5] As an initial matter, consciousness "is what it is not" because it is purely intentional—that is, it is constituted by the world of which it is intentionally aware, which founds it but never completely. But consciousness is never passively aware, and, therefore, as we have seen, it also "is what it is not" by virtue of its ability to negate various aspects of the world of which it is aware. This is what enables consciousness to imagine, interrogate, doubt, and, as we have seen, experience absence, all of which revolve around its ability to project itself toward the future. Even more fundamentally, the ability of consciousness to negate various aspects of the world might be the very condition of perception's posibility, for in the absence of this ability, being-in-itself would simply be an undifferentiated mass or what has been called a "blooming, buzzing confusion."[6]

Being-for-itself is, therefore, basically a relation (B&N, p. 472), and in addition to being mediated by its relation to being-in-itself, being-for-itself is mediated by its relation to others: "The Other is the indispensable mediator between myself and me . . . I am put in the position of passing judgment on myself as on an object, for it is as an object that I appear to the Other. . . . But at the same time, I need the Other in order to realize fully all the structures of my being" (B&N, pp. 302–303). As the indispensable condition of making the for-itself an object for itself, others are responsible for the development of the empirical ego—although, as I shall discuss in greater detail in a subsequent section, they are not responsible for all the particulars of its constitution. What is important to recognize for the moment, however, is that, according to Sartre, my "being-for-others" is on an ontological par with being-in-itself and being-for-itself. (I am essentially *for* others because our individual projects of founding ourselves invariably conflict on account of the mutual objectification that this process involves.) The other "appears as a being who arises in an original relation of being with me and whose indubitability and factual necessity are those of my own consciousness" (B&N, p. 367). Indeed, Sartre even asserts that there is a distinctive cogito that pertains to my relation to others:

> It is not in the world that the Other is first to be sought but at the side of consciousness as a consciousness in which and by which consciousness makes itself be what it is. Just as my consciousness apprehended by the cogito bears indubitable witness of itself and of its own existence, so certain particular consciousnesses—for example, "shame-consciousness"—bear indubitable witness to the cogito both of themselves and the existence of the other. (B&N, pp. 364–365)

In our being-for-others, we espy the basis for the second half of Sartre's contention that consciousness "is what it is not and is not what it is." In a manner of speaking, consciousness is the facticity of its past, which is what constitutes the empirical ego or "the Self" for both itself and for others. Yet, because the ego, which is first engendered by others, is not in consciousness, this historically determined "essence" does not, strictly speaking, determine consciousness, for consciousness can always put it "out of bounds." Accordingly, the freedom of consciousness "is characterized by a constantly renewed obligation to remake the Self which designates the free being" (B&N, p. 72). As Sartre might articulate it, consciousness must live the ego that it is, but always in the mode of not being it. Or, in other words, consciousness "is not what it is." The wellspring of this freedom for Sartre is the prereflective cogito, and it is to a consideration of this pivotal Sartrean structure that I now turn.

As we saw when considering consciousness from the standpoint of knowledge, the prereflective cogito is a nonpositional (or, put rather differently, "nonthetic") consciousness of our positional consciousness of objects. According to Sartre, all knowledge must be conscious of itself as knowledge in order to truly be knowledge, and the nonpositional consciousness of the prereflective cogito is what performs this function. This gives rise to the Fichtean problem of an infinite regress, however, and Sartre's response to this problem is to make nonpositional consciousness and positional consciousness a unitary phenomenon whose fundamental relation is one of being rather than knowing: "If we wish to avoid an infinite regress, there must be an immediate, noncognitive relation of the self to itself" (B&N, p. 12). Although the immediate, noncognitive nature of this self-relation will raise certain problems concerning Sartre's views on freedom and responsibility (which I shall discuss in the last section), it nevertheless performs the crucial theoretical function of permitting him to sublate the principal difference between the philosophies of Husserl and Heidegger, which, notwithstanding their strengths, are one-sided in diametrically opposed ways.

Boiled down for Sartre (as for Adorno), the basic difference between the philosophies of Husserl and Heidegger is that Husserl's Cartesian-inspired phenomenological method collapses the being of the object into an objectivized transcendental subject, while Heidegger's anti-Cartesian ontology collapses the subject into an object that has been unwittingly objectivized. Sartre, by way of contrast, seeks to circumvent the pitfalls of both Husserl's transcendental ego, which supports an eidetic analysis that reveals more about the structures of consciousness than the objects under analysis, and Heidegger's Dasein, whose "being-in-the-world" reveals more about the sociohistorical determinations of our world than the existential structures of Dasein. After asserting that "it makes no difference whether we consider the for-itself articulated in the in-itself as a well marked duality ["consciousness-being"] or as a disintegrated being," Sartre, referring to being as "a phenomenon," emphasizes that

> if it appears useful to employ the new notion of a phenomenon as a disintegrated totality, it will be necessary to speak of it *both* in terms of immanence and in terms of transcendence. The danger, in fact, would be of falling into either a doctrine of pure immanence (Husserlian idealism) or into one of pure transcendence which would look on the *phenomenon* as a new kind of *object*. But immanence will always be limited by the phenomenon's dimension in-itself, and transcendence will be limited by its dimension for-itself. (B&N, p. 795)

Moreover, in his 1948 lecture to the *Société française de philosophie*, in which he summarized the basic theses of *Being and Nothingness*, Sartre goes one step further by explicitly contending that the philosophies of

Husserl and Heidegger should be synthesized (which, of course, was one of the book's vital objectives, and accounts for the structure of its phenomenological ontology): "It is necessary to arrange a synthesis of the contemplative and non-dialectical consciousness of Husserl . . . with the activity of the dialectical project—but without consciousness, and hence without foundation—that we find in Heidegger, where we see, on the contrary, that the first element is transcendence."[7]

The unitary but two-tiered structure of prereflective consciousness (i.e., its positional awareness of intentional objects and the prereflective cogito's nonpositional awareness of this positional awareness) is what allows Sartre to bring about this synthesis. On the one hand, this duality "at one stroke" (B&N, p. 14) is what permits him to avoid falling prey to the unmediated duality that exists between the transcendental consciousness and an empirical or psychological consciousness. This is the problem that Kant bequeathed to Husserl, who purports to bracket the "natural attitude" (which, for Kant, was merely the stuff of anthropology). But with Husserl's recourse to transcendental consciousness, which does nothing less than ground both itself and the significance of its intentional objects, consciousness is cut off from the world in which it actually lives, which is why Sartre refers to this as a "non-dialectical consciousness," and, more broadly, Husserl's philosophy as a "doctrine of pure immanence."[8] By making the prereflective cogito, which crudely substitutes for Husserl's transcendental ego, one with the positional awareness of prereflective consciousness, Sartre plunges Husserl's transcendental consciousness back into the world. With the prereflective cogito, Sartre is still able to ground consciousness's positional knowledge of intentional objects, but now this immediate knowledge (of) our knowledge of intentional objects is non-cognitive, given its prereflective nature. Indeed, the cost of this move, as we previously saw, is that knowledge based on concepts is no longer "knowledge" in the firm (Husserlian) sense, for this kind of knowledge, which is based on the subject-object paradigm, is only probabilistic.[9] More importantly, by plunging Husserl's consciousness back into the world, *all* knowledge becomes inexorably engaged, and, therefore, perspectival: "The identity of the being of the for-itself and of knowledge does not come from the fact that knowledge is the measure of being but from the fact that the for-itself makes known to itself what it is through the in-itself" (B&N, pp. 294–295). There is no "objective" knowledge: knowledge is only *for us*.

On the other hand, although Sartre's for-itself makes known to itself what it is through its miscellaneous engagements in the world, which is a point that could just as easily be made about Heidegger's Dasein, the prereflective cogito affords the all important margin of distance between what is ultimately Sartre's robust notion of self-consciousness and Heidegger's outright rejection of it. If consciousness was truly nothing more than the positional consciousness of prereflective consciousness, there would really be no distinction between the two doctrines, for consciousness would then be nothing more than "pure" intentionality—that is, it would be entirely submerged in its object, or, to use Sartre's terminology in the passage set forth above, it would be a "pure transcendence." Before considering what this would mean from the ethical standpoint, which is my central concern here, however, it is necessary to consider the epistemological question one more time, for, in some sense, the epistemological standpoint is logically prior to the ethical one. The problem can be illuminated as follows: By all appearances, the kind of knowing that exists in Sartre's example of prereflectively counting cigarettes (B&N, p. 13) is structurally akin to the kind of knowing that exists in Heidegger's well-known example of the carpenter hammering in his shed: in both cases it is of a distinctly noncognitive nature, as the participants are seamlessly absorbed in their activities, the "I" nowhere to be found on the phenomenological horizon. On Heidegger's account, this kind of knowing needs no underlying internal structures to explain it, for Dasein's concern with its possibilities in the world comes first, and its awareness of itself arises from its concernful being-in-the-world. On Sartre's account, in sharp contrast, without the prereflective cogito, whose awareness of awareness comes first, prereflective knowing would itself be impossible. But if Sartre is wrong about this, and the prereflective cogitio can be shaved off with Ockham's razor, the cost to his key theses concerning freedom and responsibility would be enormous. The ground of Sartre's ethical mainstay, the purifying reflection, would also go by the wayside, and what Sartre says against Heidegger's denial of "the consciousness of ekstasis" in the epistemological context would continue to apply to the ethical one: the "ekstatic character of human reality [would] lapse into a thing-like, blind in-itself" (B&N, p. 120).

In her book on Sartre, Marjorie Grene argues that Heidegger's model of knowing is more than sufficient, and that Sartre's resort to the prereflective cogito involves an "invalid" argument that "distorts" his complete philosophy.[10] According to Grene, there is no compelling reason for Sartre to argue that for consciousness to have knowledge of an object, it must also be conscious of itself as having that knowledge. Grene does readily acknowledge that there is necessarily an implicit ground of knowledge, but she argues that this ground need not be self-reflexive as it is for Sartre. Rather than presuppose an immediate consciousness of knowledge, Grene contends, consciousness can be strictly oriented toward the world with a "subsidiary awareness" of what it knows—a "subsidiary awareness" that is initially constituted by the world in which we live, and only then interiorized. Grene points out that the cost of her alternative for Sartre's philosophy is high, for the denial of "the self-referential being of immediate consciousness" (the prereflective cogito) and, for that matter, "the wholly positional character of cognitive consciousness" (given that the Cartesian cogito follows from the prereflective cogito) would mean denying "the concept of consciousness as wholly active and instantaneous."[11] As my argument to this point suggests, it seems to me that Grene's last point is correct—that is, aside from its immediate, noncognitive knowledge (of) knowledge, the prereflective cogito is the linchpin of both the reflective cogito and freedom. The fashion in which Sartre deals with Heidegger's rejection of the prereflective cogito must therefore be looked at a bit more closely.

Thus, according to Sartre:

> Heidegger is so persuaded that the "I think" of Husserl is a trap . . . that he has completely avoided any appeal to consciousness in his description of Dasein. His goal is to show it immediately as care; that is, as escaping itself in the projecting of self toward the possibilities which it is. It is this project of the self outside the self which he calls "understanding." . . . But this attempt to show first the escape from self of the Dasein is going to encounter in turn insurmountable difficulties; we cannot first suppress the dimension "consciousness," not even if it is in order to re-establish it subsequently. Understanding has meaning only if it is consciousness of understanding. My possibility can exist as my possibility only if it is my consciousness which escapes itself toward my possibility. Otherwise, the whole system of being and its possibilities will fall back into the unconscious— that

> is, into the in-itself. Behold, we are thrown back again toward the cogito. We must make this our point of departure. (B&N, pp. 133–134)

On Sartre's account, Heidegger's attempt to circumvent (self-)consciousness (i.e., nonpositional or nonthetic consciousness) in busting open Husserl's self-enclosed cogito presupposes the very (self-)consciousness that he intends to reject,[12] for "my possibility" can only be "mine" if *I* am able to identify it as such, which is precisely what Heidegger's Dasein, as a "pure transcendence" submerged in the object, is not in a position to do.[13] As Sartre states above, "my possibility can exist as my possibility only if it is *my* [thetic] consciousness which escapes itself toward my possibility." This suggests that the "I" must precede its transcendence towards its possibility, which on Heidegger's account is "care," because even if, hypothetically speaking, the "I" could realize its possibility without such (self-)consciousness, it would not be in a position to recognize itself in its realized possibility. In this way, to say it again, the "I" would simply be a "thing-like, blind in-itself." What's more, as Manfred Frank argues, Heidegger's notion that Dasein comes to know itself by its engagements in the world, which reflect back to Dasein what it is, actually presupposes the "model of representation" that Heidegger rejects as being at the core of subject-centered metaphysics, and therefore, ironically, is at odds with his extreme anti-subjectivism. As Frank puts it:

> The view that the self owes the knowledge in which it carries itself to a reflection, which shines back to it from the *intentum* of a self-thematisation, uses precisely the justifiably criticized model of representation according to which a subject puts an object before it, whereby in this particular case the *intentum* is, exceptionally, the subject itself. According to this model we would have self-consciousness in analogy to the . . . consciousness of physical objects. That is obviously wrong and the argument attached to it is circular.[14]

I believe that this argument successfully responds to Grene's objections, but I shall not argue for it more vigorously because, for the purposes of my thesis, there is a more important problem that is tacitly raised by Heidegger's position that the mere existence of the prereflective cogito does not answer. The problem is that even if we get past Grene's strictly epistemological objection—that is, we grant the idea that the nonthetic consciousness of the prereflective cogito must be the "point of departure"—the "unitary duality" of consciousness that is the positional conciousness and the prereflective cogito might still not have the capacity for the robust sort of agency that Sartre presumes. In other words, Grene correctly points out that from an ontological standpoint the prereflective cogito is a necessary condition for the reflective cogito and freedom, but she does not get past her hostility to the prereflective cogito's very existence to further argue that it may not be a sufficient condition for the reflective cogito and freedom even if it does exist. Yet, given Sartre's insistence that the prereflective cogito is "in the world" by being one with positional consciousness, there is no reason to conclude that the "ideal distance" between the two insulates the prereflective cogito from colonization by "the they" in its "upsurge toward being" with purely intentional positional consciousness. This, of course, would negate Sartre's robust notions of reflection and freedom, which are necessary for a mediating subject. From a strictly "ontological" standpoint, then, Sartre's argument for the reflective cogito and freedom may fail.

Ultimately, however, Sartre's argument for reflection and freedom is not properly viewed from a strictly ontological standpoint, nor, for that matter, is it actually an "argument" at all. As I already discussed, Sartre's characterization of *Being and Nothingness* as a "*phenomenological* ontology" entails that all claims about the nature of the world must follow from the way in which we consciously experience ourselves within it, which means that Sartre's "ontological argument" actually follows from the phenomenological standpoint. Consequently, it is not the existence of the prereflective cogito that makes us free, but it is our experience of freedom—regardless of the metaphysical fact of the matter—that leads us to posit the prereflective cogito.[15] Sartre himself tends to speak in these terms:

> It would be in vain to object that the sole condition of this anguish [that reveals to me my freedom] is ignorance of the underlying psychological determinism. . . . Anguish has not appeared to us as *proof* of human freedom. . . . We wished only to show that there exists a specific consciousness of freedom, and we wished to show that this consciousness is anguish. This means that we wished to establish anguish in its essential

> structure as consciousness of freedom. Now *from this point of view* the existence of psychological [or metaphysical] determinism could not invalidate the results of our description. . . . It is not because I am free that my act is not subject to the determination of motives; on the contrary, the structure of motives as ineffective is the condition of my freedom. (B&N, pp. 70–71; italics added)

Determinism "is not given as a reflective intuition" (B&N, p. 79), according to Sartre, because despite the circumstances within which we find ourselves, we do not (unless we are in bad faith) experience them as determinative with respect to our decisions. No matter how "compelling" the circumstances, they are only persuasive. Thus, notwithstanding the actions that we have actually undertaken, we are always in a position to say that we could have done otherwise, which is the case in even those circumstances in which we did not reflect on our decision. For it is always the case that we could have reflected, and the fact that we did not was itself connected to a deeper set of freely embraced commitments or "projects." This reflection, furthermore, is not of the slight Heideggerian variety[16] (for then it would cut against the argument for freedom). Instead, due to the "reflecting-reflected-on" dyad that is innate to consciousness, we are always beyond our past and thus, in principle, able to bracket it. This is the gist of freedom, which is simply "the human being putting his past out of play" (B&N, p. 64).[17] And, finally, it is this very ability to bootstrap ourselves, to put our pasts "out of play," that points towards the "ideal distance" that suggests the existence of the prereflective cogito.

I shall return to Sartre's view of reflection and freedom in the last section of this chapter, but for now I would simply point out that we have our synthesis of Heidegger and Husserl. On the one hand, Sartre employs Heidegger's ontology to transport Husserl's transcendental ego into the world, while, on the other hand, he employs Husserl's phenomenological approach to create the necessary space for beings-in-the-world to bracket their empirical existences or "essences" (as Sartre wryly puts it) to move beyond them. Yet, this synthesis comes at a price: the objective knowledge afforded by Husserl's transcendental ego and the possibility of self-presence afforded by Heidegger's fundamental ontology both go by the wayside. But the upshot of this synthesis is nothing less than the starting point of Sartre's entire philosophy: the unique trait of human beings is to be a "freedom-in-the-world." From the phenomenological standpoint, this notion of being a freedom-in-the-world captures the very nature of what it means to be a mediating subject. As I will now show in my discussion of ego formation and the other, however, our "essence" must still be lived. It is not just an inconvenient obstacle that our freedom soars above.

BEING-FOR-OTHERS: THE EGO IN FORMATION

Sartre tackles numerous issues in his analysis of being-for-others, most of which cannot be considered at any great length here. Therefore, as the subtitle of this section implies, in what follows I shall be concerned mainly with the relation between being-for-others and the formation of the ego. The purpose of this particular inquiry is to show that Sartre's notion of subjectivity in *Being and Nothingness* is by no means as individualistic and abstract as many critics reflexively maintain.[18] To be sure, Sartre does not fill in his account with specific sociohistorical facts, for this is not the intent of his phenomenological ontology. The question, rather, is whether Sartre's phenomenological ontology tacitly incorporates sociohistorical categories into its understanding of what it means to be a person in the world, and on this score it is my position that there is no question but that it does.[19] In any event, as a preliminary matter, I shall briefly consider Sartre's response to the "reef of solipsism," for his examination of this enduring philosophical question, which more or less constitutes the first forty pages of his characterization of being-for-others, lays the groundwork for his understanding of ego formation.

Sartre contends that the classical responses of both realism and idealism to the problem of solipsism are inadequate to the task, and that, ultimately, these two archetypical positions tend to collapse into one another. On the one hand, realism, which Sartre characterizes as a "philosophy based on intuitions" (B&N, p. 304), is never actually presented with an intuition of the other's subjectivity: "It is not *the Other's* body which is present to the realist intuition but [only] a body" (B&N, p. 304), which, of course, does not preclude the possibility that the body we intuit is only a machine. Inasmuch as intuitions do not have access to the subjectivity of the Other, but only to a body, the realist must therefore proceed by analogy to his own consciousness to make out the existence of the Other. In other words, the existence of the Other's subjectivity becomes an issue of knowledge that is based on the extent to which the other's body conforms to behaviors that are akin to my own bodily behaviors—the greater the correspondence, the greater the likelihood that the other exists. But, of course, this knowledge is never more than probable, and, therefore, the realist is ultimately relegated to bridging the gap by "representing" the Other's existence, which is precisely what the idealist does. On the other hand, idealism, or, to be more precise, Kant's "critical idealism," begins with the notion that we know others through our representations of them, but the problem here is that the Other's subjectivity, which founds his own representations, is on principle outside any knowledge that the Kantian can have of it. I necessarily objectify the Other's subjectivity, just as my subjectivity is necessarily objectified by him. But this does not get the idealist any closer to the other's subjectivity than the realist's recourse to representations, which leads those idealists who do not directly collapse into an affirmation of solipsism to posit the existence of the Other as a self-contained substance, which smacks of a dogmatic realism.

The misconceived "presupposition common to both idealism and realism," according to Sartre, "is that the constituting negation is an external negation" that separates us from the Other "by a real or ideal space" (B&N, pp. 312–313). This has two consequenses. First, with respect to the problem of solipsism, it renders the Other an object of knowledge, and thus only probable. Second, and more importantly for our purposes, it suggests that the Other is only an "indifferent exteriority" who cannot affect me in my being (B&N, pp. 313–314). Therefore, after summarily examining Husserl's response to the problem of solipsism (which, by virtue of its reliance on the transcendental ego, is "not perceptibly different than Kant's" [B&N, p. 317]), as well as the responses of both Hegel and Heidegger (which I shall consider in due course), Sartre rejects this underlying presupposition by attempting to show that interpersonal relations are originally an "internal negation"—that is, "a negation which posits the original distinction between the Other and myself as being such that it determines me by means of the Other and determines the Other by means of me" (B&N, p. 315). Sartre's argument builds on the prior distinction that he made between immediate (self-)consciousness and mediated self-consciousness (or self-knowledge). To be more specific, just as reflective self-knowledge is based on an underlying immediate consciousness (of) self, reflective knowledge of the other is based on an underlying immediate consciousness (of) the Other, which, I take it, is exactly why Sartre talks in terms of a "second cogito": "Just as my consciousness apprehended by the cogito bears indubitable witness of itself and of its own existence, so certain particular consciousnesses . . . bear indubitable witness to the cogito both of themselves and of the existence of the Other" (B&N, pp. 364–365). Accordingly, by seeing our relation to others as an internal relation, or, more specifically, an internal negation, Sartre is not only saying that our knowledge (of) the Other's existence takes place on the plane of being rather than knowing. He is also saying that it is ultimately on the plane of being that human beings intersubjectively constitute one another.

In any event, as is well known, Sartre purports to establish the existence of this "internal negation" between human beings, and therefore overcome the "reef of solipsism," through the phenomenon of "the look." On Sartre's account, the look is a "fundamental" and "immediate" relation between me and the Other in which I do not grasp the Other as an object, as idealists and realists are inclined to do, but, rather, as a subject:

> If the Other-as-object is identified in connection with the world as the object which sees what I see, then my fundamental connection with the Other-as-subject must be able to be referred back to my permanent possibility of being seen by the Other. It is in and through the revelation of my being-as-object for the Other that I must be able to apprehend the presence of his being-as-subject. (B&N, pp. 344–345)

The example that Sartre uses to illustrate this phenomenon involves a voyeur who is abruptly caught in the act of peering through a keyhole. At the very moment the Other's look is apprehended, the voyeur begins to feel shame, which signifies a "*recognition* of the fact that [the voyeur is] indeed that object which the Other is looking at and judging" (B&N, p. 350). With this nonpositional consciousness (of) shame or shame-consciousness, there can be no doubt that the Other exists as a subject, for in the experience of being an "unrevealed object-ness," the voyeur "experiences the inapprehensible subjectivity of the Other directly and with [his or her] being" (B&N, pp. 361–362). Accordingly, unlike all the objects that constitute the voyeur's (self-)centered phenomenological world (which includes other persons whom the voyeur might objectify, and thus make objects of only probable knowledge), the look of the Other completely decenters this person's phenomenological world. It causes one to experience an "internal hemorrhage" in one's world in which all of its constituents—including one(self)—flow toward the Other "without limit": "The world flows out of the world and [he] flows out of himself" (B&N, p. 350).

Strictly speaking, Sartre's response to the problem of solipsism must be deemed a failure. Just as the realist and idealist cannot get beyond the probable nature of the Other's subjectivity by considering him as an object of knowledge, there can be little doubt but that Sartre cannot get beyond the probable nature of the Other as subject by immediately apprehending his look. And, indeed, it seems fairly clear that Sartre himself would agree. Thus, shortly before introducing the example of the voyeur, Sartre asserts that, "in a word, my apprehension of the Other in the world as *probably being* a man refers to my permanent possibility . . . that a subject who sees me may be substituted for the object seen by me" (B&N, p. 345). Furthermore, at a subsequent point in the argument, he explicitly concedes that although I feel shame in the presence of what I take to be the Other, the Other may not really be there at all.[20] Sartre responds to this problem, in turn, by just raising the ante—that is, he says that human beings are everywhere, and even if I mistakenly apprehend an inanimate object as a subject, there is still a world of absent subjects before whom I still feel shame: "The Other's presence in the world can not be derived analytically from the presence of the Other-as-subject to me, for this original presence is transcendent—i.e., being-beyond-the-world" (B&N, p. 370). The problem that arises with this move, however, is that Sartre has lost the phenomenological perspective—namely, the feeling of shame before another concrete subjectivity—and while shame before an absent Other is an apparent phenomenon, the phenomenological grounds on which Sartre can say that there are, in fact, other subjects in the world seems to have been lost with this generalization.

The best way to make sense of Sartre's answer to the problem of solipsism, as Robert C. Solomon indicates, is to interpret him as saying that there are certain powerful experiences of the world that, phenomenologically speaking, one is not in a position to deny inasmuch as they are constitutive of our most fundamental experiences. Thus, as we saw earlier, Sartre brackets the metaphysical fact of the matter with respect to whether we are free by contending that, from the first-person standpoint, we cannot help but apprehend ourselves as free, irrespective of the fact of the matter. So, too, with the problem of other minds, we must interpret Sartre as saying that we cannot help but apprehend ourselves as part of a world with other persons, irrespective of the fact of the matter. As Sartre's rich analysis of "hodological space" evidences,[21] whether he is present or absent, the Other is always already a fundamental constituent of my experience: "Thus the empirical concepts of absence and of presence are [only] two specifications of a fundamental presence of [the Other]" (B&N, p. 372). This implies, moreover, that the Other is not ultimately any particular Other but simply "they," for "when objectivized the prenumerical reality [that is] the Other is decomposed and pluralized" (B&N, p. 375), which suggests that the Other is always already everywhere looking at me. And, indeed, in the final analysis, Sartre indicates, it is not even on the basis of my experience of any particular person at any particular time that I can come to know that the Other actually exists: "For the appearance of a man as an object in the field of my experience is not what informs me that there are men. My certainty of the Other's existence is independent of these experiences and is, on the contrary, that which makes them possible" (B&N, p. 373). With this last turn of the screw, it becomes clear, phenomenologically, that there is no basis for actually proving the existence of the Other but, nevertheless, that our experience of the Other's subjectivity is ultimately a transcendental condition of experience that makes the Other's existence undeniable *for us*.

Although Sartre does not make it explicit, it is roughly at this point in the argument that the question of "the existence of others" slides from the less interesting question of whether the Other truly exists to the more interesting question of how the Other's existence bears on my own existence, and specifically how it bears on the existence of my ego structure. Thus, for Sartre, it is with the dawn of the look that "essential modifications appear in my structure—modifications which I can apprehend and fix conceptually by means of the reflective cogito" (B&N, p. 349). To put it simply, it is the appearance of the Other that engenders the empirical ego:

> So long as we considered the for-itself in its isolation, we were able to maintain that the unreflective consciousness can not be inhabited by a self; the self was given in the form of an object

> and only for the reflective consciousness. But here the self comes to haunt the unreflective consciousness. Now the unreflective consciousness is a consciousness of the world. Therefore for the unreflective consciousness the self exists on the level of objects in the world; this role which devolved only on the reflective consciousness—the making-present of the self—belongs now to the unreflective consciousness. Only the reflective consciousness has the self directly for an object. The unreflective consciousness does not apprehend the person directly or as its object; the person is presented to consciousness in so far as the person is an object for the Other. This means that all of a sudden I am conscious of myself as escaping myself, not in that I am not the foundation of my own nothingness but in that I have my foundation outside myself. I am for myself only as I am pure reference to the Other. (B&N, p. 349)

Sartre's argument here, which anticipatorily responds to those who would claim that he posits a free, sociohistorically unencumbered subjectivity, is that the Other, whom we have already seen can be both absent and generic, tends to inhabit consciousness at its very depths. In other words, Sartre is not just saying that the ego is generated through our encounters with others, although, as we will see, this is more or less the case. He is also saying, more radically, that at an unreflective level "I am that Ego" (B&N, p. 350). Indeed, this ego that I am, which "is never more present, more urgent than when I am *not* aware of it" (B&N, p. 360), largely determines who I am. This suggests that my worldview is innately colored by "the Other," who symbolizes not just concrete individuals that are present or absent but also the generalized "Other" (i.e., Heidegger's "the they") through whom the *zeitgeist* or existing sociohistorical situation is manifested.

On its face, Sartre's argument here, which is especially dense, bears an undeniably strong resemblance to the logic of Hegel's master-slave parable in the *Phenomenology of Spirit*. As an initial matter, according to both Sartre and Hegel, the impetus for ego (re)formation originates within the framework of our encounters with other human beings. Moreover, for "ontological" (as opposed to "psychological") reasons, these encounters culminate in a situation in which one party gains mastery over the other—although, for Hegel, the parties begin on relatively equal terms, while, for Sartre, one party, by virtue of its "project," is ripe for subordination and the other party acquires mastery over him simply by being there. But this difference results more from the form of presentation than from any actual discrepancy between Sartre and Hegel, for Sartre did not have to use the example of the voyeur in order to illustrate the ego (re)forming process of one's objectification by another. An example that involved, say, two persons seeking to stare one another down, each crudely aiming to retain his sense of "self-certainty," which is akin to the battle that took place in Hegel's master-slave parable, would have accomplished the same objective. Indeed, relations are fundamentally inscribed with conflict on Sartre's account precisely because "the Other-as-subject," who has turned me into a "being-as-object," could just as easily have been objectified by me under a different set of circumstances. And, moreover, I can, at least theoretically, always turn the tables on him, such that I could become a "being-as-subject" while he becomes an "Other-as-object." One of the most compelling reasons that "hell is other people" is that relations of domination and subordination can never be fixed or reach a final resting place. As Sartre's theoretical discussion of concrete relations implies, and the dilemma of the characters in "No Exit" graphically depicts, these relations of domination and subordination are always fluid: "there is no dialectic of my relations with the Other but rather a circle—although each attempt is enriched by the failure of the other" (B&N, p. 474).

As this excerpt already begins to attest, there are also deep differences between Sartre and Hegel on the matter of intersubjectivity, and explicating these differences will help clarify the particulars of Sartre's position. Accordingly, the most obvious difference between Sartre and Hegel (and the one suggested by this excerpt) bears on the prospects for a social reconciliation. Hegel's intersubjective dialectic, as is well known, might start with the master-slave encounter, but the unreconcilable contradictions that arise in these two forms of consciousness lead to their sublation by a new form of consciousness (stoicism) that seeks to resolve them. This movement, in which an ensuing form of consciousness incorporates the truths of the superseded forms of consciousness in the course of resolving their contradictions, is repeated until reconciling reason engenders a form of consciousness in which there is mutual recognition amongst all individuals, all of whom identify themselves with the broader social collective. In contrast, as we just saw, Sartre does not see human relations breaking out of the "circle" of domination and subordination, and although he, too, uses the term "recognition," it means something much different for him. As we saw earlier, the voyeur's shame signifies his "*recognition* of the fact that [he is] indeed that object which the Other is looking at and judging (B&N, p. 350), which means that this ego (re)forming "recognition" is actually based on a loss of subjectivity that results from the Other's objectifying look—a point, it should be noted in passing, that is taken up by more contemporary theorists, who would wrongly associate the ethical upshot of Sartre's theory of subjectivity with the very recognitive ethics that they too would stigmatize on these grounds. In any case, while the impulse toward recognition within Hegel's framework is a positive thing, as it yields richer forms of subjectivity through self-knowledge, the impulse toward recognition within Sartre's framework is a negative thing, as it testifies to the objectification of subjectivity, and therefore the usurpation of its freedom to self-determine (or, to be more exact, to determine its self). This difference, which revolves around Sartre's emphasis on the prereflective cogito, is at the heart of his critique of Hegel.

To make sense of ego (re)formation in Sartre's thought, it is necessary to look at Sartre's critique of Hegel, but to look at it from the perspective of ego (re)formation rather than from the perspective of making good the existence of others, which is nominally the impetus for Sartre's critique at that point in the chapter. Thus, according to Sartre, Hegel's great achievement is to be found in his recognition that the Other is an indispensable condition of self-consciousness. In contrast to Husserl, who saw the basic connection between people as one of knowledge, Hegel, at least nominally, saw this connection as one of being: "Consciousnesses are directly supported by one another in a reciprocal imbrication of their being" (B&N, p. 319). And as is the case with Sartre's account of our relation to the Other, this connection of being that constitutes the Other as he constitutes me is based on an "internal negation." Yet, according to Sartre, Hegel's account is flawed in a number of respects. The primary problem, he contends, is that while Hegel poses the question of self-consciousness in terms of being, the question itself is always framed in terms of knowledge: "Knowledge here is still the measure of being, and Hegel does not even conceive of the possibility of a being-for-others which is not finally reducible to a 'being-as-object'" (B&N, p. 322). Along the lines of Kierkegaard, Sartre is saying that Hegel only abstractly considers consciousness in its being, and he therefore loses its irreducible concreteness, which cannot be defined in terms of knowledge. This conflation of knowledge and being leads Sartre to level what he calls a "twofold charge of optimism" against Hegel (B&N, p. 324). On the one hand, Hegel is guilty of an "epistemological optimism," for he thinks that the for-itself of the Other can be known. But, of course, on Sartre's account, not only can I not "know" the for-itself of the other (i.e., the Other-as-subject), I cannot even "know" the for-itself of myself (i.e., my being-as-subject), given that I am always beyond my objectifications of my self. On the other hand, Hegel is also guilty of an "ontological optimism," for he deals with the question of the Other from the standpoint of "the Whole," which is where Hegel places himself. In other words, Hegel himself does not actually experience the Other because his "system" only knows the other—and, indeed, himself—from the outside, which means that his "internal negation" is finally just an "external negation." "But if Hegel has forgotten himself," Sartre declares, "we cannot forget Hegel. This means that we are referred back to the cogito. . . . The sole point of departure is the interiority of the cogito" (B&N, p. 329).[22]

While the *bildungsroman* that is the *Phenomenology of Spirit* is retrospectively recounted from the summit of "the Whole," Sartre's claim that Hegel loses the irreducible concreteness of individual experience, which is what the "interiority of the [prereflective] cogito" ensures, is not quite right. Indeed, Sartre and Hegel offer what are complementary points of view. Just as we saw Sartre presuppose the universal Other (whose "existence is independent of [our] experiences and is . . . that which makes them possible" [B&N, p. 373]) so as to investigate the way in which the particular subject is constrained to experience the Other's existence, Hegel presupposes the particular subject's experience so as to investigate the transcendental conditions of its possibility. The process of transforming Kant's hardwired categories into sociohistorically engendered ones to bring the Kantian revolution to fruition was never, in theory, supposed to be at the expense of the particular subject, either epistemologically (since the individual's changing experiences bear on the categories out of which he thinks the world) or ethically (since the individual's uncoerced reconciliation to the institutions of the modern world was Hegel's motivating concern). And, in fact, this is evidenced in the *Phenomenology of Spirit* and the *Philosophy of Right*, respectively. First, in the *Phenomenology*, Hegel, much like Sartre himself, clearly presupposes a thin notion of self-consciousness prior to the master-slave parable, such as when he says, in a well-known passage, that a "self-consciousness exists for a self-consciousness [and] only so is it in fact self-consciousness."[23] Along these lines, it should be recalled that Hegel was quite familiar with the self-grounding problem with which Fichte had struggled, and that by incorporating this moment into the *Phenomenology*, he both anticipates and agrees with Sartre's concerns.[24] So, too, while Hegel himself analyzes the movement of the "forms of consciousness" from the summit, for the particular subject existing in a particular time and place the existing form of consciousness (i.e., the category out of which he thinks the world) ties him to other particular subjects at the level of their very "being," to use Sartre's words. Second, in the *Philosophy of Right*, the first moment of the will "contains the element of pure indeterminacy or that pure reflection of the ego into itself," which affords the margin of freedom provided by the prereflective cogito[25]—a margin that must not be indeterminately fetishized when dealing with either the empirical ego (Sartre) or the social institutions of our world (Hegel), both of which concretize it.

Conversely, the prevailing form of consciousness—the transcendental, sociohistorically engendered category that is the condition of possibility of any particular subject's experience—implicitly comes through Sartre's Other, whether particular or general. The voyeur feels shame instead of pride when apprehended in the act of peeping through a keyhole by a particular person because this is what one is supposed to feel in the culture in these circumstances. And, what's more, this feeling of shame would probably also be experienced by the voyeur even if there was no particular person there to apprehend him—that is, he would feel shame before the general Other—for the Other, whether present or absent, "is the indispensable mediator between myself and me" (B&N, p. 302). This ubiquitous Other that is always already inserted "between myself and me" points to the virtual incomprehensibility of the notion of "individual authenticity" in a bad sociohistorical context, and this is why Sartre, in the context of speaking about our concrete relations with others, asserts that "these considerations do not exclude the possibility of an ethics of deliverance and salvation, [b]ut this can be achieved only after a radical conversion which we can not discuss here" (B&N, p. 534). As a necessary condition of an ethics of deliverance and salvation, which in turn is a necessary condition of individual authenticity, a radical conversion requires a radical reorganization of the social context (which means that Sartre did not evidence a "radical conversion" to Marxism, as some have simplistically contended, but rather came to see Marxism as a necessary condition for a radical conversion). In other words, not unlike Adorno, Sartre came to appreciate as early as *Being and Nothingness* that "wrong life cannot be lived rightly" (MM, p. 39).

Although there is no possibility of individual authenticity in a bad sociohistorical context, this does not mean that freedom and responsibility, which are circumscribed by the situation, are also ruled out, but even here Sartre evidences a basic ambivalence, an ambivalence that arguably goes to the core of his thought.[26] On the one hand, as I have been emphasizing in my comparison of Sartre and Hegel, with the first appearance of the Other's look, the Other penetrates me to my core: "the [empirical] self comes to haunt the unreflective consciousness." At this point, Sartre asserts, the problem is no longer finding reasons to believe that the Other exists; to the contrary, "in my inmost depths I must find . . . the Other himself as not being me" (B&N, p. 338). But this is no routine task, for the Other's "presence without intermediary is the necessary condition of all thought which I would attempt to form concerning myself" (B&N, p. 362). These comments all suggest that the Other exists at my "center"—that is, that he resides at the very core of my being and basically constitutes who I am in much the same way that Heidegger's Dasein is constituted by "the they." To say the least, under these circumstances, this makes a robust Sartrean account of freedom and responsibility quite problematical. On the other hand, however, Sartre contends that my being-for-others is my "being-outside—not a being passively submitted to which would itself have come to me from outside, but an outside assumed and recognized as *my* outside" (B&N, p. 380). This comment suggests that the Other "is not always in question at the heart of my freedom," but, instead, is merely "the limit of my freedom" (B&N, p. 351). Under these circumstances, I am still, in some sense, internally insulated from the Other, who poses only an external problem for my freedom. Sartre himself does not actually make out this ambivalence in *Being and Nothingness*, and, indeed, it seems that in the latter parts of the book he tends to vacillate between these two fundamental presuppositions.[27] Of course, in his subsequent works, the vicissitudes of the first thesis will come to dominate.

However, even in the worst case—that is, even if "the upsurge of the Other touches the for-itself in its very heart" and "fixes" the flight of the for-itself from the in-itself in such a way that "the objectivity of my flight I experience as an alienation which I can neither transcend nor *know*"—I must still, "by the sole fact that I experience it," then "turn back toward it and assume *attitudes* with respect to it" (B&N, p. 473). In other words, Sartre contends, in response to my objectification by the Other, "two things are necessary: consciousness must have to be itself and must spontaneously have to be this non-being" (B&N, pp. 377–378):

> consciousness must freely disengage itself from the Other and wrench itself away by choosing itself as a nothingness which is simply Other than the Other and thereby must be reunited in "itself." This very detachment, which is the being of the for-itself, causes there to be an Other. . . . The for-itself is what is not the Other in the nihilating mode of "reflection-reflecting." The not-being-the-Other is never given but perpetually chosen in a perpetual resurrection: consciousness cannot be the Other only in so far as it is consciousness (of) itself as not being the Other. Thus the internal negation, here as in the case of presence to the world, is a unitary bond of being. . . . If consciousness were abruptly to be something, the distinction between itself and the Other would disappear at the heart of a total undifferentiation. (B&N, p. 378)

Sartre's argument here is that the "internal negation," a "unitary bond of being," unifies me and the Other, who cascades into my consciousness by means of the look, which then causes me to bounce from being an unmediated for-itself to being an unmediated for-others. But, as Sartre asserts here, the for-itself—which, of course, is no less a fundamental ontological structure than the for-others—must reassert its own prerogatives by "wrenching away" from the Other through exercising its own nihilating nothingness. This "resurrection," in turn, gives rise to the mediated Other of knowledge—that is, the Other that I encounter as an empirical subject in the world. In other words, it is the inexorable freedom of the for-itself (which should not be confused with the robust freedom of a purifying reflection for which it is a necessary but not sufficient condition), that impels me to escape from the Other's objectifying look. Of course, this is not the end of the story, for by this wrenching away—that is, by refusing the self that the Other has made of me and reasserting my subjectivity—I tend to objectify the other, which is "the second moment in my relation to him" (B&N, p. 382). Naturally, the other will then seek to turn the tables, and at this point we are both empirical selves seeking to assert our own subjectivities, thus making our empirical selves comport with our freely chosen self-conceptions. And, as we saw earlier, there is no way out of this circle: "One of two things happens: Either I make myself not be a certain being for him, and then he is an object for me . . . or else this being is indeed the Other and makes himself not-be me, in which case I become an object for him . . ." (B&N, p. 379). Ultimately, for Sartre, we ceaselessly careen between the Other-as-object and the Other-as-subject, for the aim of equality—namely, the apprehension of the Other as simultaneously freedom (subject) and objectivity (object)—is, in principle, unobtainable (B&N, p. 529).

If Sartre is guilty of ontologizing a bad reality, this is where the charge is most apropos, for his phenomenologically based notion that interpersonal relations are characterized by conflict is arguably a reflection of the conditions in which he lived. Given that Sartre acknowledged that his philosophy of freedom was inspired by his war experiences, it seems reasonable enough to conclude that his view that human relations are founded on domination and subordination also arose from his war experiences—his life in a prisoner of war camp, under the Nazi occupation, and, more generally, under competitive capitalism. This conclusion, however, is only partially right, for just as Sartre's doctrine of freedom runs philosophically deeper than its socio-historical breeding grounds, it seems to me—although to a somewhat lesser degree—that his claim that we can no more be a for-itself-for-others than a for-itself-in-itself also strikes a deeper philosophical chord. Now, undoubtedly, the excesses of the conflict-ridden nature of his characterization of interpersonal relations do bear witness to his particular times, but his refusal to concede that the *modern* individual can be seamlessly reconciled with others under any conditions strikes me as being correct.

Accordingly, while Sartre does not preclude the prospect of collective experiences, as his analyses of the "us-object" and the "we-subject" in *Being and Nothingness* attest,[28] his notion of the for-itself as "wholly consciousness *and* wholly body" (B&N, p. 404) points to the irreducibly individual character of our emotional and biological concerns: there can be no "intersubjective totality that would attain consciousness of itself as a unified subjectivity" (B&N, p. 553). What is for Sartre the freedom of the nonidentical cogito ("nonidentical" in the sense that it is always beyond the situation that it is nevertheless constrained to live) is for Adorno the "particularity" of the individual, whose sociohistorical reconciliation with others invariably takes places more in philosophical thought than social reality. Nevertheless, both Sartre and Adorno hold on to the idea of an interpersonal reconciliation as a regulative ideal. Another regulative ideal that Sartre retains, which is strongly affected by the sociohistorical condition of interpersonal relations, is the idea of an intrapersonal reconcilation, or, more simply, "good faith."

Bad Faith and the Fundamental Project

In the introduction to this part of the book, I indicated that Sartre's philosophical works become progressively more concrete over time. *Being and Nothingness*, for example, is more concrete than the works that preceded it, such as *The Psychology of Imagination*, *Transcendence of the Ego*, and *The Emotions*. *Search for a Method* and the *Critique of Dialectical Reason*, in turn, are more concrete than *Being and Nothingness*. And, ultimately, the biographies, which culminate with *The Family Idiot*, are the most concrete of all in their analyses of what seem to be the most insignificant details of personal lives. Nevertheless, the later works do not forsake the abstract principles that are inherent in the earlier works, but, rather, merely flesh them out. This "sublating" movement toward concretion can be detected in *Being and Nothingness* itself, which, like Hegel's *Philosophy of Right*, starts with the most abstract concepts and concludes with their richest, most concrete existential instantiations. From such abstract ideas as being, nothingness, being-in-itself, being-for-itself, and the prereflective cogito, Sartre progressively guides us toward concrete insights pertaining to our relations with others, the life experiences to be unearthed in existential psychoanalysis, and, ultimately, the most concrete thing of all, "slime," which reflects being-in-itself at its most concrete (or, if you prefer, its most gelatinous). If we understand the development of *Being and Nothingness* in this way, however, certain apparent exceptions need to be explained. The most conspicuous of these exceptions is Sartre's placement of the chapter on "bad faith," which, despite its highly concrete discussion of human self-deception, precedes his explication of being-for-itself, being-for-others, "the situation," and existential psychoanalysis. This placement, moreover, makes even more problematical my contention in the previous section that bad faith must be understood as a function of social relations, which would warrant placing it no earlier than the end of part III ("Being-for-Others"). Why, then, does it appear so early in the book?

In contrast to a good deal of the recent secondary literature, which attempts to make sense of such concepts as "good faith" and "authenticity" in terms that would admit of their practical realization,[29] it is my view that on Sartre's account the phenomenon of bad faith is unavoidable for ontological reasons: human beings can never *entirely* overcome it (notwithstanding Sartre's occasional gestures toward the possibility of good faith and authenticity). When viewed in this way, it makes perfect sense that Sartre would include the phenomenon in part I of *Being and Nothingness*, which is titled the "Problem of Nothingness," for bad faith is an inescapable human problem that arises from the fact that consciousness is a nothingness that must establish its being in a world that it must simultaneously be and not be. In other words, the problem arises from the nonidentical or dualistic nature of human consciousness, which, as we saw, "is what it is not" (transcendence) and "is not what it is" (facticity) by virtue of the nothingness that separates nonpositional and positional consciousness. Moreover, although, we generally tend to speak about bad faith as an individual phenomenon, and not without good cause (given that this ontologically rooted pathology proximately expresses itself through the choices of individuals), it is my view that it is fundamentally a social, and derivatively epistemological, phenomenon—albeit, as I just implied, a social and epistemological phenomenon that must find expression in all individuals irrespective of the nature of their particular social situations and the kinds of knowledge that they engender. Crucially, however, bad faith is a phenomenon that can be more or less egregious in terms of the regulative ideal of good faith, and although bad faith must take place irrespective of the character of the individual, the particular social situation, and the kinds of knowledge that it engenders, the degree of bad faith that exists individually and collectively in a given population depends, in the first instance, on the character of the particular social situation.

To unpack this argument, I shall begin by briefly recapitulating Sartre's account of bad faith. According to Sartre, to be in bad faith is to "lie to oneself" (B&N, p. 89), but—unlike the duality that exists between the liar and the one lied to in the case of ordinary deceit—in the case of bad faith this phenomenon takes place within a single consciousness. Thus, the person in bad faith must paradoxically know in his capacity as deceiver the truth that is hidden from him in his capacity as the one deceived, but he must know it in such a way that he can successfully conceal it from himself. After he rules out the Freudian unconscious as a satisfactory explanation of this phenomenon, given that it only pushes the problem back a step (and otherwise conflicts with his primary commitment to the translucency of consciousness), Sartre contends, as we just saw, that bad faith is grounded in the "double property of the human being, who is at once a facticity and a transcendence" (B&N, p. 98). And, to be more precise, Sartre contends, it is through a person's approach to this double property of his constitution that bad faith arises: "Bad faith does not wish either to coordinate them or to surmount them in a synthesis. Bad faith seeks to affirm their identity while preserving their differences. It must affirm facticity as being transcendence and transcendence as being facticity in such a way that at the instant when a person apprehends the one, he can find himself abruptly faced with the other" (B&N, p. 98).

Although Sartre is unambiguous about the dual nature of bad faith—in other words, that it consists in overemphasizing either facticity or transcendence—there is a tendency on the part of those commentators who seek to carve out a practical space for "good faith" to see bad faith principally as an escape from freedom (i.e., as an overemphasis on facticity). And this tendency, in turn, leads them to see good faith as little more than an acceptance of freedom's ontological inalienability. For example, Ronald E. Santoni, who offers the most comprehensive analysis of the bad faith problematic, contends that "in accepting its freedom, the good faith consciousness refuses to adopt any project of giving up its freedom."[30] Or, to be more precise, good faith is "the human being's (freedom's) project of accepting its abandonment to freedom and the anxiety of its ontological distance."[31] Still, isn't it the case that this characterization of good faith applies to characters whom Sartre either implicitly or explicitly takes to be in bad faith—for example, Mathieu (*The Age of Reason*), who is only able to hold on to his freedom by clinging to a project of noninvolvement, and "the homosexual," who refuses to see his prior conduct as a function of anything more than a "restless search" (B&N, p. 107)? Isn't it the case, furthermore, that these characters gladly accept their "abandonment to freedom" because *their* anxiety derives from the fact that the "ontological distance" of which Santoni speaks isn't quite distant enough (i.e., that they might still be "glued down," as Sartre says, by their facticity)? For Sartre, these characters are classic examples of bad faith, for they focus almost completely on transcendence. Now, to be sure, Santoni also appreciates that part of what it means to be in good faith is to "accept the facticity of our freedom," which means recognizing ourselves as "the incontestable authors" of our actions and our world,[32] but, again, this takes place at an "ontological distance"—by which I mean, in this context, a standpoint that, in some sense, is above the fray.

Accordingly, this still has the feel of a "free floating 'I,'" and, like Heidegger, who uses this phrase in the context of emphatically denying that it applies to resolute, authentic Dasein,[33] Sartre would reject its application to good faith and authenticity (which, Santoni credibly argues, are distinguished by the fact that good faith is an "immediate attitude," while authenticity is a reflective way of being). However, crucially, although Santoni more or less takes Heidegger's resolute, authentic Dasein as the model for Sartrean authenticity, there are structural differences between the two that actually makes Heidegger's resolute, authentic Dasein more vulnerable to the charge. Unlike Heidegger's Dasein, which, to put it rather peculiarly, is able to attain this "ontological distance" because Heidegger retains the individuating possibility of a resolute self-presence, Sartre explicitly rules this possibility out. Rather, on Sartre's account, we must exist our sociohistorically produced facticity in a much more entangled fashion, for the "ontological distance" between nonpositional and positional consciousness, which is comprised of "nothing," is only an ideal one, which means that the kind of freedom it ultimately makes possible is better understood as arising from a *phenomenological* distance. As such, we are free only to the extent that we can choose how to plunge ourselves back into the fray, and then only within a limited range of possibilities:

> Freedom, which manifests itself through anguish, is characterized by a constantly renewed obligation to remake the *Self* which designates the free being. . . . This self with its a priori and historical content is the *essence* of man. Anguish as the manifestation of freedom in the face of self means that man is always separated by a nothingness from his essence. We should refer here to Hegel's statement: "*wesen ist was gewesen ist.*" Essence is what has been. Essence is everything in the human

> being which we can indicate by the words—that *is*. Due to this fact it is the totality of characteristics which *explain* the act. . . . Man continually carries with him a pre-judicative comprehension of his essence, but due to this very fact he is separated from it by a nothingness. (B&N, p. 72)

I shall return to the relation between freedom and what Sartre refers to as our a priori and historically determined essence momentarily. In the meantime, however, I would like to further shut the door on the notion that good faith is an attainable ideal. Accordingly, although I have rejected Santoni's account of good faith due to the fact that it conflates a bad faith overemphasis on transcendence and good faith, there is still the possibility of another practical concept of good faith that we saw Sartre himself raise in passing—namely, a valid coordination of transcendence and facticity (B&N, p. 98). The very idea of a valid coordination of transcendence and facticity presupposes that these properties are functionally discrete, however, and on Sartre's account this is simply not the case. To the contrary, transcendence and facticity are linked in such a way that they cannot be practically disengaged from one another. Thus, in contrast to Cartesian freedom, Sartre's transcendence is always already embedded in a "situation," which means that freedom is both defined and constrained by the facticity of a particular context, sociohistorical or personal. And, conversely, what constitutes Sartrean facticity is ultimately transcendence, for beyond the stripped down "fact of the matter," which in and of itself means nothing, the actual significance of facticity is only to be understood with respect to our freely chosen projects. Transcendence and facticity interpenetrate one another so totally, in other words, that the idea of disentangling them in order to effect a "valid coordination" can find no theoretical purchase: they are the torn but overlapping halves of a synthetic whole to which they can never add up.[34] When, as we saw, Sartre says that bad faith "must affirm facticity as being transcendence and transcendence as being facticity in such a way that at the instant when a person apprehends the one, he can find himself abruptly faced with the other" (B&N, p. 98), then, he is speaking about what it means to be a human being, not just a human being in bad faith. And, finally, as Sartre contends, the very attempt to be "sincere," which would ostensibly be the stamp of good faith, is itself an endeavor that is undertaken in bad faith: "For bad faith to be possible, sincerity itself must be in bad faith" (B&N, p. 112), which is precisely why the homosexual's interlocutor, the so-called champion of sincerity, is no less in bad faith than his friend. In sum, then, there is no Archimedean point either between or above transcendence and facticity that permits their valid coordination, a fact that will become even clearer as I delve into the social aspect of our facticity, or what Sartre calls the "a priori and historical content [that] is the essence of man."

Although the bad faith chapter precedes Sartre's discussion of being-for-others, social considerations are always hovering right beneath the surface. As an initial matter, Sartre begins the chapter on bad faith by referring to numerous social roles that would influence a person to direct the negating powers of consciousness outward for the purpose of negating the possibilities of another person: There are "men (e.g., caretakers, overseers, gaolers), whose social reality is uniquely that of the No . . ." (B&N, pp. 86–87). Although Sartre does not elaborate on this point, the implication is that this outwardly turned negation of another's possibilities is the necessary condition for being able to turn this negating power inward—which at this point in the analysis is how he characterizes the phenomenon of bad faith.[35] In his example involving the waiter whose "rapid movements" evidence a desire to be "the waiter," moreover, Sartre explicitly speaks in social terms:

> The waiter in the cafe plays with his condition in order to realize it. This obligation is not different from that which is imposed on all tradesmen. Their condition is wholly one of ceremony. The public demands of them that they realize it as a ceremony; there is the dance of the grocer, of the tailor, of the auctioneer, by which they endeavor to persuade their clientele that they are nothing but a grocer, an auctioneer, a tailor. A grocer who dreams is offensive to the buyer, because such a grocer is not wholly a grocer. Society demands that he limit himself to his function as a grocer. . . . There are indeed many precautions to imprison a man in what he is, as if we lived in perpetual fear that he might escape from it, that he might suddenly break away and elude his condition. (B&N, p. 102)

Sartre clearly recognizes the social compulsion to conform to a particular functional role here—indeed, while I do not want to press the point too hard, we might read this passage as an indictment of the instrumentalizing nature of capitalist society—but despite this recognition he nevertheless concludes that the waiter is in bad faith. As many commentators have pointed out, however, Sartre himself, the bourgeois patron of the café who holds the waiter's livelihood in his hands, cannot know whether the waiter is in bad faith. Indeed, the social compulsion that leads one to perform "the dance" that Sartre refers to in this passage suggests the possibility that the waiter is not trying to become "a waiter" in "the sense that this inkwell is an inkwell" (B&N, p. 102), but rather that he is putting on this performance for Sartre and the other customers. To be sure, the waiter might really seek to identify with his role (and, in fact, many people do come to identify with their roles), but Sartre cannot know that this is the case from his limited standpoint. And, in fact, Sartre cannot know that any of the people to whom he refers in this chapter are in bad faith. The "flirtatious woman," for example, has all sorts of social reasons for not abruptly extricating her hand, and, given a homophobic climate, "the homosexual" has no good reason to explicitly acknowledge his homosexuality. In any event, although Sartre cannot know whether particular acts are the result of bad faith or social expectations, he does clearly recognize that it is largely the expectations of others that precipitate the phenomenon when it does occur.

Moreover, Sartre anticipatorily discusses the ontological phenomenon of being-for-others in the bad faith chapter:

> Although this metastable concept of "transcendence-facticity" is one of the most basic instruments of bad faith, it is not the only one of its kind. We can equally well use another kind of duplicity derived from human reality which we will express roughly by saying that its being-for-itself implies complementarily a being-for-others. Upon any one of my conducts it is always possible to converge two looks, mine and that of the Other. . . . The equal dignity of being, possessed by my being-for-others and by my being-for-myself, permits a perpetually disintegrating synthesis and a perpetual game of escape from the for-itself to the for-others and from the for-others to the for-itself. (B&N, pp. 99–100)

To make the point more plainly, the transcendence of the for-itself, or the self that I project into the future, is largely constrained by my being-for-others. Any self that I can even conceive of, much less hope to be, results from the sociohistorical context in which I live, as Sartre forcefully states elsewhere: "it is in its effort to choose itself as a personal self that the for-itself sustains in existence certain social and abstract characteristics which make of it a man (or woman). . . . [It is] an undeniable fact that the for-itself can choose itself only beyond certain meanings of which it is not the origin" (B&N, p. 666).

Just as my being-for-others constrains the transcendence of my for-itself, as Sartre asserts here, it constrains the facticity of my in-itself. If others have a "deformed image of me" (B&N, p. 99), this mediates what I will take to be the facts about myself, and leads to my own deformed self-conception. Thus, just as my being-for-others mediates my self-constituting transcendent projects, it mediates the factical givens from which these projects arise (because, as we saw, for Sartre, like Nietzsche, there are no facts, only interpretations). And, indeed, according to Sartre, it would seem that others actually have a disproportionate impact on my facticity, for in contrast to the "original facticity" of the for-itself *before* its being-for-others (namely, *before* "the look" of the Other that structurally modifies it), which consciousness is free to transcend by adopting a new project, my other-engendered facticity is far more congealed:[36]

> The for-itself is not only a being which arises as the nihilation of the in-itself which it is and the internal negation of the in-itself which it is not. This nihilating flight is entirely reapprehended by the in-itself and fixed in in-itself as soon as the Other appears. The for-itself when alone transcends the world; it is the nothing by which there are things. The Other by rising up confers on the for-itself a being-in-itself-in-the-midst-of-the-world as a thing among things. This petrifaction in in-itself by the Other's look is the profound meaning of the myth of Medusa. (B&N, p. 555)

Of course, Sartre speaks rather misleadingly here about the for-itself before "the Other appears," which signifies "my original fall" (B&N, p. 352), but, as is the case with Hegel's three opening "epistemological" chapters in the *Phenomenology*, which precede the introduction of the Other, it is only to make the phenomenological point: the Other is always already there (as we saw in the previous section), which means that the facticity that exists before any number of particular empirical Others "rise up" is saturated by the Others' influence, whether these Others are present or not. In sum, both transcendence and facticity, the for-itself and the in-itself, which are the two components of bad faith, are, first and foremost, social. When we speak of transcendence and facticity thoroughly interpenetrating one another, then, this must not be understood in terms of a fictional Cartesian self that straddles the nonexistent boundary line between the freely embraced future goals of the for-itself and the past facts of the in-itself. Rather, even if it is not explicitly stated, it must be understood in terms of the freely embraced future goals of the for-itself-for-others and the past facts of the in-itself-for-others.

The ontological unavoidability of bad faith and its ultimately social nature meet within the context of what Sartre calls "the fundamental project." According to Sartre, every person's possibilities arise within the framework of a hierarchy of projects and behaviors. These projects and behaviors (which vary in duration) testify, in turn, to the existence of a more basic project that reflects a person's underlying "existential choice"—that is, an initial choice of oneself in the world, which establishes the limits of one's self-identity. (For example, Sartre speaks of stutterers, whose initial project is geared toward being inferior, which is how they finally see themselves [B&N, p. 606]). And, ultimately, this initial project, which varies from person to person, testifies to the existence of "the fundamental project," a universal project that Sartre characterizes as follows:

> The best way to conceive of the fundamental project of human reality is to say that man is the being whose project is to be God. . . . God, value and supreme end of transcendence, represents the permanent limit in terms of which man makes known to himself what he is. To be man means to reach toward being God. Or if you prefer, *man fundamentally is the desire to be God*. It may be asked, if man on coming into the world is borne toward God as toward his limit, *if he can choose only to be God*, what becomes of freedom? For freedom is nothing other than a choice which creates for itself its own possibilities, but it appears here that the initial project of being God, which "defines" man, comes close to being the same as a human "nature" or an "essence." The answer is that while the meaning

> of the desire is ultimately the project of being God, the desire is never constituted by this meaning; on the contrary, it always represents a particular discovery of its ends. These ends in fact are pursued in terms of a particular empirical situation, *and it is this very pursuit which constitutes the surroundings as a situation.* (B&N, p. 724; emphasis added)

Put more simply (and without the religious overtones), the fundamental project is the desire to be a for-itself-in-itself—namely, to be self-identical and yet absolutely free in terms of the empirical situation.

Although Sartre is quite clear on the necessity of the initial project, and, even more, the fundamental project from which it springs—not only does he say here that "man fundamentally is the desire to be God" and that "he can choose only to be God," but elsewhere he says that "my freedom is a choice of being God and all my acts, all my projects translate this choice and reflect it in a thousand and one ways" (B&N, p. 764)—commentators who attempt to carve out a space for good faith often take the position that it requires junking the fundamental project altogether in the name of freedom. What they mean by "freedom," however, is not completely clear. For example, along the lines of Santoni, Thomas C. Anderson says that in rejecting the fundamental project, "I accept the fact that I am not a substantial, necessary thing, which has a right to be, but a contingent, gratuitous freedom, which *continually* questions itself about the purpose of its existence."[37] So, too, David Detmer, who is particularly diligent in putting forth these counterexamples, ultimately says, in the context of upholding Sartre's concept of a radical conversion, that "one must pursue freedom, and abandon the impossible desire to be God."[38] In other words, like Santoni, Anderson and Detmer think that by rejecting the fundamental project, we shall see ourselves as absolutely (albeit contingently) free, but isn't this bad faith? Haven't Anderson and Detmer also conflated a bad faith overemphasis on transcendence and good faith?

Of course, the claim that human beings cannot *be* a for-itself-in-itself is trivially true—as Sartre himself says in his unpublished *Notebooks for an Ethics*, "every attempt of the For-itself to *be* In-itself is by definition doomed to failure"[39]—and the pursuit of the fundamental project undertaken in this particular way can be circumvented, as Anderson and Detmer contend. The fact remains, however, that human beings *are* a for-itself *and* an in-itself, and it is bad faith not only to overemphasize either the transcendence of the for-itself or the facticity of the in-itself but also to hypostatize them in their difference. For all intents and purposes, what this means is that we must take up the gambit of the fundamental project, all the while acknowledging that it is unattainable. Indeed, how could we even begin to understand Sartre's political commitments, which are already implicit in *Being and Nothingness*, if we do not understand them as reflecting his recognition that the freedom of the for-itself must make a factical in-itself of itself, which, for Sartre, necessitates making a sociopolitical context that broadens as best we can the universe of possible things that the for-itself can make itself be? And, in a somewhat more modest sense, isn't this just what it means to be an *ens causa sui*?[40] In effect, then, human beings must retain a dialectical tension between the two sides of their nonidentical nature. The fundamental project demands that we freely but fully invest ourselves in the in-itself of history, and more specifically "the situation," in order to make of the in-itself, which constitutes "what we are," a context with which our drive for practical freedom ("what we are not") can identify (in the mode of not being it like a mere thing). This is what Sartre means when he asserts that "freedom, which manifests itself through anguish, is characterized by a constantly renewed obligation to remake the Self which designates the free being, [and that] the self with its a priori and historical content is the essence of man."

If we must take up the fundamental project in the mode of not being it (as Sartre would put it), which is just another way of saying that bad faith is inescapable given the types of beings that we are, then it must also be the case that we all have "initial projects." That is, we all must (prereflectively, according to Sartre) choose a way of being, which follows from the existence of the fundamental project. Thus, as Sartre says in the passage set forth above, the project of being God "is never constituted by this meaning" because "these ends in fact are pursued in terms of a particular empirical situation, and it is this very pursuit which constitutes the surroundings as a situation. The desire of being is always realized as the desire of a mode of being." Sartre's point here is crucial. It is not only that we find ourselves in *a* situation, although, again, this is trivially true. More to the point, *the* situation is always already encrusted with meaning, even (or, better, especially) when we do not acknowledge it as such, for a situation's meaning is what ultimately makes it a situation in the first place. And the situation's meaning, in turn, arises from our initial project. Without an initial project, which orients us toward the world in one way or another, and thus constitutes the surroundings as a situation, the world would, quite literally, be meaningless, and we would, in a very real sense, be less than human.[41] Nevertheless, the particulars of this necessary initial choice—our most basic choice of ourselves—is itself completely unjustifiable: "This means that we apprehend our choice as not deriving from any prior reality but rather as being about to serve as foundation for the ensemble of significations which constitute reality" (B&N, p. 598).

It is with the "meaning" of the situation, or, alternatively, the "ensemble of significations which constitute reality," that we move toward the question of the relation between bad faith and epistemology. In the course of introducing the bad faith problematic, it will be remembered, I asserted that bad faith, which is ontologically rooted, is fundamentally a social phenomenon, and only then, derivatively, an epistemological one. As Robert C. Solomon nicely puts it: "Bad faith is not just self-deception because it is not primarily about belief. Of course, beliefs often follow, but bad faith is about the very nature of our engagements in the world. And then, perhaps, we form beliefs about our engagements in the world."[42] In other words, the "problem of belief" that Sartre tackles in the bad faith chapter—mostly in the brief concluding section titled "The 'Faith' of Bad Faith"—stems from the problem of self-constitution, for it is our self-constitution, which comes about on the edifice of our nonidentical nature, that both engenders and circumscribes the structure of our beliefs. Thus, according to Sartre:

> Bad faith does not hold the norms and criteria of truth as they are accepted by the critical thought of good faith. . . . The *ontological* characteristic of the world of bad faith with which the subject suddenly surrounds himself is this: that here being is what it is not, and is not what it is. Consequently, a peculiar type of evidence appears: *non-persuasive* evidence. Bad faith apprehends evidence but it is resigned in advance to not being fulfilled by this evidence. . . . [It] decides that the metastable structure is the structure of being and that non-persuasion is the structure of all convictions. (B&N, p. 113)

If bad faith trades on "the ontological characteristic" that "being is what it is not, and is not what it is," it can find that all evidence is "nonpersuasive," which means that it is in a position to let itself be persuaded by that which is nonpersuasive: it "takes refuge in 'not-believing-what-one-believes'" (B&N, p. 115).

Sartre clearly recognizes the problem with which we are left—that "every belief in good faith is an impossible belief" (B&N, p. 115)—but in an "authenticity" footnote that is, perhaps, cited as frequently as his "radical conversion footnote," he declares:

> If it is indifferent whether one is in good faith or in bad faith, because bad faith reapprehends good faith and slides to the very origin of the project of good faith, that does not mean that we can not radically escape bad faith. But this supposes a self-recovery of being which was previously corrupted. This self-recovery we call authenticity, the description of which has no place here. (B&N, p. 116)

Along the same lines, Sartre also asserts that "good faith wishes to flee the 'not-believing-what-one-believes' by finding refuge in being" (B&N, p. 115). Yet, on the next page—the same page as the "authenticity footnote"—he asserts that "good faith seeks to flee the inner disintegration of my being in the direction of the in-itself which it should be and is not" (B&N, p. 116). With this third claim about authenticity, it should be noticed, Sartre shifts from one notion of being to another. The "authenticity footnote" and the first of these two lines trade on some variant of the Heideggerian notion of Being, which, I have previously contended, is the single worst aspect of *Being and Nothingness* (and it is not something to which Sartre is entitled anyway, since, unlike Heidegger's Dasein, who at least retains the ontological potential for self-presence, Sartre's person is ontologically and not just sociohistorically riven). The third line, which speaks about being in the sense that Sartre usually does in the book—as the mundane being-in-itself—gets it right, but then the problem is that although good faith should flee the inner disintegration of its being in the direction of the in-itself that it should be, it is *not* this in-itself, and all attempts to actually become it are as attempts to become a stone, the project of Sartre's anti-Semite in *Anti-Semite and Jew* (who, of course, is in bad faith). This suggests, as I have argued, both that good faith is an ontological impossibility *and* that we must strive to be a for-itself-in-itself in accord with the meaning conferring fundamental and initial projects, but in such a way that (while sustaining the necessary dialectical tension between the for-itself and in-itself) fully recognizes its unattainability. As Sartre argues in the last pages of *Being and Nothingness*, we must seek to "symbolically appropriate" (instead of literally appropriate) being-in-itself, "but to the extent that this attempt still shares in the spirit of seriousness" by believing that it can actually "effect the existence of the in-itself-for-itself," it is doomed to failure (B&N, p. 627).[43] In other words, to use Sartre's phraseology, we must strive to be a for-itself-in-itself in the mode of not being it.

In light of this imperative, and in keeping with my initial claim—namely, that while we cannot *entirely* overcome it, bad faith exists (and exhibits itself) in more or less egregious forms with respect to the regulative ideal of good faith—I would like to sketch a rather qualified notion of good faith in somewhat different terms. And, while I have contended that the epistemological question is derivative in terms of the phenomenon of bad faith, the metastable nature of belief with which it deals is the best point of ingress for making this case. Thus, although all beliefs are metastable, there are beliefs that are more or less metastable because the larger structure of beliefs with which they are intertwined are more or less coherent. This means, in turn, that there are (sociohistorically engendered) initial projects that are more or less coherent, given that it is the initial project that establishes the ensemble that is a person's belief structure in the first place. Understood in this way, a qualified notion of good faith would surely involve a relative degree of openness, which, of course, is a condition of having a critical attitude toward new evidence, but there are ontological limits to such openness, given that, as the price of intelligibility, an initial project precludes us from being infinitely open and fluid in terms of our self-identities (for such an aim, which is tantamount to not having an initial project at all, would itself be in bad faith). As a result, to use Herbert Fingarette's phrase, it is unavoidable that we will "spell out" some things and not "spell out" others,[44] for we must be oriented toward the world in order to engage with it, and the price of this orientation is a selective seeing. The only issue, therefore, is how selective our selective seeing is—that is, how much contradictory evidence it takes for us to see the bad faith nature of our comportment, which would lead us, ideally, to another initial project, an existential comportment that, all things considered, is in less bad faith. Accordingly, if there is such a thing as a "radical conversion" to "good faith" and ultimately "authenticity," it involves a reflective understanding of this problematic that would qualitatively lessen bad faith rather than overcome it (which is itself an aim in bad faith). Put in Nietzsche's terms, it involves a reflective understanding that, in some sense, untruth, and thus bad faith, is a basic condition of life.

Bracketing the sociohistorical context, which delineates our initial projects, the question is how individuals might be open to *any* reformulation of their initial projects, and therefore their belief structures—much less what I am offering here as a reformulated notion of Sartrean "good faith." Although Sartre describes the initial project (which he also calls the "original project" or "original choice") as "the fundamental act of our freedom," he says that it is not open to the kind of reflective reformulation that I am advocating, for reflection follows from the initial project:

> When I deliberate the chips are down. And if I am brought to the point of deliberating, this is simply because it is part of my original project to realize motives by means of deliberation rather than by some other discovery. There is therefore a choice of deliberation as a procedure which will make known to me what I project and consequently what I am. And the choice of deliberation is organized with the ensemble motives-causes and ends by free spontaneity. (B&N, p. 581; parentheses omitted)

If the primary way in which we reflect on matters derives from our unreflectively adopted initial project, which our "deliberation"—what Sartre calls "accessory reflection"—inexorably reinstantiates, why the "free spontaneity" that is consciousness would come to *re*choose itself arguably becomes the matter of central importance. How it chooses itself as an initial matter, it seems to me, is well depicted by Sartre in his analysis of Jean Genet, whose fundamental way of "being-in-the-world" as a thief was crystallized when, as a very young boy, he was reproached with a "Stop Thief" (which, it should be pointed out, is a scene that implicitly incorporates in it the underlying social relations that brought Genet to that point). How it comes to rechoose itself is another matter. As I shall discuss in greater detail in the next section, Sartre himself will be rather unhelpful in dealing with this issue, for on his account any claim that the free spontaneity that is consciousness is *caused* to choose an initial project (which would make it intelligible) is essentially confused, and for this reason, this is the point at which Sartre's argument for freedom is at its weakest—a point that he, at least implicitly, recognizes himself.

In any case, to sum up, in the last paragraph of *Being and Nothingness*, which ends the part of the Conclusion that is titled "Ethical Implications," Sartre asks: "Will freedom by taking itself for an end escape all situation? Or on the contrary will it remain situated?" (B&N, p. 798). It seems to me that the answers to these questions are quite clear. Due to the nonidentical nature of our constitution, we must always be in bad faith: we cannot help but exist in a situation toward which we are oriented, and the cost of this orientation (which is dutifully sustained by "accessory reflection") is the investment of freedom into an initial project, or "way of being," that itself is prompted by the unattainable imperative of the fundamental project toward which we must strive in a qualified way. Still, while we must be in bad faith, since we cannot exist as "free floating freedoms," there are better and worse ways of being in bad faith.[45] Specifically, sociohistorical contexts that engender practices that seek to optimize our practical freedom—that is, that take freedom as the highest value—will also foster persons with initial projects that take freedom as the highest value. What this means is that our initial projects, which themselves will be less self-destructive, are more open to revision, such that we will always be in a position to freely (in the strong sense) plunge our freedom into orienting projects that will constitute our (individual and collective) situations in life enhancing ways.

How is this more modest "radical conversion" to be brought about? According to Sartre, it requires a "purifying reflection," which may ultimately be the real condition of freedom. I am now in a better position to consider this issue, as well as others issues related to Sartre's concept of freedom.

SITUATED FREEDOM AND PURIFIED REFLECTION

I began the last section by making the point that *Being and Nothingness* steadily moves from abstract concepts to their concrete instantiations, and nowhere is this more evident than in the movement of the concept of freedom itself. Thus, according to Sartre, it is only in the last quarter of the book that "we begin to catch a glimpse of the paradox of freedom" (B&N, p. 629):

> There is freedom only in a situation, and there is a situation only through freedom. Human-reality everywhere encounters resistances and obstacles which it has not created, but these resistances and obstacles have meaning only in and through the free choice that human-reality is. . . . What we have called the facticity of freedom is the given which it has to be and which it illuminates by its project. This given is manifested in several ways although within the absolute unity of a single illumination. It is my place, my body, my past, my position, *in so far as it is already determined by the indications of Others* . . . (B&N, p. 629; italics added)

If the situation in which I find myself has "already [been] determined by the indications of Others," and if my orienting initial project that "illuminates" this situation (i.e., concurrently makes it for me both *a* situation and *my* situation) arose in a collectively constituted context that was also "determined by the indications of Others" (as Sartre will come to explicitly assert in the case of Genet), then it would seem that as early as *Being and Nothingness*, freedom is ultimately "determined by the indications of others." In other words, as I have attempted to show in the last two sections, these so-called indications render exceedingly problematical the very notion of even having "freedom in situation," especially if by "freedom" we mean self-determination (and thus cuts sharply against those critics that attribute to him a hyperbolic doctrine of freedom). For as I shall discuss momentarily, even changes in my initial project, which would seem to evidence free self-determination, are themselves not subject to reasons but rather to the "pure spontaneity" of consciousness. Indeed, *this* is arguably the "paradox of freedom" in Sartre's early philosophy. To get beyond the impoverished notion of freedom with which we are left—in other words, to get beyond this paradox—Sartre emphasizes the need for a "purifying reflection" (B&N, p. 742), of which he tells us little.

Yet, even at this late point in *Being and Nothingness*, there still seems to be an asocial residuum in Sartre's notion of freedom. For instance, just a few pages before his pronouncement on the "paradox of freedom," Sartre gives us an example in which he asserts that my inability to scale "a particular crag" does not testify to a lack of freedom because this very inability derives from my freely chosen ends (B&N, p. 620). He asserts that the crag's "coefficient of adversity" could just as easily be a "coefficient of utility" if my objective is to appreciate it, or, say, depend on its impregnable nature to insulate me from the people living on the other side. Even more to the point (since it deals with my relations with Others), on the following page Sartre infamously says that even a prisoner is free, for "he is always free to try to escape (or get himself liberated)" (B&N, p. 622). And, indeed, this line of thought culminates in his well-known section at the end of this chapter titled "Freedom and Responsibility," in which Sartre not only reaffirms that we are all "absolutely free" but also declares that there are "no accidents in life" and that we all are "responsible for everything" (B&N, pp. 708–710). This characterization of freedom, to be sure, is what gives rise to the opinion that is held by Adorno and Marcuse, as well as an assortment of somewhat more contemporary critics, that Sartre's concept of freedom confuses genuine freedom with the meager ability of consciousness to reorient its projects in order to reconcile them with a bad social reality.

Even Sartre subsequently reproaches himself for this position, as is evidenced by a well-known 1969 interview that has since been titled "The Itinerary of a Thought." Referring to his earlier claim that "a man is always free to choose to be a traitor or not," Sartre declares: "When I read this, I said to myself: it's incredible, I actually believed that!"[46] Yet, even at this juncture, Sartre hangs on to a notion of freedom that presupposes some capacity for self-determination:

> For the idea which I have never ceased to develop is that in the end one is always responsible for what is made of one. Even if one can do nothing else besides assume this responsibility. For I believe that a man can always make something out of what is made of him. This is the limit I would today accord to freedom: the small movement which makes of a totally conditioned social being someone who does not render back completely what his conditioning has given him.[47]

Moreover, as I stated in the opening section of this part of the book, even in the 1975 Schilpp interview, Sartre says that freedom remains his "starting point," which, he states, is exactly what distinguishes his thought from the dominant strains of Marxist thought (which do not necessarily bear a strong relation to Marx's thought).[48] Sartre thus rejects as a "mistake" his previous claim that "existentialism is only an enclave within Marxism" because of his "idea of freedom."[49]

How are we to make sense of these seemingly divergent tendencies concerning freedom in *Being and Nothingness* itself (much less Sartre's ostensibly changing views on freedom over time)? The best way to approach this question, it seems to me, is to avail ourselves of Sartre's "regressive analysis"—that is, to begin with the specific empirical act that allegedly manifests our "freedom in situation" and then work backward to the individual's initial project or "ultimate possible," which, motivated by the fundamental project, puts the particular act in an integrated perspective (B&N, p. 592). Before proceeding, however, it is necessary to consider Sartre's definition of freedom itself, for the very ambiguity of the term gives rise to numerous problems.

As David Detmer correctly points out, there are, according to Sartre, two different senses of freedom—"ontological freedom" and "practical freedom"—and Sartre's various references to freedom in *Being and Nothingness* invariably fall into one of these two categories. For example, Sartre alternatively depicts "ontological freedom" as "freedom of choice," "abstract freedom," "intellectual freedom," and "metaphysical freedom," and, conversely, "practical freedom" as the "freedom to obtain," "concrete freedom," "political and social freedom," and "conditioned and limited freedom."[50] The crucial point, however, is that our "freedom of choice" or "ontological freedom" must never be confused with our "freedom of obtaining" or "practical freedom"—a point on which Sartre is exceedingly clear:

> It is necessary to point out to "common sense" that the formula "to be free" does not mean "to obtain what one has wished" but rather "by oneself to determine oneself to wish" (in the broad sense of choosing). In other words, success is not important to freedom. The discussion which opposes common sense to philosophers stems from a misunderstanding: the empirical and popular concept of "freedom" which has been produced by historical, political, and moral circumstances is equivalent to "the ability to obtain the ends chosen." The technical and philosophical concept of freedom, *the only one which we are considering here*, means only the autonomy of choice. (B&N, pp. 621–622; italics added)

Sartre makes this distinction right before his infamous "prisoner example," which was the basis for Marcuse's claim that Sartre's notion of freedom "declined to the level of mere ideology, an ideology which offers itself as a handy justification for the persecutors and executioners."[51] But, as we saw earlier (and are in a better position to see now), Sartre is not referring to "practical" (i.e., "political and social") freedom here, and the fact that human beings are "ontologically free" is by no means an ideological justification for persecutors and executioners. To the contrary, it is the objective basis for condemning them, since they are persecutors and executioners by virtue of persecuting and executing free beings. Thus, as Detmer indicates, this problem would not even arise in the context of causally determined robots, for freedom does not apply to robots in any meaningful sense: only an ontologically free being can be enslaved.[52] In other words, it is just because we are ontologically free that we can be understood as practically unfree. Thus, unlike certain bourgeois apologists (i.e., the sort that Marcuse rightly worries about), who see "freedom of choice" as both the necessary *and* sufficient condition of a robust practical freedom, Sartre sees ontological freedom as nothing more than a necessary condition of any practical freedom, and this is the case in *Being and Nothingness* no less than his later works.

Although Sartre claims that "success is not important to freedom" and that "there is no situation in which the for-itself would be more free than others," it does not follow that he is also claiming that ontological freedom is tantamount to "inward freedom" or "the independence of the inner life," which, he recognizes, would appropriately subject his position to "ridicule." To the contrary, ontological freedom is never a disengaged freedom: I must freely choose within a limiting situation, which itself arises within the framework of my concrete actions and goals, my initial project, and, finally, "the indications of others." Even if I see myself as "the victim"—that is, from a third-person perspective that would preclude the possibility that I can change my own conditions (much less the conditions of the world)—the unalterable fact remains that ultimately *I* am the one who chooses to see myself in this way. In other words, even if it denies its particular engagements by denying itself, the ontological freedom of the for-itself is inexorably engaged. It should thus be clear that Adorno's charge that Sartre has a Kierkegaardian concept of freedom, in which social conditions "do hardly more than provide an occasion for the action," does not hold, for such a charge is consonant with the concept of that "inward freedom" that Sartre has explicitly rejected. Unlike Kierkegaard, who, Adorno asserts, withdraws from horizontal (i.e., concrete) relations with others to retain his freedom in the face of "the present age,"[53] Sartre refuses to entertain the view that human beings can ever indeterminately withdraw from "the situation" (which, as we have seen, is his phenomenological correlate of the sociohistorical situation). Since "the situation is the subject illuminating things by his very surpassing" (B&N, p. 702)—that is, it is neither purely subjective nor purely objective because it is a synthetic relation between the freedom of the for-itself and the facticity of the in-itself—it makes no sense to analytically separate the Sartrean subject from his situation and speak in terms of a withdrawal that is effectuated to test the (indeterminate) subject's ethical or religious mettle. Sartre certainly holds open the "nihilating withdrawal," but since this withdrawal necessarily and instantaneously plunges itself right back into a situation, the subject's factical stuff, it is of a determinate nature. Indeed, Sartre's "nihilating withdrawal" might be best viewed in terms of Hegel's "determinate negativity," a notion that Adorno emphatically embraces throughout his oeuvre.

The crucial "paradox of freedom" to which I referred at the start of this section does not relate to whether we are "free to choose" even if we are not "free to obtain" (in any meaningful sense), for, as I have just argued, I think that Sartre effectively deals with this matter. Nor does this crucial "paradox of freedom" relate to what we have seen Sartre himself call "the paradox of freedom," namely, that "there is freedom only in a situation, and there is a situation only through freedom," which I also take to be right. Rather, the crucial paradox to which I referred relates to whether we are "free to choose" in any situation even if we are entirely "free to obtain" in every situation—in other words, whether our phenomenological freedom is of such a nature that we can see ourselves as self-determining irrespective of our practical freedom. As I argued earlier, I think that Sartre's phenomenological ontology in *Being and Nothingness* already implies that our initial projects are all but socially determined. But, crucially, even if this is not the case, Sartre's avowed position—namely, that our initial projects are free just because they are not determined by reasons—calls into question whether all of our choices, which are free only because they are made pursuant to our spontaneously chosen initial projects, are of such a nature that Sartre is justified in understanding us as responsible for them. Indeed, although

Adorno is referring to our more mundane choices, his claim that in Sartre's existentialism the "individual [must] choose without his choice being determined by any reason" (ND, p. 51) seems to be right on target when understood within the deeper framework of the initial choice. To see why this is the case, I shall proceed with the "regressive analysis" to which I referred earlier. And, following Sartre's lead, I shall begin with the nature of the "act" itself.

According to Sartre, an act or "action is on principle intentional"—that is, the conscious pursuit of a project—which means that an unmotivated act, such as an act of carelessness, is not, strictly speaking, an "act" at all (B&N, pp. 559–560). In seeking to bring about a state of affairs that does not presently exist, moreover, the very concept of an act, Sartre contends, implies that "consciousness has been able to withdraw itself from the full world of which it is consciousness and to leave the level of being [i.e., what is] in order frankly to approach that of non-being [i.e., what is not]" (B&N, p. 560). But Sartre's understanding of an "act" is even more restricted than this suggests, for he goes on to say that a person who is completely "immersed in the historical situation" can have no conception of its economic and political shortcomings, and although this person actively conforms to its strictures (since "he lacks the education and reflection necessary for him to conceive of a social state in which his sufferings would not exist"), "he does not act" (B&N, p. 561). That is, although being unwittingly exploited in the workplace does involve acts in the first sense because the worker intentionally acts to bring about another material reality through his work, it does not involve acts in the second sense because what he does appears to him to be "natural" (which, for Adorno, would be characterized as "second nature").

Sartre's basic point here is that a factual state in and of itself can never motivate or cause a human act. It is only because a person is able to wrench himself away from the immediacy of his experience, which means that he is able to *freely* posit alternative possibilities, that a given factual state can loosely be described as the "cause" of his ensuing actions. It is for this reason that Sartre rejects the temporally linear "cause-intention-act-end" framework in which both the proponents of free will *and* the determinists classically frame their debate. The proponents of free will, he claims, advance an "absurd" position because an "uncaused" act would necessarily be one that lacks the intentional structure of all acts (for, as we saw, acts, which are deliberative, have causes), while the determinists abortively end their inquiry by simply pointing to a "cause" or "motive" without specifying how it actually comes to be constituted as a "cause" or "motive." In response to this lack in the determinists' position, Sartre asserts that "to be a cause, the cause must be experienced as such" (B&N, p. 564), and to "be experienced as such" it must relate to an "end," a presently nonexisting state of affairs that gives both the causally induced motive and action their meanings. (It goes without saying that there are no "meanings" with respect to the full plentitude of being, which simply "is what it is.") Thus, "as the resolute project toward a change is not distinct from the act, the motive, the act, and the end are all constituted in a single upsurge. Each of these three structures claims the two others as its meaning" (B&N, p. 565). Or, to put it more clearly, as well as in opposition to both the determinists and the proponents of free will, "causes" and "motives" point back toward our freedom, which gives rise to them.

Accordingly, it cannot be emphasized too strongly that notwithstanding the conventional inclination to indiscriminately throw Sartre in with the proponents of free will, his argument, at least at this level, runs contrary to their most deeply held positions. Not only is it the case that on Sartre's account to be free is to be phenomenologically free (irrespective of the metaphysical fact of the matter), but it is also the case that the will is not autonomous (irrespective of the fact that the "autonomous will" is generally the linchpin of arguments offered by the proponents of free will). According to Sartre, classical views of the "autonomous will" are antinomical in that the will is seen both as the ground on which free acts can originate and as reflectively committed to certain ends—in other words, it is seen as causally efficacious without itself being caused and as the reflective consequence of a freedom that has already oriented itself toward particular goals. To avoid this antinomy, Sartre contends, we must understand the will in the second sense only, which means jettisoning the concept of will generally offered by the proponents of free will:

> The will, far from being the unique or at least privileged manifestation of freedom, actually—like every event of the for-itself—must presuppose the foundation of an original freedom in order to be able to constitute itself as will. The will in fact is posited as a reflective decision in relation to certain ends. But it does not create these ends. It is rather a mode of being in

> relation to them: it decrees that the pursuit of these ends will be reflective and deliberative. Passion can posit the same ends. (B&N, p. 571)

In sum, then, because the will is determined within the framework of motives and ends that have already been posited by the for-itself, it is merely "a psychic event of a peculiar structure which is constituted on the same plane as other psychic events" (B&N, p. 583).

So far so good. Practically speaking, for Sartre, each person has some complex ensemble of projects, goals, or ultimate ends to which he is committed, and, as is the case with Heidegger's carpenter in the tool shed, there is ordinarily no particular need to deliberate on them. And, in fact, even if conflicts arise among these aims, they might be adjudicated at an unreflective level, for our miscellaneous commitments vary in depth. Some aims are tertiary, others secondary, and yet others more elementary, and, as Sartre says, since we have a "pre-judicative comprehension" of this hierarchy, we might unreflectively act in accordance with the deeper commitments. Of course, at certain times there might be a more fundamental conflict, or, even more likely, it might be the case that we are unable to unreflectively achieve our aims within our habitual frames of reference, and it is only at this point, when "the chips are down," that the will reflects (B&N, p. 582). As we saw earlier, however, this predominant type of reflection, which Sartre refers to as "accessory," is by definition limited to the best or most consistent way of achieving our goals. This means that it cannot call into question our most basic project—the initial project that orients all of our other projects—but rather only tries to support or justify it. As the very foundation of accessory reflection, therefore, the initial project is itself nonreflective:

> We must insist on the fact that the question here is not of a deliberative choice. This is not because the choice is less conscious or less explicit than a deliberation but rather because it is the foundation of all deliberation and because, as we have seen, a deliberation requires an interpretation in terms of an original choice. Therefore it is necessary to defend oneself against the illusion which would make of original freedom a positing of causes and motives as objects, then a decision from the standpoint of these causes and these motives. Quite the

> contrary, as soon as there are cause and motive (that is, an appreciation of things and the structures of the world) there is already a positing of ends and consequently a choice. But this does not mean that the profound choice is thereby unconscious. It is simply one with the consciousness that we have of ourselves. This consciousness, as we know, can be only non-positional; it is we-as-consciousness since it is not distinct from our being. And as our being is precisely our original choice, the consciousness (of) the choice is identical with the self-consciousness which we have. One must be conscious in order to choose and one must choose in order to be conscious. Choice and consciousness are one and the same thing. (B&N, pp. 594–595)

It is at this point, to repeat, that Adorno's claim—that Sartre's "individual [must] choose without his choice being determined by any reason"—hits closest to home. In the course of our everyday lives, on Sartre's account, *instrumental* reasons do motivate our actions. According to Sartre, the reason for every significant act can theoretically be comprehended by progressively plumbing the depths of the hierarchical "ensemble" of tertiary, secondary, and primary projects that constitute a person's self-identity. Yet, at the deepest level, the level of the initial project, which is what enables all reasons to come into being, Sartre's "regressive analysis" can go no further: there is simply pure contingency. Of course, Sartre contends that it is precisely because our reasons do not orient our fundamental choice of ourselves in the world, but only arise from it, that we are, in fact, free. But this position, which is highly unsatisfying in terms of the kinds of freedom, responsibility, and self-determination with which we are left, since it suggests that reflection is constituted by the life-structuring initial project but cannot reconstitute it in turn, also runs contrary to other aspects of Sartre's thought. In particular, it seems to me that Sartre's notion of a "purifying reflection"—which, although arguably the linchpin of his ethical thought, is obscurely described as a "katharsis" (B&N, p. 218)—is utterly compromised on this account.

As an initial matter, the conceptual distinction between a purifying reflection, which, for Sartre, enjoys a privileged epistemic status, and ordinary accessory reflection, which is part and parcel of that very initial project that a purifying reflection is able to call into question, is easy enough to make: the purifying reflection yields a knowledge—or, better put, awareness—that is immediate rather than the mediate knowledge yielded by accessory reflection. Thus, accessory reflection is based on the classical subject-object paradigm, in which the subject that knows and the object of its knowledge are at a remove, and the subject, in some sense, represents the object of its knowledge, which makes this knowledge only probable. On Sartre's particular account, as we know, consciousness spontaneously, although ineluctably, generates an empirical self, and consciousness's knowledge of both self and other is wholly mediated by the imperatives of the initial project that underlies the empirical self formed. A purifying reflection, conversely, entails a "simple presence of the reflective for-itself to the for-itself reflected on" (B&N, p. 218), which "at one stroke" yields an intuitive self-knowledge that not only reveals the unjustifiability of the initial project but also the motivation for it, the fundamental project of *being* a for-itself-in-itself. As a result, while in one sense we are always free because our initial project arises from the free spontaneity of consciousness, with the "immediate reflection" of a purifying reflection we evolve to a moral sense of freedom. And this moral sense of freedom, Sartre thinks, would translate into practical freedom if such a "radical conversion" took place on a larger social scale.

This account, nevertheless, has (at least) two crucial problems. First, what is the impetus for a purifying reflection? In *Being and Nothingness*, Sartre sidesteps this question by informing us that "this is not the place to describe the motivation and the structure of the katharsis" entailed in pure reflection (B&N, p. 224). Yet, if everything about us can be traced to the initial project, it would stand to reason that there is no standpoint from which resistance to our initial choice of ourselves (as well as the impure reflection that it generates) could establish itself. Second, how could one sustain a purifying reflection and live in accordance with its insights in the event that it could somehow establish itself? Although Sartre often denigrates the initial project or choice, he also views it as the most basic organizing principle: as we have already seen, by both structuring our perceptual field and providing the motivating reasons of accessory reflection (rather than being determined by reasons), it is the fount of intelligibility. Thus, even if a purifying reflection could arise, it could bear no relation to our personal practices, which presuppose the accessory reflection of an empirical self that is created by consciousness through its initial choice of itself. In other words, in the face of this ontologically unavoidable initial choice, a purifying reflection would be either fleeting (i.e., existing only in "the instant") or impotent.

If the secondary literature is a reasonable judge, and I believe that it is, there is no good answer to the first problem. In "Self-Consciousness and the Ego in the Philosophy of Sartre," for instance, Phyllis Berdt Kenevan says that "the troubling question, why does consciousness purify itself spontaneously, what motivates it? is one that Sartre cannot answer."[54] Kenevan then goes on to point out that in his talk to the *Société Française de Philosophie*, Sartre himself admitted that he was unable to answer this question:

> Is it possible to pass from an immediate consciousness to pure reflection? I know nothing about it. . . . What is most frequently encountered is, I believe, people who pass calmly from the immediate to impure reflection. The type who is thirsty, who hasn't enough money, who has difficulties with his wife, is plunged into all of this and one fine day exclaims: "How miserable I am!" It is a reflection welling up from an impure psyche. But I can't imagine the individual going on from this to see the ontological reality of his being, which is perhaps leading him to leave his wife and change his job; and we would be on the level of morality. I don't think there would be a transition from one to the other.[55]

It would seem that without a transcendental ego, which itself gives rise to innumerable problems, Sartre's Husserlian-inspired purifying reflection is not able to identify its own impetus. Francis Jeanson, whose 1947 book on Sartre's work was one that Sartre wholeheartedly endorsed, sees the problem and tries to respond, but he does so inadequately. After asserting that "the purifying reflection is none other than Husserl's famous 'reduction'"[56]—a contention that is only arguably in accordance with Sartre's actual position[57]—Jeanson declares that the impetus for a purifying reflection derives from freedom itself: "freedom is no more than an appeal from within, which we are free to disregard."[58] Ostensibly, this "appeal from within" would have to be from the prereflective cogito, which, as we have already seen, is simultaneously one with prereflective consciousness and, in its awareness of the awareness of prereflective consciousness, at a remove (thus accounting for our freedom from the world of objects of which we are positionally aware). But, to my mind, this only replicates the problem at a deeper level.

Now, perhaps Jeanson's "appeal from within" points us toward intuitions—by "intuition" here I mean only the immediate apprehension of a given principle or phenomenon—for Sartre certainly seems to privilege this prereflective form of "knowing." And, it will be recalled, early in *Being and Nothingness*, Sartre contends that through boredom, nausea, and other such feelings we intuit the phenomenon of being. In fact, as I have already indicated, although I reject the idea that such intuitions tell us something about being—again, to my mind, the emptiest philosophical concept, as Hegel says in the *Logic*—I do think that at times intuitions can reveal to us the nature of our empirical existences in a way that we are not otherwise able to reflectively articulate. But, ultimately, even if we understand intuitions as pointing toward the deficiencies of our empirical existences when measured against our prereflective expectations, I do not believe that they are particularly reliable guides in the absence of a reflective knowledge that could elaborate on them. And, indeed, without "the labor of the concept"—that is, without the very reflective knowledge that has been invalidated as a degrading form of knowing—Sartre's intuitions, now mistakenly ontologized, might be used to justify any irrational end, which is exactly Adorno's point against Heidegger. In any case, the question of what brings about Sartre's purifying reflection remains.

The second problem that I raised earlier—namely, whether one could sustain a purifying reflection and live in accordance with its insights even if it could somehow establish itself—is no more amenable to a satisfactory answer than the first problem. Along these lines, it would be helpful to recall that in Sartre's talk to the *Société française de philosophie* he stated that the aim of *Being and Nothingness* was "to arrange a synthesis of the contemplative and nondialectical consciousness of Husserl, who alone leads us to the contemplation of essences, with the activity of the dialectical project, but without consciousness and hence without foundation, that we find in Heidegger"[59]—that is, to arrange a synthesis of Husserl's phenomenological reduction and Heidegger's notion of us as beings-in-the-world. Ultimately, however, Sartre fails to pull this synthesis off. Even if the Husserl-inspired purifying reflection was able to arise within Sartre's existential phenomenology, it would bracket nothing less than the sociohistorically engendered lifeworld—the progenitor of what Husserl refers to as "the natural attitude"—in its entirety, lest it remain captive to the kinds of reasons that are intrinsic to accessory reflection. Thus, such a "purifying" stance—an ideal that arises in "the instant" and takes as its paradigmatic activity the "entirely gratuitous" activity of play because it is not "of the world" (B&N, pp. 740–741)—is necessarily typified by an utter lack of practical efficacy. Indeed, like Marcuse's "body lived as flesh," such an individual "conversion" would turn into its opposite under the existing conditions (assuming that it would not pass away in "the instant" due to the inexorability of consciousness's plunge into another initial project).

Things are no better when viewed from the other side of the coin. Although, for Sartre, Heidegger's "dialectical project" is problematical because it is "without consciousness and hence without foundation," the moral element in their respective philosophies founders in roughly the same way. Heidegger, of course, does not speak in terms of consciousness, much less purifying reflections, but he does speak in terms of "authenticity," which is what the purifying reflection allegedly attains. But, in much the same way that Dasein is locked into its hermeneutic horizon, human beings are locked into the rigid determinism of their initial choice of themselves, which arises within the context of a world of collective practices.[60] So, too, in much the same way that Dasein individuates itself from "the they" through anxiety in the face of death, which (as its ownmost possibility) enables it to bring its being into question, consciousness, Sartre contends, liberates itself from its own bad faith construct (the empirical ego or self) through anguish in the face of freedom, which is the "essential" nature of consciousness: "it is in anguish that freedom is, in its being, in question for itself" (B&N, p. 65). And, finally, when Heidegger contends that an authentic comportment does not "float above falling everydayness" but is "only a modified way in which such everydayness is seized on,"[61] or when he contends that authenticity "can not evade its ownmost non-relational possibility,"[62] he testifies to the impotence of his concept of authenticity, which lacks any vestige of either social or personal efficacy. For what else does it mean to live the same "fallen" life in a "modified way," or to contend that your relation to *your* authentic life is "nonrelational"? Yet, it would seem that Sartre also falls into this trap, for there is absolutely no basis for mediating a purifying reflection that brackets the natural attitude and an initial choice of oneself that is mired in it.

In the final analysis, however, I think that there is a better way to interpret Sartre so as to bring about his attempted synthesis—a way in which a space for a truly self-determining agent remains open—for on Sartre's account here there is not even space for the sort of modestly mediating subject that he later speaks about in "The Itinerary of a Thought" (i.e., the person that "can always make something out of what is made of him"). Because Sartre's characterization of Heidegger's philosophy as a "dialectical project" is mistaken, since there can be no dialectical project "without consciousness," what is actually needed is Hegel's genuinely dialectical project for the purpose of sublating the undialectical projects of Husserl and Heidegger. And, indeed, because much of Sartre's phenomenological ontology is patterned on Hegel's categories anyway, the possibility of this further synthesis is present.

On the one hand, although it is not entirely clear whether Sartre's purifying reflection brackets the natural attitude like Husserl's phenomenological reduction or erupts "in the instant" within the natural attitude, both of these interpretations are based on the notion that a purifying reflection stands in an unmediated relation to the natural attitude, and this is a notion that must be rejected. Whether it is "purifying" or "accessory," all reflection—albeit with varying degrees of self-consciousness—ineluctably bears the mark of the particular sociohistorical situation within which it arises. Yet, this does not mean that we are merely left with accessory reflection, which concerns technical questions of means instead of ends. Rather, it means that reflection must take place within a moral framework in which practical freedom itself is understood as the end that both orients and delimits our instrumental reflections (not freedom understood as the immediate self-consciousness of our "ontological lack," i.e., our noncoincidence with our selves, as Sartre implies toward the end of *Being and Nothingness*). It means that it is incumbent on freedom, our highest value, to foster the grounds of its own most optimal expression (which is by no means the same thing as extirpating anything that might tether it, as Hegel's discussion of "the French Terror" illustrates). Finally, it means that just as practical freedom presupposes ontological freedom as its ground—which, it will be recalled, was Sartre's response to Marcuse—ontological freedom presupposes practical freedom as its telos (lest we devolve into the sort of claim, which is occasionally made by Sartre, that it makes no difference what we do because "man is a useless passion" [B&N, p. 784]). In any event, there is a vital difference between this kind of situated, purposeful, "purifying" reflection that takes place over time and is oriented toward its practical freedom, which is inherently dialectical, and either a purifying reflection that suspends the object under inquiry or anarchically arises in the instant for no reason at all.

On the other hand, we must also reject Sartre's monolithic concept of the initial project, which is what gives rise to the view that freedom can consist only in the ever present possibility of choosing a new initial project, and that this choice is not the result of reasons but instead just spontaneously occurs. This totalizing "mystery in broad delight," as Sartre describes the initial project, deprives us of the means that "ordinarily permit analysis and conceptualization" (B&N, p. 729), and, therefore, precludes any meaningful notion of critical self-determination (not unlike Heidegger's Dasein). Properly understood, our orientation toward the world is predicated on a subjective constitution that is a function of a highly differentiated, multilayered ensemble of social, historical, and psychological factors, and the foundation of a "purifying" reflection—or, put somewhat better, "nonaccessory" reflection, which has a more dialectical ring—is to be found *within* the framework of this significantly expanded subjective constitution. Thus, on this account, freedom is the ability to take a different point of view. It is the ability to reflectively call into question (or, as Fingarette characterizes it, "spell out") aspects of our existing initial orientation from another standpoint that does not spontaneously arise outside of our prevailing subjective constitution but, to the contrary, reflects the wide-ranging nature of the experiences that are a part of it—albeit a part of it that has not been ascendant with respect to the dominant orientation, and, indeed, for this reason, has the ability to critique it.[63] Without pressing the point too strongly, this notion of the initial project is, in certain respects, not unlike an Hegelian "form of consciousness," at least to the extent that it sublates previous orientations (or, at least, leaves the space for their inclusion in the larger subjective constitution of which it is a part) and only gradually breaks down due to the possibility of a continuing nonaccessory reflection that, unless the initial project is wholly in bad faith, at least hazily perceives internal contradictions (rather than spontaneously breaks down all at once).

In sum, then, with these modifications, nonaccessory reflection ideally plays an essential role in the empirical ego's ongoing self-formation by mediating a far more expansive subjective constitution (which includes a far less reductive initial project), and therefore the actions that are undertaken on its behalf (which is not to say that on very rare occasions more abrupt subjective reorientations do not take place). What is involved here is a perpetual exchange between, on the one hand, nonaccessory reflection, and, on the other hand, the assemblage that is comprised of action, accessory reflection, project, and orientation (i.e., that aspect of our subjective constitution that motivates them). And this perpetual exchange is in the service of the individual's effort to achieve a genuine understanding of himself for the purpose of effectuating a more felicitous self-constitution—although, of course, as discussed in the context of bad faith, this ideal is merely a regulative one for Sartre, given that the subject (consciousness) that is trying to know is always beyond the self (or ego) that would be known.[64] Thus, while one must still be geared toward the world by some specific subjective orientation—one is always already in some way engaged—its empirical content is always up for grabs, and *fluid* alterations to it (or, indeed, those exceedingly rare outright changes of it) are generated in the natural attitude itself. On this account, in other words, a space is opened for the possibility—indeed, the predominance—of incremental changes within a far more flexible fundamental orientation (i.e., initial project), which itself is simply an aspect of a larger subjective constitution. When Sartre says that freedom "is characterized by a *constantly renewed* obligation to remake the Self which designates the free being, [and that] the self with its a priori and historical content is the essence of man" (B&N, p. 72), therefore, he cannot reasonably be interpreted as saying that we must perpetually careen from one totalizing initial project to another, but rather that we must take into account what experience teaches to refine our initial project, and therefore our self-conception—that is, until such a point that experience teaches that, in its broad outline, the existing initial project is untenable. Moreover, it is at this point that we see the ethical necessity for practical freedom. Beyond the particular ends that he seeks to obtain, the individual must be oriented by the desire to expand the range of practical freedom within his sociohistorical context because it delineates the range of possible subjective orientations that determine, in a fundamental way, how he is able to "remake [his] Self." As Adorno succinctly puts it, "there is no available model of freedom save one: that consciousness, as it intervenes in the total social constitution, will through that constitution intervene in the complexion of the individual" (ND, p. 265).

These changes, it must be emphasized, are implicit in *Being and Nothingness* itself, and an overview of Sartre's entries in *Notebooks for an Ethics*, which (although not published during his lifetime) were written in the mid-1940s, just a few years after *Being and Nothingness*, draws them out. In his notebooks, for example, Sartre states that the purifying reflection does not spell the death of the underlying project, and, moreover, that it does not suppress the natural attitude: "The project is not absolutely suppressed by pure reflection, any more than the natural attitude is suppressed in the phenomenological epoché. It fully remains as deeply rooted in my original choice. But at the same time it is thematized and becomes the object of a question."[65] This new possibility of thematizing the initial project, in turn, develops the position that Sartre takes in *Being and Nothingness* in two key ways: first, there is "a new relation of man to his project: he is both inside and outside"[66] (and I have just offered an account of our subjective constitution that might help to make sense of this "outside"); and, second, for pure reflection to accomplish this task it cannot only arise in "the instant," since, "for there to be attention to the instant, there must be a duration that temporalizes itself."[67] Moreover, if the initial project can be thematized by a subject over time who is both inside and outside of it, then the negativity that the subject brings to bear on the situation, which is now designated as "historical," is more clearly of a determinate nature: "freedom does not limit itself to negating A (conceived of as a situation) [for] negation is also specifying with regard to A."[68] And, lastly, there is no more talk about an indifference with respect to ends, for "the ultimate end is always the founding of a reign of concrete freedom."[69]

By the time Sartre writes *Search for a Method*, the dialectical movement that I have been advocating comes fully to fruition, and, indeed, it comes to fruition in terms that are homologous with those in *Being and Nothingness*. The book's third (and by far largest) section, in particular, "The Progressive-Regressive Method," is constituted almost entirely by a subsection titled "The Project," in which Sartre explicitly reaffirms that "man defines himself by his project" (SM, p. 150). No longer speaking specifically in terms of the totalizing initial project, which abstractly brought sociohistorical considerations through the back door (but brought these "indications of others" through it no less forcefully all the same), he now speaks in terms of an all too concrete social conditioning. Yet, crucially, Sartre still refuses to objectivistically dissipate subjectivity in the historical unfolding that yields such conditioning precisely because his analysis *is* dialectical:

> We refuse to confuse the alienated man with a thing or alienation with the physical laws governing external conditions. We affirm the specificity of the human act, which cuts across the social milieu while still holding on to its determinations, and which transforms the world on the basis of given conditions. For us, man is characterized above all by his going beyond a situation, and by what he succeeds in making of what he has been made. (SM, p. 91)

While many claim that the space for self-determination narrows in Sartre's later works, it seems to me that the opposite is really the case, for in these works there is no longer a totalizing initial project, determined by "the indications of others," that wholly instrumentalizes reason and thus can only change for no reason at all (i.e., in a nondeliberate, spontaneous way). Rather, as I have been arguing, there is now a larger subjective constitution that is constituted by numerous conflicting perspectives that one must assume within the framework of a far more nuanced basic orientation. For Sartre, it now becomes a matter of analyzing the contradictory but dialectically interconnected "roles which compose us and tear us apart"—roles that also retain "the traces left by our first revolts, our desperate attempts to go beyond a stifling reality, and the resulting deviations and distortions, [because] to surpass all that is also to preserve it" (SM, p. 101). Thus, these roles neither remain static over a (frozen) life nor are they precipitously discarded more or less rapidly within a (disjointed) life: "Life develops in spirals, [and] it passes again and again by the same points but at different levels of integration and complexity" in pursuit of increasingly concrete syntheses (SM, p. 106). And the ability to perform these syntheses, which incorporate "need, negativity, surpassing, project, and transcendence" (each of which contains all the others) is on account of the existence of situated non-accessory reflection: "the reflective operation—as a particular dated act—can be indefinitely repeated. Thereby the dialectic develops indefinitely and wholly in each dialectic process, whether it be individual or collective" (SM, pp. 173–174).[70]

Last, while Sartre's focus is now on practical rather than phenomenological freedom, and, more specifically, the severe limits on practical freedom in the modern social world (which, of course, is also the focus of the Frankfurt School philosophers), "this recognition of freedom's extreme limitations," as William McBride puts it, "does not dethrone it as the supreme Sartrean value."[71] Sartre unequivocally restates one of his earliest and most important propositions—"to be sure, man can be enslaved only if he is free" (SM, p. 180)—and he goes on to contend that while the extreme limitations of practical freedom are "grasped only as the permanent, concrete condition of his servitude," it is still necessary for "the historical man" to thematize this state-of-affairs, and in its very thematization he can, in some sense, move beyond it:

> It is necessary that the questioner understand how the questioned—that is, himself—*exists his alienation*, how he surpasses it and is alienated in this very surpassing. It is necessary that his very thought should at every instant surpass the intimate contradiction which unites the comprehension of man-as-agent with the knowing of man-as-object and that it forge new concepts, new determinations of Knowledge which emerge from the existential comprehension and which regulate the movement of their contents by its dialectical procedure. Yet this comprehension—as a living moment of the practical organism—can take place only within a concrete situation, insofar as theoretical knowledge illuminates and interprets this situation. (SM, p. 180)

Since, in the mode of non-accessory reflection, the "man-as-agent" is the "man-as-object" in the mode of not being it, given the thin transcendent space that he forms by thematizing his situation, he can "forge new concepts," and therefore, like Münchhausen, (incrementally) pull himself out of any particular social bog by his pigtail in what must be an "indefinitely repeated" operation. And, viewed more broadly, since "every man is defined negatively by the sum total of possibles which are impossible for him by a future blocked off," and "the most individual possible is only the internalization and enrichment of a social possible" (SM, p. 95) defined by a particular social bog, it becomes ethically incumbent on us as such agents to expand the realm of social possibles that is the very stuff from which we are produced as objects (because, going back to *Being and Nothingness*, this is where the stuff of the empirical ego is produced). To enrich the milieu that constitutes us individually and collectively—this is the ultimate ethical task of "man-as-agent." Nevertheless, it should be recognized, it is only when "there will exist for everyone a margin of real freedom beyond the production of life" that we shall *first* have a "philosophy of freedom" (SM, p. 34), which is the type of philosophy that befits beings who, within the particular range of social, historical, and psychophysiological existents, have the ability for self-determination—or, as Nietzsche (who also rejects the "free will" hypothesis) might state it, that befits beings who have the ability "to give style to [their] character."

At the end of the day, this modest capacity for self-determination, which arises from the phenomenology of freedom that Sartre offers throughout his works, is a sociohistorical product rather than an ontological one, and this is why I have repeatedly contended that what we get from Sartre is a "phenomenology of freedom" rather than "ontological freedom." As I argued in the previous chapter, Sartre's "phenomenological ontology" is ultimately phenomenological, which means that the abstract ontological structures that underlie his subject in *Being and Nothingness* are no less sociohistorically produced than the concrete sociohistorical structures that underlie his subject in *Search for a Method* and the *Critique of Dialectical Reason*. What Sartre provides throughout his works, when viewed in their unfolding, is a dialectical analysis of what it means to claim "that every being which cannot act otherwise than under the idea of freedom is thereby free in a practical respect" (irrespective of whether he is free in a "theoretical aspect")[72]—which drives him beyond this Kantian formulation (and the more general "reciprocity thesis" of which it forms a part) to Hegel. And, understood on Hegel's dialectical model, this phenomenology of freedom is a hard won historical achievement (and, it must be added, no less a historical disaster to the extent that it has been sophistically pressed into the service of justifying the domination of others—which, nevertheless, had previously needed no justification at all). Yet, unlike Hegel's dialectical model, Sartre hangs on to the Kantian moment not only by refusing to abandon for Spirit the individual who experiences the world, but also by holding this individual both free and responsible in the face of a social world that is increasingly looking to bury him. In this sense, he is and has been an indispensable antidote to not only Hegel but also to orthodox Marxists, structuralists, and poststructuralists—all of whom, in their different ways, have ratcheted up Hegel's unfortunate claim "that the individual must all the more forget himself, as the nature of Science implies and requires."[73] And, indeed, as the later works of Foucault and Derrida, in particular, demonstrate, even if Sartre's phenomenology of freedom is "only" a sociohistorically produced self-understanding, it is a self-understanding in which we (post)moderns must continue to believe.

Throughout his works, then, Sartre's approach remains markedly phenomenological in the sense that his philosophical analysis begins from the first-person standpoint and builds out to the world. Even in the *Critique of Dialectical Reason*, he starts with free, but totally concretized, individuals who progressively come together in larger and increasingly self-conscious collectives (i.e., the series, the group, the organization, and the institution). Crucially, however, to balance this first-person, phenomenological perspective, which is inherently one-sided because it begins from the concrete individual as a simple given, we must also consider the sociohistorical context from the third-person perspective (i.e., the perspective from which the identities of these concrete individuals are formed), provided that, at bottom, this third-person perspective also presupposes a free individual. Such is the perspective of Adorno, who plays, in Hegel's words, the "objective subject-object" to Sartre's "subjective subject-object," but who, like Sartre, rejects the totalizing movement that is, in some sense, Hegel himself.

PART III

Adorno's Dialectic of Subjectivity

Because Adorno emphasizes the relation between enlightenment subjectivism and an oppressive historical dialectic, many commentators claim that he all but rejects the subject. This conclusion, which is often based on Adorno's analysis of the subject's genesis and historical development in *Dialectic of Enlightenment* (but at least nominally finds support in virtually all of his principal works), is fundamentally misguided. As Adorno himself declares in *Negative Dialectics*, "it is not the purpose of critical thought to place the object on the orphaned royal throne once occupied by the subject. The purpose of critical thought is to abolish the hierarchy" (ND, p. 181). Much like Sartre, whose synthetic approach also explicitly rejects the hierarchies that are inherent in classical versions of both idealism and materialism—Husserl's transcendental phenomenology, Heidegger's fundamental ontology, orthodox Marxism's material dialectic, and Anglo-American positivism—it is Adorno's intention to revitalize the subject rather than to reject him. Moreover, although they differ methodologically in that Sartre's concrete phenomenological depiction of the subject takes place in an abstract sociohistorical context,[1] while Adorno's concrete dialectical analyses presuppose a subject who remains largely abstract, both are committed to the dialectical mediation of the opposite pole—and, finally, of subject and object, universal and particular.

The abstractness of the subject for Adorno is not due to an oversight, therefore, but rather to his refusal to be pinned down on its meaning by virtue of his methodological starting point, a sociohistorical dialectic that mediates even the most basic of concepts. In "Subject and Object," an essay published shortly before his death, Adorno makes this very point. As an initial matter, however, Adorno declares that the very term "subject" is "patently ambiguous," for it can mean either a "particular individual" or "consciousness in general." These meanings, moreover, are themselves mutually defining because the view of the subject as a "consciousness in general" idealistically abstracts from the concrete beings in the world that give rise to this meaning, and the view of the subject as a "particular individual" collapses into meaninglessness without a generic concept that could be applied to it.[2] Yet, crucially, Adorno does not ask that we give up on the attempt to grasp the term, for this would be tantamount to conceptually hypostatizing it in accordance with its presently given meaning, and thus giving it a final meaning. Instead, Adorno argues, reflection should take up its meaning "as the well-honed philosophical language hands it to us as a historical sediment—not, of course, sticking to such conventionalism but continuing with critical analysis."[3]

Still, critical analyses rely on a standpoint of critique, and, as the following excerpt from a conversation between Adorno and the sociologist Arnold Gehlen illustrates, the type of subject that Adorno presupposes shares much in common with the (Sartrean) enlightenment subject that he is often alleged to have rejected:

> GEHLEN: Mr. Adorno, you see the problem of emancipation here once again, of course. Do you really believe that the burden of fundamental problems, of extensive reflection, of errors in life that have profound and continuing effects, all of which we have gone through because we are trying to swim free of them—do you really believe that one ought to expect everyone to go through this?
>
> ADORNO: I can give you a simple answer: Yes! I have a particular conception of objective happiness and objective despair, and I would say that, for as long as people have problems taken away

> from them, for as long as they are not expected to take on full responsibility and full determination, their welfare and happiness in this world will merely be an illusion. And it will be an illusion that will one day burst.[4]

Of course, while Adorno advocates the principles of self-responsibility and self-determination, poststructuralists are correct when they claim that he unequivocally attacks the kind of subject that is offered in the works of Descartes, Kant, and Husserl, in which the subject is purged of every natural desire. But, as this passage implies, Adorno also attacks with no less vehemence those various philosophies that uniformly reject the traits that are associated with such a subject. Thus, it will be recalled, at the beginning of *Negative Dialectics*, Adorno contends that what he will attempt to do is "use *the strength of the subject* to break through the fallacy of constitutive subjectivity" (ND, p. xx). Given this commitment to the subject, which is not synonymous with a commitment to the "constitutive subjectivity" of idealism, Adorno sees it as no less important to use the strength of the subject to break through the fallacy of "a self-denying subjectivity," which, he argues, "recoils into objectivism" (ND, p. 70). Against Heidegger's "incapacitation of the subject," and, more generally, all thought that would reject the subject, he states: "Doctrines which heedlessly run off from the subject . . . are more easily brought into accord with the world's hardened condition and with the chances of success in it than is the tiniest bit of self-reflection by a subject pondering upon itself and its real captivity" (ND, p. 68).[5] All such doctrines, in other words, give rise to a deformed subjectivity, for the subject "as an element is ineradicable."[6] The notion of a "subjectivity without a subject," which has recently been advanced as an aim, is, therefore, no more acceptable than the notion of a "subject without a subjectivity." I shall now consider these two terms, which are arguably the broken halves that comprise the subject under late capitalism.

A "subject without a subjectivity" relates to Adorno's "objectless subject," who abstracts from his natural desires and sociohistorical conditions in the course of practical deliberation, and, therefore, unwittingly transforms his subjectivity into something that is objectlike in the pursuit of self-realization. For Adorno, Kierkegaard's philosophy reflects the theological variant of this impulse, and (as we saw in chapter 1), according to Adorno, Kierkegaard's thought culminates in the renunciation of its own subjectivity. But the very same charge can also be directed against Kierkegaard's chief target of attack, the rational subject of classical thought. This approach is reflected in Kant's philosophy, in which "the natural" is seen as pathological—but, of course, it also has strong Platonic resonances. In both cases, the ideal subject is self-identical, since he is the subject of the laws of formal reason. Happiness, which has nothing to do with such a subject because it is grounded in nature, is the bone thrown out to induce compliance with the laws of formal reason, but this bone is illusory, for in the very process of abstracting from his internal nature to make himself worthy of happiness, the subject bars the possibility of ever attaining it.

A "subjectivity without a subject," conversely, relates to the more recent inclination to reject the subject, who is taken to be an insidious embodiment of the washed out metaphysical tradition, as well as the perpetrator of its ongoing propensities for objectification and domination. Still, for Adorno, who readily agrees that the enlightenment subject has evinced these tendencies, it is no less a mistake to simply do away with the subject altogether. As we saw in part I, it is his position that the subject's self-destruction causes it to identify all the more with the (subjectively constituted) objective context that it purports to flee. In other words, the theoretical space that constitutes the slight difference between the subject and his subjectivity, which is what gives the basis for Adorno's "tiniest bit of self-reflection" (and, indeed, Sartre's nonaccessory reflection), is negated, and the subject becomes one with his situation, which is ontologized. This diagnosis, which was applied to Heidegger's thought,[7] is no less applicable to Heidegger's linguistically oriented legatees (hermeneuticists and poststructuralists), second generation critical theorists, and philosophers of the body (who dissolve the subject into the play of bodily forces). For these theorists, the problem is not reconciling the individual subject with "its other," which for Adorno means transcending the repression of both nature (internal and external) and other human beings, but rather facilitating an idealistic reconciliation among human beings in language (Habermas), mourning the inability to bring about a reconciliation between human beings and their idealized "other" through language (Derrida), or materialistically celebrating the libido in a way that either explicitly (Lyotard) or implicitly (Deleuze) results in a high-energy collapse into late capitalism.

In contrast to these assorted positions, and despite his unwillingness to pin the subject conceptually, I would argue that Adorno embraces the notion of a mediating subject, and that he does so in a way that suggests that this notion of the subject provides him with both a norm (i.e., *this* is where "the strength of the subject resides") and a standpoint from which to carry out his critical analyses of the subject's predicament under late capitalism (although he worries about the continuing viability of this historically engendered standpoint).[8] This notion of a mediating subject is indicated by Adorno, for example, when he refers to Münchhausen pulling himself out of the bog by his pigtail as representative of an approach to (self-)knowledge that is "at every moment both within things and outside them" and "more than either verification or speculation" (MM, p. 74). Moreover, although the following passage in *Negative Dialectics* (from the section "Reversal of the Subjective Reduction") seems to censure the mediating subject, which is called by its name, it actually supports the notion of the mediating subject that I am arguing is properly attributable to Adorno:

> The means employed by the philosophical tradition to distinguish the concept of subjectivity from entity are copied from entity. That philosophy, suffering of deficient self-reflection to this day, forgot the mediation in the *mediating subject* is no more indicative of meritorious sublimity than any forgetting. As though to punish it, the subject will be overcome by what it has forgotten. It no sooner turns into an object of epistemological reflection than it will share that objective character whose absence is so often cited as elevating it above the factual realm. (ND, p. 176)

Adorno's criticism of the mediating subject, as it is characterized here, is that it unreflectively absolutizes the thin space that separates it from its prereflective engagements in the world, and that in this absolutization, it makes itself into something sublime rather than recognizing that it is always already tethered to the social, historical, and psychophysiological grounds that engender it. (This is analogous to those Sartreans who would mistakenly overemphasize transcendence at the expense of facticity in the belief that this is what constitutes good faith.) In this way—that is, by virtue of its belief that it mediates its own ground but is not first mediated by this ground—it becomes self-identical, just like the entities that it manipulates. Put in terms of the Münchhausen metaphor, this concept of the mediating subject understands itself only as "outside" that to which its knowledge refers, and is therefore woodenly speculative. But, it must be emphasized, Adorno is not criticizing the existence of this space altogether, which is what constitutes the space of the genuinely mediating subject, lest the subject entirely collapse into the "inside" of its knowledge, and therefore become a wooden instrument of verification.

Although Adorno refuses to construct an ontology of the subject, as Sartre heuristically does, they share similar presuppositions. The mediating standpoint in Sartre's phenomenological characterization of the subject, which is the prereflective cogito, is not "indicative of meritorious sublimity," for in itself it is "nothing." Thus, although the prereflective cogito is the basis for mediating reflection, it does not "constitute" its objects—rather, since it is one with prereflective consciousness, which is none other than the objects of which it is intentionally aware, it is thrust into the world. The world is not "forgotten" on Sartre's view but rather is the very stuff of his philosophy. (As Sartre illustrates in *The Age of Reason*, the more the subject idealistically views himself as other than his world to retain his freedom, the more his "bad faith" causes him to be overcome by the world.[9]) Moreover, as against those philosophers who forget "the body," such as Kant *and* Heidegger (who otherwise oppose one another on the matter of the subject), Sartre, like Adorno, views the body as an essential part of who we are: "Consciousness exists its body" (B&N, p. 435).

Like Sartre, indeed, Adorno is ultimately a humanist of sorts. Such a claim, to be sure, is a controversial one, for Adorno himself often repudiates the term. Yet, as the following passages show, he is just as quick to repudiate antihumanism:

> The truth that expels man from the center of creation and reminds him of his impotence—this same truth will, as a subjective mode of conduct, confirm the sense of impotence, cause men to identify with it, and thus reinforce the spell of second nature. (ND, p. 68)

> Heidegger promotes slave thinking. With the standard gesture against the market place of public opinion he spurns the word "humanism." . . . The current talk of humanism is awful enough, but one may well ask whether Heidegger would not end the talk solely because his doctrine would end the matter. (ND, p. 89)

The "current talk of humanism is awful enough," according to Adorno, because it implies the repression of both external and internal nature, and a static, ahistorical concept of human nature that justifies social repression against those who do not conform to it (allegedly for humanitarian reasons but generally for reasons that are far less noble). As his rejection of Heidegger's antihumanism also suggests, however, Adorno does not want to simply end all talk of humanism, for this would (in Nietzschean terms) promote "slave thinking." Thus, as Alfred Schmidt contends, Adorno might be best understood as a "real humanist"—a phrase that was first used by Marx in *The Holy Family*, in which he criticizes Feuerbach's ahistorical humanism.[10] And, indeed, after emphasizing that "the core of truth is historical" in the Preface to the 1969 edition of *Dialectic of Enlightenment*, Adorno and Horkheimer go on to state that "critical thought demands support for the residues of freedom, and for tendencies toward *true humanism*, even if these seem powerless in regard to the main course of history" (DOE, p. x). This third alternative is in accordance with Adorno's refusal either to jettison the subject-object paradigm or bring its internal dialectic to a premature conclusion by privileging one of the two sides.

My focus in this part will revolve around my attempt to justify this claim. In chapter 7, I shall consider Adorno's understanding of the relation between the subject's formation and reason for the purpose of showing that the "dialectic of enlightenment" to which his most pessimistic work refers is a historical tendency that is being contingently expressed rather than a historical necessity. In chapter 8, I shall try to show that Adorno's own notion of "negative dialectics," which is grounded in enlightenment thought, does not jettison the enlightenment notion of an autonomous subject but rather reworks it for the purpose of doing justice to it.

7

The (De)Formation of the Subject

In contrast to *Being and Nothingness*, which considers the subject from the phenomenological standpoint, and therefore does not call into question such "first person" notions as freedom and responsibility (because, practically speaking, we must operate under these ideas), *Dialectic of Enlightenment* considers the subject from the historical or "third person" standpoint. From this standpoint, notions such as freedom and responsibility, which constitute "the subject" as such, become quite problematical—indeed, with the ineluctable march of history as a backdrop, they tend to all but disappear from view (even if they are implicitly presupposed, as is the case with Adorno). It is for this reason that a variety of poststructuralists see *Dialectic of Enlightenment* as a prototypical poststructuralist work. Accordingly, Peter Uwe Hohendahl asserts:

> The obvious and most promising point [for the poststructuralist accretion of Adorno] is Adorno and Horkheimer's critique of the western philosophical tradition in *Dialectic of Enlightenment*. Adorno's critique of the enlightenment project—with its emphasis on universal history, the autonomy of the subject, and the unity of reason and rationality through the transparency of language and communication—becomes the focus for the poststructuralist readings.[1]

Moreover, according to Hohendahl, the motivation that impels poststructuralists to appropriate Adorno's thought is their own repudiation of Marxism:

> What characterizes the poststructuralist approach to Adorno is its deliberate attempt to distinguish his work from the body of Marxist theory and to underscore the difference between his thought and the conceptual apparatus of Marxist theory. . . . In other words, the question of reason and rationality becomes the touchstone for the poststructuralist reading. . . . This reading wants to subvert what Marxist theory had, by and large, taken for granted and therefore ascribed to the writings of Adorno: namely, a stable concept of subjectivity and agency (as opposed to the state of fragmentation and passivity found in advanced capitalism, for instance). The poststructuralist reading would emphasize Adorno's critique of subjectivity, a critique that does not merely focus (as does Lukács) on fragmentation under monopoly capitalism but rather calls the entire Western tradition—the very constitution and identity in Greek culture—into question.[2]

Although Habermas does not approach Adorno in this way, like the poststructuralists he rejects "the conceptual apparatus of Marxist theory" and engages in a "critique of subjectivity" that calls not just the subject under late capitalism into question but what he calls "the philosophy of the subject," which crosses much of the "Western tradition." Yet, unlike the poststructuralists, Habermas does not eschew "universal history," for he proffers a grand narrative in which it is he who brings the enlightenment project to fruition. And, indeed, the centerpiece of Habermas's philosophy, his theory of "communicative rationality," is based on the idea that there is a "unity of reason and rationality"—if not "through the transparency of language and communication" then, in some qualified sense, through the pragmatic structures that undergird them. It is on this basis that Habermas splits with the poststructuralists—and then reductively characterizes Adorno as one of them. In the very first paragraph of his chapter on *Dialectic of Enlightenment* in *The Philosophical Discourse of Modernity*, for instance, Habermas declares that he will "forestall the confusion" that arises from poststructuralism, whose "moods and attitudes" are "confusingly like those of Horkheimer and Adorno."[3] For both sets of thinkers, Habermas states, "it is no longer possible to place hope in the liberating force of the enlightenment."[4]

Although popular with *both* poststructuralists and Habermas, this depiction of *Dialectic of Enlightenment* is just plain wrong. Far from "surrendering . . . to an uninhibited scepticism regarding reason,"[5] *Dialectic of Enlightenment* tries to do justice to the most basic impulses of enlightenment rationality—albeit a notion of enlightenment rationality that manifestly differs from Habermas's formal account (which is possibly why Habermas tries to depict Adorno as an irrationalist). In the Introduction, for example, Adorno and Horkheimer unequivocally say: "We are wholly convinced—and therein lies our *petitio principii*—that social freedom is inseparable from enlightened thought. . . . If enlightenment does not accommodate reflection on the recidivist element then it seals its own fate" (DOE, p. xiii). (This recidivist element is what distinguishes "pure" and "impure" reflection for Sartre.) A scant two pages later, Adorno and Horkheimer contend: "The point is that the Enlightenment must consider itself, if men are not to be wholly betrayed" (DOE, p. xv). Again, on the very next page, they declare: "The accompanying critique of enlightenment is intended to prepare the way for a positive notion of enlightenment which will release it from entanglement in blind domination" (DOE, p. xvi). Notwithstanding their piercing critique of how enlightenment rationality and subjectivity has played out to this point in time, moreover, there is no reason to think that Adorno and Horkheimer change their minds about the need for enlightenment thinking once they get beyond the Introduction. In the last pages of their opening essay ("The Concept of Enlightenment"), they speak in hopeful terms about the enlightenment's ability to bring about the material conditions for a world that is free of coercion: "While bourgeois economy multiplied power through the mediation of the market, it also multiplied its objects and powers to such an extent that for their administration not just the kings [or middle classes] are necessary, but all men. They learn from the power of things to at last dispense with power" (DOE, p. 42). In the last line in the last section of their theses on anti-Semitism (which immediately precedes the book's concluding notes and drafts), Adorno and Horkheimer declare: "Enlightenment which is in possession of itself and coming to power can break the bounds of enlightenment" (DOE, p. 208). In sum, then, *Dialectic of Enlightenment* is nothing other than a critique of reason by (dialectical) reason—that is, a critique of *verstehen* by *vernunft*—and as such resonates with the projects of such "irrationalists" as Kant and Hegel.

Having made clear the enlightenment impulse that lies at the very heart of *Dialectic of Enlightenment*, I am now in a position to consider the particulars of the book, which immanently critiques enlightenment subjectivity and rationality as they have historically unfolded.[6] In the opening section, I shall look at the first excursis, "Odysseus or Myth and Enlightenment," which analyzes the genesis of the enlightenment subject. In the second section, I shall consider "The Concept of Enlightenment" (the introductory essay), "Juliette or Enlightenment and Morality" (the second excursis), and "The Culture Industry: Enlightenment as Mass Deception" (the first appendix), which I take to be analyses of the enlightenment subject's fate within the present day contexts of science, morality, and culture. Last, in the third section, I shall compare "Elements of Anti-Semitism: Limits of Enlightenment" (the second appendix) and Sartre's *Anti-Semite and Jew*, and then cursorily lay out Adorno's psychoanalytic account of the ego, as well as defend it from attacks made by current theorists.

THE DAWN OF THE SUBJECT

If myth is already enlightenment and enlightenment reverts to mythology, as the central thesis in the introductory essay of *Dialectic of Enlightenment* holds, its analogue in "Odysseus or Myth and Enlightenment" is that self-denial is already self-assertion and self-assertion reverts to self-denial. Thus, as the form of mythic self-denial, sacrifice "already appears as the magical pattern of rational exchange, a device of men by which the gods may be mastered" (DOE, p. 49) so that they could guarantee their own self-*preservation*—that is, their preservation as biological organisms. And, conversely:

> In class history, the enmity of the self to sacrifice implied a sacrifice of the self, inasmuch as it was paid for by a denial of nature in man for the sake of domination over non-human nature and other men. This very denial, the nucleus of all civilizing rationality, is the germ cell of a proliferating mythic

> irrationality; with the denial of nature in man not only the telos of the outward control of nature but the telos of man's own life is distorted and befogged. . . . Man's domination over himself, which grounds his selfhood, is *almost* always the destruction of the subject in whose service it is undertaken. (DOE, p. 54; emphasis added)

This form of *self*-preservation, which exemplifies enlightenment self-assertion, does not relate to biological self-*preservation* but to the preservation of the particular ego structure that separates a human being both from nature and other human beings. And, when taken to the extreme, it not only destroys its bid for *self*-preservation, as Adorno states here, but ultimately threatens its self-*preservation* as well.

On the cusp between mythic self-denial as self-assertion and enlightenment self-assertion as self-denial is Hegel's master-slave parable in the *Phenomenology of Spirit*, the ur-moment of human history. Mythic self-denial as self-assertion—the belief that sacrifice ensures (biological) survival—might chronologically follow from an early kind of enlightenment thinking, based on the notion of rational exchange, but conceptually it is a prior moment for Hegel, since it is based on the drive for self-*preservation* that is intrinsic to all animals. What actually makes us human, according to Hegel, is our innate human drive for recognition, which is the very condition of the "self" (in the egological sense). Accordingly, Hegel argues that when two indeterminate, selfless self-consciousnesses—"self-conscious" in the sense of a thin self-awareness that if it could utter it would say "I = I"—initially meet in the state of nature, they must risk their biological selves so as to retain their newly generated ego structures, the provisional outcome of each having been objectified by the acknowledging look of the biologically independent other. This is the moment when the concern with self-*preservation* metamorphoses into the concern with *self*-preservation:

> It is only through staking one's life that freedom is won; only thus is it proved that for self-consciousness, its essential being is not [just] being, not the immediate form in which it appears, not its submergence in the expanse of life, but rather that there is nothing present in it which could not be regarded as a vanishing moment, that it is only pure *being-for-self*.[7]

From this key passage in the *Phenomenology*, it is easy enough to see Adorno and Horkheimer's point about enlightenment self-assertion being self-denial. Despite Hegel's antipathy toward all that is unmediated, this passage implies that it is on the very concept of an indeterminate "pure being-for-self" that all ensuing self-development is based. And what is this "vanishing moment" if not the moment of the pure subject, stripped of all natural residuum, that is the basic stuff of Kant's (empirical) self-abnegating moral idealism—with which Hegel otherwise disagrees. In other words, although Hegel makes the Kantian self determinate by bringing it into relations with others, it becomes determinate only as a social being, not a natural being. Of course, this initial "social" moment in the *Phenomenology*, in which the social self is generated at the price of the natural self, is nominally sublated in an ever-expanding determinate subject (as is also the case with the first moment in Hegel's *Philosophy of Right*, the "pure reflection of the ego"). But the real question for Adorno is whether this first moment, in which we sought to dominate the other human being at the expense of our own internal nature (as well as the Other's), is picked up by this ever-expanding determinate subject on the "recidivist element" of enlightenment reflection (DOE, p. xiii). And, with respect to Hegel's philosophy, with which he otherwise agrees, it is Adorno's belief that it is not.

For Adorno, this internally and externally violent (albeit necessary) initial moment—in which human beings experienced both relief and anxiety at having been catapulted from their undifferentiated oneness with nature—circumscribes all others in the absence of a recidivistic (or purifying) reflection (which, as we will see in the next chapter, relies on a mimetic component). This idea is captured by Adorno's renowned statement in *Negative Dialectics* that "no universal history leads from savagery to humanitarianism, but there is one leading from the slingshot to the megaton bomb" (ND, p. 320). Of course, this is yet another way in which Adorno differs from Hegel and (to a lesser extent) Marx—that is, in his rejection of a universal history that concludes in some ultimate reconciliation. It must be emphasized, however, that Adorno no more rejects universal history than he accepts it, for the idea of a universal history is what gives his thought a critical edge. In an anticipatory reply to those postructuralists who would claim that he rejects universal history in favor of pure discontinuity, Adorno declares: "Discontinuity and universal history must be conceived together. To strike out the latter as a relic of metaphysical superstition would spiritually consolidate pure facticity as the only thing to be known and therefore to be accepted. . . . Universal history must be construed and denied" (ND, pp. 319–320). To drive the point home, while Hegel and Marx might have all too unproblematically embraced universal history from Adorno's point of view, it is in their construal of universal history that they find the critical impulse that is inherent in Adorno's thought no less than their own. As Adorno states the matter, "the prohibition against any brushed-in portrait of utopia that the dialectical theories of both Hegel and Marx issued keenly sniffs out any betrayal of utopia."[8]

It is therefore incorrect to contend that *Dialectic of Enlightenment* posits a philosophy of history that essentially runs against the grain of Marx's thought (although it does help to explain the underlying tendencies that led to those authoritarian state structures that opportunistically styled themselves as "Marxist"). In fact, the first draft of *Dialectic of Enlightenment*, which was titled *Philosophical Fragments*, was written in Marxian terminology, and it was only in reaction to the fear of reprisal from an anticommunist West German regime that Adorno and Horkheimer customized their language.[9] More importantly, from a substantive standpoint, by identifying a destructive *propensity* within the dialectic of enlightenment—that is, by not overtly calling into question capitalism itself but rather the abstract, classifying logic of enlightenment rationality as it has unfolded—Adorno and Horkheimer do not mean to supplant Marx's critique of capitalism. Rather, they construe a universal history that qualifiedly broadens that critique to cover what are, strictly speaking, precapitalist periods. Thus, Adorno and Horkheimer assert that Odysseus is "a prototype of the *bourgeois* individual" (DOE, p. 43).[10]

Indeed, in sharp contrast to (even) Hegel, who fails to comprehend the leveling impulse of the market economy (and on certain accounts actually saw it as a model for Spirit), it is Marx who clearly perceives that the more nettlesome forms of enlightenment rationality and capitalist phenomena such as abstract labor, exchange value, and money are homologous in that they are part and parcel of the instrumentalizing propensity of modernity itself. As the abstract, ordering currencies that arise in nascent bourgeois society and function to strip the haloes from all prior mystifications,[11] money and reason finally turn into mystifications themselves, as do the qualities that comprise the actual individual, who is first transvalued and then destroyed. With respect to money, for example, Marx declares:

> Being the external, common medium and faculty for turning an image into reality and reality into a mere image (a faculty not springing from man as man or from human society as society), money transforms the real essential powers of man and nature into what are merely abstract conceits and therefore imperfections—into tormenting chimeras—just as it transforms real imperfections and chimeras—essential powers which are really impotent, which exist only in the imagination of the individual—into real powers and faculties. In the light of this characteristic alone, money is thus the general overturning of individualities which turns them into their contrary and adds contradictory attributes to their attributes. . . . Since money as the existing and active concept of value confounds and exchanges all things, it is the general confounding and compounding of all things—the world upside-down—the confounding and compounding of all natural and human qualities. He who can buy bravery is brave, though he be a coward.[12]

With respect to enlightenment reason, Marx declares in *The German Ideology* that Kant's rationalistic moral philosophy reflects the alteration of French liberalism by the German burgher, who "recoils in horror" at "shameless bourgeois profit-making": Kant thus "made the materially motivated determinations of the will of the French bourgeoise into pure self-determinations of *free will*, of the will in and for itself . . . and so converted it into purely conceptual ideological determinations and moral postulates."[13] This, too, as has been contended by Marxist and non-Marxist alike, "turns the world upside-down" and is "the confounding and compounding of all natural and human qualities." Moreover, Marx's claim that Kant's philosophy exhibits the bad conscience of the petty bourgeois class finds support in the third formulation of the categorical imperative (i.e., that we should always treat people as an ends and not exclusively as a means), which seems to apologetically reflect the dawning awareness that bourgeois society has already relegated the individual to precisely that—a means alone. Yet, Marx's claim rightly implies that the very same thing could also be said about Kant's moral self notwithstanding Kant's intentions. And, indeed, as Hegel's section in the *Phenomenology* titled "Reason as Testing Laws" suggests, the moral self, although putatively indifferent to content, frames his maxims in accordance with society's norms, which operate through him, and due to the way in which the maxim is framed, the society's norms are validated through the use of the categorical imperative.[14] In sum, then, for Marx no less than for Adorno and Horkheimer, reason and money are part and parcel of the ordering logic of modern bourgeois society—an ordering logic that both lays the groundwork for human beings (individually and collectively) to actualize their full potential and, when ultimately fetishized at the expense of sensuous particularity, precludes them from doing so.

Although "Odysseus or Myth and Enlightenment" deals mostly with the relation between Odysseus's *self*-preservation/development and his adventures on the high seas, it is incumbent on Adorno and Horkheimer to at least glimpse the domestic life of their "prototypical bourgeois," which first forms the self that is to be preserved and developed. The episode from the *Odyssey* that they recount for this purpose is Penelope's challenge to Odysseus's dominion over sex and property—a challenge that takes the form of her attempt to move the marital bed that he had built, which was anchored in an olive tree that itself served as their bedroom's ballast:

> Furious, her husband [provides] her with a detailed account of his longlasting [*sic*] piece of woodwork. He is the prototypical bourgeois—the with-it hobbyist. His do-it-yourself effort is an imitation of the actual labor of a craftsman, from which, in the framework of differentiated conditions of property ownership, he has long been necessarily excluded. He enjoys this for the freedom to do what is really superfluous as far as he is concerned confirms his power of disposal over those who have to do precisely that kind of work in order to live. (DOE, pp. 74–75)[15]

In this passage, Adorno and Horkheimer allude to the bourgeois division of sex and labor, which they consider more thoroughly in their analysis of Odysseus's encounter with the Sirens. Although, chronologically speaking, the Sirens episode is not the first of the adventures in the *Odyssey* with which Adorno and Horkheimer deal, it is the first one that is presented in *Dialectic of Enlightenment*—in fact, it is primarily discussed in the concluding pages of the introductory essay itself. As I interpret it, the Sirens episode is highlighted in the introductory essay because it exemplifies the entanglement of myth, domination, sex, and labor in a way that not only best supports their contention that the Homeric world is prototypically bourgeois but also parallels the first moment of self-formation in the *Phenomenology* (the master-slave parable), although with crucial substantive differences. In concluding this section, therefore, I shall recount Adorno and Horkheimer's consideration of this episode, as well as (to a lesser degree) Odysseus's encounters with the Lotus-Eaters, Circe, and Polyphemus, in order to explicate their cryptic claim that "the establishment of the self cuts through that fluctuating relation with nature that the sacrifice of the self claims to establish. Every sacrifice is a restoration by the actual historical situation in which it occurs" (DOE, p. 51).

Before proceeding, however, it must be emphasized that my consideration of Adorno and Horkheimer's treatment of these adventures must be appropriately framed by the actual historical conditions in which *Dialectic of Enlightenment* itself arises, which is only in keeping with their own approach. Written by German Jews during World War II and published during the early stages of the Cold War and nuclear arms race, *Dialectic of Enlightenment* is well positioned to see the negative aspects of the enlightenment project. And, to be sure, there can be little question but that Adorno and Horkheimer are using these Homeric adventures for the purpose of showing that the formation of the subject is inextricably intertwined with the contemporary dynamics of domination and subordination. How, then, are we to reconcile the lesson of the Odysseus essay, and, indeed, all of the book's essays, with its Introduction, which, as we saw, emphatically seeks to make good the promise of the enlightenment? The answer, quite simply, is to recognize that Adorno and Horkheimer intend *Dialectic of Enlightenment* to be a diagnostic tool that reveals the coercive element that is inherent within enlightenment thought, and therefore the enlightenment subject, but reveals it not for the purpose of discarding enlightenment rationality and subjectivity altogether, but rather for encouraging the sort of self-reflection that would enable it to overcome this inherent propensity (which is in accordance with what they say in the Introduction, as well as other points throughout the book).[16] Consequently, although the episodes that I shall consider do emphasize the innately coercive nature of the early stages of self-formation, they are no more Adorno's last word on the issue than the early stages of self-formation in the *Phenomenology* are Hegel's last word on the issue,[17] and to think otherwise is to confuse genesis with validity. In the next chapter, in which I shall address Adorno's notion of negative dialectics, I shall lay out a more positive model of subject formation.

If, as I have already evidenced an inclination to do, Homer's "highway of adventure" is to be compared with Hegel's phenomenological "highway of despair" (and the Sirens episode is to be compared with the master-slave parable), given that both works are narratives about self-formation, it is for the purpose of emphasizing the essential differences between them—essential differences that help flesh out Adorno and Horkheimer's assorted positions on subject formation. Accordingly, to begin with, while, for Hegel, who is not particularly sensitive to class dynamics, the difference between master and slave is merged in stoicism due to their respective inabilities to resolve the basic contradictions of the master-slave relation, for Adorno and Horkheimer there is no such merger, since Homer's story of subject formation is conveyed from the standpoint of the master alone. In some sense, of course, this is precisely the opposite of Kojéve's account, in which it is only the slave who moves beyond the master-slave parable, but the difference that makes this opposition asymmetrical is that Adorno and Horkheimer (through Homer) recognize the continuation of the slave, who (like nature, which includes the master's own internal nature) is the one exploited in this historical movement. As I see it, then, for Adorno and Horkheimer, the "dialectic of enlightenment" that they recount is part and parcel of the bourgeois perspective on the world, which has positive and negative ramifications. Positively, what is supposed to be their categorical indictment of reason and the subject can be understood as *only* a historically situated indictment of bourgeois reason and the bourgeois subject. And yet, negatively, what is only supposed to be a story about bourgeois reason and the bourgeois subject, which is merely one side of the story, tends to become *the* story—and this manifests what is arguably Adorno's most troubling tendency, namely, to make sense of the modern predicament in totalizing terms.

Moreover, although Odysseus's encounter with the Sirens gives rise to the same sorts of considerations as Hegel's master-slave parable in the passages that immediately follow from the fight-to-the-death, since it analyzes the asymmetrical relations between master, slave, and nature, the real upshot in terms of self-formation in the two accounts is essentially different. Of course, as an initial matter, the underlying similarity is that the master and Odysseus interpose the slave and oarsmen between themselves and nature, a parallel that Adorno and Horkheimer explicitly point out. Like the master, "Odysseus is represented in labor," and, like the slave, the oarsmen "despite their closeness to things cannot enjoy their labor because it is performed under pressure" (DOE, p. 35). Of course, unlike the master, Odysseus is not "represented in labor" so much as he is represented in manual labor, for Odysseus's intellectual labor is essential to the survival of the oarsmen, and, unlike the slave, who must bring his intellect to bear on his work, since he is the sole laborer, the oarsmen only represent manual labor. However, what Odysseus and his oarsmen share as against master and slave is what makes the two accounts essentially different. As I stated earlier, Hegel loses the moment of happiness because he loses the moment of internal nature, the ultimate source of happiness, as desire becomes social. Yet, this is precisely what is in question in the Sirens episode. The Sirens' song is the call of nature, and while humanity is relieved at its having been sprung from nature, it is no less the case that nature is the fount of happiness, which means that *self*-preservation and happiness seem to be essentially at odds:

> The strain of holding the I together adheres to the I in all stages; and the temptation to lose it has always been there with the blind determination to maintain it. The narcotic intoxication which permits the atonement of deathlike sleep for the euphoria in which the self is suspended, is one of the oldest social arrangements which mediate between self-preservation and self-destruction—an attempt of the self to survive the self. The dread of losing the self and of abrogating together with the self the barrier between oneself and other life, the fear of death and destruction, is intimately associated with a promise of happiness which threatened civilization in every moment. Its road was that of obedience and labor, over which fulfillment shines forth perpetually—but only as illusive appearance, as devitalized beauty. (DOE, p. 33)

When faced with the beauty of the Sirens' call, Odysseus has only two possible choices, and he opts for both—one for his oarsmen, one for himself. One choice involves shutting out the call of happiness altogether, which is the one that he imposes on his oarsmen. By plugging their ears with wax, Odysseus makes sure that they will not deviate from their labors: "They must doggedly sublimate in additional effort the drive that impels to diversion. And so they become practical" (DOE, p. 34). The other option, the one that Odysseus chooses for himself, involves listening to the call of the Sirens while being bound impotently to the mast, and the more he is tempted to heed the call, the more he has his bonds tightened by his oarsmen:

> The bonds with which he has irremediably tied himself to practice, also keep the Sirens away from practice: their temptation is neutralized and becomes a mere object of contemplation—becomes art. The prisoner is present at a concert, an active eavesdropper like later concert-goers, and his spirited call for liberation fades like applause. Thus the enjoyment of art and manual labor break apart as the world of prehistory is left behind. (DOE, p. 34)

Crucially, then, while Odysseus and his oarsmen are "prisoners" of a nascent dialectic that has not yet satisfactorily worked out the relation between self-*preservation*, *self*-preservation, and happiness (which at the present historical juncture should be more amenable to reconciliation), and are thus prototypes of the modern self, the master and slave are less than human. Neither one receives even the minimal recognition that is needed for the purpose of sustaining a *self* (i.e., the master refuses to recognize the slave, and, in turn, he can get no recognition from a "thing" that does not justify his recognition), which means that neither has a *self* to preserve. Neither one is concerned with happiness (which is by no means the same thing as "the satisfactions of self-consciousness"). And, finally, the master is not even appropriately concerned with his self-*preservation*, for unlike the slave he has not yet faced the daunting prospect of his own mortality.

These last facts point toward a crucial difference that exists between Hegel's master-slave parable and the episode with the Sirens. While the episode with the Sirens is set in history, the master-slave parable, which comes up in the hypothetical "state-of-nature," is the transcendental condition of history. Of course, there can be no question but that the very purpose of Hegel's parable is to refute "state-of-nature" theorists like Hobbes, Locke, and Rousseau, who view the individual in monadic terms. But by conceptually (if not historically) presupposing this parable, and in no small part permitting it to set the dynamic for all that follows in the *Phenomenology*, Hegel might well be inadvertently smuggling some aspects of the parable into his own historical account, which might be the reason that he valorizes both the monarchy and bourgeois society (provided, of course, that the interests of its opposing camps are reconciled by the "universal" class of civil servants). In other words, from the master-slave parable through the *Philosophy of Right*, what concerns Hegel is reconciling starkly different classes, as if such differentiations are natural, not sublating the social hierarchy that gives rise to the necessity of such a reconciliation (which, for Hegel, I believe, is incorrectly seen as indifferentiable from the indeterminate notion of freedom that he rightly attacks in the context of the French Terror). According to Adorno and Horkheimer, in contrast, these hierarchies arise in society itself—that is, they are fundamentally historical phenomena—and therefore there is nothing necessary about them. Thus, a scant two pages after detailing the Sirens episode, they assert:

> The impotence of the worker is not merely a strategem of the rulers, but the logical consequence of the industrial society into which the ancient Fate—in the very course of the effort to escape it—has finally changed. *But this logical necessity is not conclusive*. It remains tied to domination, as both its reflection and its tool. Therefore its truth is no less questionable than its evidence is irrefutable. (DOE, p. 37; emphasis added)

Much like the Sirens, the Lotus-eaters and Circe broach the question of the loss of the self to pleasure (i.e., they represent nature's attempt to bring about Odysseus's *self*-dissolution by way of a return to primordial happiness), and thus we need not dwell on these episodes. Still, it must be reemphasized that although Adorno and Horkheimer are of the belief that any possibility of happiness must arise from nature—or, to be more precise, "the remembrance of nature in the subject" (DOE, p. 40)—they explicitly reject the reunion with nature that both the lotus (drugs) and Circe (ceaseless sexual pleasure) offer. This is because they see not just the futility but also the undesirability of trying to break off the historical dialectic in the name of happiness, as if the slate could be wiped clean without a bad return of the repressive history that this break represses. What's more, speaking of the lotus, they assert: "It is actually the mere illusion of happiness, a dull vegetation, as meager as an animal's bare existence. . . . *But happiness holds truth*, and is of its nature a result, revealing itself with the abrogation of misery" (DOE, p. 63). And, similarly, speaking of Circe, they assert: "Like the idyllic interlude of the Lotus-eaters, [Circe] brings about, however delusive it may be, the illusion of redemption. But because they have already been men, the civilized epic cannot represent what has happened to them as anything other than unseemly degradation" (DOE, p. 70).[18]

Finally, I shall look at Odysseus's encounter with Polyphemus, an encounter that perhaps best illustrates not only the essential core of the dialectic of subject formation, but also Adorno and Horkheimer's emphasis on the fact that this formation must be grasped within the framework of particular historical preoccupations. As Adorno and Horkheimer declare in the Introduction to *Dialectic of Enlightenment*, they are not concerned with abstract forms of life but rather with the "actual movement of civil society as a whole in the aspect of its idea as embodied in individuals and institutions" (DOE, p. xiv). Thus, if Odysseus is the prototype of the bourgeois individual, then in the episode with Polyphemus we see that the institution with which he and his men are associated is the prototype of the bourgeois institution from whose historical standpoint Adorno and Horkheimer were writing—the institution of imperialism.

As Adorno and Horkheimer point out, Polyphemus represents hunters and herdsmen, and thus represents a more advanced stage of development than any of Odysseus's prior adversaries. Indeed, although Homer characterizes the one-eyed Cyclops as an asocial barbarian, after Odysseus blinds Polyphemus, his fellow tribesmen come to his aid, which at least partly belies this characterization. The actual basis for Homer's condemnation of the Cyclopes, according to Adorno and Horkheimer, is, in fact, the unrationalized nature of both their economic and legal processes. As Homer (disparagingly) states, however, "their crops grow without any planning and plowing," which precludes the need for economic rationalization (but only fuels Homer's envy of this society, in which plentitude rather than scarcity is the rule), and "they have neither laws nor assemblies" but rather mete out a rough form of justice (DOE, p. 64), which, however, is not so rough that it does not incorporate a genuine concern for their livestock (DOE, p. 66). It is really the Cyclopes' utter lack of artifice that makes them the object of Homer's scorn (i.e., they lack "the cunning of reason"), and this is what finally leads to Polyphemus's downfall. More to the point, if "artifice is the means by which the adventuring self loses itself in order to preserve itself" (DOE, pp. 48–49), the simple Cyclops is not yet a self, and he is therefore not worthy of Homeric respect.

Although Adorno and Horkheimer do not make the point, the Cyclopes are not so lacking in reason that they do not see through Odysseus's designs. On initially confronting Odysseus and his crew in the cave, Polyphemus asks: "Strangers . . . Who are you? And where from? What brings you here by sea ways—a fair traffic? Or are you wandering rogues, who cast your lives like dice, and ravage other folk by the sea?"[19] Questions of this sort are not at all dissimilar to those that arise in the contemporary world, in which highly rationalized economic systems that are based on the shibboleth of "free trade" paternalistically profess to bring less economically advanced countries into their "fair traffic" but largely do so for the purpose of "ravaging" their populations (and, in the process, their own "uppity" domestic working classes as well). To be sure, in contrast to Odysseus, who needs no lofty justifications for ravaging the "uncivilized" other, the modern bourgeois have raised wordplay to an art form so as to justify the perpetration of imperialistic (and domestic) injustices. However, although they may justify these injustices on humanitarian grounds, they ultimately have the same fundamental orientation as Odysseus. Like Odysseus's Cyclops, who is guilty of nothing more than anatomical differences and a much simpler form of life, the racially different and less economically advanced other—now under the rubric of culture rather than biology—is fair game.

In any case, the crucial dialectical point concerning the formation of the self in the Polyphemus episode involves the cunning that Odysseus uses to escape from the intellectually outmatched Cyclops. After first getting Polyphemus drunk and then blinding him, Odysseus ultimately escapes the community of Cyclopes by wordplay—specifically, by referring to himself as "Udeis" (literally: "nobody") rather than the similarly sounding "Odysseus," Odysseus stops the other Cyclopes from coming to Polyphemus's aid when he yells that "Nobody" has attacked him. This double-entendre (which crudely augurs the early twentieth-century philosophical preoccupation with language, and, more specifically, "naming") is far beyond the understanding of this simple creature, who is not a subject. Yet, in this very process, Adorno and Horkheimer contend, Odysseus denies himself no less than his adversary:

> In reality, the subject Odysseus denies his own identity, which makes him a subject, and keeps himself alive by imitating the amorphous. He calls himself Nobody because Polyphemus is not a self, and the confusion of name and thing prevents the deceived savage from evading the trap: his call for retribution stays, as such, magically bound to the name of the one on whom he would be avenged, and this name condemns the call to impotence. Since Odysseus inserts the intention in the name, he withdraws it from the realm of magic. But his self-assertion—as in all epics, as in civilization as a whole—is self-denial. Thereby the self enters that coercive circle of the very natural context from which it tries to escape by imitation. He who calls himself Nobody for his own sake and manipulates approximation to the state of nature as a means of mastering nature, falls victim to hubris. (DOE, pp. 67–68)

From this example, we can understand what Adorno and Horkheimer mean when they claim that "the establishment of the self cuts through that fluctuating relation with nature that the sacrifice of the self claims to establish. Every sacrifice is a restoration by the actual historical situation in which it occurs" (DOE, p. 51). It is in the sacrificial denial of the natural self that "the subject" is engendered, but by rejecting the natural self, and therefore ostensibly separating itself from the fluctuations of nature, the rigidified subject becomes like a thing of nature that is imprisoned in the natural context (DOE, p. 54), although the fluctuations of the "natural context" are now really the fluctuations of the existing historical situation. This argument, it will be recalled, is the very same one that Adorno makes when considering Kierkegaard, but it is no less applicable today, when petrified social relations are fetishistically viewed as the outcome of ineluctable economic laws that are no less forgiving than the laws of nature. In these laws of "second nature," the self is lost and the wholly abstract "economic man" arises.

Finally, Odysseus must blind Polyphemus since the latter sees through him, thus usurping "the field of vision."[20] To articulate this with respect to Hegel's master-slave parable, the master blinds the slave once the master sees that the slave recognizes the master's dependence on him. Under these conditions, however, the Hegelian dialectic is broken off, for the Other that would decenter the master is effectively neutralized—he has no field of vision—thus precluding the kind of mutual recognition of differences that Hegel's dialectic, at least ideally, seeks. History thus unfolds from only one point of view (which is one of the basic ideas of Francis Fukuyama's *The End of History and the Last Man*, an otherwise bad recycling of Kojève's dubious reading of Hegel). Under these conditions, the master's increasingly self-identical (or, as Sartre would say, stonelike) nature parallels the movement of his increasingly hegmonic abstract socioeconomic structures, and this, at least implicitly, reveals a line from Odysseus to the anti-Semite—the most rabid of which, however, is the blinded slave, who now identifies with his own oppressor at the expense of other victims. I shall consider the anti-Semite in the third section, while, in the next section, I shall briefly consider how the enlightenment subject fares within the modern realms of science, morality, and art.

SCIENCE, MORALITY, ART

At the start of this chapter, I asserted that *Dialectic of Enlightenment* deals with science, morality, and art in "The Concept of Enlightenment," "Juliette or Enlightenment and Morality," and "The Culture Industry: Enlightenment and Mass Deception," respectively. As I interpret it, "The Concept of Enlightenment" is the opening essay because Adorno and Horkheimer believe that science's instrumental approach to reason and nature has delimited the standards of all other spheres of human experience. Indeed, even the analysis of self-formation in "Odysseus or Myth and Enlightenment" does not come before this essay because the Odysseus essay is designed to show how the modern instrumental approach to reason and nature considered in "The Concept of Enlightenment" is already present in—indeed, is an inextricable part of—the earliest moments of self-formation. In turn, "Juliette or Enlightenment and Morality" and "The Culture Industry," which come after the Odysseus essay, are meant to show how the instrumental approach of the sciences has historically overdetermined the spheres of morality and art.

In *The Philosophical Discourse of Modernity*, Habermas also contends that "The Concept of Enlightenment," "Juliette or Enlightenment and Morality," and "The Culture Industry" probe science, morality, and art.[21] Yet, it is Habermas's position that Adorno and Horkheimer fail to appreciate what he calls "modernity's specific dignity," which he depicts as "the differentiation of value spheres in accord with their own logics,"[22] and that this failure causes them to wrongly infer that the instrumentalization of reason is inherent in the modern "differentiation of value spheres" itself:

> In respect to science, morality, and art, the argument follows the same figure: Already the separation of cultural domains, the collapse of the substantive reason still incorporated in religion and metaphysics, so greatly disempowers the moments of reason (as isolated and robbed of their coherence) that they regress to a rationality in the service of self-preservation gone wild. In cultural modernity, reason gets definitively stripped of its validity claim and assimilated to sheer power.[23]

It would seem to be Habermas's position that Adorno and Horkheimer either (1) reject reason's emancipatory possibilities altogether due to the "separation of cultural domains"; (2) impotently hold on to these possibilities in the context of an antiquated "metaphysical" viewpoint, which (in Heideggerian fashion) Habermas understands as tantamount to a "philosophy of the subject"; or (3) reject reason's emancipatory possibilities altogether *just because* they buy into a "philosophy of the subject"—but without a corresponding confidence in either immanent critique (which is no longer viable given the one-dimensional mass consciousness that capitalism has produced) or any other ground that such an allegedly metaphysical position might have otherwise historically provided. This third alternative would seem to be Habermas's actual position,[24] but his depiction of *Dialectic of Enlightenment* in this way is not only way off the mark, but way off the mark in such a way as to unfairly reject it as even a rival modernist account (bracketing the merits).

In this section, I shall use Habermas as a foil to broach the fate of the "enlightenment subject" in *Dialectic of Enlightenment*. First, I intend to show that Adorno and Horkheimer do not indiscriminately reject the enlightenment's "differentiation of value spheres" but rather that they are more discerning than Habermas himself on the prospects for morality and art under the enlightenment as it has unfolded (i.e., under late capitalism's subordination and universalization of science's instrumental impulses). Specifically, I shall argue that in anticipation of Habermas's idealistic emphasis on science, morality, and art as the three wholly differentiated rationalization processes that are the hallmark of the enlightenment, Adorno and Horkheimer correctly perceive that these "differentiated" spheres can no more be hermetically sealed off from one another than they can be conflated, and that the instrumental rationality that typifies the scientific approach *as it is presently socially constituted* dialectically penetrates the spheres of morality and art. This obviously does not justify Habermas's claim that the book harbors an irrationalistic component. Second, I shall try to show that Habermas's characterization of *Dialectic of Enlightenment* as a "philosophy of the subject," and therefore "metaphysical," is highly misleading, and that in his rejection of "the subject," Habermas opens up his own "theory of communicative action" to the charge that it is "metaphysical." Third, I shall try to show that Adorno and Horkheimer's critique of enlightenment morality in "Juliette or Enlightenment and Morality" anticipates and undermines Habermas's own concept of an ideal speech community. In sum, therefore, despite Habermas's characterization of *Dialectic of Enlightenment* as an irrationalistic work, Adorno and Horkheimer are no less committed than Habermas to what the latter calls "the unfinished project of modernity," and it is Habermas whose theory is regressive in these terms.

As an initial matter, neither "Juliette or Enlightenment and Morality" nor "The Culture Industry" holds that there is a necessary evolution of enlightenment morality and culture, which means that notwithstanding Habermas's contention, Adorno and Horkheimer do not think that in "cultural modernity" reason must be "definitively stripped of its validity claim and assimilated to sheer power." Instead, as I have already argued, the book does not consider these disciplines abstractly or as part and parcel of a "negative" universal history but rather in the sociohistorical circumstances in which they dialectically unfolded. Adorno was working on a book that dealt with a more positive notion of enlightenment morality when he died, which, in conjunction with the initial remarks in *Dialectic of Enlightenment*, belies the contention that he saw enlightenment reason as *necessarily* coercive. So, too, as Fredric Jameson analogously asserts with respect to art, "The Culture Industry" essay "is not a theory of culture," which would imply that, culturally speaking, the enlightenment must culminate in Hollywood. To the contrary, it is "the theory of an industry, of a branch of the interlocking monopolies of late capitalism that makes money out of what used to be culture."[25]

More to the point, while Adorno and Horkheimer clearly contend that there is a coercive element indigenous to science in its underlying concept (i.e., when considered abstractly), and, moreover, clearly contend that this coercive element could—and, indeed, did—manifest itself in a coercive, instrumental approach not only to the way in which science is undertaken and applied but to the total range of human endeavors (i.e., to morality and culture), they do not even contend that science is *necessarily* coercive in its unfolding, as is reflected in a passage set forth at the beginning of "The Concept of Enlightenment":

> The human mind, which overcomes superstition, is to hold sway over a disenchanted nature. Knowledge, which is power, knows no obstacles: neither in the enslavement of men nor in compliance with the world's rulers. . . . What men want to learn from nature is how to use it in order wholly to dominate it and other men. That is the only aim. Ruthlessly, in despite of itself, the Enlightenment has extinguished any trace of its own self-consciousness. The only kind of thinking that is sufficiently hard to shatter myths is ultimately self-destructive. (DOE, p. 4)

This is a particularly emblematic passage, for its tenor is such that one could easily conclude that Adorno and Horkheimer do see science as necessarily coercive, since they seem to be indicating that the only thing that is "sufficiently hard to shatter myths" is, for the most part, another ("self-destructive") myth. And yet, inserted between this claim and their claim that "the only aim" of (scientific) knowledge is to learn how to "wholly dominate nature and other human beings" is the claim that "ruthlessly, *in despite of itself*, the Enlightenment has extinguished any trace of its own self-consciousness." It is the possibility of becoming self-conscious—which implies that with sufficient self-reflection things could have been, and still might be, otherwise—that points to the fact that, from the beginning, Adorno and Horkheimer are only dealing with a particular historical unfolding of science (however compelling it might seem to be). And, of course, this is just in keeping with what they state throughout the Introduction.

Accordingly, their attack on science is actually an attack on scientism, the substitution of science for *Wissenschaft* (or, perhaps worse, the ultimate equation of science and *Wissenschaft*). In making this argument, I am not attempting to dilute Adorno and Horkheimer's position that enlightenment thought inherently contains coercive elements, which means that I am not saying that they buy into the sunny (but ultimately coercive) systematicity of Hegel's *Wissenschaft*. To the contrary, I am saying that it is exactly because emancipatory enlightenment thought harbors a coercive element that it requires self-reflection on the *meaning* of our goals and activities—nonscientific and scientific alike[26]—which is just what a more modest notion of *Wissenschaft* would presuppose. And, in fact, it is the lack of any attempt to ascertain such a meaning that lies at the core of unreflective enlightenment thought: "On the road to modern science, men renounce any claim to meaning" (DOE, p. 5). This point is made by Adorno himself in a small piece titled "Philosophy and Teachers." Referring to his philosophy students, he states:

> The surrogate they take in its stead [specifically, instead of self-understanding] is the concept of science. This concept once used to mean the requirement that nothing be accepted without first being examined and tested: the freedom and emancipation from the tutelage of heteronomous dogmas. Today one shudders at just how pervasively scientificity has become a new form of heteronomy for its disciples. They imagine that their salvation is secured if they follow scientific rules, heed the ritual of science, surround themselves with science. The approbation of science becomes the substitute for the intellectual reflection upon the facts, once the very foundation of science. The armor masks the wound. Reified consciousness installs science as an apparatus between itself and living experience. The more the suspicion grows that the best has been forgotten, the more the operation of the apparatus itself serves as consolation.[27]

As I see it, this passage supports my contention that what troubles Adorno about science is its historically contingent displacement of "intellectual reflection upon the facts, once the very foundation of science." Reminiscent of Nietzsche, who in *Human, all too Human* had valorized science's experimental nature as a counterpoise to religious dogmatism but subsequently turned on science when he perceived that it itself had become the new dogma, Adorno aims to revitalize the deeply existential concern with "living experience," which has been progressively emptied of meaning. And, indeed, for the most part,

Adorno would agree with Nietzsche's diagnosis of this phenomenon: as the "highest value," science was in the process of devaluing even itself because its corrosive reason devalued the very lifeworld that it depended on for its own valuation, which opens the door to nihilism[28]—and thus "the fully enlightened earth radiates disaster triumphant" (DOE, p. 3). Yet, crucially, this means that science must be put in its proper place rather than demonized. It will be remembered from chapter 2 that Adorno ridicules what Rolf Wiggershaus characterizes as Heidegger's "genteel aversion to science . . . [as well as] the world of motorways and modern technology, and his way of offering 'comfort for the heart' that relieved him of any need to criticize reality."[29] As to Adorno himself, Wiggershaus states:

> Adorno's relationship to science was ambivalent. When he criticized science, it often remained unclear whether he really meant (a) the positivist conception of science, (b) the sciences in their existing form (whether or not this form was adequately grasped by positivist scientific theory) or (c) the individual scientific disciplines with their division of labor.[30]

As is suggested by the nature of my discussion to this point, it seems to me that Adorno's criticisms of science are, for the most part, of the (b) variety—namely, criticisms of the sciences in their existing form. Since, according to Adorno, "the idea of scientific truth cannot be split off from that of a true society,"[31] it makes little sense to speak of the scientific enterprise in general terms that would circumscribe the nature of science "in itself." Nevertheless, having said this, if the universalizing, instrumentalizing impulse that undeniably is, and ought to be, at the heart of science is allowed to run rampant—both in terms of the larger society, and, indeed, even in terms of the scientific enterprises's own self-understanding—it is actually a reflection on society rather than science. This way of delineating the problem, it seems to me, is in accord with Adorno's general inclination to both hold on to the discrete poles of any inquiry without conflating them (i.e., subject-object, universal-particular, concept-intuition) and to mediate these discrete poles in such a way as to preclude the possibility of demarcating clear boundaries. From this it follows that, with respect to (c), Adorno both recognizes the necessity of some "division of labor" in the individual scientific disciplines, albeit not the one that has historically evolved, and, with respect to (a), recognizes the necessity of certain positivistic conceptions of science, albeit not the ones that have historically evolved (such as logical positivism's or Popper's). Far from *subject-ing* (i.e., submitting to the self-reflection of the subject) science's innate predisposition for unifying qualitatively different natural phenomena by reducing them to numbers that are plugged into equations, which would lead society to judiciously delimit the scientific sphere (and would thus be in accord with Habermas's own aims), this predisposition is manifested and expanded beyond its bounds by a society structured along the same lines: "The same equations dominate bourgeois justice and commodity exchange. . . . Bourgeois society is ruled by equivalence. It makes the dissimilar comparable by reducing it to abstract quantities" (DOE, p. 7). It is only in the absence of self-reflection—an absence that analogously culminates in a capitalist society that is based on relations of domination that aim to ideologically piggyback on to the unifying, instrumentalizing tendencies of science—that science runs amok.

Indeed, although it is true that early Critical Theory divided crudely along two lines—a theory of society based on mediating a historical convergence of philosophy's theoretical norms and (social) scientific facts as they manifested themselves in practices (Horkheimer, Marcuse) and an immanent critique of philosophy's norms and the larger culture of which they are a part, but with little expectation that social practices would make good philosophical theory (Adorno, Benjamin)—I would argue that it is easy to overemphasize these differences. And, in particular, I would argue that there is little in Horkheimer's early piece, "Notes on Science and the Crisis," that either Horkheimer *or* Adorno would utterly reject at the time that they composed *Dialectic of Enlightenment*. Horkheimer's claim that "it is not for social interests to decide what is or is not true [since] the criteria for truth have developed in connection with progress at the theoretical level" is something with which Adorno would agree, and he would also agree with Horkheimer's claim that "even though science is subject to the dynamisms of history, it may not be deprived of its own proper character and misinterpreted for utilitarian ends."[32] All of this, it seems to me, is in keeping with Adorno's commitment to the notion that truth must be strived toward by way of the subject-object dialectic: reducing science to a social construct would break off the subject-object dialectic every bit as much as orthodox Marxism's dialectic of nature, the difference being that while the latter idealistically absolutizes nature by purging the subjective aspect, the former idealistically relativizes nature by purging the objective aspect. In its fallibilistic way, science must strive toward the truth. Moreover, Adorno would agree with Horkheimer's claim that the limitations of science are "conditioned by the increasing rigidification of the social situation," which entailed "limiting scientific activity to the description, classification, and generalization of phenomena,"[33] and that "scientific effort mirrors an economy filled with contradictions"—a mirroring that is reflected in the fact that "the setting of tasks lacks a theoretical grounding and seems to be taken arbitrarily," which arises from the fact that science has "no realistic grasp" of how its work relates to the society on which it depends.[34] Thus, Habermas's well-known claim that Adorno somehow corrupted Horkheimer, who had it right in the earlier days of his project, is not correct. Not only are the concerns that motivated Horkheimer in "Notes on Science and the Crisis" still fully present in *Dialectic of Enlightenment*, but these concerns are ones with which Adorno never really disagreed.

In sum, it is not Adorno and Horkheimer's claim that the recognition of "different value spheres" invariably causes reason to "regress to a rationality in the service of self-preservation gone wild," unless, of course, these different value spheres are idealistically posited (in theory or in practice) as altogether autonomous—that is, beyond the pale of the subject's own mediating reflections—which is the case with Habermas. Indeed, while Habermas rejects all "philosophies of the subject," his differentiation of value spheres nevertheless tacitly presupposes a subject—a subject that is completely fragmented. It was Kant, of course, who first divided reason into three differentiated spheres, and in this way constructed the archetype for Habermas's own theory of communicative action, but, in contrast to Habermas, Kant explicitly recognized the fragmented nature of the subject in his architectonic. For Kant, of course, human beings are, in one sense, completely determined, and yet, in another sense, completely free, and it is the task of aesthetic reflection to mediate the split. Conversely, for Habermas, who only nominally rejects Kant's dualistic metaphysics, and seems to have no real use for the notion of aesthetic reflection, the spheres of instrumental reason or "system" (i.e., science and capitalism) and practical reason or "lifeworld" (i.e., morality) either are mediated by communicative relations of some type or are discrete. On the one hand, if they are mediated, what, precisely, is their grounding? Habermas cannot buy into a metalanguage, which would de-differentiate the internal language and logics of these spheres, and therefore run afoul of what he calls "modernity's specific dignity." And if he would acquiesce to putting the system under the aegis of the lifeworld, how would this come about? Habermas himself says that the system has "colonized" the lifeworld. How, then, would laborers who are instrumentalized in the system (and appropriately so, according to the logic of his account) acquire the necessary language competencies in the lifeworld to communicate fully and competently for the purpose of bringing the system under control? Any language that might arise would already be "colonized." On the other hand, because the lifeworld has been colonized by the system—indeed, if we drop the fiction, the instrumental reason of system as it is exhibited in capitalism and science is not only historically but also conceptually an always already part of the enlightenment lifeworld[35]—it is (always) already too late to speak about the spheres as being autonomous. But, even if they were autonomous, this amalgam would produce a schizophrenic human being—that is, one who is wholly exploited in the system, but comes home, changes his work clothes, and becomes a full and equal communicative partner in the democratic lifeworld. In other words, it produces the very stuff of capitalist mythology. Put succinctly, Habermas's different spheres cannot be autonomous, and it is only because he has a metaphysical account of both the human subject and language that he claims otherwise. In what follows, I shall flesh out this claim.

Because Habermas explicitly rejects what he refers to as "philosophies of the subject" or "philosophies of consciousness," and, indeed, says that it is *Dialectic of Enlightenment* itself that evidences the exhaustion of this paradigm,[36] my claim that he has a metaphysical account of the subject (which is what he claims to skirt with his paradigm shift to a linguistic or communicative theory) may seem somewhat baffling. But, of course, the upshot of philosophical theories often differ from their intentions, and to illustrate that this is the case with Habermas, it is necessary for me to start with a summary of the grounds on which he attacks the various "philosophies of the subject." Thus, while Habermas only began to attack this paradigm in earnest in *The Theory of Communicative Action*, and did not make this one of the centerpieces of his theory until *The Philosophical Discourse of Modernity*, the position reiterates his attack on Hegel in *Theory and Practice*—specifically, the seminal essay titled "Labor and Interaction: Remarks on Hegel's Jena Philosophy of Mind." In "Labor and Interaction," Habermas says that although Hegel opted for the primacy of interaction (i.e., mutual recognition) over labor and language in the master-slave dialectic in the *Phenomenology*, and Marx opted for the primacy of labor over interaction and language, what should be privileged is language, which is presupposed by interaction and labor.[37] And, according to Habermas, this is exactly what Hegel did privilege in the Jena works, in which individuals are always-already rooted in a linguistic community. But with his movement from the Jena works to the *Phenomenology*, Habermas claims, Hegel abandoned this always-already existing dialogic community in favor of the idea of Absolute Spirit, which Habermas depicts in "Labor and Interaction" as the embodiment of a monological process of self-reflection. On this account, there is an identity between Absolute Spirit and nature, and Absolute Spirit actualizes this identity by initially externalizing itself in nature and then reappropriating this externalization through action: "Under the presupposition of this thesis of identity Hegel has always interpreted the dialectics of representation and of labor idealistically."[38]

Habermas's reduction of Hegel's rich portrayal of spirit's growth process to the abstract concept of monological Absolute Spirit engaging in a stilted two-step process of externalization through representation and reappropriation through action is essentially flawed[39]—unfortunately, however, it cannot be considered in detail here. More importantly for our present purposes is the fact that Habermas sticks to this abstract characterization of Hegel's "philosophy of the subject" when he scrutinizes the theoretical underpinnings of *Dialectic of Enlightenment*.[40] According to Habermas, the goal toward which subjects are oriented on this model is "self-maintenance": "to secure their continued (and contingent) existence. In this way, Horkheimer and Adorno conceive of subjective reason as instrumental reason."[41] This compels the social subject to collectively exploit external nature (through the representation-reappropriation "two-step") and to internally repeat this process within society—with respect to both the relation between individuals and the relation between the individual and his instinctual nature. However, according to Habermas, if Adorno and Horkheimer had come to recognize that it is "the remembrance of *language* in the subject" (i.e., a subject-subject or ego–alter ego paradigm of communication) that produces the emancipatory moment, and not "the remembrance of nature in the subject" (i.e., the subject-object paradigm), they would have been able to break out of the aporias that are wrought by the "philosophy of the subject."[42] In other words, he claims, it is because Adorno and Horkheimer emphasize the liberating role of nonconceptual mimesis in *Dialectic of Enlightenment*—that is, the imitation of nature rather than its collective conceptual (or actual) domination—that they preclude any chance of breaking out of a purely instrumental rationality either theoretically (since they have precluded the possibility of providing untainted conceptual grounds for critique) or historically (since this position culminates, politically, in Adorno's so-called resignation).

Aside from the fact that Habermas indiscriminately subsumes the philosophies of such varied thinkers as Descartes, Leibniz, Kant, Hegel, and Adorno and Horkheimer under the rubric of "philosophies of the subject," in certain important respects he shares more with these earlier "philosophers of the subject" than Adorno and Horkheimer. Nowhere is this more evident than in his position with respect to nature, in general, and, more particularly, his position with respect to Adorno and Horkheimer's privileging of mimesis—namely, that because mimesis escapes all conceptual determinations, their emphasis on it effectively closes off any possibility of salvaging the enlightenment project. As we saw with his attacks on Heidegger, Adorno takes great pains to make clear that a mimetic approach unmediated by concepts is as regressive as a conceptuality that forgets its mimetic component. Nevertheless, this does not deter Habermas from contending that "Adorno is in the end very similar to Heidegger as regards his position on the theoretical claims of objectivating thought and of reflection: The mindfulness of nature comes shockingly close to the recollection of being."[43] And, to add insult to injury, he further states: "the rational core of mimetic achievements can be laid open only if we give up the paradigm of philosophy of consciousness . . . in favor of the paradigm of linguistic philosophy."[44]

Habermas does not bother to flesh out this claim—nor, in fact, could he. What this throwaway line does clearly reveal, however, is his own bad conscience, for other than the individual subject (with which it is inextricably intertwined), the one thing that gets left out of Habermas's neo-Heideggerian hermeneutical philosophy is nature. Much like Descartes, the prototypical "philosopher of the subject," Habermas's sprawling architectonic deals with nature in a wholly instrumental fashion: it is only the stuff on which "the system" (i.e., the sphere of instrumental reason) works. Along the lines of Descartes (who, in contrast to Hegel, Marx, and Adorno and Horkheimer actually does conceive of the subject-object paradigm in such a way that it "tears loose from an intersubjectively shared lifeworld"[45]), Habermas essentially sees the world from the standpoint of what might be called a "subject-subject" paradigm—he refers to it as an "ego–alter ego" paradigm—that does not even attempt to mediate (or have mediated) its relation to the object, or, more specifically, external nature, which drops out of the picture. And, more importantly, as Joel Whitebook says, because Habermas begins from the fact of communication, the unconscious or internal nature is an entirely derivative phenomenon for him—in other words, like Lacan, internal nature for Habermas is "linguistified."[46] Habermas's theory thus completely grounds itself in "the sovereignty of ideas," and therefore "progressively distances itself from the object" (DOE, p. 11), which is inimical to mimesis, not its "rational core." As a result, he ends up unwittingly implicating himself in the very *dialectic* of enlightenment that he so airily rejects.

Habermas's attempt to foster the enlightenment project through the regulative ideal of an "ideal speech situation," which is transcendentally grounded in a "universal pragmatics" (i.e., a combination of structural linguistics and more empirically oriented speech-act theories), ignores the fact that the abstract thinking of an unmediated universalism is what provides the grounds for the counterenlightenment ideologies with which *Dialectic of Enlightenment* grapples:

> The horde which so assuredly appears in the organization of Hitler Youth is not a return to barbarism but the triumph of repressive equality, the disclosure through peers of the parity of the right to injustice. . . . Every attempt to break the natural thralldom, because nature is broken, enters all the more deeply into that natural enslavement. Hence the course of European civilization. Abstraction, the tool of enlightenment, treats its objects as did fate, the notion of which it rejects: it liquidates them. Under the leveling domination of abstraction (which makes everything in nature repeatable), and of industry (for which abstraction ordains repetition), the free themselves finally came to form that "herd" which Hegel had declared to be the result of the enlightenment. (DOE, p. 13)

Hegel's admixture of enlightenment rationality and romanticism, in contrast, grasps the necessity of reconciling universal and particular if the enlightenment project is actually to be brought to fruition. According to Adorno, however, Hegel does not go far enough in giving particularity its due. As a result, Adorno emphasizes the need to open ourselves to the fluid, nonidentical nature of the particular, which, by its very nature, can never be completely captured by any conceptual determination—and yet, to use a Sartrean circumlocution, the concept must nevertheless strive to capture particularity in the mode of not striving to capture it. In other words, because concepts cannot absolutely subsume particulars in their particularity, conceptual hypostatization does not really strive to capture particularity but rather gives up on it, content with a subjective positing that is an illusive capture: it strives not to capture particularity in the mode of capturing it. The concept that opens itself up to particularity, conversely, strives to capture it, but in the mode of not capturing it, since it recognizes that the particular's ever changing multifariousness can never be completely captured. It is in this way that the concept does the least violence not only to the object but also to the subject (whose underlying brittleness increases as its conceptually mediated distance from the object increases). In its unfolding, this conceptual deportment, is what Adorno and Horkheimer see as the enlightened core of Hegel's thought: determinate negation. "With the notion of determinate negativity, Hegel revealed an element that distinguishes the Enlightenment from the positivist degeneracy to which he attributes it. By ultimately making the conscious result of the whole process of negation—totality in system and in history—into an absolute, he of course contravened the prohibition and himself lapsed into mythology" (DOE, p. 24).

In sum, then, by positing the overly formal "ideal speech community" for the purpose of grounding the enlightenment project, it is ultimately Habermas's philosophy that is antagonistic to its true aims, and in this way his philosophy lapses into mythology. From the neo-Hegelian–Marxist standpoint of Adorno and Horkheimer, he regresses beyond Hegel and Marx to Kant—a "philosopher of the subject" who shares his philosophical commitment to the "differentiation of value spheres." This commitment, I have contended, presupposes a conception of the subject, and although Habermas plainly does not speak in Kantian terms along *these* lines, he implicitly presupposes such a concept, which has resonances of the Kantian subject. To be sure, in contrast to Kant's procedural account, which commands the individual subject to bracket his empirical interests in the service of what is right, Habermas's procedural account commands ego and alter ego to conform to what is right (i.e., the formal conditions of an unconstrained consensus) in the service of dialogically working out some shared conception of the good. However, both Kant's subject and Habermas's subject (ego–alter ego) are alike in that they seek to liquidate all natural residues in an attempt to supply universal grounds for moral experience—universal grounds that abstract from the sociohistorical situation and, in their very abstractness, end up validating a bad sociohistorical given. The conditions that ensure Habermas's ideal speech situation are therefore the latest target of Hegel's "Reason as Testing Laws": indifferent to content they ultimately afford moral cover for the bad existing social content, as putatively "uncoerced" consensuses, produced by a one-dimensional sociopolitical totality, mask its coercive nature. And, finally, by virtue of Habermas's recent acceptance of a more or less unalloyed political liberalism, which brings this dynamic to fruition, even the echos of what once thematized this as a concern in his philosophy, the problem of a "colonized" lifeworld, grow ever dimmer, as does Habermas's Kantian concept of the moral subject who could bracket his instrumentalization in the system to become a full and equal participant in the lifeworld.

Adorno and Horkheimer's analysis of Kant's morality in "Juliette or Enlightenment and Morality" anticipates much of this critique of Habermas, and one passage, in particular, is pretty much right on target:

> The difficulties in the concept of reason caused by the fact that its subjects, the possessors of that very reason, contradict one another, are concealed by the apparent clarity of the judgment of the Western Enlightenment. In the *Critique of Pure Reason*, however, they are expressed in the unclear relation of the transcendental to the empirical ego, and in other unresolved contradictions. Kant's concepts are ambiguous. As the transcendental, supraindividual self, reason comprises the idea of a free, human social life in which men organize themselves as the universal subject and overcome the conflict between pure and empirical reason in the conscious solidarity of the whole. This represents the idea of true universality: utopia. At the same time, however, reason, constitutes the court of judgment,

> which adjusts the world for the ends of self-preservation and recognizes no function other than the preparation of the object from mere sensory material in order to make it the material of subjugation. The true nature of schematism, of the general and the particular, of concept and individual case reconciled from without, is ultimately revealed in contemporary society as the interest of industrial society. (DOE, p. 84)

Of course, for Habermas, we are not speaking of the transcendental and empirical ego so much as the jointly determining ego and alter ego of the lifeworld and the ego coercively determining its alter ego in the system, but, structurally, the analogy holds. The transcendentally grounded ideal speech situation aims "to overcome the conflict between instrumental and practical reason in the conscious solidarity of the whole," and this represents "the idea of true universality" or "utopia" for Habermas—although it is not clear how "the rational core of mimetic achievements is laid open" here under the "paradigm of linguistic philosophy," as Habermas says that it would be. At the same time, the instrumentalizing reason of the system is the true "court of judgment," and, as we saw, Habermas makes no bones about the fact that the object is "the material of subjugation." And, finally, the instrumentalizing reason of the system, which is in the interest of the contracting core of policy-making politicoeconomic elites, also reveals itself in contemporary society as the essential stuff of the lifeworld. The "colonization of the lifeworld" thesis, which Habermas has not spoken all that much about in his more recent works, is effectively bracketed, and now the pressing problem is how the predominant mass of (effectively colonized) lifeworld participants can have any access at all to the formation of social policy, to which Habermas has no satisfactory answer—his atherosclerotic "sluices" (i.e., communicative channels leading from the political periphery to the political core) to the contrary notwithstanding.

In any case, in much the same way that for Kant "the conceptual apparatus determines the senses even before perception occurs" (DOE, p. 84), for Habermas (despite his intentions) a language sedimented by the imperatives of the system's ruling elite determines the senses even before perception occurs, especially given the fact that the unconscious is itself linguistified. In other words, in much the same way that the categorical imperative inadvertently lapses into a reaffirmation of the existing power relations—Adorno and Horkheimer tacitly seize on Hegel's critique of Kant in "Reason as Testing Laws" (see DOE, pp. 87–88)—Habermas's metaphysical-like reliance on language does the same. When Adorno and Horkheimer lament at the beginning of *Dialectic of Enlightenment* that "there is no longer any available form of linguistic expression which has not tended toward accommodation to dominant currents of thought, and that what a devalued language does not do automatically is proficiently executed by societal mechanisms" (DOE, p. xii), they are not only speaking to the colonization of the lifeworld problem but to the colonization of language itself, which is even more troubling, for it suggests that colonized ego and alter ego in the lifeworld no longer have, even in theory, the means through which they can articulate their colonization. A colonized lifeworld still has at its disposal immanent critique, even if its application is impotent by virtue of the very extent to which the lifeworld has been colonized, but a colonized language closes even this thin space down, as there is an absolute identity between word and object, which brings to a catastrophic end Derrida's "endless death of metaphysics" (and leads Adorno to ask whether, after Auschwitz, metaphysics is still possible):

> As a mere means of reinforcing the social power of language, ideas became all the more superfluous as this power grew, and the language of science prepared the way for their ultimate desuetude. The unity of collectivity and domination is revealed in the universality necessarily assumed by the bad content of language, both metaphysical and scientific. Metaphysical apology betrayed the injustice of the status quo least of all in the incongruence of concept and actuality. In the impartiality of scientific language, that which is powerless has wholly lost any means of expression, and only the given finds its neutral sign. *This kind of neutrality is more metaphysical than metaphysics.* (DOE, p. 22; emphasis added)

Habermas is well aware of the problem that this "colonization of language" thesis holds for his theory of communicative action, as is best reflected in his various exchanges with critics after *The Theory of Communicative Action* was published. In particular, in Habermas's reply to Charles Taylor's claim that *The Theory of Communicative Action* failed to adequately capture the world-disclosing function of language,[47] Habermas accuses Taylor of falling into a "philosophy of consciousness" by treating "the whole of language as a self-referential subject," as opposed to grasping that the syntheses performed by language are accomplished "solely within those forms taken by the diffracted intersubjectivity of dialogue."[48] What concerns Habermas is that Taylor's understanding of language's world-disclosing nature here, which always already presupposes a highly sedimented world as the backdrop of all discursive deliberations, could operate as a drag on the validity claims arrived at by lifeworld conversants. Thus, according to J. M. Bernstein, Habermas is actually "objecting to the logical anteriority of language (as world-disclosing) over communication," and thus he "folds the world-disclosive aspect of language into communicative interaction."[49] In this way, as I suggested above, Habermas has a metaphysical-like reliance on language: language is entirely neutral, the unsedimented stuff from which new communicative agreements are reached. And it is this very neutrality that Adorno and Horkheimer characterize as "more metaphysical than metaphysics." What's more, although I would certainly agree with Habermas that our thoughts cannot simply be reduced to language, which fetishizes language by ignoring how it is appropriated and transformed by human beings engaged in their individual and collective practices, "language *is* the organon of thought" (ND, p. 56). Consequently, to contend that communicative agreements are independent of the way in which language has dialectically unfolded prior to our appropriation of it is to return to the position held by earlier "philosophers of the subject" (which includes neither Adorno nor Sartre). Habermas's inclination to neutralize language reflects an inclination to neutralize the unfolding historic dialectic whose sediments it bears, such that ego and alter ego are no more weighed down by their historically sedimented language than Kant's moral self is weighed down by its empirical interests. When Habermas claims to mediate his Kantian inclinations with a variant of Hegel's theory of recognition, then, the latter performs little work: Habermas wants Hegelian intersubjectivity without the baggage of a dialectic formed by the movement of intersubjective life, which strips Hegel of his dialectic.

Finally, under the aegis of late capitalism, the system colonizes not only the moral part of the lifeworld but also the cultural part, and correlatively it colonizes not only moral language but also cultural language. Referring to the cultural sphere as the "culture industry"—an ironical term that reflects the commodification of culture, which used to (nominally) hold itself out as a bastion of humanistic values offering an experiential alternative to profane capitalism—Adorno and Horkheimer state that culture is now mired in the language of advertising. This transition in culture parallels the transition from competitive to monopoly capitalism, which views critical language as a hindrance that would point to the "incongruence of concept and actuality," and would thus pose a threat to its counterfeit reconciliation of culture and society. Thus, as in the moral sphere, in the cultural sphere language serves to water down the possibility of resistance by watering down the language in which it might be asserted: "The more completely language is lost in the announcement, the more words are debased as substantial vehicles of meaning and become signs devoid of quality; the more transparently words communicate what is intended, the more impenetrable they become" (DOE, p. 164). And again: "Innumerable people use words and expressions which they have either ceased to understand or employ only because they trigger off conditioned reflexes; in this sense, words are trade-marks which are finally all the more firmly linked to the things they denote, the less their linguistic sense is grasped" (DOE, p. 166). To put it succinctly, culture turns into its opposite. It no longer serves to broaden our horizons but rather serves to narrow them—and thus the very content about which we can communicate.

Ultimately, then, if the aim is to offer a "critical theory of society," Habermas's linguistic turn is no more promising than Kant's categorical imperative. In "Juliette or Enlightenment and Morality," Adorno and Horkheimer go on to assert that Kant's moral theory leads directly into the moralities of Sade and Nietzsche, who made explicit the idea that enlightenment rationality's historic propensity to abstractly classify and administer the world is no less (and really far more) in step with domination than universal humanity. Like "the unleashed market economy," their theories were "both the actual form of reason and the power which destroyed reason" (DOE, p. 90). Unfortunately, however, these analyses cannot be considered here. Nevertheless, Adorno and Horkheimer conclude this essay with a provocative line that arguably speaks to Habermas's philosophical project. Pointing out that Nietzsche viewed compassion as a threat and thus denied it, they state: "With his denial he redeemed the unshakeable confidence in man that is constantly betrayed by every form of assurance that seeks only to console" (DOE, p. 119). As a reaction to Adorno and Horkheimer's penetrating critique, isn't Habermas's "ideal speech community" just such an assurance?

ADORNO, SARTRE, ANTI-SEMITISM, AND PSYCHOANALYSIS

In accord with Nietzsche's claim that the best way to get at the truth of a phenomenon is to look at it from as many different perspectives as possible, the concluding essay in *Dialectic of Enlightenment*, "Elements of Anti-Semitism: Limits of Enlightenment," looks at anti-Semitism from seven different perspectives. This essay, moreover, anticipates Adorno's more empirically oriented analysis of the anti-Semitic phenomenon in *The Authoritarian Personality*, in which he and his fellow researchers remark on the first page of the Conclusion that

> there is a marked similarity between the syndrome which we have labeled the authoritarian personality and "the portrait of the anti-Semite" by Jean-Paul Sartre. Sartre's brilliant paper became available to us after all our data had been collected and analyzed. That his phenomenological "portrait" should resemble so closely, both in general structure and numerous details, the syndrome which slowly emerged from our empirical observations and quantitative analysis, seems to us remarkable. (AP, p. 475)

Sartre's "portrait of the anti-Semite" refers, of course, to *Anti-Semite and Jew*. And, if, as I am contending, Adorno and Sartre share similar presuppositions concerning the nature of the subject despite the fact that one looks at the subject from the third-person standpoint of the dialectic and the other from the first-person or phenomenological standpoint, this coincidence in their analyses of the anti-Semite is not nearly as remarkable as it first seems. Both philosophers are, of course, what poststructuralists and Habermas-inspired critical theorists alike call "philosophers of the subject." Yet, as "philosophers of the subject" that essentially problematize the very status of the subject—thus their shared concerns with the anti-Semitic, authoritarian personality—they are less naive about the subject than either of these more contemporary groups.

In the previous two sections, we saw that it is Adorno's position that the universalizing propensity in enlightenment thought culminates in authoritarian tendencies when enlightenment thought does not reflect on its own underlying dynamic. However, as I have argued throughout, in contrast to many poststructuralists (such as Deleuze, who is the most prominent on this score), an antienlightenment fall into pure particularity would surely constitute no less a regress to these authoritarian tendencies, since it would either directly reaffirm the authoritarian tendencies that are inherent in "the tradition" or indirectly reaffirm these authoritarian tendencies by abstractly valorizing our unmediated libidinal impulses, which tend to reaffirm the concrete sociohistorical framework in which they are acted out.[50] The particularizing propensity in antienlightenment thought is, therefore, no more emancipatory than unreflectively embracing the universalizing propensity in the enlightenment project. Thus, in their opening thesis on anti-Semitism, which approaches the phenomenon from a political perspective, Adorno and Horkheimer compare anti-Semitism, which views Jewish characteristics as "the embodiment of the negative principle," to (unreflective) liberal theory, which holds that Jews "have no national or racial characteristics" (DOE, p. 168), and they conclude that both form "the dialectical link between enlightenment and domination" (DOE, p. 169). In the final analysis, then, "the harmony of society which the liberal Jews embraced turned against them in the form of the harmony of a national community" (DOE, pp. 169–170).

In *Anti-Semite and Jew*, Sartre articulates this very same dialectic. It is in the opening section, which I shall return to shortly, that he "brilliantly" characterizes the personality of the anti-Semite. For the moment, however, it is the concise second section that interests me, because it is in this particular section that Sartre considers the Jews' "helper," the enlightenment subject (whom he refers to as "the democrat"), and tacitly reaffirms many of the points that are made by Adorno and Horkheimer in *Dialectic of Enlightenment* concerning the leveling impulse at work in enlightenment thought. According to Sartre, "the democrat," who asserts that "all men have equal rights," opted for the "analytic spirit" during the eighteenth century, and since that period "has no eyes for the concrete syntheses with which history confronts him." By "resolving all collectivities into individual elements," he acknowledges "neither Jew, nor Arab, nor Negro, nor bourgeois, nor worker, but only man," and by the individual man he just "means the incarnation in a single example of the universal traits which make up human nature" (AS&J, p. 55). Thus, "like the scientist, he fails to see the particular case," and from this "it follows that his defense of the Jew saves the latter as a man and annihilates him as a Jew." Accordingly, this enlightenment subject, who acts like the scientist, really "fears that the Jew will acquire a consciousness of the Jewish collectivity—just as he fears that a 'class consciousness' may awaken in the worker" (AS&J, pp. 56–57). Ultimately, then, "there may not be so much difference between the anti-Semite and the democrat. The former wishes to destroy him as a man and leave nothing in him but the Jew, the pariah, the untouchable; the latter wishes to destroy him as a Jew and leave nothing in him but the man, the abstract and universal subject . . ." (AS&J, p. 57).

Although Sartre does not proceed to flesh out this thesis, he ends *Anti-Semite and Jew* by emphatically rejecting both the democrat's abstract emphasis on "*the man* [who] does not exist" (AS&J, p. 144) and his "drastic measures of coercion, [which] would mean the annihilation of a spiritual community" (AS&J, p. 145). In lieu of this approach, he contends, anti-Semitism must be responded to by emphasizing the "concrete community engaged in a particular fight having nothing to do with universalist abstractions of morality" (AS&J, p. 153).[51] This emphasis on "concrete particularity" brings Sartre close to Adorno, and, moreover, in the short excerpts set forth from *Anti-Semite and Jew* above, which by no means exhaust the matter, we can see that the similarities that exist in their respective analyses of the enlightenment subject are also quite striking. From these excerpts alone, it is clear that, like Adorno, Sartre thinks:

1. that science serves as the model for the way in which "the democrat" (i.e., the enlightenment subject) thinks about matters that go beyond the scientific sphere;
2. that so constituted, enlightenment thought is basically coercive in that it levels the particulars that differentiate concrete human beings, and therefore, in the final analysis, does not differ as much from anti-Semitism as appears at first blush; and
3. that while abstract, enlightenment thought smuggles in the presuppositions of capitalist society, which means that while

> bourgeois consciousness is implicitly taken to be the ahistorical norm, the "class consciousness" of the worker is taken to be an inappropriate, particularistic deviation from this norm.

Interestingly, in a section of *The Authoritarian Personality* written by Adorno, he remarks that "subjects whose scores are at the lowest extreme [which indicates the least amount of prejudice] often tend to simply deny the existence of any Jewish traits, sometimes with a violence that seems to be due more to the impact of their own conscience than to an objective appraisal of the minority members" (AP, p. 341). "To the low scorer, racial discrimination violates the basic principle of the equality of all men" (AP, p. 339). In other words, in accordance with Sartre's analysis, Adorno is asserting that those people who attack anti-Semitism from an "enlightened" standpoint feel the need to disregard those particularities that do, in fact, characterize some subset of the Jewish population.

Moreover, in describing the Jew's own response to anti-Semitism, which is taken up on enlightenment grounds precisely because enlightenment thought *does* seek to level the particular differences that have made the Jew the object of the anti-Semite's disdain, Sartre states:

> In the very name of universal man, [the Jew] refuses to lend an ear to the private messages his organism sends him. . . . Universality being for him at the summit of the scale of values, he conceives of a sort of *universal and rationalized body*. . . . Insofar as he does not actually forget it, he treats it as an instrument, which he concerns himself with only in order to adapt it with precision to his ends. (AS&J, p. 121; emphasis in original)

This is similar to Adorno and Horkheimer's emphasis on the way that the body is instrumentally rationalized under enlightenment precepts, and, of course, is as an anticipation of Foucault's later analyses of the unfolding historical processes that facilitated this comportment toward our bodies (thus necessitating Adorno and Horkheimer's "remembrance of nature in the subject").

Conversely, with respect to the anti-Semite, Adorno and Sartre both see that what is most significant is "the anti" rather than "the Semite"—that is, the reactive mode of self-understanding that Nietzsche perceptively dissected in *On the Genealogy of Morals*. As Sartre aptly puts it, "if the Jew did not exist, the anti-Semite would invent him" (AS&J, p. 13). To sustain his object of hate, and thus solidify his own (reactive) self-understanding, the anti-Semite must close himself off to the richness of experience since the truths of experience tend to undermine the stereotypes that provide the very stuff of the anti-Semite's identity. Thus, Adorno contends, "the less anti-Jewish imagery is related to actual experience and the more it is kept 'pure' from contamination by reality, the less it seems to be exposed to disturbance by the dialectics of experience, which it keeps away through its own rigidity" (AP, p. 311). From Sartre's phenomenological standpoint, this means that anti-Semites are "attracted by the durability of a stone. They wish to be massive and impenetrable; they wish not to change. They have a basic fear of oneself and truth. What frightens them is not the content of truth, of which they have no conception, but the form itself of truth, that thing of indefinite approximation" (AS&J, pp. 18–19). And because the anti-Semite "chooses for his personality the permanence of a rock, he [also] chooses for his morality a scale of petrified values" (AS&J, p. 27). This "closed circle of eternal sameness becomes a substitute for omnipotence" (DOE, p. 190), Adorno says, and gives rise to what he refers to as "the ticket mentality," which is "as anti-Semitic as the anti-Semitic ticket" (DOE, p. 207). In this way, experience is replaced by clichés, and the imagination active in experience by eager acceptance" (DOE, p. 201).

Like Nietzsche, both Adorno and Sartre also assert that this "substitute for omnipotence" takes the form of a leveling mediocrity. Accordingly, Sartre asserts that "the anti-Semite has no illusions about what he is. He considers himself an average man, modestly average, basically mediocre, [and] he takes pleasure in it. . . . However small his stature, he takes every precaution to make it smaller, lest he stand out from the herd and find himself face to face with himself. He has made himself an anti-Semite because that is something one cannot be alone" (AS&J, p. 22). More importantly, and in contrast to Nietzsche, both Adorno and Sartre see the impetus for this pseudo-egalitarianism as developing from capitalist society's institutional structures, which have exploited anti-Semitism for their own purposes. Accordingly, Adorno and Horkheimer assert that "bourgeois anti-Semitism has a specific economic reason: the concealment of domination in production" (DOE, p. 173). And, in their third thesis on anti-Semitism, which approaches the phenomenon from an economic perspective, they assert that under the conditions of capitalism's historic unfolding, the Jews, as financiers, "were always a thorn in the side of the craftsmen and peasants who were declassed by capitalism." To be sure, this was only due to the fact that prior forms of anti-Semitism had already determined that for the Jews commerce would not be their vocation but their fate (DOE, p. 175), but as the most visible representatives of capital, as well as the most identifiable representatives of "otherness," they were seen as the outside perpetrators of injustice—all to the benefit of "the knights of industry," whose own anti-Semitism constituted "the bad conscience of the parasite" (DOE, p. 176). Sartre, too, recognizes not only that the Jews "filled a vital economic function as traffickers in money" (AS&J, p. 68), but also that the modern forms of anti-Semitism are inextricably intertwined with capitalism: "They have chosen anti-Semitism as a means of establishing their status as possessors. The Jew has more money than they? So much the better: money is Jewish, and they can despise it as they despise intelligence. . . . Thus I would call anti-Semitism a poor man's snobbery. And it would appear that the rich for the most part exploit this passion for their own uses . . ." (AS&J, pp. 25–26).

It would serve no purpose to continue to catalog the convergences that exist between Adorno and Horkheimer's dialectical analysis of anti-Semitism and Sartre's phenomenological one. Accordingly, in what follows, I shall attempt to deepen rather than merely widen my own discussion of these convergences, which, for pedagogical purposes, can roughly be classified in either social (i.e., political, economic, cultural) or psychological terms. I shall deal with these particular groupings in turn.

From a social perspective, the point that bears greatest emphasis is that the anti-Semite's predilection for a "leveling mediocrity" does not really make him less committed to "equality" than the enlightenment subject, and that like Adorno and Horkheimer, Sartre sees the anti-Semite and the liberal enlightenment subject as two distorted sides of the same coin. And, indeed, since both sides of this coin embrace "equality" in a one-sided manner, each side tends to careen to the other extreme. Thus, at the beginning of their second thesis on anti-Semitism, which investigates the phenomenon from a social standpoint, Adorno and Horkheimer contend that "anti-Semitism as a national movement was always based on an urge that its instigators held against the Social Democrats: the urge for equality. Those who have no power to command must suffer the same fate as ordinary people" (DOE, p. 170). And, in the "Note and Drafts" that end the book, they flesh out this claim:

> The bourgeois form of reasoning must lay claim to universality and at the same time seek to set limits. Just as in the process of exchange each person is given his due while social injustice still occurs, so the form of reflection in an economy founded on exchange is just, general, and at the same time biased—an instrument of privilege in equality. The Fascists reveal this form of reasoning in its true colors. They openly defend particular interests and therefore show the limits of the rationale based on generality. (DOE, p. 210)

In a strikingly similar way, Sartre also contends that the particular interests that the anti-Semite defends within the context of *his* "urge for equality" are a reaction to an economic system that belies the ideology of abstract equality that sustains it:

> The equalitarianism that the anti-Semite seeks with so much ardor has nothing in common with that equality inscribed in the creed of democracies. The latter is to be realized in a society that is economically hierarchical, and is to remain compatible with a diversity of functions. But it is in protest against the hierarchy of functions that the anti-Semite asserts the equality of Aryans. . . . Each of them does his part in constituting a community based on mechanical solidarity. (AS&J, pp. 28–29)

Ultimately, then, as both *Dialectic of Enlightenment* and *Anti-Semite and Jew* suggest, the enlightenment approach to equality, which levels particularity in the name of the "universal man," ends up valorizing not "universal man" qua "universal man" but rather the particular man that stands behind this abstraction and alleges that it is tantamount to it—namely, the bourgeois. Particularity inexorably fills the void of an abstract universality, and by equating the numerous traits of the bourgeois to human nature, the bourgeois has sought to justify his own particular interests—and nothing more. Accordingly, Adam Smith's claim that human beings are by nature acquisitive, which helped establish capitalism's particular claim to universality, is no truer today than it was back then, and Marx's reply that such is the case only under capitalism is no less apt. If this is the "end of history," as Fukyama says, it is not because human beings have universally realized their essence. Conversely, while anti-Semites "openly defend particular interests," they do so with the intent of wiping out all other particular interests, for fascism cannot tolerate what is not identical to it. But in wiping out all other particularities, which are what make the fascist determinate, fascism would raise itself to an abstract universal principle. Its own drive toward a universal unfreedom results in the same "vanishing point" that Hegel discusses in the context of the enlightenment's drive toward (abstract) universal freedom—that is, it culminates in universal terror. If absolute freedom "removes the antithesis between the universal and the individual will" because the pure negativity of (abstract) individual freedom perceives its own negative will in the universal will,[52] the absolute unfreedom of fascism also removes the antithesis between the universal and individual will because the pure positivity of (concrete) individual (and collective) unfreedom perceives its own positive will in the stonelike positive will of its leader's individual will, which unifies, and is purportedly one with, the wills of those whom he leads. (Thus, "while appearing as a superman, the leader must at the same time work the miracle of appearing as an average person, just as Hitler posed as a composite of King Kong and the suburban barber."[53])

From a psychological perspective, Sartre, like Adorno and Horkheimer, recognizes that the anti-Semite's outlook is largely based on its own projections. As Sartre says, the anti-Semite can "glut himself to the point of obsession with the recital of obscene or criminal actions which excite and satisfy his perverse leanings; but since at the same time he attributes them to [the Jews] he satisfies himself without being compromised" (AS&J, p. 46). Yet, despite the fact that Adorno and Horkheimer also emphasize that the anti-Semite projects his own propensities on to the Jews ("Anti-Semitism is based on a false projection" [DOE, p. 187]), they closely adhere to a Freudian interpretation of anti-Semitism, which, at least superficially, is in contrast to Sartre's anti-Freudian approach. In particular, Adorno, who facetiously declares that "in psychoanalysis nothing is true but the exaggerations" (MM, p. 49), more or less follows the Freudian line not only in *The Authoritarian Personality* but also in "Sociology and Psychology" and "Freudian Theory and the Pattern of Fascist Propaganda." After briefly indicating why I think that Sartrean psychoanalysis stands in closer proximity to Freud and Adorno than appears at first blush, I shall conclude this section by discussing Adorno's Freudianism and some recent criticisms of it.

It would seem that Adorno and Sartre directly contradict one another on the question of unconscious libidinal drives, for even a quick survey of Adorno's psychoanalytic works reveals that he puts a fair bit of emphasis on this Freudian staple. In "Freudian Theory and the Pattern of Fascist Propaganda," for example, he says that "it is one of the basic tenets of fascist leadership to keep primary libidinal energy on an unconscious level so as to divert its manifestations in a way suitable to political ends."[54] Conversely, Sartre notably rejects the idea of the unconscious, and his so-called Cartesianism would certainly seem to repudiate the causal affects of libidinal drives. These differences are not nearly as pronounced as they are frequently made out to be, however, and in many (although not all) respects they are nothing more than terminological.

What Sartre rejects about the Freudian notion of the unconscious is the ontological claim that it constitutes some discrete realm of the mind that is primarily hidden from consciousness, which is directly at odds with his own view that consciousness is both unitary and translucent. Nevertheless, Sartre readily agrees that we are not aware of most of the objects of which we are, in a minimal sense, conscious. It is necessarily the case that there are huge swaths of conscious life of which we are unaware, for consciousness must nihilate (i.e., in some sense "intentionally" become unaware of) a good deal of the world to constitute a coherent experience, which depends on raising only particular aspects of the world to awareness. This phenomenon, as we saw in the last chapter, gives rise to the inevitability of bad faith, which is based on the fact that we can be only prereflectively conscious of objects (and, even then, with varying degrees of awareness). Ultimately, the level of awareness that we actually have with respect to objects of which we are conscious is symptomatic of our hierarchy of projects, which, for the most part, goes back to the initial project—our most basic self-orienting project that is generally not brought to awareness without the benefit of existential psychoanalysis. At this point, the similarities with Freudian psychoanalysis are rather clear. Moreover, while our actions arise from our underlying projects instead of libidinal drives, as is the case with Freudian theory, this does not imply that Sartre altogether denies the notion of the libido. While considering Freudian theory's attempt to deal with the phenomenon of bad faith, Sartre does deny the contention that "the libido is a blind conatus toward conscious expression," and that "the conscious phenomenon is a passive, faked result" (B&N, p. 94). Yet, as I read him, he is only denying the idea that the libido blindly issues from "the unconscious" and lacks an intentional object, not the idea that there are truly libidinal drives (which, for Sartre, can be thematized, and therefore do not determine our actions). After all, "consciousness exists [the material drives of] its body" (B&N, p. 434), and these drives may not be brought to awareness if they are inconsistent with a person's underlying project. Indeed, some variations of Sartre's "frigid woman" example would seem to reflect just this phenomenon. In sum, Sartre does believe in the notion of libidinal drives of which we are unaware—provided that we recognize that we choose not to be aware of them by dint of our spontaneously conceived underlying projects—which brings him much closer to the Freudian framework.

In contrast to Sartre, Adorno relies on the idea of unconscious libidinal drives not only to articulate the psychological inducements of fascism—which seek to camouflage the existence of these frustrated drives while simultaneously giving them a distorted sociopolitical outlet—but to also provide a locus for emancipatory urges. As an initial matter, however, it must be pointed out that while this does imply that Adorno has a somewhat more classical approach to Freudian psychoanalytic theory than Sartre, as I asserted above, Adorno's critique of the unconscious does bear certain important resemblances to the Sartrean critique. Specifically, while Sartre, given his first-person phenomenological method, breaks down the division of consciousness that Freud's theory of the unconscious posits by holding that consciousness is unitary, and that even libidinal drives of which we are unaware have intentionality, Adorno, given his third-person dialectical method, reverses the direction of the criticism and holds that Freud's division of consciousness is broken down by the sociohistorical, which penetrates to the center of the unconscious. Thus, in "Sociology and Psychology," Adorno says that Freud's idea of the unconscious is undialectical:

> The psyche that has been extracted from the social dialectic and investigated as an abstract "for itself" under the microscope has become an object of scientific inquiry all too consistent with a

> society that hires and fires people as so many units of abstract labor-power. . . . *The more strictly the psychological realm is conceived as an autonomous, self-enclosed play of forces, the more completely the subject is drained of his subjectivity.* The objectless subject that is thrown back onto himself freezes into an object. It cannot break out of its immanence and amounts to no more than equations of libidinal force.[55]

Adorno is right to say that the psyche must be dragged back into the social dialectic, which is the position that Marcuse takes in *Eros and Civilization*, and he is right to say that when conceived as an abstract, autonomous "for itself," it has the effect of draining the subject of his subjectivity. However, this attack on Freud's notion of the psyche belies a certain tension in his own thought, and it is the same tension that was previously discussed in the context of Marcuse's *Eros and Civilization.* If the ego fails to differentiate itself by virtue of the fact that it has been colonized by the institutional structures of society (bourgeois or fascist), it not only effectively cancels itself out as an agent, but, in the process, it also immediately transmits to the unconcious those social aims that would otherwise be subject to the critical capacities of a well-functioning, mediating ego—aims that actually contradict the goals of the primary libido.[56] In other words, if the primary libido is what Adorno intends by the "nature in the subject," which ideally serves as a reminder of the nondominating possibilities of genuinely enlightened thought (DOE, p. 40), the transposition of societal aims directly into the unconscious (due to a colonized ego structure's inability to filter out the irrational) would effectively negate the possibility of the "remembrance" that would permit the libido to serve as this source of resistance. And, indeed, this is exactly the aim of fascist propaganda, which seeks to reinforce its program of "malicious egalitarianism" by foisting on the collective psyche the idea that individual (as opposed to collective) instinctual gratification is unacceptable. Thus, as Adorno declares in "Freudian Theory and the Pattern of Fascist Propaganda": "The less they want the inherent social structure changed, the more they prate about social justice, meaning that no member of the 'community of people' should indulge in individual pleasures."[57]

If once the subject's ego structure is colonized the "internal nature" of the subject moves more or less in lock step with it, then "the remembrance of the nature in the subject" is, in effect, negated as one of the dwindling loci of resistance. And, analogously, if the social world has been more or less colonized, such that it becomes second nature, mimesis is, in effect, also negated as one of the dwindling loci of resistance: "the progressive distancing from the object" that is at odds with the mimetic impulse in the context of external nature is precisely what is called for in the context of second nature, which dialectically informs what cannot be viewed as the "in-itself" of external nature. Under these circumstances, the locus of resistance must be whatever remains of the historically engendered mediating ego, which seems to be Adorno's view—thus he speaks of "the withdrawal to the individual sphere" of the "social force of liberation" (MM, p. 18). But, of course, as to the continuing viability of this possibility, he is not particularly sanguine:

> The social power-structure hardly needs the mediating agencies of ego and individuality any longer. An outward sign of this is, precisely, the spread of so-called ego psychology, whereas in reality the individual psychological dynamic is replaced by the partly conscious and partly regressive adjustment of the individual to society. . . . A brutal, total, standardizing society arrests all differentiation, and to this end it exploits the primitive core of the unconscious. Both conspire to annihilate the mediating ego; the triumphant archaic impulses, the victory of id over ego, harmonize with the triumph of the society over the individual.[58]

According to Jessica Benjamin, this passage from "Sociology and Psychology," which was first published in 1955, as well as other passages from later works, points to an "unacknowledged reversal" of Adorno's position on the ego. In *Dialectic of Enlightenment*, she states, Adorno and Horkheimer hold the view that "the ego creates an increasingly hostile world through its exercise of domination and control," while in passages such as this one, Adorno holds the view that the ego is necessary to control the unconscious's innate destructiveness.[59] Although, at first blush, this claim would seem to be right, it is ultimately wrong, and to see why this is so it is necessary to consider Benjamin's broader critique of Adorno, which in many ways helps to more clearly elucidate Adorno's actual position.

The crux of the matter for Benjamin, who critiques Adorno from the standpoint of object relations theory, is that he buys into Freud's idea of internalization. In particular, while Adorno views the internalization of external authority as the deeply problematic outcome of the dialectic of enlightenment, he privileges its fleeting manifestation in the contemporary social milieu by clinging to Freud's Oedipal Complex, in which the father's authority (and through him society's authority) is internalized by the son. According to Adorno (who is certainly of the view that the Oedipal Complex is itself a manifestation of untoward authority), it is only by working through the Oedipal Complex that the critical reason needed for opposing authority is engendered, but in contemporary times the "totally administered society" goes over the head of the father to directly exercise control over the child, and in this way it precludes the critical reason that could one day undermine it—therefore "the end of internalization." Paradoxically, then, although he views the Oedipal Complex as a perpetuator of the enlightenment's regressive tendencies, he laments its passing, as its internalization processes held open the space for a mediating ego that could serve as a site of resistance. Justifiably dissatisfied, Benjamin rhetorically asks: "If reason, reflection, and individuation are historically tied to the process of internalizing authority, is not the result that authority is in some sense seen as necessary or even vindicated?" She implicitly answers in the affirmative, and goes on to say that "this paradox is only surmountable through an alternative not considered by critical theory," which she characterizes as "the potential for emancipation grounded in an intersubjective theory of personality, rather than the individual psychology of internalization."[60]

The problem with Benjamin's critique is that it simultaneously overstates and understates various aspects of Adorno's thought. In accord with my general argument, it overstates certain aspects of Adorno and Horkheimer's critique in *Dialectic of Enlightenment* by unsubtly holding that they view ego formation in negative terms rather than as a tangled historical achievement that contains violent elements. And, indeed, although these violent elements are necessary for the ego's genesis and are built into its structure such that they can never be altogether purged, they also provide the basis for ego coherence. The strength that constitutes what Adorno calls the "strength of the subject" arises from a more profound understanding of the ego's relation to these violent elements, and if this strength is able to "break through the fallacy of constitutive subjectivity" (ND, p. xx), which manifests a rigidified ego structure cowering before its Other, it is because it has recognized the necessity of minimizing the violent moment that makes it cohere. This "breakthrough," the strong ego recognizes, redounds to its own benefit every bit as much as it redounds to the benefit of its Other. (Homologously, the concept necessarily does violence to the phenomenon, but Adorno does not view the concept in negative terms, for it affords the basis for experiential coherence. Again, the key is to open up the concept to its Other to minimize this violent moment that makes experience cohere, and in this way the concept is benefited no less than the phenomenon, to which it now has a much greater felicity.) Accordingly, for Adorno, the ego—in wresting us from the absolute violence that was inherent in our undifferentiated oneness with nature—must be understood as offering a promissory note on a future reconciliation whose redemption is endangered by subjects that continue to fetishize the threat that scarcity presents for self-preservation even after the objective conditions that gave rise to this threat have been largely overcome. As he states in "Sociology and Psychology," "what society, for the sake of its survival, justly demands of each individual is at the same time unjust for each individual and, ultimately, for society itself," but at this historical stage it is now the case that "given objective possibilities, adjustment to society should no longer be a necessity": "*Self-preservation succeeds only to the extent that, as a result of self-imposed regression, self-development fails.*"[61] In sum, then, while it discusses how in its earliest moments "the ego creates an increasingly hostile world through its exercise of domination and control," the Odysseus essay should not be understood as holding that this phylogenetic necessity is a continuing historical necessity. If the modern ego yields to this dynamic, which Adorno and Horkheimer present to diagnose and treat the modern ego rather than disparage it, this is not because the history that we have made (and continue to make) could not have been otherwise.

Nevertheless, ontogenically speaking, even under the best of social circumstances—that is, in a (relatively) nonrepressive society, in which "nonrepressive" is defined by the objective historical possibilities—the appropriate socialization of the child necessarily presupposes *some* conduit through which "legitimate" authority is internalized. This necessary, albeit historically conditioned, moment of violence, which is the condition of the ego's possibility, is "legitimate" to the degree that it does not entail, in Marcuse's words,"surplus-repression." When he laments that in Freud's system "there is a total lack of any adequate criteria for distinguishing 'positive' from 'negative' ego-functions, above all, sublimation from repression, [but] instead the concept of what is socially useful or productive is rather innocently dragged in," and when he laments "the often *senseless* renunciations" imposed on the individual,[62] Adorno is implicitly saying that while the forms that internalization might take are historically variable, the necessity of some form of internalization is not. The vital point, according to Adorno, is that society, under cover of ego psychology (which has contemporary legatees), equates what is "objectively necessary" with "what is socially useful or productive," or, simply, with what "makes sense" (since this is how senselessness is generally packaged). For Adorno, then, a "nonregressive ego ideal" must not be confused with a "nonrepressive ego ideal": a "nonregressive ego ideal" is one that can be historically attained, provided that it is an ego ideal shorn of *surplus* repression, while a "nonrepressive ego ideal," like Sartrean good faith, is a regulative ideal toward which we must strive but one that, in principle, is unobtainable.[63]

Adorno thus buys into the notion that the ego, which initially depends on some process of internalization, is a historical achievement, and that what is problematical is its hypostatization in an antagonistic society that does not liberate its true potential. In this sense, I disagree with Joel Whitebook, who states in *Perversion and Utopia* that "there exists a remarkable convergence" between Adorno and Lacan, and that it is only at the last minute, as it were, that Adorno, unlike Lacan, "refuses to abandon the standpoint of rationality and the ego."[64] This conclusion mistakes Adorno's attacks on the ego as it has historically unfolded for an attack on the notion of the ego itself, and thus makes it seem as if the commitment to rationality and the ideal of an unrepressed ego structure is something other than a deep and abiding one that goes to the heart of his thought. If ego deformations are relentlessly attacked in the name of an ideal that society refuses to honor by redeeming the ego's existing historical potential, it is so much the worse for society instead of this ideal. Indeed, I would argue, on this score, Adorno is actually much closer to Sartre than to Lacan (who took more than a little from Sartre), since Lacan's antihumanist line is inconsistent with Adorno's thought. In *Being and Nothingness*, Sartre also extols an egological openness (in the name of freedom), perceives the way in which "the indications of others" tend to hypostatize our ego formations (by providing the historically regressive categories that form the stuff of our initial projects, which constitute that minimal level of violence that is necessary for egological and experiential coherence), and calls for a "radical conversion" to change the existing state of affairs (which entails his move to Marxism, which he hoped would facilitate the sociohistorical conditions that would permit us the freedom to open ourselves up in such a way as to do justice to the phenomenological freedom of consciousness).

Although Benjamin overstates Adorno and Horkheimer's attack on the enlightenment subject in *Dialectic of Enlightenment* by asserting that they see the ego (per se) as committed to the exercise of domination and control, and that they take shelter in the authoritarian process of internalization because the individual that it engenders is, in essence, the only remaining (quasi-)viable option in terms of providing a locus of resistance,[65] she also understates the role that a socially reconciled individual plays in his thought:

> The principle of self-interest was understood in bourgeois society as an individual rather than a collective principle. The possibility of a different form of ego, based not on individual self-interest but on social membership and mutuality of interest is not wholly unrecognized in critical theory. But only the principle of individual interest, that is, individual self-preservation, is raised to a category of endopsychic process, of nature. Furthermore, only the struggle against nature, rather than an impulse to satisfy a desire for the other—sociability—can ultimately elicit the human potential for conscious social existence. . . . The crucial problem in both this conception of the ego and of nature is therefore the lack of a concept of intersubjectivity—of subject to subject relations or societal interaction. Consciousness appears to be a property of the individual monad. . . . The source of their objectification of the outside world, as well as their inability to transcend the reason which objectifies, is the development of the categories of reflection and self-reflection out of the relation between subject and object.[66]

Although Benjamin admits that the idea of an ego "based not on individual self-interest but on social membership and mutuality is not wholly unrecognized in critical theory," she treats Adorno as if this idea of the ego is unrecognized by him. Yet, in "Subject and Object," Adorno belies this characterization:

> If speculation on the state of reconciliation were permitted, neither the undistinguished unity of subject and object nor their antithetical hostility would be conceivable in it; rather, the communication of what was distinguished. Not until then would the concept of communication, as an objective concept, come into its own. The present one is so infamous because the best there is, the potential of an agreement between people and things, is betrayed to an interchange between subjects according to the requirements of subjective reason. In its proper place, even epistemologically, the relationship of subject and object would lie in the realization of peace among men as well as between men and their Other. Peace is the state of distinctness without domination, with the distinct participating in each other.[67]

In this passage, we can see that Adorno takes "subjective reason" to be no less troubling than Benjamin, who asserts that he is trapped in "the categories of reflection and self-reflection." The difference between Adorno and Benjamin, however, is that if Adorno's thought is truly unable to "transcend the reason which objectifies," it is because he lives in a society that makes it so. And, indeed, in contrast to Adorno, who is particularly wary of the traps that are laid by theoreticians promulgating false reconciliations, Benjamin's object relations approach has the potential to fall into just these sorts of traps.

Object relations, which emphasizes Hegel's theory of recognition and, more generally, the construction of a nurturing social environment in which authority need not be internalized because the ego is developed in a nonauthoritarian familial framework, is an ideal with much to recommend it. Unlike Habermas's philosophical approach—which is anticipated by Adorno's observation that "the concept of communication" will not "come into its own" until a reconciled social context exists—it is not overly formal or abstract. And, what's more, it speaks in terms of "subject-subject" relations (instead of "ego–alter ego" relations), which means that it holds on to the moment of internal nature that Habermas has rejected. Yet, in the final analysis, it, too, puts the cart before the horse. Although Benjamin is more right than not when she contends that "the absence of authority and power, rather than identification with a powerful father, *could* form the basis for autonomous ego development,"[68] she is undialectically embracing this psychoanalytical model under late capitalism, in which coercion is the rule—a coercion which indubitably pierces every familial dynamic. Although we might be able to "*imagine* that some form of development toward sociability would occur in the presence of other subjects who do not exercise coercion,"[69] therefore, it is another thing to say that there are currently such subjects who are free of capital's coercive legacy. The idea that individuals can truly be raised free of coercive tendencies under the existing sociohistorical conditions is a mistaken one, but what is not mistaken is Adorno's claim that the idea of this possibility can be ideologically appropriated by those who would turn it against its own best intentions:

> The well-balanced person who no longer sensed the inner conflict of psychological forces, the irreconcilable claims of id and ego, would not thereby have achieved an inner resolution of social conflicts. He would be confusing his psychic state—his personal good fortune—with objective reality. His integration would be a false reconciliation with an unreconciled world, and would presumably amount in the last analysis to an "identification with the aggressor," a mere character mask of subordination.[70]

Like Benjamin, Seyla Benhabib also asserts that Adorno has an inadequate account of intersubjectivity. After referring to Benjamin's criticisms of Adorno, she asserts that "it is not illegitimate to ask what intimations of otherness, of other modes of being, [Adorno's] negative dialectics can offer," for he seems to reject all possible accounts of otherness.[71] Indeed, although Adorno's thought is indebted to Hegel, Benhabib goes on to say, he believes that even "Hegel's definition of freedom as 'being-by-oneself-in-otherness' is inadequate insofar as the World Spirit reduces otherness to a mere vehicle in which it can actualize itself."[72] This description of "World Spirit" as "reducing otherness to a mere vehicle in which it can actualize itself" has far more in common with Habermas's characterization of Spirit as "monologically self-positing" than it does with Adorno's view of Spirit. However, the kernal of truth here, as it relates to Adorno's critique of Hegel, is that for the sake of a reconciliation that he precludes in the very process of positing it, Hegel privileges the universal subject (in the form of the institutional structures that comprise society) over both the individual subject and the object. Under these circumstances, in which the universal subject trumps all, "being-by-oneself-in-otherness" means that the individual is both assimilated by the collective and split off from the object (because the "constituting subjectivity" that is the universal subject conceptually blocks the way to this relation). It is in this way that Benhabib is correct when she contends that, according to Adorno, "Hegel's definition of freedom as 'being-by-oneself-in-otherness' is inadequate." Like Habermas, Benhabib advocates a return to Hegel's Jena writings, in which he "distinguishes love from recognition" within the midst of an always-already existing communal framework, while Adorno, she contends, "opts neither for [the concreteness of] love nor for [the abstract equivalence of] justice" but instead rejects social ideals in favor of aesthetic ones.[73]

This is not the occasion to consider in any great detail Benhabib's *Critique, Norm, and Utopia*, but at least with respect to this particular critique of Adorno, it should be indicated that, like Benjamin, she seems to be promoting the very sort of premature reconciliation that Adorno explicitly rejects in the passage above. Thus, as I suggested earlier, if Adorno "opts neither for love nor justice," it is only because *abstractly* opting for one (or both, as Benhabib does) tends to give undue credence to its manifestation in late capitalist society, where it is badly disfigured. On the one hand, in considering Adorno's refusal to opt for justice, we must come to grips with his contention in *Dialectic of Enlightenment* that "the blindfold over Justitia's eyes does not only mean that there should be no assault upon justice, but that justice does not originate in freedom" (DOE, p. 17). The point is not simply that Justitia must be blind to the legal combatants before her because in a deeply antagonistic society there is no way to step outside of justice's formal, universalistic framework to take into account the sorts of particulars that would constitute a free, actualized justice. More to the point, Justitia is supposed to be blind to the concerns of whole classes of people who have been left out of the dialectic (i.e., Habermas's public "conversation"), for if their interests do not find expression in the law, they are persona non grata. Under these circumstances, what does it mean to opt for (formal) justice? On the other hand, Benhabib is incorrect when she contends that Adorno does not opt for love simply because he adheres to an "orthodox Freudian view of desire" that is based on the release of blind libidinal energy, which makes Hegel's early idea of love seem like a "romantic rhapsody."[74] Instead, citing

Freud, he declares at the end of "Sociology and Psychology" that the concept of love when elevated to a universal principle "goes along with contempt for mankind": "The undifferentiated concept under which it subsumes deviations is invariably another instrument of domination."[75] Indeed, while Sartre's rather paranoid characterization of love, and, more generally, being-for-others in *Being and Nothingness* ontologizes the bad intersubjective relations that exist under capitalism, there is more than a grain of truth in his description of these relations as they presently exist, and in this sense it yields greater truths from an Adornian standpoint than those exegeses that simply seek to reconcile. In any case, in the final analysis, Benhabib's work itself has moved beyond any explicit concern with love, as she has moved closer to Habermas's deliberative democratic framework, which cannot cognize it as a concern. And, of course, if Benhabib were to reply that it still remains an implicit concern—albeit one that cannot be accommodated in any framework dealing with the complex pluralistic societies with which she deals—the same could also be said of Adorno, albeit from his far more antagonistic position.

In sum, then, Adorno will have no truck with theories that purport to offer foundations for a social reconciliation. Rather than abstractly elevate candidates such as love and justice to this role, we must concretely consider these concepts as they have been dialectically bequeathed to us. This means that we must work through the fallen nature of these otherwise lofty concepts to make something more of them rather than simply do an end run, which would only make them adequate to their concepts in thought rather than reality (and probably not even that, since they would drag along the bad reality into thought). To get at the truth content of these concepts, as they currently exist, which is the only way to actually make something more of them, Adorno offers a methodology of sorts, which is part and parcel of his notion of negative dialectics.

8

Subjectivity and Negative Dialectics

During 1963, Adorno published three monographs on Hegel—"Aspects of Hegel's Philosophy," "The Experiential Content of Hegel's Philosophy," and "Skoteinos, or How to Read Hegel"—in a small book titled *Hegel: Three Studies*. In the Preface to this book, Adorno says that "the work as a whole is intended as a preparation for a revised conception of the dialectic,"[1] and in 1966 this revised conception was tendered in *Negative Dialectics*.

Adorno starts *Negative Dialectics* with a section titled "The Possibility of Philosophy." "Philosophy," he begins, "which once seemed obsolete, lives on because the moment to realize it was missed.... Having broken its pledge to be as one with reality or at the point of realization, philosophy is obliged to ruthlessly criticize itself" (ND, p. 3). These words, purposely evocative of Marx's claim that "you cannot abolish philosophy without realizing it,"[2] which is itself tied to the fortunes of the working classes ("philosophy can only be realized by the abolition of the proletariat, and the proletariat can only be abolished by the realization of philosophy"[3]), should not be taken to mean that Adorno has effectively split with Hegelian-Marxism by virtue of the fact that "the attempt to change the world miscarried" (ND, p. 3). Indeed, Adorno sees Hegelian-Marxism as the highest achievement of the philosophical tradition, which is why it is nothing less than "philosophy" itself that must "ruthlessly criticize itself." The problem in "reopening the case of dialectics," however, is that its "non-idealistic form has since degenerated into dogma as its idealistic one did into a cultural asset"—and, yet, there is no question of going back to "a traditional mode of philosophizing," which is concerned with "the actuality of the philosophical structure of cognitive concepts," a form of philosophizing that Hegel's substantive thinking had rightly seen as "empty and, in an emphatic sense, null and void" (ND, p. 7).

Even in the light of this rather scant discussion of the first lines of *Negative Dialectics*, it should be relatively clear that Adorno is neither a "post-Marxist" nor a "postmodernist" *avant la lettre*, which Fredric Jameson describes as "the two most influential misreadings of Adorno."[4] The important problem that Adorno does not address—which might, at least in part, provide the grounds for such "misreadings"—is not whether his negative dialectics is actually breaking with the dialectical tradition (the answer to which is plain enough) but whether his negative dialectics is actually justified notwithstanding the fact that "the attempt to change the world miscarried." Adorno is quite clear on the fact that "theory cannot prolong the moment its critique depended on" (ND, p. 3), which suggests that with the passing of the moment there is also a passing of the theory. Thus, the problem, which is reflected in certain variants of postmodernism, is whether there is any concept of philosophy left that has not been completely assimilated by the "totally administered society," such that philosophy has been abolished by virtue of the very fact that it has ultimately *not* realized itself. Of course, theory lives on—but the issue is whether it lives on as *critical* theory. As analytically powerful as it might be, Habermas's theory of communicative action–cum–theory of deliberative democracy is of a piece with the traditional variety, and so is J. M. Bernstein's recent reconstruction of Adorno's negative dialectic itself.[5] In any case, while I believe that Adorno could have made good the continuing viability of negative dialectics by making good the argument that the sociohistorical grounds that could support it are still extant (and, indeed, I believe that even now they are still extant), it was incumbent on him to do so.

Adorno is well aware of the problem. In "The Possibility of Philosophy," he asserts that "critical self-reflection must not halt before the highest peaks of its history [but instead] its task would be to inquire whether and how there can be philosophy at all" (ND, p. 4), and in the very next section, "Dialectics Not a Standpoint," he admits that "the self-righteous conviction that my own theory is spared the fate [of assimilation by the market] would surely deteriorate into self-advertising" (ND, p. 4). Nevertheless, Adorno declares, dialectics need not "be muted by such criticism" because "the name of dialectics says no more, to begin with, than that objects do not go into their concepts without leaving a remainder," which "contradicts the traditional norm of adequacy" (ND, pp. 4–5). With respect to the "standpoint problem," then, this is the fundamental turn, for at this point Adorno can take the position that "dialectics is the consistent sense of nonidentity" and, therefore, is presumably more than a transitory historical notion. Particularly in Adorno's philosophy, however, there is something a bit odd about this claim, given his aversion to ahistorical absolutes. And, in certain respects—albeit from the standpoint of the object rather than the subject—it is not unlike Sartre's "ontological" claim that there is an ideal space between our positional awareness of objects (one of which is the empirical ego) and our nonpositional awareness of this awareness, which is what affords the thin space for the purifying reflection that constitutes the foundation of our freedom. In other words, not unlike Sartre's freedom, which is grounded in the transphenomenality of the subject, Adorno's negative dialectics is grounded in the transphenomenality of the object, but both of their philosophies are ultimately grounded in history, and therefore, in principle, could go away. And, indeed, this is something that Adorno, in particular, must take into account, for his concept of "the totally administered society" seems to render negative dialectics obsolete. Yet, it is exactly because I reject as extreme this totalizing thesis that I can accept negative dialectic's continuing viability.

In any case, although Hegel's dialectic has "fallen" (ND, p. 4), it is the point of departure for reviewing philosophy's fate: "If Hegel's dialectics constituted the unsuccessful attempt to use philosophical concepts for coping with all that is heterogenous to those concepts, the relationship to dialectics is due for an accounting insofar as his attempt failed" (ND, p. 4).[6] It is Adorno's view that dialectics ossifies in both Hegel and Marx because of the drive for identity inherent in both systems—a drive that is manifested in a tendency to hypostatize concepts and to posit final ends (i.e., Absolute Spirit and communism)—which reproduces the very kind of mythological thinking that he and Horkheimer had previously diagnosed in *Dialectic of Enlightenment*. As a result, in response to the drive for identity that exists in both the Hegelian and Marxist dialectics, in which objects are subsumed by their concepts without leaving any remainder, "the hinge of [Adorno's] negative dialectics" is "to change the direction of conceptuality, to give it a turn toward nonidentity" (ND, p. 12).

At the outset, it must be made clear that this turn toward nonidentity sharply differs from nominally similar turns later made by certain poststructuralists. Adorno does not want to discard the moment of identity altogether—"the appearance of identity is inherent in thought itself," or, put more simply, "to think is to identify" (ND, p. 5). Rather, he asserts, philosophy "must strive by way of the concept to transcend the concept" (ND, p. 15). While Hegel famously advocates the "identity of identity and non-identity" and various poststructuralists advocate "nonidentity" in itself, Adorno argues for the "non-identity of identity and non-identity"—that is, the need for conceptual fluidity to adequately (and therefore never completely) describe the actual objects of a fluid reality. In some sense, therefore, as I asserted in part I of this book, although Adorno rejects phenomenology's "pure intuition" in favor of socially mediated concepts, since he thinks that pure intuitions unwittingly smuggle in the stuff of the conceptual apparatuses they purport to "bracket," his negative dialectics shares phenomenology's fundamental impulse to surmount the "constitutive subjectivity" of German idealism "to return to the things themselves." Thus, he asserts: "We want to adhere as closely to the heterogenous as the programs of phenomenology. . . . Philosophical contents can only be grasped where philosophy does not impose them. The illusion that it might confine the essence in its finite definitions will have to be given up" (ND, p. 13). Indeed, it is Adorno's view that his desire for "full, unreduced experience in the medium of conceptual reflection" (ND, p. 13) makes good the phenomenological impulse, which had gone badly astray: "Phenomenology, which once was animated by the need for contents, became an invocation of being, a repudiation of any content as unclean" (ND, p. 7).

By freeing the object from philosophy's drive toward identity, crucially, Adorno thinks that a richer subjectivity will be redeemed. The drive toward identity, which, for Adorno, is no less predominant in Husserl and Heidegger than in Kant and Hegel, levels subjective experience, and therefore the subject of that experience. To overcome this drive is to permit the subject to experience the richness of the world, which, in turn, enriches subjectivity. As Jameson puts it:

> At the threshold of a philosophical analysis of identity, it seems appropriate to insist on the face it wears and turns on

> daily life—namely repetition as such, the return of sameness over and over again, in all its psychological desolation and tedium: that is to say, neurosis. In that limited appropriation which Adorno makes of Freudian conceptuality, neurosis is simply this boring imprisonment of the self in itself, crippled by its terror of the new and unexpected, carrying its sameness with it wherever it goes, so that it has the protection of feeling, whatever it might stretch out its hand to touch, that it never meets anything but what it knows already. To put it that way, however, is to begin to wonder—not merely "psychologically"—what it would take to have the strength to stand the new, to be "open" to it; but even more: what that new might be, what it might be like, how one would go about conceptualizing and imagining what you can by definition not yet imagine or forsee; what has no equivalent in your current experience. At that point, there slowly emerges the counter-image or –mirage of the neurotic self locked utterly into its own "identity."[7]

As we saw in the last chapter, moreover, Adorno thinks that hanging behind these philosophical and psychological drives toward self-*identity* (i.e., the self-identical self) is the drive toward self-preservation, which finds its (artificially perpetuated) expression in capitalism itself. As Marx's piercing analysis of the phenomenon of commodity fetishism reveals, the commodity's sensuous particularity for its producer (i.e., its "use value") and the producer himself (the sensuous person) are subordinated to the categories of "exchange value" and "abstract labor," respectively, which are designed to make both commodities and human beings fungible. This progressively tends to alientate human beings from themselves, and this alienation, in turn, manifests itself in the drive toward identity, in which one's genuine "self" tends to be viewed as something that is outside of experience (as is the case with Kant's transcendental ego or Kierkegaard's interiority, which still drag "bad" experience into their innermost being) or one with experience (as is the case with the individual's reconciliation with existing social institutions under the rubric of Hegel's Absolute or Heidegger's Being, which reflect variations on the Freudian "introjection of the oppressor" phenomenon). In both types of cases, there is an identity. Thus, it is not by accident that early in *Negative Dialectics* Adorno equates the utopian idea of particularity defying subsumption under identity with "the 'use value,' in Marxist terminology" (ND, p. 11).

At its core, negative dialectics is Adorno's attempt to immanently think through identity thinking in the service of what he takes to be "the concern of philosophy"—namely, "cognitive utopia," which "would be to use concepts to unseal the non-conceptual with concepts, without making it their equal" (ND, p. 10). When J. M. Bernstein asserts that "Adorno's concern is with an analytic structure rather than an historical process,"[8] he is thus half right. Adorno's concern *is* with an analytic structure, an analytic structure that is constituted by the entwinement of myth and enlightenment: mythic rationalization processes, which are already instrumentally rational, betoken enlightenment rationalization processes, which harbor a mythic core in that they banish the nonconceptual from the concept to better instrumentalize it (theoretically and practically). Moreover, Bernstein is right when he asserts that Adorno is "not proposing an alternative history or replacing genealogy with a dialectical history of his own" and "nowhere does Adorno suggest a narrative of secularization that is meant to compete with existing narratives."[9] Yet, Bernstein mythologizes the very "analytical structure" that he seeks to demythologize because he strips it from the unfolding sociohistorical processes in which it is manifested, which, in different ways, leads him to be overly pessimistic and overly optimistic by turns. On the one hand, as was stated in chapter 2, he is overly pessimistic in that he summarily contends that "there is now no viable or available alternative" to "the institutional forms of liberal democracy and a market economy," which then absolves him of the burden to account for praxis (or the lack thereof) and throws the utopian moment so important to Adorno overboard. On the other hand, he is overly optimistic in that he ahistorically reincorporates the utopian moment in his brand of ethical modernism, which entails a "utopian form of particularistic moral realism" that "involves a re-enchantment of the world to this extent: empirical ethical predicates are not mere projections of human valuings onto a wholly indifferent object domain, but rather conceptions of things (events, happenings, actions) as conceived in the light of natural human interactions in the world."[10] When considered in the light of Bernstein's penetrating criticisms of Habermas, there is something rather odd about this, for in at least one important respect, this position is very close to Habermas's: although Bernstein rejects Habermas's attempt to neatly split system and lifeworld, which would allow Habermas's lifeworld participant to bracket what has been made of him in the system, Bernstein's moral agent can bracket what has been made of him under "the institutional forms of liberal democracy and a market economy," which he takes to be invariant.

Adorno himself offers a methodology of sorts to disenchant the concept—that is, to mine the nonconceptual that the enchanted concept has sealed up in the name of control, which would plug external and internal nature back into the picture, and therefore fulfill not only the concept but the human subject who uses it. Crucially, however, this methodology self-reflectively builds into itself the historical processes that, for better or worse, inform it in any event. Rejecting the subsumptive linear style that is part and parcel of abstract identity thinking, Adorno opts for nonhierarchical "models" or "constellations." These puzzle-like constructions (as was discussed in the first chapter) are designed to release the repressed truths in identity thinking by juxtaposing the different concepts that are operative in a particular sociohistorical context so as to reveal their limitations—limitations that point toward the repressed difference between identifying concepts and the objects that they purport to capture. Yet, before considering the constellation's structure, it is necessary to emphasize that Adorno sees the constellation as something that is historically mandated. Its nonhierarchical form, he thinks, is required by the nature of late capitalism itself, which, increasingly, has the tendency to undermine the possibility of clear-cut, hierarchically structured causal explanations:

> Although barter and its problematics would certainly be unthinkable without rationality . . . the capitalist system's increasingly integrative trend, the fact that its elements entwine into a more and more total context of functions, is precisely what makes the old question of cause—as opposed to the constellation—more and more precarious. We need no epistemological critique to make us pursue constellations; the search for them is forced upon us by the real course of history. (ND, p. 166)

Moreover, if the nonhierarchical form of the constellation is historically mandated, so, too, is its content. The subject that fashions the constellation is itself a historical product (but a historical product who, in the fashioning, injects his subjective share), as are the concepts and objects that constitute his constellation. As Adorno stated in his 1932 essay "The Actuality of Philosophy" and restates in *Negative Dialectics*, by putting concepts and objects into different configurations or trial combinations within a constellation, which is as fleeting as the particular sociohistorical context that gives rise to it (in its whole and parts), insights into the concepts and objects under consideration can be "unriddled" through the novel interplay of the particulars:

> The object opens itself up to a monadological insistence, to a sense of the constellation in which it stands; the possibility of internal immersion requires that externality. But such an immanent generality of something individual is objective as sedimented history. The history is in the individual thing and outside it; it is something encompassing in which the individual has its place. Becoming aware of the constellation in which a thing stands is tantamount to deciphering the constellation which, having come to be, it bears within it. The *chorismos* of without and within is historically qualified in turn. The history locked in the object can only be delivered by a knowledge mindful of the historic positional value of the object in its relation to other objects—by the actualization and concentration of something which is already known and is transformed by that knowledge. Cognition of the object in its constellation is cognition of the process stored in the object. As a constellation theoretical thought circles the concept it would like to unseal, hoping that it will fly open like a lock of a well-guarded safe-deposit box; in response, not a single key or a single number, but to a combination of numbers. (ND, p. 163)

As this passage suggests, although he is committed to the particulars over which a bad social totality runs roughshod, Adorno is also committed to the Hegelian-Marxist view that these particulars must be understood within the context of the bad social totality in which they exist, for "absolute individuality is [itself] a product of the very process of abstraction that is begun for universality's sake" (ND, p. 162). What this means is that any approach to the "truth content" of the particular must be by way of the mediating social totality or "the whole"—even if, contrary to Hegel's aphorism, "the whole is the false"

(MM, p. 50). This is because "totality," as Sartre puts it in the *Critique of Dialectical Reason*, "while radically distinct from the sum of its parts, is present in its entirety, in one form or another, in each of these parts."[11] Therefore, for Adorno, the bad social totality and an identity driven conceptuality are homologous: they are just different expressions of a petrified universal moment. And, just as conceptuality is a necessary aspect of cognition and cannot be discarded to get around the failings of an identity driven conceptuality in the name of the nonconceptual, the social moment is a necessary aspect of cognition and cannot be discarded to get around the bad social totality in the name of particularity. These notions are an anathema to many poststructuralists, which is the reason that Adorno has not caught on with poststructuralists in quite the same way as Benjamin. Indeed, while Adorno actually took the constellatory approach from Benjamin, one of his basic disagreements with Benjamin concerns the latter's tendency to see the truths unriddled by his method in an intuitively immediate, rather than dialectically mediated, way. Lamenting the loss of any interpretive mediation by the subject in Benjamin's work, which relied on direct "images" of truth, Adorno declares: "The mediation which I miss, and find hidden by materialistic-historiographic invocation, is in fact nothing other than just that theory which your work bypasses."[12]

Negative Dialectics itself, more broadly, is best viewed as a constellation of sorts. It is a constellation that is fashioned to show how the enlightenment's most fundamental philosophical concepts have turned against the basic commitments that inspired them (perhaps, most of all, the commitment to the individual, whose self-determination was perhaps the enlightenment's core); to unriddle the truth content that still continues to subsist in these concepts, and that might point the way to better redeeming the enlightenment project; and to "unfold" the "paradoxical title" of the book itself (ND, p. xix), which, for Adorno, is connected to redeeming the enlightenment project. Because this is a constellation that is self-consciously fashioned by Adorno himself, it is absolutely necessary not only to mention all the sections that make up the book but to also make clear their precise placement, since, given Adorno's commitments, the book's structure must be considered as inextricably intertwined with its content. After a lengthy Introduction, in which he considers a variety of current philosophical topics, Adorno interrogates Heidegger's fundamental ontology in Part One, "Relation to Ontology." (It will be recalled that Part One was considered in the second chapter of this book.) As its title implies, in Part Two, "Negative Dialectics. Concept and Categories," Adorno introduces his own theory of negative dialectics. And, finally, according to Adorno, Part Three, "Models," "elaborates models of negative dialectics . . . models that are to make plain what negative dialectics is and to bring it into the realm of reality, in line with its own concept" (ND, p. xx). Part Three is thus a constellation within the larger constellation that is the book itself, and in it Adorno juxtaposes Kantian freedom (subpart I), Hegelian history (subpart II), and speculations on the fate of philosophy itself in the wake of Auschwitz (subpart III).

At this juncture, two important points must be made. First, although there are many who say that Adorno's decision to include Heidegger's fundamental ontology in *Negative Dialectics* evidences his recognition that there are affinities between negative dialectics and fundamental ontology (especially given Part One's title, "Relation to Ontology"), this conclusion is mistaken. The mere placement of Heidegger's philosophy within the larger constellation that is *Negative Dialectics* just points to the indisputable fact that it plays a prominent role in the philosophical (not to mention larger cultural) debates of Adorno's time. There could be no true constellation of the kind that Adorno is fashioning that would be complete without Heidegger's philosophy, for, as we saw in chapter 2, even if negatively, it reflects the truth content of its time. Thus, in many respects, Heidegger's thought, as well as the support that it garners, is a manifestation of enlightenment thought gone bad, but this is no reason to privilege it, and if Adorno's intent is to redeem enlightenment thought, Heidegger has very little to say. What is most significant, then, is not Heidegger's inclusion in the constellation that is *Negative Dialectics* but his placement within it. By addressing Heidegger's fundamental ontology before introducing his own negative dialectics (for the purpose of clearly differentiating it), and then, more importantly, omitting it entirely from the *philosophical* constellation that is Part Three—which we saw Adorno describe as "models of negative dialectics"—Adorno must be understood as saying that, unlike Kant and Hegel, Heidegger's philosophy has nothing to contribute to his own project. Adorno thus rejects Heidegger's rejection of the subject-object paradigm—the thread that unifies the philosophical approaches that are contained within his own constellation. Thus, while Adorno largely shares Heidegger's concern about the overinflated subjectivism of the enlightenment subject, he holds, in contrast to Heidegger, that we must fully emancipate the subject, not reject him:

> Wherever, in the current manner of speaking, judgment is too subjective at the present historical stage, the subject, as a rule, will automatically parrot the *consensus omnium*. To give the object its due instead of being content with the false copy, the subject would have to resist the average value of such objectivity and to free itself as a subject. It is on this emancipation, not on the subject's insatiable repression, that objectivity depends today. The superiority of objectification in the subjects not only keeps them from becoming subjects; it equally prevents a cognition of objectivity. This is what became of what used to be called "the subjective factor." It is now subjectivity rather than objectivity that is indirect, and this sort of mediation is more in need of analysis than the traditional one. (ND, pp. 170–171)

It is just this notion of subjectivity that Adorno seeks to unriddle within his own constellation in Part Three. In particular, while Kant and Hegel both embrace the subject-object paradigm—one from the standpoint of individual freedom, the other from the standpoint of world history—both also emphasize the universal moment of the subject, and thereby give short shrift to the sensuous particular subject. Hegel's emphasis on the universal subject or spirit evidences this tendency clearly enough, but even in Kant's moral philosophy, which emphasizes the role of the particular agent to the virtual exclusion of sociohistorical concerns, "the principle of particularization is a universal. In honor of universality, Kant draws a terminological line between personality and the person" (ND, p. 292).

Second, it should be readily apparent that Adorno's constellatory juxtaposition of Kant and Hegel in Part Three of *Negative Dialectics* for the purpose of salvaging a vigorous notion of subjectivity is not at all unlike my juxtaposition of Sartre and Adorno in this book. By bringing freedom and historical determinism into a dialectical relation, Adorno is basically doing what I am attempting to do here—namely, he is interrogating these first- and third-person standpoints so as to show how each leads back to the other. Kant's antinomical freedom model ultimately splits apart, and through its cracks pours the social totality. And, although Hegel's world history gives short shrift to the individual, it presupposes him as it rejects him. Moreover, as far as my thesis here is concerned, what Sartre and Adorno bring to the table that goes beyond Kant and Hegel is just this concern with the sensuous, particular subject. In what follows, then, I shall integrate my own analyses of Sartre and Adorno into Adorno's analyses of Kant and Hegel. Accordingly, in the first section of this chapter, which will consider Adorno's critique of Kantian freedom in his "Freedom" model, I shall integrate Sartre's notion of freedom into the discussion to show how he circumvents the antinomies of Kantian freedom. In the second section, I shall consider Adorno's critique of Hegel's idea of history in his "World Spirit and Natural History" model, emphasizing the way in which Adorno circumvents Hegel's so-called totalizing impulse without discarding the all important notion of "totality." And, in the final section of this chapter (and book), I shall discuss the affinities between Sartre's phenomenology and Adorno's negative dialectics in terms of promoting a richer notion of individual experience.

FREEDOM MODEL

In the freedom model, Adorno aims to unseal what he sees as the truths of Kant's concept of freedom, which, in certain respects, represents the final breaking point in the concept's classic philosophical exposition—that is, in its exposition as the "free will–determinism *problem*." It is in Kant's dichotomous philosophy that the abstract concepts of both free will and determinism, as discussed in the Third Antinomy of the *Critique of Pure Reason* and the *Critique of Practical Reason*, turn around into their opposites, and this explodes their "binary opposition" (thus setting the stage for Hegel, who rightly states that freedom can only be understood in its objective social context—but then gives freedom short shrift in the name of that context). Still, for Adorno, the "problem" of freedom is an actual one, even if its classic philosophical exposition does not make it appear as such, and in the freedom model, he seeks, even if only negatively, to unriddle it.

Adorno roughly structures his freedom constellation as follows: In the first two sets of fragments, he shows that all concepts of unfreedom presuppose some concept of freedom, and, conversely, that all concepts of freedom presuppose some concept of unfreedom, which means that freedom and unfreedom dialectically entail one another. Then, in the third and fourth sets of fragments, Adorno seeks to undo the Third Antinomy in Kant's *Critique of Pure Reason* for the purpose of liberating not only the concept of freedom but also the concept of causality, which he thinks is lost in the peculiar form of social integration that marks late capitalism. In the fifth set of fragments, Adorno considers some of the more contemporary alternatives to Kant's concept of freedom. And, finally, in the sixth set of fragments, he considers Kant's idea of the "intelligible world," with particular emphasis on where the "truth content" in this concept continues to lie.[13] Despite the fact that there are many important insights to be gleaned from Adorno's analysis, in which he attempts to bring the very concept of freedom to life, in this section I shall not follow the movement of Adorno's dialectical exposition through its various twists and turns. Instead, I shall emphasize what I take to be his most important points, and then juxtapose them to Sartre's various notions concerning freedom—with which, I shall attempt to show, they bear more than a passing resemblance.

As an initial matter, however, it should be emphasized that Kant's concept of freedom, which might well be viewed as the philosophical model for bourgeois freedom during the early days of capitalism, reflected for Adorno the antinomies of early capitalism itself. Roughly thirty-four years prior to the publication of *Negative Dialectics*, Adorno contended in "The Actuality of Philosophy" that Kant's thing-in-itself problem, which is what hangs behind his antinomical idea of freedom, is actually a philosophical expression of Marx's analysis concerning the fetishization of commodities. Thus, Adorno argued, "it might be possible that, from a sufficient construction of the commodity structure, the thing-in-itself problem absolutely disappeared. Like a source of light the historical figure of commodity and exchange value may free the form of a reality, the hidden meaning of which remained closed to investigation of the thing-in-itself problem."[14] In fact, he believed, more broadly, that such a diagnosis could lead to the unveiling of virtually all of the metaphysical problems in Kant's thought. As Susan Buck-Morss states, Adorno sensed that the "indifferent relationship between Kant's subject and object was the reified relationship between worker and product; the abstractness of Kant's formalism was the abstractness of exchange value; the irrationality of the thing-in-itself was the resulting opacity of commodities; the acceptance of the given world of experience was the acceptance of class relations as second nature."[15]

By the time he writes *Negative Dialectics*, however, Adorno thinks that late capitalism's tendency to artificially perpetuate a condition of economic scarcity has led not to the unveiling of the metaphysical problems surrounding the concept of freedom in Kant's philosophy but rather to their demise. In other words, if once it was hoped that freedom would disappear as a problem because it would be realized, now it is feared that freedom will disappear as a problem precisely because it can no longer be realized (which, it will be recalled, parallels my earlier discussion of the problem of philosophy itself). Thus, Adorno asserts, "indifference to freedom, to the concept and the thing itself is caused by the integration of society, which happens to subjects as if it were irresistible. Their interest in being provided for has paralyzed the interest in freedom which they fear would leave them unprotected" (ND, p. 216). Under these circumstances, Adorno fears, the very concept of freedom itself might come to be "wholly extinguished, perhaps without leaving a trace" (ND, p. 218). The problem of freedom, then, becomes nothing less than the problem of keeping it alive: "Where freedom will hide out at any moment in history cannot be decreed once for all. Freedom turns concrete in the changing forms of repression, as resistance to repression. There has been as much free will as there were men with the will to be free" (ND, p. 265).

It is for this very reason that Adorno asserts in the opening section of the freedom model that "the either-or exacted by the question of free will is both succinct and worth asking" (ND, p. 212), which is a position that anticipatorily rejects the postmodern inclination to relegate the idea of freedom to the dust bin of the "history of ideas" or an outdated "system of thought." What's more, freedom is not just a "pseudoproblem" in the sense that a certain strain of Anglo-American philosophy would speak about it—in other words, a problem only because "the concept used [is] unclearly defined" (ND, p. 211):

> Reflections on freedom and determinism sound archaic, as though dating from the early times of the revolutionary bourgeoise. But that freedom grows obsolete without having been realized—this is not a fatality to be accepted; it is a fatality which resistance must clarify. Not the least of the reasons why

> the idea of freedom lost its power over people is that from the outset it was conceived so abstractly and subjectively that the objective social trends found it easy to bury. (ND, p. 215)

Ironically, although Adorno is setting the stage for a Hume-like reformulation of the very idea of "freedom" here, he does not want to reformulate the idea for the purpose of showing that it is just a "pseudoproblem" that disappears once we "get clear on our use of language." Instead, Adorno aims to show that the concept of freedom poses an actual problem that has only been turned into a pseudoproblem by virtue of its failure to be properly articulated in the first instance—a failure that owes its very existence to just those "objective social trends" that sought to bury the concept once the idea of it no longer served the ruling interests. In other words, for Adorno, the abstract idea of freedom served the interests of the rising bourgeoise, who relied on it to commercially maneuver while they extracted surplus value from those who "freely" offered themselves up as wage laborers. However, under advanced, neoliberal, monopoly capitalism, with its close (but unacknowledged) ties to the state, even the idea of freedom became a hindrance, and if it was not "buried" outright it was ideologically modified to accord with the new realities.

To emancipate the truth content inherent in Kant's concept of freedom, we must first see not only that it was open to being progressively undermined by capitalism due to its abstract and subjective formulation, which contributed to its obsolescence, but also that it was of a piece with capitalism as an initial matter. The formal space that Kant carves out for his concept of freedom, which is allegedly beyond the reach of capitalism's demonstrated penchant for instrumentalizing human beings like the pure means that his third variation of the categorical imperative prohibits, is really already a partisan of bourgeois thought, which tends toward formalism: "Formality in itself is a bourgeois trait: on the one hand, it frees the individual from the confining definitions of what has come to be just so, while on the other hand it has nothing to set against things as they are, nothing to base itself upon except domination, which has been raised to the rank of a pure principle" (ND, pp. 250–251). Much like Adam Smith's "invisible hand" (whose harmonization of particular and universal interests had a strong impact on Hegel's notion of relations in civil society), Kant's concept of wills that cohere under the formal condition of freedom gives the nod to individual freedom, but for both Smith and Kant this freedom demands the subordination of our natural instincts *and* our self-conscious reason to the "law above" that actually controls—but controls in the name of particular interests fostering unfreedom: "Laws receive the encomiastic epithet 'constant,' which is to raise them above the dread specter of anarchy without allowing the suspicion to dawn that they precisely are the old evil of unfreedom" (ND, p. 252).

According to Adorno, moreover, this principle of domination, in which we are supposed to subordinate our natural inclinations in the name of freedom, is rolled into the very structure of the Kantian subject itself—that is, in the distinction between the pure transcendental subject and the pathological empirical self. The transcendental ego that dominates the external phenomena it constitutes for epistemological reasons, Adorno suggests, also implicitly dominates the empirical self's natural drives: "The unity of the person [is] the equivalent of the epistemological unity of self-consciousness. The backstage expectation of the Kantian system is that the supreme concept of practical philosophy will coincide with the supreme concept of theoretical philosophy: with the ego principle that makes for theoretical unity and tames and integrates the human drives in practice. . . . The principle of particularization is a universal" (ND, p. 292). Thus, the subject is both free and unfree—unfree in that it is its own object and thus subjected to the lawful synthesis of the categories, but free insofar as it essentially is the subject of this lawful synthesis. Yet, just as Kierkegaard's interiorized self unwittingly drags along the bad reality that it seeks to escape, so does Kant's "free" transcendental ego, which is only individuated by its "unfree" empirical nature. "The transcendental subject needs the irreducible nonidentity which simultaneously delimits the legality," and this "nonidentity," which is not reflected on because it is not admitted, turns out to be none other than the substance of society itself: "The identifying principle of the subject is itself the internalized principle of society. This is why in the real subjects, in social beings, unfreedom ranks above freedom to this day. Within a reality modeled after the principle of identity there exists no positive freedom" (ND, p. 241). It is for this reason that the objective social trends found it easy to bury Kant's abstract and subjective concept of freedom. Through the back door, these social trends provide the very stuff that make it determinate, as Hegel's "Reason as Testing Laws" section in the *Phenomenology* amply demonstrates.[16]

Looked at from the flip side, however, Adorno sees it as neither feasible nor desirable to simply collapse Kant's transcendental subject back into the empirical self. Since the mind-body duality that this distinction reflects is part and parcel of the unfolding dialectic itself, it makes no sense to speak in these terms: our historically conditioned sense of ourselves, which is based on the distinction, would not permit it. And, indeed, even if all memory of the distinction could be wiped out (as it sometimes seems postmodern capitalism seeks to do), it would not wipe out the history that engendered and perpetuated this distinction, and this history would be all the more controlling because of our loss of memory with respect to it. More importantly, the concerns that gave rise to the distinction are not illegitimate ones—even if they were regressively fetishized in our concepts of the subject—and Adorno seeks to do justice to these concerns by holding open a space for them. Thus, he declares that there is "a moment which we may call the addendum"—a moment in which "the subject's decisions do not roll off in a causal chain [but] what occurs is a jolt"—and that traditional philosophy "rationalistically narrows" this addendum to "nothing but consciousness" (ND, pp. 226–227). The addendum, described by Adorno as an impulse that is "intramental and somatic in one" (ND, pp. 228–229), is what constitutes the something more that provides the basis for "rational insight"—which, emphatically, "is not simply the same as a free act [and which] we cannot flatly equate with the will" (ND, p. 227). In other words, Adorno's addendum is neither "nothing but drives and inclinations" nor is it "nothing but consciousness," but rather it is some amalgam of the two that permits "subjectivity [to] laboriously, ephemerally raise its head" (ND, p. 227). And, bearing some resemblance to Hegel's emphasis on circularity in his epistemology, Adorno says that the moment of the addendum is both something that was left behind sometime after subjectivity sprung from its undifferentiated oneness with nature and something that stands in for the promise of subjectivity's reconciliation with nature: "It is a flash of light between the poles of something long past, something grown all but unrecognizable, and that which might some day come to be" (ND, p. 229).

Ironically, although Sartre is mentioned only once in the freedom model (despite the fact that he is the staunchest modern defender of the concept of freedom), it occurs in a footnote that directly precedes the section in which Adorno introduces the concept of the addendum.

As will be recalled from the fourth chapter, Adorno attacks Sartre for ontologizing a bad social situation ("many of Sartre's situations are derived from fascism and true as indictments of fascism, not as a *condition humaine*" [ND, p. 226]), and, as far as it goes, Adorno is undoubtedly right: Sartre's description of human relations, as I previously suggested, does have an ahistorical component, which reflects phenomenology's one-sided or "first person" perspective. Nevertheless, there is no other philosopher that comes closer to offering a notion of Adorno's addendum than Sartre, and on this point Adorno does not say a word.

To begin with, contrary to Kant's rationalized account of the will, it is only by virtue of the somatic component of the addendum, Adorno contends, that there can be a will at all: "If the motor form of reaction were liquidated altogether, if the hand no longer twitched, there would be no will" (ND, p. 230). And, more generally, he contends, it is only by virtue of the stuff that constitutes our empirical selves (namely, the drives, desires, and inclinations that constitute our interests)—which is demarcated by "countless moments of external, notably social, reality [that] invade the decisions designated by the [concepts] 'will' and 'freedom'" (ND, p. 213)—that there can be any such concepts at all. It is roughly along the same lines that Sartre rejects the classic conception of the will. As an initial matter, despite Sartre's Cartesianism—which critics crudely reference for the purpose of summarily dismissing his thought instead of working through it—he is one of the first philosophers to not only take seriously the body but to reject as incoherent the mind-body split: "Being-for-itself must be wholly body and it must be wholly consciousness; it can not be *united* with a body" (B&N, p. 404). Or, put more simply, "consciousness exists its body" (B&N, p. 434), which is its point of departure onto the world. Accordingly, Sartre also rejects as incoherent any division of the for-itself into pure will and bodily emotion, and for much the same reason as Adorno: there must be ends other than those posited by the *ratio* of pure will for us to will: "The will in fact is posited as a reflective decision in relation to certain ends but it does not create these ends. . . . It decrees that the pursuit of these ends will be reflective and deliberative" (B&N, pp. 571–572). These ends, it will be recalled, are fashioned within the framework of the initial project, and the stuff of the initial project, the ultimate "decision," is, in turn, fashioned by "the indications of others"—the point at which, as Adorno puts it, social reality "invades." The "free" will is, therefore, ultimately a function of both bodily drives and social realities.

If freedom "needs what Kant calls heteronomous" (ND, p. 237) in terms of simple bodily drives and complex orienting societal interests, it is also the case, to put it rather awkwardly, that unfreedom "needs what Kant calls autonomous" to bring these simple bodily drives and complex orienting social interests to fruition. As Sartre states, "in order to be a cause, the cause must be experienced as such" (B&N, p. 564), which means that "no factual state whatever it may be (the political and economic structure of society, the psychological 'state,' *etc.*) is capable by itself of motivating any act whatsoever" (B&N, p. 562). Sartre's phenomenological stance, which holds that it is an individual's initial free choice of himself that first brings into play the ensemble of cause, motive, will, and end, is somewhat reminiscent of Kant's "incorporation thesis"—namely, that an incentive can move the will to action only if the individual incorporates it into his maxim. And, as Bernstein points out, the claim that "reasoning activities, as normative, are not reducible to drives and inclinations, and drives and inclinations on their own are not, for rational animals, unconditionally self-authorizing reasons," is a claim with which Adorno concurs—"this much of . . . 'the incorporation thesis' is granted by Adorno."[17] Thus, although Adorno contends that a will without physical impulses would not be a will, "at the same time," he contends, "the will settles down as the centralizing unit of impulses, as the authority that tames them and potentially negates them. . . . It is the force that enables consciousness to leave its own domain and so to change what merely exists" (ND, p. 241). In this way, ironically, Adorno accords more freedom to the will than does Sartre, who sees the will in purely instrumental terms. Yet, although Sartre does not call this "centralizing unit" the "will" as such, he does provide a space for it one step back, as it were—namely, in the free initial choice of oneself, which then circumscribes the will. And, what's more, Sartre comes even closer to this conception in *Search for a Method*, in which he speaks of our ability to make something of what has already been made of us. Both bodily drives and social realities are, therefore, ultimately organized by the freedom of consciousness (if not "*free* will" per se) in a particular sort of way.

For both Adorno and Sartre, then, the linked dualities freedom and unfreedom, autonomy and heteronomy, and necessity and chance dialectically entail one another not only externally but also internally.

Sartre's characterization of the "paradox of freedom"—that "there is freedom only in a situation, and there is a situation only through freedom" (B&N, p. 629)—captures what Adorno means by such statements as "freedom . . . is entwined, not to be isolated" (ND, p. 219), "the two concepts," freedom and unfreedom, "are not a simple antithesis; they are interwoven" (ND, p. 220), and "freedom itself and unfreedom are so entangled that unfreedom is not just an impediment to freedom but a premise of its concept" (ND, p. 265). For Adorno, to investigate either one of these poles in isolation from the other (and not only the first in isolation from the second)—that is, freedom *or* unfreedom, autonomy *or* heteronomy, necessity *or* chance—is to fall into a theory of identity that does violence to both poles. And, from his phenomenological perspective, the same can also be said for Sartre, who expresses this problem in the violence that the subject does to himself by overemphasizing either his nonidentity (i.e., his transcendence, or freedom) or his identity (i.e., his facticity, or unfreedom), both of which end up identifying with their situations, albeit in different ways. For this reason, then, both Adorno and Sartre relativize the absolute space that internally exists between all of these pairs on Kant's account, and if the "either-or exacted by the question of free will is both succinct and worth asking," as we have seen Adorno contend, it is only because the question testifies to, and thus illuminates, social (un)truths rather than metaphysical truths.

In sum, then, while Kant perceives the indispensability of the nonidentical moment, and, in some respects, honors it more than Hegel—the idea of the noumenon holds that we can never get a conceptual stranglehold on the object—his philosophy turns into one based on identity by virtue of the fact that he hypostatizes the identical and the nonidentical in their difference. Both the phenomenal and noumenal realms thus become statically self-identical—the former because the world is *for us* as it must be, given that we overdetermine it through our concepts (which then rebound in our maxims), and the latter because it is absolutely indeterminate. This problematic, according to Adorno, is expressed in the Third Antinomy:

> All that the subject needs to do to be lost is to pose the inescapable alternative: the will is free, or it is unfree. Each drastic thesis is false. In their innermost core the theses of determinism and of freedom coincide. Both proclaim identity.

> The reduction to pure spontaneity applies to the empirical subjects the very same law which as an expanded causal category becomes determinism. . . . [And yet] the antinomy between the determination of the individual and the social responsibility that contradicts this determination is not due to a misuse of concepts. It is a reality, the moral indication that the universal and the particular are not reconciled. (ND, p. 264)

Adorno's point here is not merely that by hypostatizing freedom and determinism (or, indeed, the transcendental and empirical egos) in their difference, Kant makes both abstractly self-identical, indeterminate, and therefore false. His point is also that Kant is unwittingly capturing an actual sociohistorical truth—namely, that practical freedom itself, which would be genuinely exhibited in the reconciliation of universal and particular, does not exist. In this sense, Adorno is returning to his crucial insight in "The Actuality of Philosophy" (i.e., that Kant's metaphysical thought is a reflection of the social world[18]).

Because this reconciliation, which practically serves as a regulative ideal, does not obtain (nor, for that matter, does Adorno's addendum, which would presumably be heralded by it), this lack of reconciliation must find expression in even the more dialectical philosophies of Adorno and Sartre. Indeed, along these very lines, implicit in Adorno's claim in this passage—that "the reduction to pure spontaneity applies to the empirical subjects the very same law which as an expanded causal category becomes determinism"—is a potent critique of Sartre. For Sartre, as we saw in part II, spontaneity, which is what he attributes to the choice of an initial project, is the source of our freedom. And, it will be recalled, it is Sartre's claim that it is precisely because the spontaneity of the initial choice is not determined by reasons that it is free. What Adorno is suggesting here, however, is just what I suggested in part II—namely, that such spontaneity, drawing on "the indications of others," just reincorporates the bad social context. Thus, Adorno further states, "the individual himself forms a moment of the merchandise society [and] the pure spontaneity that is attributed to him is the spontaneity that society expropriates" (ND, p. 264). It is for this reason that I suggested that Sartre's overly reductive orienting initial project must be loosened up, and, in essence, that this moment of spontaneity must be understood in terms of reflective choices with respect to a broader array of sociohistorically engendered alternatives, for to sever spontaneity from its sociohistorical context is to simply reproduce that sociohistorical context in the name of a false freedom. Thus, when Adorno contends, in accordance with his notion of the addendum, that "the possibilities of a truly progressive consciousness" depend on one's "nerval reactions" and "idiosyncrasies" (i.e., on one's peculiar somatic reactions to social phenomena), which constitutes the moment of spontaneity, he quickly goes on to say that those reactions must be sublimated into a theory[19]—otherwise these spontaneous somatic responses, much like Sartre's free initial choice of oneself, would reflect nothing more than the conditioning of a bad social context.

Conversely, it is in his critique of Sartre in the freedom model that, ironically enough, Adorno evidences the way in which the unreconciled social totality finds expression in his own thought. After contending that Sartre turns a bad social reality into a *condition humaine*, Adorno goes on to declare that "a free man would only be one who need not bow to any alternatives, and under existing circumstances there is a touch of freedom in refusing to accept the alternatives. Freedom means to criticize and change situations, not to confirm them by deciding within their coercive structure" (ND, p. 226). If by "refusing to accept the alternatives," Adorno only means to say that thought must not shirk its responsibility to continually think through changing social circumstances in the process of aligning itself with the most emancipatory political alternative, which it then seeks to positively affect, he is right. And, indeed, Sartre, who committed himself to the left but never ceased to criticize its tendencies toward reification, is (along with Marcuse) a perfect example of this approach. But when Adorno incorrectly accuses Sartre of "cling[ing] to the decision alone" (ND, p. 226) in the context of political practice (rather than in the context of the spontaneous choice of an initial project), and, moreover, when he abstains from participating in the new left, one must understand his claim in a much stronger sense—namely, that one must not even critically and self-consciously choose to align oneself with the best alternative within a "coercive structure" (which, historically, is, of course, ubiquitous). In this way, it is Adorno, not Sartre, who fails to embrace a dialectical approach, for Sartre recognizes not only that we remake ourselves regardless of the position that we take with respect to prevailing political practices, but also that we cannot dodge moral responsibility by refraining from political practice, since we are always already up to our elbows in blood in the "coercive structure" in which we find ourselves.

Adorno himself clearly acknowledges this point, for elsewhere in the freedom model he states that the moral high ground is no more to be found in refraining from political practice than in engaging in it: "Whatever an individual or a group may undertake against the totality they are part of is infected by the evil of that totality; and no less infected is he who does nothing at all. This is how original sin has been secularized" (ND, p. 243). Yet, Adorno eschews virtually all political practice. When Adorno speaks to "resistance," he is usually speaking only to theoretical resistance, which—even when self-reflectively aware of its own inherent limitations—tends to approach the sort of Kierkegaardian inwardness that he otherwise rejects. And, indeed, as with Kierkegaard, this has serious implications for subjectivity: consciousness tends to draw into itself the mean reality from which it tries to withdraw. Although we can wholeheartedly agree with Adorno when he asserts that "theory and practice . . . cannot be glued together in a synthesis" (ND, p. 286), then, it is no more the case that theory and practice can be split off from one another, for this presupposes the very separation that he is properly rejecting in Kant's dualistic subject, and it collapses into an identity theory that is no less virulent. Indeed, in terms of practice, it might well put Adorno only one step behind Kant, who says in "What Is Enlightenment?" that the need for the absolute freedom of critique must be offset by practical obedience. Ultimately, then, just as practically committed resistance must preserve its theoretical wits, lest it fall into apologetics, theory must engage with the most emancipatory form of practice that is available in a coercive world, lest the world move beyond not only the possibility of any emancipatory form of practice but also the possibility of any emancipatory theory. Practice is required to keep critical theory alive, for in the absence of oppositional practices that might staunch the movement toward the "totally administered society," there will no longer be any space open for oppositional theories.

In sum, then, freedom requires engagement and disengagement, action and reflection, for while Adorno rightly resists breaking off the subject-object dialectic in theory, he tends to break it off in practice, and if subject and object are not mediated in practice, in the long run they will not be mediated in theory either. When Adorno declares that "freedom calls for reflection" (ND, p. 237), he is, of course, right, but reflection that does not balance itself by action collapses into itself, and thus becomes self-identical. A "mediating" reflection, which is the aim, is one that is neither entirely engaged nor entirely disengaged. Or, put in Sartre's terms, albeit against Sartre's own intentions, it must be neither entirely "accessory" nor entirely "purifying." (The former is entirely engaged in the service of a project that arises from an orienting initial choice, which is invariably the heteronomous stuff of the social totality; the latter is entirely disengaged from the social totality in "the instant," which, in the name of autonomy, hides from itself the fact that it is the heteronomous stuff of that social totality into which it must again plunge itself with another orienting initial choice in any case.) If we view the Sartrean subject's orienting initial choice in the more variegated fashion that I suggested in part II, we get a subject that avoids these poles of reflection—a subject capable of the sort of mediating reflection that is part and parcel of what Marjorie Grene refers to as Sartre's "negative dialectic."[20] Sartrean consciousness neither stands wholly apart from the world nor collapses into it, both of which would subject it to the principle of identity. To the contrary, by virtue of its intentionality, consciousness is always-already in the world, but, by virtue of its negativity, consciousness is also able to both reflect on and change its particular projects, and therefore does not wholly collapse into the world of which it is a part.

To reflectively remake the world that has made you is the sign of a mediating subject, and, in the freedom model, Adorno equates the notion of a mediating subject with freedom itself:

> Freedom turns concrete in the changing forms of repression, as resistance to repression. There has been as much free will as there were men with the will to be free. . . . There is no available model of freedom save one: that consciousness, as it intervenes in the total social constitution, will through that constitution intervene in the complexion of the individual. (ND, p. 265)

For Sartre, too, freedom is to be found in the notion of a mediating subject, and in *Search for a Method* he not only enriches his phenomenological commitment to this notion by offering a more thoroughgoing dialectical analysis than exists in *Being and Nothingness*, but he also provides a method for making sense of it. The so-called progressive-regressive method discards neither history nor freedom: the first moment, which is really the regressive element, works backward to analyze the particular historical factors that have gone into the construction of subjectivity, while the second moment, the progressive element, involves the way in which subjectivity synthesizes and transcends these factors in pursuit of its future projects. Or, put differently, it is through "the internalization of the external" and "the externalization of the internal" that the subject, through its actions, freely makes the history that has made him. Sartre describes the process as follows:

> Praxis, indeed, is a passage from objective to objective through internalization. The project, as the subjective surpassing of objectivity toward objectivity, and stretched between the objective conditions of the environment and the objective structures of the field of possibles, represents in itself the moving unity of subjectivity and objectivity. . . . The subjective appears then as a necessary moment in the objective process. If the material conditions which govern human relations are to become real conditions of praxis, they must be lived in the particularity of particular situations. (SM, p. 97)

Sartre's method here resonates with Marx's contention in "The Eighteenth Brumaire of Louis Bonaparte" that "men make their own history, but they do not make it just as they please; they do not make it under circumstances chosen by themselves, but under circumstances directly found, given and transmitted from the past."[21] Yet, there is one crucial difference: Subjectivity plays a much larger role in the contemporary context because history no longer seems unproblematically inclined to realize philosophy's ideals by virtue of capitalism's own internal dynamics (if, in fact, this was ever really the case), and this requires a much greater self-consciousness with respect to the nature of our activities—especially in light of the vastly more sophisticated mechanisms for obfuscating the nature of what we take to be our emancipatory aims. Thus, there is a need for careful attention to the regressive element—or the objective, rather than subjective, aspect of the subject-object dialectic—and this finds expression in Adorno's history model.

HISTORY MODEL

Adorno's constellatory scheme in this section of *Negative Dialectics* must be seen as an adjunct to *Dialectic of Enlightenment*, which, in some sense, is itself a sustained "history model." And, in fact, my discussion of the issue of universal history in the last chapter drew on Adorno's history model in *Negative Dialectics*. Accordingly, this model, which is a good deal shorter than the "freedom model," need not detain us for very long. In both its sustained emphasis on Hegel and its placement in the broader constellation that is *Negative Dialectics*, however, the history model does go beyond *Dialectic of Enlightenment*, which it clarifies in certain respects, and thus deserves to be considered in its own right. In *Dialectic of Enlightenment*, it will be remembered, Adorno and Horkheimer cast their lot with Hegel's notion of "determinate negativity" but further argue that Hegel himself was ultimately not true to this notion:

> Determinate negation rejects the defective ideas of the absolute, the idols, differently than does rigorism, which confronts them with the Idea that they cannot match up to. Dialectic, on the contrary, interprets every image as writing. It shows how the admission of its falsity is to be read in the lines of its features—a confession that deprives it of its power and appropriates for it truth. With the notion of determinate negativity, Hegel revealed an element that distinguishes the Enlightenment from the positivist degeneracy to which he attributes it. By ultimately making the conscious result of the whole process of negation—totality in system and in history—into an absolute, he of course contravened the prohibition and himself lapsed into mythology. (DOE, p. 24)

In the history model of *Negative Dialectics*, Adorno largely seeks to support this claim—namely, that Hegel "contravened the prohibition" on positivism, and therefore was not true to the notion of determinate negativity—by contending that he uncritically valorized the Absolute and World Spirit, which are ultimately based on the "given" empirical facts. Or, as Adorno states it: "In the concept of the world spirit, the principle of divine omnipotence was secularized into the principle that posits unity, and the world plan was secularized into the relentlessness of what happens" (ND, p. 305).

As was the case with my analysis of the freedom model, I will not follow the movement of Adorno's dialectical analysis through its various twists and turns in the history model. Rather, I shall emphasize what I take to be the vital points with respect to my present concern—namely, the mediating individual that Adorno takes to be buried beneath the various Hegelian universals. Preliminarily, however, the history model is broadly structured as follows: In the first three sets of fragments, Adorno considers Spirit, individuality, and history from the universal standpoint, which means that he considers the construction and predominance of World Spirit, the way in which World Spirit overrides the individuals that nevertheless make it up, and universal history. In the fourth set of fragments, Adorno considers what he takes to be the essential shortcomings in Hegel's dialectics. And, finally, in the last three sets of fragments, Adorno considers Spirit, individuality, and history from the particular standpoint, which means that he considers the spell woven by Popular Spirit, the way in which Popular Spirit manifests itself in the psychology of the individuals it tamps down, and natural history. In this section, I shall begin with some basic, orienting comments about the history model, and then I shall assemble Adorno's miscellaneous positions in this model into a somewhat more discernible movement from the World Spirit to the individual (and analogously, although more abstractly, from universal to particular). Moreover, when appropriate, I will include Adorno's observations in *Hegel: Three Studies*, which anticipates the history model in *Negative Dialectics*.

On the whole, while in the freedom model Adorno aims to fracture Kant's hermetically sealed concept of freedom for the purpose of showing that it is always already permeated by the sociohistorical truths that it seeks to marginalize as merely anthropological, in the history section he reverses the process for the purpose of showing that Hegel's idea of history, which is based on the universal or World Spirit, turns out to be merely an empty abstraction because the individuals that would concretize it are left way behind: "If philosophy were what it is proclaimed to be in Hegel's *Phenomenology*—the science of the experience of consciousness—it could not, as Hegel does more and more, blithely dismiss the individual experience of the prevailing universal as an unreconciled evil, and lend itself to the role of defending power from an allegedly higher vantage point" (ND, pp. 307–308). As we saw in part II, Sartre makes a rather similar argument from the phenomenological standpoint when he contends that Hegel suffers from an undue "ontological optimism" by (abstractly) adopting the vantage point of "the Whole": "When Hegelian monism considers the relation of consciousnesses, it does not put itself in any particular consciousness. . . . If Hegel can assert the reality of this surpassing, it is because he has already given it to himself at the outset. In fact, he has forgotten his own consciousness" (B&N, p. 328).[22] Actually, not only has Hegel forgotten his own consciousness, which is also a stand-in for the consciousnesses of all individuals, but he unknowingly projects the bad subjectivism inherent in his own consciousness on to the "objective" World Spirit, which had first "contracted" into Hegel's own consciousness: "the universal he vindicates, as a higher objectivity, correlatively declines to a bad subjectivity, to the mean value of particularities" (ND, pp. 330–331).

The recognition that "society's law of motion has for thousands of years been abstracting from its individual subjects," and that ultimately "there would be nothing without individuals and their spontaneities" (ND, p. 304), is a fact that is also appreciated by Marx (who arises frequently in the history model). Thus, while Marx, like Hegel, approaches matters from the sociohistorical standpoint—the Marxian law of exchange value is analogous to Hegel's world spirit in that both "come into force without men being conscious of it" (ND, p. 300)—Marx does not mistakenly valorize this universal, as does Hegel in his emphasis on the "cunning of reason," but, instead, he strives to demystify it by contending that the "substrate" of history is nothing but "real individual subjects": "History does nothing, does not possess vast wealth, does not fight battles. It is man, rather, the real, living man who does all that, who does possess and fight; it is not history that uses man as a means to pursue its ends, as if it were a person apart. History is nothing but the activity of man pursuing his ends" (ND, p. 304).[23] What's more, much like Marx, Adorno (and, for that matter, Sartre) recognizes that Hegel's concept of reason is itself partisan because what it takes to be "realized reason" is only "the particular reason of the universal" (ND, p. 318)—that is, particular reason representing particular interests justified in universal terms.

Thus, although dialectics is innately a "challenge from below" (ND, p. 303), by "siding with the universal" (ND, p. 326), the deified World Spirit, which actually means siding with the modern state, unbridled capitalist production, and positive law, Hegel gives short shrift to the mediating moment, the challenge from below, and positivistically hypostatizes these universals. The particular interests of the ruling classes are thereby reified and turned around to subjugate the individual, whose plight becomes another "problem" to be managed from above—ultimately, by the so-called universal class of civil servants, who must ameliorate the condition of, among others, Hegel's aggressively discontented "rabble." Hegel's aim, the individual's reconciliation with World Spirit, in sum, ultimately takes place more in thought than in reality, which remains antagonistic, and the demand that individuals "reconcile" themselves to it because it supposedly reflects their interests (which is the Right Hegelian side of the equation) is really only a demand for submission:

> The ideology of the idea's being-in-itself is so powerful because it is the truth, but it is the negative truth; what makes it ideology is its affirmative reversal. Once men have learned about the preponderance of the universal, it is all but inescapable for them to transfigure it into spirit, as the higher being which they must propitiate. Coercion acquires meaning for them. And not without all reason: for the abstract universal of the whole, which applies the coercion, is akin to the universality of thought, the spirit. . . . Ideology hypostatizes the world spirit because potentially it was already hypostatized. The cult of its categories, however . . . reinforces only the consciousness of the spirit's difference from everything individual, as if it were an ontological difference; it thus reinforces antagonism. (ND, pp. 316–317)

In some sense, Hegel himself recognized the unmediated relation that he had posited, which is why he introduced the idea of "world historical individuals," who would "function as a bridging concept, a hypostatized intermediary between the world spirit and the individuals" (ND, p. 338). According to Adorno, however, these world historical individuals are not up to this task, for the concept of a world historical individual is a reactionary one that is evidence of a strong nationalistic bent. Yet, as his emphasis on the Prussian state suggests, Hegel himself was by no means immune from this bent: "His precept that individuals have to 'align themselves, to form themselves according to the substantial being' of their people, is despotic" (ND, p. 340). As we saw above, moreover, because the "substantial being" of a people is not even the reflection of an overbearing popular will but rather is meant to conceal underlying antagonisms, the demand for reconciliation with the existing national spirit is not only a demand for a reconciliation with the particular interests of the capitalist class but is also a demand by Hegel that his own dialectic not be taken too seriously: Hegel "confirms the state's prerogative to be above dialectics because—a matter he did not delude himself about—dialectics will drive men beyond bourgeois society. He does not put his trust in dialectics, does not look upon it as the force to cure itself, and disavows his own assurance that identity will produce itself in dialectics" (ND, pp. 336–337). In "Aspects of Hegel's Philosophy," Adorno articulates this point even more clearly: "The free play of forces in capitalist society, whose liberal economic theory Hegel had accepted, has no antidote for the fact that poverty increases with social wealth. . . . The state is appealed to in desperation as a seat of authority beyond this play of [dialectical] forces."[24] Analogously, positive law, which, Hegel argues, the individual should view as the objectification of his own interests in the legal sphere, is actually the medium through which his interests are thwarted. According to Adorno, even in its theoretical form—in other words, before the incursion of class-related issues—positive law evidences the fracture between individual interests and the whole that is their abstract aggregate. For this reason, Adorno argues, although the idea of natural law leads to antinomies when it is analyzed in its own right, it nevertheless "critically maintains the untruth of positive law" (ND, p. 310). Yet, even worse, is positive law in capitalist society, in which the abstract equivalence of all individuals under the law merely reinforces the underlying social relations that give rise to the abstract equivalence of social labor: "In law the formal principle of equivalence becomes the norm. . . . An equality in which differences perish secretly serves to promote inequality; it becomes the myth that survives amidst an only seemingly demythologized mankind" (ND, p. 309). Thus, Adorno argues, if individuals are "reconciled" with the law, it is "only because, to survive, they have to make an alien cause their own" (ND, p. 311).

This discussion of how Hegel ultimately "sides with the universal," undertaken from a sociopolitical standpoint (i.e., by looking at World Spirit, the state, capitalism, and positive law), can also be undertaken from the standpoint of Hegel's dialectical logic, and his dialectical logic, in turn, opens back on to the sociohistorical, since Hegel views the categories of his dialectical logic and his sociohistorical account as homologous (ND, p. 317). It is exactly this reversal that Adorno undertakes in the history model, and in a passage that epitomizes his own interpretation of Hegel's dialectic, Adorno declares:

> The principle of absolute identity is self-contradictory. It perpetuates nonidentity in suppressed and damaged form. A trace of this enters into Hegel's effort to have nonidentity absorbed by the philosophy of identity, indeed to define identity by nonidentity. Yet Hegel is distorting the state of facts by affirming identity, admitting nonidentity as a negative—albeit a necessary one—and misconceiving the negativity of the universal. He lacks sympathy with the utopian particular that has been buried underneath the universal—with that nonidentity which would not come into being until realized reason has left the particular reason of the universal behind. (ND, p. 318)

As I interpret Adorno, the chief utopian particular that has been buried underneath the particular reason of the universal is the sensuous, self-determining individual—that is, the individual with "a certain degree of ego firmness,"[25] whose autonomy resides in the self-conscious recognition of his own heteronomy, and whose aim is a world in which he can afford to be heteronomous. I shall return to this theme shortly. In the meantime, however, Adorno's attack on the compulsion of identity in Hegel's logic shifts here to an attack on what he takes to be the logical necessity with which history itself unfolds in Hegel's philosophy. This analysis deals with the idea of universal history, which, of course, was dealt with in the previous chapter. Still, I should briefly point out that while I do largely agree with Adorno's claims that "objectivity ranks ahead of the individual and his consciousness" in Hegel's philosophy (ND, p. 314), and, more generally, that Hegel's logic does not think about the particular qua particular but instead as the already abstract conceptual category of "particularity" (ND, p. 328), I am far less inclined to agree with his claim that there is any historical necessity in Hegel's thought. Hegel does not believe that there are any logical deductions or inevitabilities with respect to the unfolding of the national consciousness, much less the consciousness of the World Spirit, for he acknowledges that the development of consciousness depends on all sorts of contingent factors, both natural and historical. Only under propitious circumstances, to use Hegel's *bildung* metaphor, will the acorn become the oak. The problem in Hegel's thought, rather, is his assumption of "the end of history" standpoint, which does not deny that things might have turned out otherwise but definitively holds that they did not, and that universal history has been realized.

Adorno is even further off the mark when he contends that the idea of historical necessity also operates in Marx's thought. According to Adorno, Marx and Engels "deify history" and are thus "enemies of utopia for the sake of its realization" (ND, pp. 321–322). Like Hegel, however, Marx (if not Engels) is a deeply historical thinker, and while Hegel, admittedly, might give rise to certain confusions by taking himself to stand at the point of "the Absolute," there is no such corollary in Marx's thought. Marx does not speculatively predicate future or concluding stages of history, and this is especially so in his mature works, such as the *Grundrisse* and *Capital*. To the contrary, he concretely sets forth structural analyses of capitalism and the antagonisms that it produces, which include analyses of existing underlying tendencies. However, these tendencies are not crudely hypostatized, as if they are historical givens, but are retheorized in the light of changing socioeconomic conditions. The ahistorical guarantees based on "historical necessity" are made by those who had already perverted Marx's thought. Despite this particular mistake, however, Adorno, as I have attempted to show, often draws on Marx's thought, and nowhere is this more evident than in his analysis of "natural history," the subject matter of the short final set of fragments in the history model. Since I have already dealt with the issue of natural history in the context of my discussion of *Dialectic of Enlightenment* (and, for that matter, *Kierkegaard: Construction of the Aesthetic*), I will not reopen the matter. I would merely point out that the following passage from *Negative Dialectics*, which includes a quote from *The German Ideology*, clearly illustrates Adorno's indebtedness to Marx on the topic of natural history:

> The youthful Marx expressed the unending entwinement of the two elements with an extremist vigor bound to irritate dogmatic materialists: "We know only a single science, the science of history. History can be considered from two sides, divided into the history of nature and the history of mankind. Yet there is no separating the two sides; as long as men exist, natural and human history will qualify each other." The traditional antithesis of history and nature is both true and false—

> true insofar as it expresses what happened to the natural element; false insofar as, by means of conceptual reconstruction, it apologetically repeats the concealment of history's natural growth by history itself. (ND, p. 358)

As we saw in the last chapter, it is this "concealment of history's natural growth by history itself" that has perpetuated enlightenment thought's regression to myth. Yet, crucially, as this passage attests, this "traditional antithesis" is not one into which Marx falls.

Finally, although Adorno emphasizes that the spontaneities of individuals are what first gives rise to the hegemonic World Spirit when he speaks about individuality from the universal standpoint in the second set of fragments (see, for e.g., ND, p. 315), these spontaneities disappear on Adorno's account when he reverses the direction of his analysis and considers the individual from the subjective standpoint in the fifth set of fragments. In a small section titled "Subject and Individual," Adorno essentially separates the two, arguing that "due to its hypostasis as spirit, the subject, the substrate of freedom, is so far detached from live human beings that its freedom in necessity can no longer profit them at all" (ND, p. 350). This is only another way of saying that there is no mediating subject because subjectivity itself is so totally overrun that the individual can no longer be deemed an actual subject at all, and that all that remains of the individual is the *principium individuation* itself, which fetishizes the scarcity principle on which capitalism relies. In this empty, abstract way—in which the regress to myth is so complete that the individual is no less intertwined with "second nature" than the characters of Homer's *Odyssey* were intertwined with (first) nature—"the individual survives himself" (ND, p. 343). In the following section, "Dialectics and Psychology," Adorno thus speaks of "the loss in commitment, in that strength to approach the universal which individuality would need to come to itself" (ND, p. 351). What's more, according to Adorno, because essentiality lies with the bad universal, even the individual who would seek to get out from under its yoke would regress to "accidental traits"—in other words, assertions of individuality under the yoke of a bad universal manifest themselves in terms of neuroses, which become the "essence" of "individuality."

This is not to say that Adorno is utterly bereft of hope, but in many respects the hope that he does offer is a cold comfort, as is exhibited in a section titled "The Spell." Adorno begins this section by comparing the spell woven by Hegel's numerous universals to Marx's commentary on the phenomenon of commodity fetishism, and he seems to be suggesting that there is absolutely no way to break out of it: "The self-made thing becomes a thing-in-itself, from which the self cannot escape anymore; in the dominating faith in facts as such, in their positive acceptance, the subject venerates its mirror image. In the spell, the reified consciousness has become total" (ND, p. 346). Nevertheless, Adorno does not completely give up hope, but it is hope that is predicated on a rather undialectical reversal. He gives us reason to hope that the spell might be broken, but the reason that he offers for such hope tends to have a lifeless sort of quality, for it does not arise out of anything that we can make sense of:

> The universal that compresses the particular until it splinters, like a torture instrument, is working against itself, for its substance is the life of the particular; without the particular, the universal declines to an abstract, separate, eradicable form. . . . It is not altogether unlikely that the spell is thus breaking itself. For the time being a so-called pluralism would falsely deny the total structure of society, but its truth comes from such impending disintegration, from horror and at the same time from a reality in which the spell explodes. . . . Total socialization objectively hatches its opposite, and there is no telling yet whether it will be disaster or liberation. (ND, p. 346)

My concern here is that although the individual might be vindicated, this vindication is the result of chance—that is, of objective historical processes auspiciously working themselves out over the heads of individuals—which has the sort of mechanistic ring that Adorno generally rebels against. Of course, Adorno will have no truck with a metaphysics of history, for he rejects mechanistic historical accounts—if by "mechanistic" we mean that history will ineluctably work itself out in a particular way. Elsewhere in the history model, he emphasizes that "things might have gone differently," and, moreover, that "*if* [the totality's] claim to be absolute is broken . . . a critical social consciousness [will] retain its freedom to think that things might be different some day" (ND, p. 323). In terms of the present, however, this suggests that the individual to whom Adorno is committed has, at least in any meaningful political sense, all but ceased to exist, which is my basic concern with his theory. It will be recalled that Adorno criticizes Hegel's "general structure" because the particular is not dealt with qua particular but instead is dealt with at the level of "particularity," which is already a "conceptual category" (ND, p. 328), but roughly the same might be said of Adorno's "general structure" with respect to "individuality": although his third-person dialectical standpoint is theoretically committed to "the individual," the individual qua individual, or first-person standpoint, is seemingly lost in the process.[26] Still, Adorno does hold out a glimmer of hope—a glimmer of hope that refuses to pronounce the historical subject dead once and for all (which, poststructuralists largely claim, he always already was in any case):

> The methexis wrought between each individual and the universal by conscious thinking—and the individual is no individual until he goes in for such thinking—transcends the contingency of the particular vis-à-vis the universal, the basis of both Hegel's and subsequently the collectivists' contempt for individuality. Experience and consistency enable the individual to see in the universal a truth which the universal as blindly prevailing power conceals from itself and from others. The reigning consciousness puts the universal in the right because of the mere form of its universality. Universality, itself a concept, comes thus to be conceptless and inimical to reflection; for the mind to perceive and to name that side of it is the first condition of resistance and a modest beginning of practice. (ND, p. 344)

What all of this suggests is that, like Sartre, Adorno is fundamentally committed to the individual but that, methodologically, he begins from the opposite pole: Adorno's third-person dialectical approach, undertaken from the standpoint of a sedimented history, presupposes the individual in much the same way that Sartre's first-person dialectical approach, undertaken from the phenomenological standpoint, presupposes the sedimented history that has made it. In the same way that Sartre's phenomenological approach requires the complement of a third-person historical approach even after it moves into history, then, Adorno's dialectical approach requires the complement of a first-person phenomenological approach even if it penetrates history all the way to the level of the individual, for what it cannot grasp is the irreducibility of consciousness living its body in its upsurge into the world. Ronald Aronson beautifully states the problem from Sartre's side of the equation but in a fashion that anticipates Adorno's side as well:

> The thinking individual may indeed discover his or her own thinking to be self-evident and therefore the correct starting point. But a second kind of self-evidence is also needed: the self-evidence of all that is presupposed by the first thought or act. . . . Without both "poles," the self-evident self-consciousness and the self-evident society, being given at the outset, there is no thought, no knowledge. Most "solutions" of the problem take hold of a single pole when the truth needs rather the tension between the two, the constant going-and-coming of concrete reality. In reacting against one side, Sartre tends to hypostatize the other. . . . At the same time, Sartre was far too penetrating to rest easy, and, refusing to avoid the issue, actually took his starting point as the guiding thread to the other pole.[27]

To maintain the tension between the two poles—this is the mark of what I take to be a mediating subjectivity. A mediating subjectivity is not only a notion to which the philosophies of Adorno and Sartre share a commitment but it is also one that incorporates their standpoints, which constitute the two necessary moments of its very being. Unlike Kant's static third-person and first-person standpoints, the philosophies of Adorno and Sartre are predominantly informed by Hegel's dialectical approach, but unlike Hegel's dialectical approach, which ultimately effects a false reconciliation that requires the individual to "all the more forget himself," their respective philosophies, by virtue of their commitment to "negativity" or "nonidentity," remain committed to a genuine reconciliation that precludes Hegel's conflation of these two Kantian standpoints. And for this reason, paradoxically, they are, for all intents and purposes, also necessary moments of any ideal of reconciliation that is worth having. Still, for these philosophies to be brought into a dialectical tension, it must be the case that the underlying presuppositions of their particular third-person and first-person accounts can be mediated, and in the final section I shall summarily follow up on earlier indications to the effect that they can be.

Negative Dialectics, Phenomenology, and Subjectivity

In Part Two of *Negative Dialectics*, titled "Negative Dialectics. Concept and Categories," Adorno sets forth his most comprehensive account of negative dialectics. As is the case with his consideration of both the freedom and history models in the first two models of Part Three, Part Two, which is made up of only one model (Adorno's), is composed of six sets of fragments. In this section, I shall not peruse Part Two, many of whose fundamental concepts were set forth in the introductory pages of this chapter. Rather, I shall consider these concepts within the context of my own interest in fleshing out Adorno's notion of a mediating subject and then show how they complement what I take to be a corresponding notion in Sartre's phenomenology.

In the opening passages of this chapter, it will be recalled, I indicated that Adorno shares Hegel's belief that the epistemological issues of the philosophical tradition are interwined with the issue of subjectivity formation. To the extent that we misconceive our relation to the objects of our experience, we deform our experiences, and, therefore, ultimately our selves, given that subjectivity is the result of our experience. Unlike Hegel, however, Adorno does not understand dialectics as a "science of experience," for in Adorno's mind (and, evidently, in Hegel's as well), such a description implies that there is an overarching movement within the fabric of experience toward some ultimate, all-embracing truth (i.e., "absolute knowing"). Adorno, of course, rejects this idea, and contends that in idealistically conceiving of such a tendency toward unification, a good deal is actually left out. For this reason, Adorno contends in a section titled "Synthesis," negative dialectics is "not only an advancing process but a retrograde one at the same time. To this extent, the picture of the circle describes it correctly. The concept's unfoldment is also a reaching back, and synthesis is the definition of the difference that perished. . . . [It] is not ashamed to recall the famous procession of Echternach: one jump forward, two jumps back" (ND, p. 157). Although Hegel, too, privileges the "picture of the circle," then, on his account what went before is now synthesized in the "identity of identity and nonidentity," and in his drive toward unity, the "retrograde" moment in dialectical reflection is tacitly revoked: the difference (or the nonidentical) that was left behind is pounded into

Hegel's burgeoning conceptual apparatus without ever having actually been given its due. Thus, although Adorno insists that we "start out from the concept," as did Hegel, he emphasizes the need for a counterbalance to the overdetermining nature of Hegel's concepts, which obstruct the rich personal experience to which his dialectic is otherwise committed. This counterbalance is what Adorno calls "mimesis."

In some sense, mimesis, on Adorno's account, is the truly "experiential" moment in the process of experience. In contrast to the preconceived concept, which dominates the object that is perceived by hierarchically classifying it before it is really experienced—this, of course, is the procedure of the "constitutive subjectivity" to which Adorno is so fervently opposed—mimesis opens itself up to the object, and thus attempts to grasp it in its multifariousness. In *Dialectic of Enlightenment*, for instance, Adorno and Horkheimer state that mimesis does not "progressively distance itself from the object" (DOE, p. 11), and that we have this ability to abandon ourselves to the object, and thus come to know it better, because we, too, are ultimately a piece of nature. "To be an object is part of the meaning of subjectivity" (ND, p. 183), and, what's more, it is that part of the meaning of subjectivity that engenders the cognitive process: "The subject's cognitive achievements are somatic. . . . Physicality emerges at the ontical pole of subjective cognition, as the core of that cognition" (ND, pp. 193–194). Still, Adorno's emphasis on mimesis, as should already be clear, is no substitute for the moment of conceptuality, which, as was asserted above, is the "starting point." A great work of art, which results from the artist giving himself up to the object, surely recompenses the artist's initial relinquishment of the subjective component with much greater conceptual dividends by releasing universal themes in new and different ways that can then be mediately pondered. However, this does not mean that the mimetic component is "the first," for the artist who undertook this project of self-relinquishment undertook it from the standpoint of a subjectivity formed within a particular sociohistorically engendered conceptual framework. Thus, if the concept is the condition of possibility for experience—a Kantian and Hegelian commitment that I do not see Adorno calling into question—mimesis is the condition of possibility for any experience truly worth having. It is the indispensable mediator in concept formation, and, therefore, is not held at arm's length from conceptuality, as is arguably the case in Kant and Hegel. Conceptualization and mimesis are, in sum, dialectically intertwined.

If, then, it is only after we have given ourselves up to the object that we can judiciously reconceptualize it, the very way in which we give ourselves up to the object points to its always already conceptual nature. According to Adorno, reconceptualization should be facilitated by the constellational process, which tends to break with the existing conceptual hierarchy, but it breaks with this hierarchy by using its own concepts: "By gathering around the objects of cognition, the concepts [of the constellation] potentially determine the object's interior" (ND, p. 162). While this might seem counterintuitive, Adorno, in contrast to certain strains of poststructuralism, sees that "individuality is not the ultimate either," for "absolute individuality is a product of the very process of abstraction that is begun for universality's sake" (ND, pp. 161–162).[28] The object, in other words, is not a sense datum that is or could be immediately at hand (ND, pp. 186–189), and it is only by framing it within the context of a nonhierarchical constellation that the "something more" within it has the chance of being emancipated: "The inside of nonidentity is its relation to that which it is not, and which its managed, frozen self-identity withholds from it. It only comes to in relinquishing itself, not hardening. . . . The possibility of immersion requires that externality. Such an immanent generality of something individual is objective as sedimented history" (ND, p. 163). In other words, the subject's relinquishment to the object must be matched by the object's relinquishment to the subject, for unconceptualized nonidenticalness is, literally, meaningless. It is in this way that the constellation, although subjectively produced, becomes "readable as sign of an objectivity: of the spiritual substance" (ND, p. 165). This must be a perpetual process, of course, for the objective social processes that reveal themselves through our selves, and provide the stuff of the subjectively established constellation, are themselves in flux. And, crucially, the process of giving oneself up to the object, and seeking to release its meaning from its ossified placement in the existing hierarchy of concepts, redounds to the existential benefit of the *subject*:

> What transmits the facts is not so much the subjective mechanism of their pre-formation and comprehension as it is the objectivity heteronomous to the subject, the objectivity behind that which the subject can experience. This objectivity is denied to the primary realm of subjective experience. . . . To give the object its due instead of being content with the false

> copy, the subject would have to resist the average value of such objectivity and to free itself as a subject. It is on this emancipation, not on the subject's insatiable repression, that objectivity depends today. The superiority of objectification in the subjects not only keeps them from becoming subjects; it equally prevents a cognition of objectivity. This is what became of what used to be called "the subjective factor." It is now subjectivity rather than objectivity that is indirect, and this sort of mediation is more in need of analysis than the traditional one. (ND, pp. 170–171)

Adorno's emphasis on the object, it should be clear, is largely for the sake of the subject. If it is "now subjectivity rather than objectivity that is indirect," it is because an objectivity produced by identity thinking preforms the subject's world, and subjectivity becomes a mere function of it. If "the subjective factor" was not overrun by objectivity's "false copy"—a social lowest common denominator that constitutes the "average value of objectivity"—it would not fail to identify but would identify in such a way that it would contribute this "subjective factor," which is the result of "self-reflection": "Nonidentity is the secret telos of identification. . . . Dialectically, cognition of nonidentity also lies in the fact that this very cognition identifies—that it identifies to a greater extent, and in other ways, than identity thinking" (ND, p. 149). Self-reflection, the "subjective factor" that is currently overwhelmed, is the mediating moment in the subject, and this mediating moment, in turn, presupposes the subject-object paradigm, which Adorno spends a good deal of time discussing in Part Two of *Negative Dialectics*. Before concluding with Adorno's analysis of the subject-object paradigm, however, I should reiterate that there is much in this approach to cognition that resonates with Sartre.

As we saw in part II, Sartre's version of intentionality, which is based on the notion that consciousness is itself "nothing" without the objects of which it is aware, sees that the subject is always-already plunged into the world of its experience and that it is basically (but, of course, by no means absolutely) constituted by the objects that make up this experience. On this account, it will be recalled, the problems that arise from the dualisms of classic epistemology are supplanted by a new dualism—namely, that of the "finite and infinite." And, according to Sartre, it is "the infinite" that takes priority in this dualism, for phenomena "can not be reduced to a finite series of manifestations since each one of them is a relation to a subject constantly changing" (B&N, p. 5). This subject constantly changing, I argued in part II, ineluctably imports the sociohistorical context into its perception of phenomena, for it is a changing sociohistorical context that is what engenders these changes in the subject. Knowledge thus becomes a matter of (sociohistorical) interpretation. Sartre thereby circumvents what Adorno describes as "peephole metaphysics," in which "the subject [is] locked up in its own self by that metaphysics," and merely sees reified shadows of its own making when it peers over its self-imposed walls at the world (ND, pp. 139–140). Rather, the only limits to experience on Sartre's account, as I previously argued, are those that are sociohistorically imposed by "the indications of others," which is not at all inconsistent with Adorno's contention that problems of knowledge are essentially the result of an antagonistic sociohistorical context. Moreover, according to Sartre, it is not only consciousness that is thrust into the world. In his discussion of "the body," Sartre, like Adorno, identifies the somatic nature of knowledge when he unequivocally rejects the idea of a disembodied "pure knowledge" (B&N, p. 419)—which, in some sense, is still the ideal in the philosophies of Husserl and Heidegger.

The conception of reason that emanates from Adorno's constellational method, moreover, stands in roughly the same relation to the scientifically inspired system of hierarchically ordered instrumental concepts that he assails as Sartre's notion of "purified" reason stands in relation to his depiction of instrumental reason. For both Adorno and Sartre, instrumental reason stands in the way of a self-reflective reason that would reveal to the subject his inadvertent capitulation to the leveling "objective" reason of the collective. Similarly, for both Adorno and Sartre, there is no higher order, more comprehensive theory of reason that can be assembled so as to surmount the problem of instrumental reason without ultimately contributing to it. (Along these lines, it will be recalled, Sartre goes so far as to claim that it is the hierarchically structured matrix of our individual projects that gives rise to our reasons in the first place.) However, in some sense, both Adorno and Sartre hold out the instant. According to Adorno, who depicts negative dialectics as a "logic of disintegration" (ND, p. 144), constellations do not reveal permanent ahistorical truths, but merely historical ones that must be perpetually reinterpreted by the subject, who, in Sartre's words, "is constantly changing." In other words, the conceptual truths that are engendered by Adorno's constellational method should not be hypostatized when they are "unriddled" by the subject, because they are as ephemeral as the moment itself (as well as the objects that they try to cognitively capture). Phenomenologically speaking, Sartre says much the same thing when he asserts that the moment of freedom, which actually comes about only on the heels of a purifying reflection, "is characterized by a constantly renewed obligation to remake the self which . . . with its a priori and historical content is the essence of man" (B&N, p. 72). In sum, then, for both Adorno and Sartre, there must be a constant exchange between a reflection that furnishes fleeting truths and the accumulates of lived experience.

This dialectical phenomenon—the phenomenon of a laborious, ongoing self-reflection that can neither tether itself to an already existing higher order ends-oriented theory of reason nor ever realize such a theory of reason but must incessantly produce nonaccessory reflection from out of itself—points to the notion of a "mediating subject," whose mediating standpoint is often referred to by Adorno as the subjective "share" or "surplus." To comprehend this phenomenon, which Adorno refuses to concretize (and, consequently, ontologize), one must comprehend, more generally, Adorno's view of the subject-object relation. Thus, in a section titled "Subject-Object Dialectics," he states:

> The polarity of subject and object may well appear to be an undialectical structure in which all dialectics takes place. But the two concepts are resultant categories of reflection, formulas for an irreconcilability; they are not positive primary states of fact but negative throughout, expressing nothing but nonidentity. Even so, the difference between subject and object cannot be simply negated. They are neither an ultimate duality nor a screen hiding ultimate unity. They constitute one another as much as—by virtue of such constitution—they depart from each other. . . . The only possible course is definite negation of the individual moments whereby subject and object are turned into absolute opposites and precisely thus are identified with each other. In truth, the subject is never quite the subject, and the object never quite the object; and yet the two are not pieced out of any third that transcends them. (ND, pp. 174–175)

This formulation closely conforms to Sartre's conception of the nonidentical relation that exists between "being-for-itself" and "being-in-itself" (with "being-for-others" straddling both sides of the duality). Of course, Adorno would eschew the ontological language, which, I contended in part II, is only heuristically used by Sartre. But, as we observed, isn't it fair to say that for Sartre "the self" is the always provisional result of the negative relation that exists between these terms, each of which perpetually reconstitutes the other? The "subject is never quite the subject" for Sartre because, as being-for-itself, the subject is, quite literally, a (nihilating) "nothingness," and it is only in a trivial sense that the object actually exists without the subject. Moreover, as is the case with Adorno, and in contrast to Hegel, whose dialectic, nevertheless, informs the thought of both, Sartre sees no higher-order third term that will transcend this nonidentical relation.[29]

So, too, on the issue of self-identity, Adorno and Sartre tend to converge, as the following passage attests:

> On its subjective side, dialectics amounts to thinking so that the thought form will no longer turn its objects into immutable ones, into objects that remain the same. Experience shows that they do not remain the same. The unstable character of traditional philosophy's solid identity can be learned from its guarantor, the individual human consciousness. To Kant, this is the generally predesigned unity underlying every identity. In fact, if an older person looking back has started early on a more or less conscious existence, he will distinctly remember his own distant past. It creates a unity, no matter how unreal the elusive picture of his childhood may seem. Yet the "I" which he remembers in this unreality, the I that he was at one time and potentially becomes again—this I turns simultaneously into another, into a stranger to be detachedly observed. (ND, p. 154)

Of course, for Sartre, "the individual human consciousness" is *not* the "guarantor" of identity with respect to either the objects that it thinks or its self but rather is the very root of nonidentity. Yet, as Adorno asserts, consciousness is not only "distant" from the "I" but is "simultaneously" unified with it, which is another way of saying, in Sartrean terms, that consciousness is always already beyond the self (both past and present) that it must nevertheless be. This reflects the fact that the subject-object relation is an interior one that is based on negativity—or, as Adorno states above, it is "neither an ultimate duality nor a screen hiding ultimate unity." Accordingly, on the one hand, consciousness's distance from the self, it will be recalled, is what provides the grounds for Sartre's phenomenological notion of freedom, and it is because Adorno is also a philosopher of nonidentity or negativity that he, too, can put forth a philosophy of freedom, albeit, of course, negatively. In other words, it is because the "I turns simultaneously into another, into a stranger to be detachedly observed" that Adorno's subject is also free to thematize its unfreedom, and thus, in some sense, move beyond it. Indeed, this is the very distance that provides the grounds for Adorno's negative social critique, and it is what allows the subject to imaginatively construct his own constellational model, for in the absence of such distance, the impetus for such a model (and the ability to put its constituents into novel "trial combinations") would not even arise. On the other hand, with respect to consciousness's unity with the self, Adorno goes on to discuss the relation between "origins" and "goals" in strikingly Sartrean terms:

> Karl Kraus's line "The origin is the goal" sounds conservative, but it also expresses something that was scarcely meant when the line was uttered: namely, that the concept "origin" ought to be stripped of its static mischief. Understood this way, the line does not mean that the goal had better make its way back to the origin, to the phantasm of "good" nature; it means that nothing is original except the goal, that it is only from the goal that the origin will constitute itself. There is no origin save in ephemeral life. (ND, pp. 155–156)

What Adorno is broaching here closely correlates with Sartre's basic claim that a person's past is necessarily mediated by his future goals. This is not to say that the past can be disavowed, which plainly would be denied by both Adorno and Sartre, for the past is the stuff of our goals. Rather, it is to say that it is only through our goals, which are circumscribed by the past, that the past, in turn, acquires meaning. And, finally, it is to say that it is the hope of both Adorno and Sartre that sociohistorical conditions, the origin, will pan out in such a way as to make these goals more the individual's own, or the result of his own subjective "share" or "surplus."

It would serve no good purpose to continue cataloging the similarities that exist between Adorno and Sartre. In concluding, I would like to offer two (very rare) speculative comments by Adorno on what the individual might look like under the "right" sociohistorical state of affairs:

> We cannot anticipate the concept of the right human being, but it would be nothing like the person, that consecrated duplicate of its own self-preservation. From the viewpoint of a philosophy of history, this concept, which on the one hand assuredly presupposes a subject objectified into a character, presupposes on the other hand the subject's disintegration. (ND, p. 277)

> In a state of freedom, the individual would not be frantically guarding the old particularity . . . but neither would that state of freedom agree with the present concept of collectivity. (ND, pp. 283–284)

If we consider these passages in tandem, we should see that while the free individual (in the free society) would not be "guarding the old particularity," there would still be an "old particularity" or "subject objectified into a character" to be continuously reworked. The individual would be a work of art ceaselessly in progress. And, indeed, it is each individual constantly reworking his self (and, impliedly, the collective of which he is a part), that is the essence of the notion of a mediating subject. In contrast, what impels the individual to hypostatize the "old particularity" in its presently existing form—that is, to undertake the "bad faith" project of making himself into a thing—is the fear that by not making himself into a thing (like Sartre's waiter, who depends on the goodwill of his customers), he will die under the weight of an indifferent economic system. Under the right state of affairs, there would be no such fear, and the individual would feel free to open himself up to the world. And, by opening himself up to the world, which would mean that self-identity would become more fluid, the individual would be in a position, as Nietzsche states, to become who he is. Openness to a world to which the individual can actually afford to be open is therefore the very condition of the liberated subject, *not* his demise. Yet, as the works of both Sartre and

Adorno testify, this does not mean that there is no such thing as a "mediating subject" under the present state of affairs. Whether ultimately amenable to actualization or not, the very ideal of the liberated subject, which continues to inspire innumerable acts of resistance, testifies to its existence.

Notes

Introduction

1. Peter Dews, *The Limits of Disenchantment: Essays on Contemporary European Philosophy* (New York: Verso, 1995), p. 169 (emphasis added).

2. Rudi Visker, *Michel Foucault: Genealogy as Critique*, tr. Chris Turner (London: Verso, 1995), p. 89 citing Rainer Schürmann, "On Constituting Oneself as an Anarchistic Subject," *Praxis International*, 6, 3, pp. 294–310.

3. Jacques Derrida, "Force of Law: The 'Mystical Foundation of Authority,'" in *Deconstruction and the Possibility of Justice*, eds., Drucilla Cornell, Michel Rosenfeld, and David Gray Carlson (New York: Routledge, 1992), pp. 19–22.

4. Even the two thinkers who are arguably the most hostile of all toward the notion of the subject, Deleuze and Guattari, cannot manage to juggle the subject out of their materialist ontology. In *A Thousand Plateaus*, they say that "you have to keep enough of the organism for it to reform each dawn; and you have to keep small supplies of significance and subjectification, if only to turn them against their own systems when the circumstances demand it, when things, persons, even situations, force you to; and you have to keep small rations of subjectivity in sufficient quantity to enable you to respond to the dominant reality." Gilles Deleuze and Félix Guattari, *A Thousand Plateaus*, tr. Brian Massumi (Minneapolis: University of Minnesota Press, 1987), p. 160.

5. Slavoj Zizek, *The Ticklish Subject: The Absent Centre of Political Ontology* (London: Verso, 1999), p. 1.

6. See, for example, Patricia J. Huntington, *Ecstatic Subjects, Utopia, and Recognition: Kristeva, Heidegger, Irigaray* (Albany: State University of New York Press, 1998) and Martin J. Matustik, *Postnational Identity: Critical Theory and Existential Philosophy in Habermas, Kierkegaard, and Havel* (New York: The Guilford Press, 1993).

7. Slavoj Zizek, *The Ticklish Subject*, p. 2.

8. Ibid., p. 160.

9. Ibid., p. 62.

10. Julia Kristeva, *Revolution in Poetic Language*, tr. Margaret Waller (New York: Columbia University Press, 1984), p. 129.

11. See, for example, Charles Taylor, *Hegel* (Cambridge: Cambridge University Press, 1975).

12. Jürgen Habermas, *The Philosophical Discourse of Modernity*, tr. Frederick G. Lawrence (Cambridge, Mass: MIT Press, 1987), p. 36.

13. G. W. F. Hegel, *Phenomenology of Spirit*, tr. A. V. Miller (Oxford: Oxford University Press, 1977), p. 45.

14. G. W. F. Hegel, *Philosophy of Right*, tr. T. M. Knox (Oxford: Oxford University Press, 1967), p. 156.

15. Marx thus rightly states that "the outstanding achievement of Hegel's *Phenomenology* and of its final outcome [is] the dialectic of negativity, [which is] the moving and generating principle." Karl Marx, *The Economic and Philosophic Manuscripts of 1844*, ed. Dirk J. Struik, tr. Martin Milligan (New York: International Publishers, 1964), p. 177. And his critique of Hegel's concept of the state—that it ignores the class contradictions inherent in capitalist society, and thus incorrectly views the state as the neutral mediator of differences when it is actually the advocate of the dominant class—is no less on target.

16. Fredric Jameson, *Late Marxism: Adorno, or, The Persistence of the Dialectic* (London: Verso, 1990), p. 46.

17. Jean-Paul Sartre, "The Itinerary of a Thought," in *Between Existentialism and Marxism*, tr. John Mathews (New York: William Morrow and Co., 1979), p. 35.

18. Theodor W. Adorno, *Prisms*, tr. Samuel and Shierry Weber (Cambridge, Mass: MIT Press, 1994), p. 235.

PART I: ADORNO'S RELATIONSHIP TO THE EXISTENTIAL AND PHENOMENOLOGICAL TRADITIONS

1. In the Preface to *Negative Dialectics*, Adorno states: "to use the strength of the subject to break through the fallacy of constitutive subjectivity—this is what the author felt to be his task ever since he came to trust his own mental processes" (ND, p. xx). (The transcendental metasubject to which I parenthetically refer is best understood as Kant's transcendental ego; the historical metasubject is Hegel's *Geist*.)

2. By rejecting the subject-object paradigm that operates in the thought of Kierkegaard and Husserl, which supposedly estranges humankind from its proper home in Being, Heidegger seems to pursue truths that are at once existential *and* epistemological.

3. Adorno asserts that "the only philosophy which can be responsibly practiced in face of despair is the attempt to contemplate all things as they would present themselves from the standpoint of redemption" (MM, p. 247).

4. In "Aspects of Hegel's Philosophy," Adorno declares that "only the doctrine of the identity of subject and object inherent in idealism—an identity that amounts in terms of form to the primacy of the subject—gives it the strength of totality that per-

forms the negative labor—the dissolution of individual concepts, the reflection of the immediate and then the sublation of reflection." See Theodor W. Adorno, *Hegel: Three Studies*, tr. Shierry Weber Nicholsen (Cambridge, Mass.: The MIT Press, 1993), p. 10.

5. Theodor W. Adorno, "The Actuality of Philosophy," *Telos* no. 31 (Spring 1977), p. 122.

6. This is, of course, a necessary first step for making out my larger thesis that Sartre's philosophy is actually a beneficial complement to Adorno's thought.

Chapter 1: Adorno and Kierkegaard

1. The book appeared in German bookstores the day that Hitler suspended freedom of the press.

2. I will recount Adorno's discussion of Heidegger in *Kierkegaard: Construction of the Aesthetic* at the end of the first section of this chapter.

3. Susan Buck-Morss, *The Origin of Negative Dialectics: Theodor W. Adorno, Walter Benjamin, and the Frankfurt Institute* (New York: The Free Press, 1977), p. 121.

4. See Rolf Wiggershaus, *The Frankfurt School: Its History, Theories and Political Significance*, tr. Michael Robertson (Cambridge, Mass: The MIT Press, 1995), p. 609. See also p. 606 (in his review of *Negative Dialectics*, Wiggershaus contends that Adorno was aware of how certain of his views were "close" to "existential philosophy").

5. This analysis serves as a reply to those who would see Adorno as a poststructuralist before the fact. In the first sentences of the book, Adorno says: "All attempts to comprehend the writings of philosophers as poetry have missed their truth content. Philosophical form requires the interpretation of the real as a binding nexus of concepts. . . . Only in communication with critical thought may philosophy be tested historically" (K, p. 3). Poststructuralism's rejection of Hegel's "labor of the concept" in favor of an open analysis of "the text" would be rejected by Adorno.

6. Soren Kierkegaard, *Fear and Trembling* and *Repetition*, ed. and tr. Howard V. Hong and Edna H. Hong (N.J.: Princeton University Press, 1971), p. 90.

7. There is a good deal of hostility toward Adorno's interpretation of Kierkegaard—much of it revolving around this very point. (Indeed, I had the chance personally to encounter some of this hostility when presenting an earlier draft of this chapter at the Society for Phenomenology and Existential Philosophy.) Still, not all Kierkegaard scholars would disagree with Adorno on this point. See, for example, Louis Mackey, "The Loss of the World in Kierkegaard's Ethics," in his *Points of View: Readings of Kierkegaard* (Tallahassee: Florida State University Press, 1986).

8. Walter Benjamin, whose own work inspired Adorno's depiction of the bourgeois *interieur*, presciently stated that it is "very possible the author's later books will spring from this one" (K, p. xii [translator's foreword]).

9. My following explication of the ambigous phrase "construction of the aesthetic" draws upon both Buck-Morss and Wiggershaus.

10. See, for example, Theodor W. Adorno, "The Idea of Natural History," *Telos* no. 60 (Summer 1984), pp. 111–112

11. Theodor W. Adorno, "The Actuality of Philosophy," p. 126.

12. Ibid., p. 127.

13. See Louis Mackey, *Kierkegaard: A Kind of Poet* (Philadelphia: University of Pennsylvania Press, 1971), pp. 3–4.

14. See, for example, John D. Caputo, "Instants, Secret and Singularities: Dealing Death in Kierkegaard and Derrida," in *Kierkegaard in Post/Modernity* ed. Martin J. Matustik and Merold Westphal (Indianapolis: Indiana University Press, 1995).

15. See, for example, Martin J. Matustik, *Postnational Identity: Critical Theory and Existential Philosophy in Habermas, Kierkegaard, and Havel* (New York: The Guilford Press, 1993), which seems to have been inspired by Habermas's 1987 Copenhagen lectures.

16. Soren Kierkegaard, *Concluding Unscientific Postscript to Philosophical Fragments*, tr. and ed. Howard V. Hong and Edna H. Hong (N.J.: Princeton University Press, 1992), pp. 72–73.

17. Siegfried Kracauer (who taught Adorno when he was a young man, and subsequently became a colleague at the Frankfurt School), wrote to Leo Lowenthal that "if Teddie one day makes a real declaration of his love . . . it will undoubtedly take such a difficult form that the young lady will have to have read the whole of Kierkegaard . . . to understand Teddie at all." Leo Lowenthal, "Recollections of Adorno," *Telos* no. 61 (Fall 1984), p. 160.

18. Along these lines, Adorno and Horkheimer state in *Dialectic of Enlightenment* that "with the notion of determinate negativity, Hegel revealed an element that distinguishes the Enlightenment from the positivist degeneracy to which he attributes it. By ultimately making the conscious result of the whole process of negation—totality in system and in history—into an absolute, he of course contravened the prohibition and himself lapsed into mythology" (p. 24).

19. "Philosophical Fragments" was the book's title when it was first circulated among the other members of the exiled Institute for Social Research. Robert Hullot-Kentor, "Back to Adorno," *Telos* no. 81 (Fall 1989), p. 6.

20. Soren Kierkegaard, *Philosophical Fragments*, tr. and ed. Howard V. Hong and Edna H. Hong (N.J.: Princeton University Press, 1985), pp. 44–45.

21. "Mediately to affirm immediacy, instead of comprehending it as mediated within itself, is to pervert thought into an apologia of its antithesis, into the immediate lie. This perversion serves all bad purposes, from the private pig-headedness of 'life's-like-that' to the justification of social injustice as a law of nature. . . . Dialectical mediation is not a recourse to the more abstract, but a resolution of the concrete in itself" (MM, pp. 73–74).

22. Without putting too fine a point on it, even certain substantive aspects of Kierkegaard's thought, albeit his earlier thought, tend to approach Adorno's concern with trying to experience otherness in its concreteness. In the *Concept of Irony*,

Kierkegaard compares the concept to a philosophical knight and the phenomenon to a woman, and asserts that "even if the observer does bring the concept along with him, it is still of great importance that the phenomenon remain inviolate and that the concept be seen as coming into existence through the phenomenon." As far as it goes, this resonates with Adorno's claim that the concept is true only to the degree that it is false—that is, a true concept is a concept that is not "true" in a metaphysical sense, for only a concept that is not "true" in the metaphysical sense retains the fluidity to let itself continually pass away in response to the ever changing nature of the phenomenon. See Soren Kierkegaard, *The Concept of Irony*, tr. and ed. Howard V. Hong and Edna H. Hong (N.J.: Princeton University Press, 1989), p. 9.

23. Kierkegaard, *Concluding Unscientific Postscript*, p. 8.

24. Ibid., pp. 81–82.

25. See ibid., pp. 191–192.

26. Theodor W. Adorno, "On Kierkegaard's Doctrine of Love," in *Soren Kierkegaard: Modern Critical Views*, ed. Harold Bloom (New York: Chelsea House Publishers, 1989), pp. 19–34.

27. Ibid., p. 28.

28. Ibid., p. 29. Kierkegaard even had the beginnings of a critique of capitalism that augurs certain Adornian themes. While battling the *Corsair*, he laments that "when passion and commercial interests determine the issue, when there is no room for the harmony of category relations but only the rattle of money in the cash box, and when passion is propelled to the extreme that even the subscriber buys along with the paper the right contemptibly to dispatch what is being written —this is another matter." As James Marsh says, much of the critique is already present, namely, the corrupting influence of money, the way that money smooths over category differences, the ability of the media to arouse a debased form of passion, and the license to dismiss complicated works that are not easily reduced to the lowest common denominator. See James L. Marsh, "Kierkegaard and Critical Theory," in *Kierkegaard in Post/Modernity*, pp. 199–215.

29. Kierkegaard, *Concluding Unscientific Postcript*, p. 233.

30. Ibid., p. 75.

Chapter 2: Adorno and Heidegger

1. *Jargon of Authenticity*, published in 1964, was to be a part of *Negative Dialectics*, but its size and tenor caused Adorno to carve it out from the rest of the book, which was published in 1966.

2. See, for example, Martin Jay, *Adorno* (Cambridge, Mass: Harvard University Press, 1984), p. 52.

3. See, for example, Fred Dallmayr, *Between Freiburg and Frankfurt: Toward a Critical Ontology* (Amherst: University of Massachusetts Press, 1991): "Needless to say,

Adorno's antagonism was greatly deepened and intensified by Heidegger's pro-Nazi affiliation" (p. 54). Dallmayr's view, which shall be considered in greater detail in the second part of this chapter, builds on Hermann Mörchen's *Adorno und Heidegger: Untersuchung Einer Philosophischen Kommunikations verweigerung* (Stuttgart: Klett-Cotta, 1981).

4. Dallmayr, *Between Freiburg and Frankfurt*, p. 45.

5. Heidegger's philosophy also expresses an "ontological need," as the title of part I, section I of *Negative Dialectics* suggests. The "ontological need," Adorno says, is the "emphatic need . . . that Kant's verdict on a knowledge of the Absolute should not be the end of the matter" (ND, p. 61).

6. In contrast to Heidegger, even Kierkegaard, whose conception of inwardness Heidegger draws on, grasped this phenomena quite well. In the wake of the "Corsair Affair," Kierkegaard speaks quite elegantly about, *inter alia*, the way in which money tends to obliterate category differences. See James L. Marsh, "Kierkegaard and Critical Theory," in *Kierkegaard in Post/Modernity*, ed. Martin J. Matustik and Merold Westphal (Indianapolis: Indiana University Press, 1995).

7. As Heidegger's own words attest, Adorno's charge is right on the money: "authentic existence is not something which floats above falling everydayness [but is] existentially only a modified way in which everydayness is seized upon." Heidegger, *Being and Time*, p. 224. The content of subjectivity is thus beside the point; the right "comportment" is what matters.

8. Given their Heideggerian inheritance, poststructuralists who would read Adorno as one of their own must reconcile, or at least dull the differences, between Adorno and Heidegger. Conversely, second-generation critical theorists, such as Habermas, feel the need to discredit Adorno as an irrationalist to justify the necessity of their own neo-Kantian linguistic turn. It is better to lump Adorno with Heidegger as an irrationalist than recognize that Adorno's dialectical use of reason to critique reason could be used to critique their own notion of an "ideal speech community."

9. Dallmayr, *Between Freiburg and Frankfurt*, p. 53, quoting Adorno, "A Portrait of Walter Benjamin," in *Prisms*, tr. Samuel and Shierry Weber (Cambridge, Mass: The MIT Press, 1994), p. 231.

10. Adorno, "A Portrait of Walter Benjamin," in *Prisms*, p. 231.

11. Ibid., p. 235. It is clearly not by accident that poststructuralists, like Derrida, have been much quicker to embrace Benjamin than Adorno.

12. Simon Jarvis, *Adorno: A Critical Introduction* (New York: Routledge, 1998), p. 199.

13. See Fredric Jameson, *Late Marxism: Adorno, or, the Persistence of the Dialectic* (New York: Verso, 1990), p. 73.

14. Jürgen Habermas, *The Theory of Communicative Action, Vol. 1: Reason and the Rationalization of Society*, tr. Thomas McCarthy (Boston: Beacon Press, 1984), p. 385.

15. Habermas, whose desire to differentiate theoretical (or instrumental) reason, practical reason, and art harks back to Kant, would do well to recall that the *Critique of Pure Reason* deals with the limits of reason, not its untrammeled ascendance, and that the *Critique of Judgment*, which deals with aesthetic matters, performs a crucial mediating function in Kant's architectonic.

16. This paper was presented by Adorno at the Frankfurt chapter of the Kant Society in 1932. See Theodor Adorno, "The Idea of Natural History," *Telos* no. 60 (1984).

17. Ibid., p. 114.

18. Indeed, Adorno broke with Benjamin, who was the one that initially formulated the idea of juxtaposing phenomena in constellations, exactly on this point. Adorno believed that Benjamin relied too much upon the moment of intuition, and not enough on theoretical interpretation. See Buck-Morss, *The Origin of Negative Dialectics*, pp. 113–114.

19. Dallmayr, *Between Freiburg and Frankfurt*, p. 49.

20. See, for example, Robert C. Solomon, *In the Spirit of Hegel* (New York: Oxford University Press, 1983), p. 328, n.15. (Hegel suggests that "given vastly different sensory inputs, the universality of our concepts would nevertheless yield similar experiences of the world; in other words, our experience is overdetermined by our concepts.")

21. Dallmayr, *Between Freiburg and Frankfurt*, p. 50.

22. Buck-Morss, *The Origin of Negative Dialectics*, pp. 58–59.

23. Dallmayr, *Between Freiburg and Frankfurt*, p. 47.

24. According to Wiggershaus, "Adorno criticized Heidegger's genteel aversion to science, which merely served to confirm its impotence. He criticized Heidegger's aversion to the world of motorways and modern technology. . . ." See Wiggershaus, *The Frankfurt School*, p. 593.

25. Along these lines, see Jameson, *Late Marxism*, pp. 109–110.

26. Dallmayr, *Between Freiburg and Frankfurt*, p. 47.

27. Ibid., p. 48.

28. Martin Heidegger, "Letter on Humanism," *Martin Heidegger: Basic Writings*, ed. David Farrell Krell (New York: HarperCollins 1993), p. 254 (emphasis added).

29. Peter Hohendahl, *Prismatic Thought: Theodor W. Adorno* (Lincoln, Nebraska: University of Nebraska Press, 1995), p. 232.

30. See part III, pp. 173–179.

31. In *Being and Time*, Heidegger says that "in Dasein's everydayness the agency through which most things come about is one of which we must say that 'it was no one'" (p. 165).

32. J. M. Bernstein, *Adorno: Disenchantment and Ethics* (Cambridge: Cambridge University Press, 2001), p. 4.

33. Ibid., pp. 38–39 (emphasis in original).

Chapter 3: Adorno and Husserl

1. Adorno, "The Actuality of Philosophy," p. 122.

2. Theodor W. Adorno, "Husserl and the Problem of Idealism," *The Journal of Philosophy* no. 37 (1940), p. 6.

3. Ibid., p. 9.

4. Ibid., p. 17.

5. Adorno acknowledges that empiricists have never clearly defended the idea of "the absolutely first" like rationalists, but he asserts, nevertheless, that even empiricism falls prey to the impulse. By accepting as given that which is apprehended, empiricists, in some sense, privilege the object, while ignoring "the moment of freedom and spontaneity" that the subject contributes to existence. What is apprehended, therefore, is not "sheer existence," but rather a human made world that is not simply a given (AE, pp. 23–24).

6. See, for example, Adorno, "Husserl and the Problem of Idealism," pp. 10–11.

7. This example is taken from Maurice Natanson, *Edmund Husserl: Philosopher of Infinite Tasks* (Evanston, Ill.: Northwestern University, 1973), p. 68.

8. Another way that Husserl falls behind Kant is in his reversal of the relation between sensations and perceptions. For Husserl, the perception of things by consciousness is "originary" and unmediated, thus causing the moment of brute materiality that classically has been understood to cause perceptions via sensations to fall out of the picture. For Kant, in contrast, perception is understood to be a performance of thought (see AE, pp. 151–155).

9. "One could say that the doctrine of categorial intuition is the necessary consequense of logical absolutism with respect to the thinking subject." Adorno, "Husserl and the Problem of Idealism," p. 12.

PART II: SUBJECTIVITY IN SARTRE'S EARLY PHILOSOPHY

1. Michel Rybalka and Oreste Pucciano, "An Interview with Jean-Paul Sartre," in *The Philosophy of Jean-Paul Sartre*, ed. Paul Schilpp (La Salle, Ill.: Open Court Publishing Co., 1981), p. 12.

2. Leo Fretz, "An Interview with Jean-Paul Sartre," in *Jean-Paul Sartre: Contemporary Approaches to His Philosophy*, ed. Hugh Silverman and Frederick Elliston (Pittsburgh: Duquesne University Press, 1980), pp. 225–226.

3. Ibid., p. 226.

4. Jean-Paul Sartre, *The Emotions: Outline of a Theory*, tr. Bernard Frechtman (New York: Citadel, 1975), p. 82.

5. Ibid.

6. In the Schilpp interview Sartre admits that "what is particularly bad in *Being and Nothingness* is the specifically social chapters . . ." Rybalka and Pucciano, "An Interview with Jean-Paul Sartre," p. 13.

7. Thomas Flynn makes this point in his *Sartre and Marxist Existentialism* (Chicago: University of Chicago Press, 1984), p. 29.

8. In a wonderfully prescient remark, Sartre states that "people have made of speech a language which speaks all by itself. This is an error which should not be made with regard to speech or any other technique. . . . [Otherwise] we shall have lost forever the possibility of meeting the technician" (B&N, p. 662).

9. The example of Foucault, whose antihumanistic impulses led him to describe his academic appointment as a "Chair in the History of the Systems of Thought," is instructive here. More than any other poststructuralist, Foucault was dedicated to the idea of social resistance, but given his genealogical framework the normative grounding for his advocacy of this resistance is less than clear. This problem is only exacerbated when Foucault turns to an ethics of self care in his last works. As Richard J. Bernstein says, Foucault's ethics "presupposes the notion of an ethical or moral agent that can be free and that can 'master' itself. But Foucault not only fails to explicate this sense of agency, his genealogical analyses seem to effectively undermine any talk of agency which is not a precipitate of power/knowledge regimes. Who or what is left to transgress historical limits?" Richard J. Bernstein, *The New Constellation* (Cambridge: MIT Press, 1995), p. 164. At any rate, there can be no question but that Foucault himself viewed the *Critique of Dialectical Reason* as an extension of Sartre's earlier work, which is why he described the book as "the magnificent and pathetic attempt by a man of the nineteenth century to think the twentieth century."

Chapter 4: The Frankfurt School's Critique of Sartre

1. See Martin Jay, *The Dialectical Imagination* (Boston: Little, Brown and Company, 1973), pp. 273–274.

2. Herbert Marcuse, *Studies in Critical Philosophy*, tr. Joris De Bres (Boston: Beacon Press, 1972), pp. 157–190.

3. See Theodor W. Adorno, "Commitment," in *The Essential Frankfurt School Reader*, ed. Andrew Arato and Eike Gebhardt (New York: The Continuum Publishing Company, 1993), pp. 300–318.

4. Jean-Paul Sartre, "Kierkegaard: The Singular Universal," in *Between Existentialism and Marxism*, tr. John Mathews (New York: Morrow Quill Paperbacks, 1974), p. 168. I would like to point out that Sartre's criticisms here could be applied to Heidegger without changing a word.

5. See Seyla Benhabib's Introduction to Marcuse's *Hegel's Ontology and the Theory of Historicity*, tr. Seyla Benhabib (Mass: The MIT Press, 1987), p. xxxi.

6. Marcuse, *Studies in Critical Philosophy*, p. 161.

7. In contrast to French existentialism's less insightful critics, who see it as a revolt against reason, Marcuse begins "Sartre's Existentialism" by pointing out that the impetus for French existentialism was the same as it was for Cartesianism, that is, a social situation that defies rational precepts. Like Descartes, the French existentialists put great stock in the mind's lucidity, but while Descartes believed that God had founded a rational universe that must be accessible to humankind, the atheistic French existentialists believe that thought operates within an indifferent universe that deprives us of a transcendental refuge. Thus, Camus posits "the Absurd," which stresses our "consciousness and revolt" in the face of a world in which we must live "without appeal." But unlike Camus, who will not try to philosophically explicate "the Absurd," which is inexplicable by its own terms, Sartre uses "the Absurd" as the starting point for a philosophy of concrete human existence.

8. Marcuse, *Studies in Critical Philosophy*, p. 162.

9. Ibid., pp. 162–163.

10. Ibid., p. 171.

11. Ibid., pp 173–174.

12. Ibid., p. 176.

13. Ibid., p. 178.

14. Ibid., p. 179.

15. See Jay, *The Dialectical Imagination*, p. 275.

16. Marcuse, *Studies in Critical Philosophy*, p. 180.

17. Ibid.

18. Ibid.

19. See Herbert Marcuse, *One-Dimensional Man* (Boston: Beacon Paperback, 1964), pp. 71–78.

20. Marcuse, *Studies in Critical Philosophy*, pp. 183–184.

21. At the start of "Materialism and Revolution" Sartre says in a footnote that his "criticisms are not directed against [Marx], but against the Marxist scholasticism of 1949." Jean-Paul Sartre, "Materialism and Revolution," *Literary and Philosophical Essays*, tr. Annette Michelson (New York: Criterion Books, 1955), p. 198.

22. Ibid., pp. 244–245.

23. Ibid., pp. 235–236

24. Ibid., pp. 201–202.

25. Ibid., p. 247.

26. Marcuse, *Studies in Critical Philosophy*, p. 183.

27. Karl Marx and Frederick Engels, *The Marx-Engels Reader* (2nd ed.), ed. Robert C. Tucker (New York: W. W. Norton & Company, 1978), p. 60.

28. Marcuse, *Studies in Critical Philosophy*, p. 189.

Chapter 5: Sartre's Relation to His Predecessors in the Phenomenological and Existential Traditions

1. Arthur C. Danto, *Sartre* (London: Fontana Press, 1991), pp. 35–37.

2. Ibid., p. 37.

3. Hubert C. Dreyfus, *Being-in-the-World: A Commentary on Heidegger's Being and Time, Division 1* (Cambridge, Mass: MIT Press, 1994), p. 13.

4. Jacques Derrida, "The Ends Of Man," in *Margins of Philosophy*, tr. Alan Bass (Chicago: The University of Chicago Press, 1982), p. 115 (parentheses omitted).

5. Jean-Paul Sartre, *Nausea*, tr. Lloyd Alexander (NewYork: New Directions Publishing Corp., 1964), p. 127.

6. Ibid., p. 151.

7. Ibid., p. 128.

8. Danto makes a similar argument in *Sartre* at pp. 7–8.

9. Sartre's idea of nothingness thus precludes pre-representational knowing in any strong sense. In contrast, for Heidegger, the overcoming of nothingness, which is a theoretical possibility given fundamental ontology's account of nothingness, is tantamount to the overcoming of the problem of representation. And, as we have seen, Adorno exposes the fascistic implications of this move. For this reason, as well as others that cannot be addressed here, I do not see why poststructuralists honor Heidegger almost as much as they dishonor Sartre.

10. Jean-Paul Sartre, "Existentialism Is a Humanism," in *Existentialism and Human Emotions*, tr. Bernard Frechtman (New York: Philosophical Library, 1957), pp. 49–50.

11. This idea of Derrida moving "upstream" towards *différance* is offered by Peter Dews, who contends that Adorno, by comparison, "moves 'downstream' towards an account of subjectivity as emerging from and entwined with the natural and historical world." Peter Dews, *Logics of Disintegration: Poststructuralist Thought and the Claims of Critical Theory* (London: Verso, 1987), p. 19.

12. Aron's comment, which was made during the course of his Gifford Lectures, is quoted in Thomas R. Flynn, "Praxis and Vision: Elements of a Sartrean Epistemology," *Philosophical Forum* 8 (1976–1977), p. 21.

13. Rybalka and Pucciani, "An Interview with Jean-Paul Sartre," p. 10.

14. Strictly, the question becomes whether the consciousness of nonpositional consciousness corresponds to the objects that are present to positional consciousness, which is translucent.

15. In the example that accompanies this statement, Sartre contends that consciousness of a table requires "consciousness of being consciousness of the table" (B&N, p. 11), which suggests that "knowledge" is being used here in its most generic sense—that is, as mere awareness. Indeed, it's not clear to me that this sort of "knowl-

edge" is even intuitive "knowledge," which for Sartre has a more revelatory quality than mere awareness. In any case, when speaking of "knowledge" that is nonconceptual in nature, I shall continue to use quotation marks.

16. Thomas R. Flynn, "Praxis and Vision: Elements of a Sartrean Epistemology," p. 25.

17. Jean-Paul Sartre, *Truth and Existence*, tr. Adrian van den Hoven, ed. Ronald Aronson (Chicago: The University of Chicago Press, 1992), p. 61.

18. Ibid., p. 67.

19. Ibid.

20. Thomas R. Flynn, "Praxis and Vision: Elements of a Sartrean Epistemology," p. 23.

21. I shall consider the distinction between "purifying" and "accessory" reflections in connection with my discussion of the "fundamental project" in the next chapter. At this juncture, however, there is one point worth noting. Although Sartre equivocally denies that pure reflection is the same as Husserl's phenomenological reduction in this passage, certain commentators, like Francis Jeanson, contend that the two are actually one and the same thing: "Phenomenology, in describing the planes of unreflectivity and accessory reflection, makes use of a purifying reflection that is none other than Husserl's famous 'reduction.'" See Francis Jeanson, *Sartre and the Problem of Morality*, tr. Robert V. Stone (Bloomington: Indiana University Press, 1980), p. 183. But as Jeanson rightly points out, this purifying reflection, which Sartre describes as a "katharsis" (B&N, p. 224), is more ethical than epistemological in nature.

22. Heidegger, *Being and Time*, p. 299.

23. Gillian Rose makes a strong argument against this approach in *Mourning Becomes the Law: Philosophy and Representation* (New York: Cambridge University Press, 1996).

24. Nor for that matter, as we saw, will Adorno, who sums up his opposition to the philosophical use of death with a remark by Horkheimer. In response to a disciple of Heidegger who remarked that at least Heidegger had once again placed human beings before death, Horkheimer replied that Ludendorff had done it much better. Adorno, *The Jargon of Authenticity*, p. 138.

25. Jean-Paul Sartre, "The Wall," in *The Wall and Other Short Stories*, tr. Lloyd Alexander (New York: New Directions, 1975), p. 8. See also Jeanson, *Sartre and the Problem of Morality*, p. 186.

Chapter 6: Sartre's Mediating Subjectivity

1. My reason for italicizing the "must" in this sentence will become clear in connection with my discussion of bad faith and the fundamental project.

2. While many seize upon the phrase that "man is a useless passion" to read into Sartre nihilistic impulses, the book's overarching moral concerns tend to give short shrift to this ontologically driven thesis.

3. Along these lines, Sartre points out that there is no such thing as "destruction" when strictly speaking in terms of the in-itself. A massive earthquake, for example, does not destroy anything; it only rearranges existing matter, such that the result is a "different" material configuration. But even this characterization of difference understates the point, for the recognition of this difference requires a witness who can make the comparison. The point is that "in order for destruction to exist, there must first be a relation to man" (B&N, p. 39).

4. For the moment I would briefly like to point out that some commentators press this point a bit too hard, for the prereflective cogito's nonpositional consciousness (of) consciousness is not "intentional" with respect to objects like, more generally, prereflective consciousness's positional consciousness of objects. This is an important point, for if the prereflective cogito were purely intentional with respect to objects, it could be reconciled with Heidegger's rejection of "the subject," that is, it would be at one with positional consciousness's immediate awareness of objects-in-the-world. Under these circumstances, consciousness would lose its efficacy.

5. Although the epitome of nonidentity, Sartre's concept of the subject is nevertheless portrayed by poststructuralists as a reversion to the classical, pre-Heideggerian self-coincidental subject. Matters are, of course, far more complicated.

6. David Detmer makes this point in *Freedom as a Value* (La Salle, Ill.: Open Court, 1986), pp. 29–30.

7. Jean-Paul Sartre, "Consciousness of Self and Knowledge of Self," trs. N. Lawrence and L. Lawrence, in *Readings in Existential Phenomenology*, eds. N. Lawrence and D. O'Connor (Englewood Cliffs, N.J.: Prentice-Hall, 1967), p. 132.

8. According to Sartre, Husserl "shut himself up inside the cogito" out of the fear that he would fall into the Cartesian "error of substance." He thus "remained timidly on the plane of functional description," which suggests that he is actually "a phenomenalist rather than a phenomenologist" (B&N, p. 119).

9. See, for example, Sartre, "Consciousness of Self and Knowledge of Self," p. 119 ("Inasmuch as becoming is in progress and we can never know where it will stop, since we cannot determine if there is an end to history, we always postpone the sum total of knowledge and the particular claims to knowledge. . . . As a result, it is impossible to conceive knowledge by referring to this totality, since that makes it pure probability . . .)

10. Marjorie Grene, *Sartre* (Lanham, Md.: University Press of America, Inc., 1983), p. 119.

11. Ibid., p. 123.

12. In the secondary literature, the term "self-consciousness" is frequently used to refer to both the prereflective cogito's tacit consciousness of self and a knowledge of "the (empirical) self." I have found that this can occasionally be confusing. Thus, in keeping with Sartre's use of parentheses around the "of" in "consciousness (of) self" to distinguish this tacit consciousness of self from a knowledge of self, I will put parentheses around the "self" in "(self-)consciousness" to make this same distinction.

13. It seems to me that Sartre's response to Heidegger's rejection of (self-)consciousness here is roughly a replay of Kant's response to Hume's rejection of the self—namely, that just by asserting "I never can catch myself at any time without a perception, and never can observe anything but the perception," Hume already presupposes the "I" he cannot find. See David Hume, *A Treatise of Human Nature* (New York: Penguin Books, 1989), p. 300. As I argued earlier, there are numerous similarities between Kant's transcendental unity of apperception and Sartre's prereflective cogito, not the least of which is that both are a necessary condition for reflection. Thus, like Kant, Sartre avoids falling prey to Hume's claim that my "self" (the "empirical ego") is not to be found in my perceptions, for both Kant and Sartre would agree. But in contrast to the transcendental unity of apperception, which stands "behind" experience and makes it possible, the preflective cogito is actually one with experience—albeit nonthetically.

14. Manfred Frank, "Is Self-Consciousness a Case of Presence to Self," tr. Andrew Bowie, *Derrida: A Critical Reader*, ed. David Wood (Oxford: Blackwell Publishers, 1992), quoted in Roger Frie, *Subjectivity and Intersubjectivity in Modern Philosophy and Psychoanalysis: A Study of Sartre, Binswanger, Lacan, and Habermas* (Lanham, Md.: Rowman and Littlefield Publishers, 1997), p. 49.

15. In his lecture to the *Société française de philosophie*, Sartre contends, for example, that "it is advisable to conceive" of the prereflective cogito. See "Consciousness of Self and Knowledge of Self," p. 122.

16. In Heidegger's "hammer example," reflection is what takes place when an object that is ready-to-hand breaks and becomes merely present-to-hand. The laborer then "reflects" upon the broken hammer, but he does not (neither, by implication, does he ever) reflect upon the broader nature of his specific project, much less his deeper projects, such as, say, choosing to be a carpenter in the first place. Heidegger's argument for authenticity notwithstanding, this seems to be just the kind of reflection that he wants to close off.

17. Gregory McCulloch, who also relies on this quotation, likewise holds that freedom for Sartre is ultimately phenomenological in nature. See McCulloch's *Using Sartre* (London: Routledge, 1994), pp. 38–45.

18. Even a relatively sympathetic critic such as Thomas C. Anderson maintains that as late as *Being and Nothingness* "the notions of human reality and human freedom that [Sartre] presents remain almost as unreal or abstract as those of his earlier works. See Anderson's *Sartre's Two Ethics* (Chicago: Open Court Publishing Co., 1993), p. 11.

19. At this time, I would remind the reader of my basic thesis, namely, that while the standpoints of phenomenology and Critical Theory are both necessary, neither is sufficient in itself. The phenomenological standpoint, which captures our subjective experience of the world, *must* be augmented by Critical Theory, just as Critical Theory needs a certain kind of phenomenological understanding if it is to meet its emancipatory aims. To flesh out a phenomenological ontology, then, it must, in principle, be compatible with the standpoint of Critical Theory, and it is my claim here that in its general contours, Sartre's phenomenological ontology—as opposed to Heidegger's—meets this requirement.

20. Along these lines Sartre states that "it is possible that I am mistaken; perhaps the objects of the world which I took for eyes were not eyes; perhaps it was only the wind that shook the bush behind me; in short perhaps these concrete objects did not really manifest a look" (B&N, p. 368).

21. "Hodological space" points to the fact that we experience the world's spatiality in human terms, or, more precisely, in terms of human projects. With respect to the relation between hodological space and the Other, Sartre states: "I am situated by the infinite diversity of the roads which lead me to the object of *my* world in correlation with the immediate presence of transcendent subjects. . . . These roads represent only the ensemble of instrumental complexes which allow me to cause an Other-as-object to appear as a "this" on the ground of the world, an Other-as-object who is already implicitly and really contained there" (B&N, pp. 372–373).

22. Sartre's response to Hegel here obviates the need to detail his response to Heidegger on the issue of others. If Hegel, who, like Sartre, adheres to the subject-object paradigm, is reproached for failing to give the prereflective cogito its due, this will also clearly be the charge against Heidegger's anti-Cartesian, antisubjective ontology, and, in fact, it is. Accordingly, while Sartre commends Heidegger for seeing interpersonal relations as purely a question of being, that is, knowledge truly plays no role, he claims that Heidegger's failure to start from the cogito results in an inability to capture the concreteness of specific conciousnesses. Indeed, much like Adorno, Sartre contends that there is an unbridgeable gap between the abstractness of Heidegger's "ontological relation between me and an abstract Other" and "a particular ontic relation between me and Pierre" (see B&N, pp. 334–335).

23. G. W. F. Hegel, *Phenomenology of Spirit*, tr. A. V. Miller (Oxford: Oxford University Press, 1977), p. 110.

24. In contrast to Hegel, however, Sartre also has a thin notion of *reflective* self-consciousness, or reflective knowledge concerning my self, that precedes an encounter with another human being. As we previously saw, in *Transcendence of the Ego*, which is adopted by reference in *Being and Nothingness* (B&N, pp. 155–156), there is an individualistic notion of an "I" or "me" that is just consciousness's reflection on its own activities over time. This leads consciousness to wrongly see itself as made up of "qualities" and "states." And this "transcendent unity" of consciousness, as the title of his prior work states, is "the ego." However, this solipsistic ego is neither the thin (self-)consciousness that I am referring to here (i.e., an immediate awareness of our awareness), nor the empirical ego.

25. G. W. F. Hegel, *Philosophy of Right*, tr. T. M. Knox (Oxford: Oxford University Press, 1967), p. 21.

26. I owe this insight to Michael Theunissen, *The Other: Studies in the Social Ontology of Husserl, Heidegger, Sartre, and Buber*, tr. Christopher Macann (Cambridge, Mass.: MIT Press, 1986), pp. 234–238.

27. I will return to this problem in the next two sections in connection with my discussions of the "fundamental project" and "purifying reflection," respectively.

28. While both the "us-object" and the "we-subject" involve what Heidegger would call *Mitsein*, that is, "being-with" (as opposed to "being-for") others, these two

ways of "being-with" derive from the experiences of "particular consciousnesses," and are thus only derivative in nature: "the 'we' is a certain particular experience which is produced in special cases on the foundation of being-for-others in general" (B&N, pp. 536–537). Moreover, Sartre makes a basic distinction between these two types of "being-with": the "us-object," which entails the collective objectification by a Third, is "ontological" because it derives from the phenomenon of being-for-others; in contrast, the "we-subject" is only "psychological" in nature, for it merely testifies to a way of feeling in the midst of others. Sartre's discussion of the "us-object" in particular, which deals, among other things, with questions of class consciousness, is rich in social insights.

29. See, for example, Ronald E. Santoni, *Bad faith, Good faith, and Authenticity in Sartre's Early Philosophy* (Philadelphia: Temple University, 1995) and Thomas C. Anderson, *Sartre's Two Ethics* (Chicago: Open Court Publishing Co., 1993).

30. Ibid., p. xxvi.

31. Ibid., p. 86.

32. Ibid.

33. Heidegger, *Being and Time*, p. 344.

34. Sartre himself states that "it is impossible to determine in each particular case what comes from freedom and what comes from the brute being of the for-itself. The given in-itself as resistance or aid is revealed only in the light of the projected freedom" (B&N, p. 627).

35. "Consciousness instead of directing its negation outward turns it toward itself. This attitude, it seems to me, is bad faith" (B&N, p. 87).

36. See Theunissen, *The Other: Studies in the Social Ontology of Husserl, Heidegger, Sartre, and Buber*, pp. 222–224.

37. Anderson, *Sartre's Two Ethics*, p. 54 (italics added).

38. Detmer, *Freedom as a Value*, p. 112.

39. Jean-Paul Sartre, *Notebooks for an Ethics*, tr. David Pellauer (Chicago: University of Chicago Press, 1992), p. 472.

40. In *Sartre's Two Ethics*, Anderson quotes Sartre's statement in *Notebooks for an Ethics* that pure reflection "renounces being as in-itself-for-itself, that is, as the cause of itself" (p. 53). Of course, this is done in the name of autonomous and contingent freedom. But Anderson omits the rest of this passage, which seems to support my position. Thus, Sartre continues, in spite of this renunciation, "to acquire this autonomy and this regaining of contingency, the existent must first accept and take up its mode of being, which is precisely the mode of diasporic being. More exactly, the assumption of this mode of being is, radically, one with the regaining of the self on the basis of contingency." See Jean-Paul Sartre, *Notebook for an Ethics*, p. 479.

41. I have argued elsewhere that Camus gives us just such a character in *The Stranger*. Because Meursault has no projects, and, ultimately, no initial project because he has prereflectively rejected Sartre's fundamental project, he comes across as dis-

tinctly less than human. See David Sherman, "Camus's Meursault and Sartrian Irresponsibility," *Philosophy and Literature* 19: 60–77 (1995).

42. Robert C. Solomon, *Dark Feelings, Grim Thoughts: Experience and Reflection in Camus and Sartre* (New York: Oxford University Press, 2006).

43. In *Notebooks for an Ethics*, Sartre once again emphasizes the need to "renounce the category of *appropriation*," and to acknowledge "the unappropriable aspect of the reflected-upon *Erlebnis*" (p. 479). I emphasize this, as well as the fact that Sartre often refers to seriousness as "bourgeois seriousness," to make clear that we must not throw the baby out with the bathwater. Although we cannot appropriate and forever possess the for-itself-in-itself, as the bourgeois consciousness mistakenly strives to appropriate and possess everything in its path (with the unwitting aim of becoming for-itself-in-itself), we still must continue to strive toward it, albeit in a different spirit.

44. Herbert Fingarette, *Self-Deception* (London: Routledge & Kegan Paul, 1969).

45. In a 1949 interview, Sartre depicted the "problem of morality" as the seeming unavoidability of taking others as a means when engaging in action: "In the choice I make of my freedom, that [i.e., the freedom] of others is also demanded; but when I move to the plane of action, I have to take the other person as a means and not an ends. Here we are obviously faced with an antinomy." This antinomy, according to Robert V. Stone, is what led Sartre to abandon his work on ethics. See the Translator's Introduction to Jeanson, *Sartre and the Problem of Morality*, p. xiv. It is somewhat ironic that Sartre is more fussy here than Kant, who at least only demands that others not be treated *exclusively* as a means.

46. Sartre, "The Itinerary of a Thought," in *Between Existentialism and Marxism*, p. 34.

47. Ibid., pp. 34–35.

48. Rybalka and Pucciani, "An Interview with Jean-Paul Sartre," p. 21.

49. Ibid., p. 20.

50. Detmer, *Freedom as a Value*, p. 59.

51. Marcuse, *Studies in Critical Philosophy*, p. 174.

52. Detmer, *Freedom as a Value*, p. 66.

53. See also Louis Mackey, "The Loss of the World in Kierkegaard's Ethics," *The Review of Metaphysics*, vol. XV, no. 4 (June 1962), p. 613.

54. Phyllis Berdt Kenevan, "Self-Consciousness and the Ego in the Philosophy of Sartre," in *The Philosophy of Jean-Paul Sartre*, p. 207.

55. Ibid.

56. Jeanson, *Sartre and the Problem of Morality*, p. 183.

57. We saw earlier that Sartre states in *The Transcendence of the Ego* that a "pure reflection . . . is not necessarily phenomenological reduction" (TE, p. 64), but in *Being and Nothingness* he seems to suggest otherwise. For instance, near the beginning of his discussion of the structures of the for-itself, Sartre contends that "it is on the reflective

level only that we can attempt an epoche, a putting between parentheses, only there that we can refuse what Husserl calls *mitmachen*" (B&N, p. 122).

58. Jeanson, *Sartre and the Problem of Morality*, p. 192. Jeanson goes on to say that "we cannot smother the calls of doubt, of negation, of revolt, and of challenge that rise within us" (p. 200).

59. Sartre, "Consciousness of Self and Knowledge of Self," p. 132.

60. Thus, I am confronted by "collective and already constituted techniques which aim at making me apprehend the world in a form whose meaning has been defined outside of me," which means that "to be free is not to choose the historic world in which one arises—which would have no meaning—but to choose oneself in the world whatever this may be." (B&N, pp. 657–658).

61. Heidegger, *Being and Time*, p. 224.

62. Ibid., p. 299.

63. Bracketing the question of the movie's overall merit, *Schindler's List* offers a good example of this. When Schindler sits atop a horse on the summit of a peak overlooking a pogrom below, a little girl in a red coat stands out against what is now the black-and-white backdrop of the larger mayhem. At this moment, one senses that Schindler's initial project changes from an exploitive war profiteer, who would not have "spelled out" this girl, to a rescuer of the innocent. The point, however, is that Schindler's larger subjective constitution, his complete set of previous experiences, had to be of such a nature that the transition to such a project, looked at retrospectively, could (at least in theory) be made intelligible.

64. Francis Jeanson makes roughly the same argument. See Jeanson, *Sartre and the Problem of Morality*, pp. 200–202. And, according to Sartre, who penned a letter-foreward to *Sartre and the Problem of Morality*, Jeanson "so perfectly followed the development of [Sartre's] thought" that he had "come to pass beyond the position [Sartre] had taken in his books at the moment [Sartre] was passing beyond it himself" (p. xxxix). Crucial differences remain between my account and Jeanson's, however. To truly "pass beyond" Sartre's position, I am arguing, requires rejecting, among other things, the idea that the exercise of freedom is not subject to reasons, the overly reductive notion of the initial project, and, more generally, as I argued in the last section, a hard ontological notion of "authenticity" itself.

65. Sartre, *Notebook for an Ethics*, p. 473.

66. Ibid., p. 474.

67. Ibid., p. 557.

68. Ibid., p. 57.

69. Ibid., p. 393.

70. See also SM, p. 32n.: "The methodological principle which holds that certitude begins with reflection in no way contradicts the anthropological principle which defines the concrete person by his materiality. For us, reflection is not reduced to the simple immanence of idealist subjectivism; it is a point of departure only if it throws us back immediately among things and men, in the world."

71. William L. McBride, *Sartre's Political Theory* (Bloomington: Indiana University Press, 1991), p. 202.

72. Immanuel Kant, *Foundations of the Metaphysics of Morals* (2nd ed.), tr. Lewis White Beck (Upper Saddle River, N.J.: Prentice Hall, 1997), p. 65.

73. Hegel, *Phenomenology of Spirit*, p. 45.

Part III: Adorno's Dialectic of Subjectivity

1. As I maintained in part II, although *Being and Nothingness* does not look at the *concrete* sociohistorical conditions in which its subject moves, given that it builds from the standpoint of consciousness, critics should not minimize the importance of the "situation," which implicitly incorporates these conditions. It is for this reason that Sartre says in *Notebooks for an Ethics* that "*Being and Nothingness* is an ontology before conversion." Jean-Paul Sartre, *Notebooks for an Ethics*, tr. David Pellauer (Chicago: University of Chicago Press, 1992), p. 6. This means that the phenomenological structures of consciousness characterized in *Being and Nothingness* must be considered from the standpoint of a social world in need of a "radical conversion," which would bring about "an ethics of deliverance and salvation" (B&N, p. 534).

2. Theodor W. Adorno, "Subject and Object," in *The Essential Frankfurt School Reader*, eds. Andrew Arato and Eike Gebhardt (New York: Continuum Publishing Co., 1993), pp. 497–498.

3. Ibid., p. 498.

4. Rolf Wiggershaus, *The Frankfurt School: Its History, Theories, and Political Significance*, tr. Michael Robertson (Cambridge, Mass.: MIT Press, 1995), p. 589.

5. This charge, as we saw, also pertains to Benjamin, who attacks not merely an "over-inflated subjectivism, but rather the subjective dimension itself." See Theodor W. Adorno, "A Portrait of Walter Benjamin," in *Prisms*, tr. Samuel and Shierry Weber (Cambridge: Mass.: The MIT Press, 1994), p. 235.

6. Adorno, "Subject and Object," p. 509.

7. For Heidegger, "subjectivity" presupposes self-reflection and the representation of experience, or the Cartesian subject. But as I am using the term, "subjectivity" refers to one's own particular experience of the world, and the hermeneutical self-understanding that this particular experience engenders. Thus, even Heidegger's carpenter in *Being and Time* has a "subjectivity" in that he necessarily experiences his world in a particular way due to being situated in his time and place. As I see it, what Heidegger objects to is the space between the subject and his subjectivity that I am arguing for here, which presupposes personal freedom and self-determination.

8. See, for example, Theodor W. Adorno, "Sociology and Psychology," *New Left Review* 47 (1968), which shall be considered below.

9. Jean-Paul Sartre, *The Age of Reason*, tr. Eric Sutton (New York: Vintage Books, 1973).

10. Martin Jay refers to Schmidt's article, "Adorno—ein Philosoph des realen Humanismus," in *The Dialectical Imagination* (Boston: Little, Brown and Co., 1973), p. 348, n. 45.

Chapter 7: The (De)Formation of the Subject

1. Peter Uwe Hohendahl, *Prismatic Thought: Theodor Adorno* (Lincoln: University of Nebraska Press, 1995), p. 7.

2. Ibid., pp. 7–8.

3. Jürgen Habermas, *The Philosophical Discourse of Modernity*, tr. Frederick G. Lawrence (Cambridge, Mass: MIT Press, 1987), p. 106.

4. Ibid.

5. Ibid., p. 129.

6. I am thus in agreement with Douglas Kellner, who asserts that "*Dialectic of Enlightenment* is best read as a history and pre-history of the bourgeois subject and that subject's project of the domination of nature, rather than as an ontological history of the relationship between the human species and nature. In other words . . . the authors' philosophy of history is best read as a philosophical analysis of a certain epoch of history, rather than an essay in universal history and ontology." Douglas Kellner, *Critical Theory, Marxism, and Modernity* (Baltimore: The Johns Hopkins University Press, 1989), pp. 87–88

7. G. W. F. Hegel, *Phenomenology of Spirit*, tr. A. V. Miller (Oxford: Oxford University Press, 1977), p. 114.

8. Theodor W. Adorno, "Progress," in *Critical Models: Interventions and Catchwords*, tr. Henry W. Pickford (New York: Columbia University Press, 1998), p. 151.

9. Among other changes, according to Robert Hullot-Kentor, "proletariat became worker, capitalist became employer, and exploitation became suffering." Robert Hullot-Kentor, "Back to Adorno," *Telos* no. 81 (fall 1989), p. 6.

10. As Martin Jay says, "the brightest star in Adorno's constellation, to begin with, would be that of Marxism, or more precisely the heterodox tradition of Western Marxist thought." Martin Jay, *Adorno* (Cambridge: Harvard University Press, 1984), p. 15. *Dialectic of Enlightenment* thus represents no break with Marxism, a point that is clearly reflected in one of Adorno's last essays: "Society remains class struggle, today just as in the period when that concept originated . . ." Theodor W. Adorno, "Society," in *Critical Theory and Society: A Reader*, ed. Stephen Bronner and Douglas Kellner (New York: Routledge, 1989), p. 272.

11. The reference to haloes is from *The Communist Manifesto*. Karl Marx and Friedrich Engels, *The Communist Manifesto*, tr. Paul M. Sweezy (New York: Monthly Review Press, 1954), p. 6.

12. Karl Marx, *The Economic and Philosophic Manuscripts of 1844*, tr. Martin Milligan (New York: International Publishers, 1964), pp. 168–169.

13. Karl Marx, *The German Ideology*, ed. C. J. Arthur (New York: International Publishers, 1993), p. 99.

14. In "Reason as Testing Laws," Hegel states: "But that is the reason why this testing does not get very far. Just because the criterion is a tautology, and indifferent to the content, one content is just as acceptable to it as its opposite. Suppose the question is: Ought it to be an absolute law that there should be property? . . . Property, simply as such, does not contradict itself; it is an isolated determinateness, or is posited as merely identical. Non-property, the non-ownership of things, or a common ownership of goods, is just as little self-contradictory. . . ." G. W. F. Hegel, *Phenomenology of Spirit*, pp. 257–258.

15. In *Adorno*, Simon Jarvis also emphasizes this passage, albeit to different ends. Juxtaposing it to another passage in "The Culture Industry: Enlightenment as Mass Deception" essay, in which Adorno and Horkheimer allude to the modern day film producer as a medieval theologian, Jarvis contends that the two passages are examples of "the oldest literary means for registering the gap between the ancient and modern: burlesque and mock-heroic." Unheroically describing Odysseus in terms of modern life and describing the bougeois film producer in a (mock) poignant fashion, he says, is a way for Adorno and Horkheimer to avoid the twin evils that might arise in comparing our experience to its historical precedents—that is, either ahistorically seeing Odysseus as the bearer of timeless human truths or seeing his experience as fundamentally incommensurable with our own. An approach based on the juxtaposition of burlesque and the mock-heroic, however, permits us to see both the identity and difference between the ancient and modern, thus permitting Adorno and Horkheimer both to point to the dominating nature of rationality as a constant theme and yet argue that things could also be otherwise. I agree. Simon Jarvis, *Adorno: A Critical Introduction* (New York: Routledge, 1998), pp. 23–24.

16. In this way, it is like Nietzsche's *Genealogy of Morals*, which was also both a genealogy of the subject and a response to the concrete sociohistorical circumstances in which it arose. If Nietzsche warns us about slave morality's inclination to progressively extirpate the Dionysian component in humanity, and ruthlessly unmasks the psychological underpinnings of this project, it is not for the purpose of lamenting the genesis of slave morality nor ridding humanity of its Apollonian element so as to reintroduce the blond beast (which is assuredly not Nietzsche's idea of the übermensch); instead, it is for the purpose of revealing to (some) people that which has operated to make them less than they could be so that they might ultimately become more than they are. It is a response to what he perceived to be the most pressing challenge of *his* time. And, indeed, without pushing the comparison too hard, the same may be said of Marx's *Capital*. Notwithstanding the positivistic readings of certain self-described Marxists, Marx's *Capital* is a concrete sociohistorical analysis that was meant to be used as a tool by the working classes.

17. As I related earlier, Adorno aims to both construe and deny universal history. At least in one sense, then, the adventures of the Odyssean subject should be seen in a way that is analogous to the early stages of Hegel's *Phenomenology*—that is, as very early stages in subject formation whose contradictions are to be surmounted. Adorno,

of course, denies any inevitability here, but the fact that he sees at least the possibility of a positive universal history is implied, ironically, in his rather pessimistic opening remark in *Negative Dialectics*: "Philosophy, which once seemed obsolete, lives on because the moment to realize it was missed" (ND, p. 3).

18. The episodes involving Circe and the Sirens, in particular, have given rise to various feminist readings, which, unfortunately, cannot be considered here. See, for example, Sabine Wilke and Heidi Schlipphacke, "Construction of a Gendered Subject: A Feminist Reading of Adorno's *Aesthetic Theory*," in *The Semblance of Subjectivity*, eds. Tom Huhn and Lambert Zuidervaart (Cambridge, Mass.: MIT Press, 1997) and Andrew Hewitt, "A Feminine Dialectic of Enlightenment? Horkheimer and Adorno Revisited," *New German Critique* 56 (1992), p. 147.

19. See Michael Clark, "Adorno, Derrida, and the *Odyssey*: A Critique of Center and Periphery," *Boundary 2*: 16 (winter/spring 1989), p. 123.

20. Ibid., p. 126.

21. See Habermas, *The Philosophical Discourse of Modernity*, p. 111.

22. Ibid., p. 112.

23. Ibid.

24. See ibid., p. 129.

25. Fredric Jameson, *Late Marxism: Adorno, or, the Persistence of the Dialectic* (New York: Verso, 1990), p. 144.

26. It is here that Adorno and Horkheimer surpass Georg Lukács's critique of science. That is, although Lukács recognizes in *History and Class Consciousness* that science is smoothly adapted to the imperatives of capitalist society, and that in the hands of the bourgeoise it is an ideological weapon, he does not recognize that in its domineering approach to nature the scientific method in and of itself has the *propensity* to foster hierarchical social relations. See Georg Lukács, *History and Class Consciousness: Studies in Marxist Dialectics*, tr. Rodney Livingstone (Cambridge, Mass.: MIT Press, 1971).

27. Adorno, "Philosophy and Teachers," in *Critical Models*, p. 32.

28. Robert Pippin, *Modernism as a Philosophical Problem* (Oxford: Blackwell Publishers, 1999).

29. Wiggershaus, *The Frankfurt School*, p. 593.

30. Ibid., p. 594.

31. Theodor W. Adorno et al., *The Positivist Dispute in German Sociology*, tr. Glyn Adley and David Frisby (London: Heinemann, 1976), p. 27

32. Max Horkheimer, "Note on Science and the Crisis," in *Critical Theory: Selected Essays* (New York: Continuum Publishing Co., 1992), p. 3.

33. Ibid., p. 5.

34. Ibid., p. 8.

35. J. M. Bernstein, *Recovering Ethical Life: Jürgen Habermas and the Future of Critical Theory* (London: Routledge, 1995), pp. 169–170.

36. Jürgen Habermas, *The Theory of Communicative Action: Volume 1*, tr. Thomas McCarthy (Boston: Beacon Press, 1984), p. 386.

37. Jürgen Habermas, "Labor and Interaction: Remarks on Hegel's Jena Philosophy of Mind," in *Theory and Practice*, tr. John Viertel (Boston: Beacon Press, 1973), p. 159.

38. Ibid., p. 163.

39. This two-step jig is reminiscent of the more popular three-step jig of various strains of "official" Marxism—namely, "thesis, antithesis, synthesis."

40. See Habermas, *The Theory of Communicative Action: Volume 1*, p. 387. ("The two attitudes of mind are representation and action.")

41. Ibid., p. 388.

42. This is the way that Albrecht Wellmer puts it. See Albrecht Wellmer, "The Dialectic of Modernism and Postmodernism: The Critique of Reason since Adorno," in *The Persistence of Modernity: Essays on Aesthetics, Ethics, and Postmodernism*, tr. David Midgley (Cambridge, Mass.: The MIT Press, 1993), p. 74.

43. Habermas, *The Theory of Communicative Action: Volume 1*, p. 385.

44. Ibid., p. 390.

45. Habermas, *The Philosophical Discourse of Modernity*, p. 29.

46. See Joel Whitebook, *Perversion and Utopia: A Study in Psychoanalysis and Critical Theory* (Cambridge, Mass.: MIT Press, 1995), pp. 179–196.

47. In this brief discussion of Habermas's reply to Taylor, I shall draw heavily on the much more detailed discussion of this encounter in J. M Bernstein, *Recovering Ethical Life*, pp. 213–221.

48. See ibid., p. 214, which quotes these same passages.

49. Ibid., p. 218.

50. As I suggested in the introductory segment of this part, an example of this propensity is to be found in Jean-Francois Lyotard's works. In particular, see *Libidinal Economy*, tr. Iain Hamilton Grant (Indianapolis: Indiana University Press, 1993).

51. This is somewhat reminiscent of Adorno and Horkheimer's claim that "the blindfold over Justitia's eyes does not only mean that there should be no assault upon justice, but that justice does not originate in freedom" (DOE, p. 17).

52. Hegel, *Phenomenology of Spirit*, p. 363.

53. Theodor W. Adorno, "Freudian Theory and the Pattern of Fascist Propaganda," in *The Culture Industry*, ed. J. M. Bernstein (London: Routledge, 1991), p. 122.

54. Ibid., p. 118.

55. Adorno, "Sociology and Psychology," p. 81

56. See ibid., pp. 87–88.

57. Adorno, "Freudian Theory and the Pattern of Fascist Propaganda," p. 126.

58. Adorno, "Sociology and Psychology," p. 95.

59. Jessica Benjamin, "The End of Internalization: Adorno's Social Psychology," *Telos* no. 32 (1977), p. 46.

60. Ibid., pp. 42–44.

61. Adorno, "Sociology and Psychology," pp. 85–86 (emphasis added).

62. Ibid., pp. 86–87.

63. I make this distinction because, as I read her, Seyla Benhabib conflates these two concepts. See Seyla Benhabib, *Critique, Norm, and Utopia: A Study of the Foundations of Critical Theory* (New York: Columbia University Press, 1986), p. 207.

64. Whitebook, *Perversion and Utopia*, pp. 132–133.

65. Thus, Benjamin contends, because the "moment of historical possibility failed, [bourgeois] individuality remains the last preserve of critical opposition and consciousness—a form which is dying out. Despite their exhaustive critique of liberal individualism, Adorno and Horkheimer now return to the individual, if only as an explanatory concept for their post mortem." See Benjamin, "The End of Internalization: Adorno's Social Psychology," p. 45.

66. Ibid., pp. 48–49.

67. Adorno, "Subject and Object," pp. 499–500.

68. Benjamin, "The End of Internalization: Adorno's Social Psychology," pp. 59–60.

69. Ibid., p. 60 (emphasis added).

70. Adorno, "Sociology and Psychology," p. 83.

71. Benhabib, *Critique, Norm, and Utopia*, p. 209.

72. Ibid., p. 211.

73. Ibid.

74. Ibid.

75. Adorno, "Sociology and Psychology," p. 97.

Chapter 8: Subjectivity and Negative Dialectics

1. Theodor W. Adorno, *Hegel: Three Studies*, tr. Shierry Weber Nicholsen (Cambridge, Mass.: MIT Press, 1993), p. xxxvi.

2. Karl Marx, "Contribution to the Critique of Hegel's *Philosophy of Right*: Introduction," *The Marx-Engels Reader* (2nd ed.), ed. Robert C. Tucker (New York: W. W. Norton and Co., 1978), p. 59.

3. Ibid., p. 65.

4. Jameson, *Late Marxism*, p. 15.

5. J. M. Bernstein, *Adorno: Disenchantment and Ethics* (Cambridge: Cambridge University Press, 2001).

6. As I indicated earlier, Hegel seems to believe that the universality of our culturally constructed concepts gives rise to similar experiences of the world for persons who otherwise have considerably different sense impressions. Robert C. Solomon, *In the Spirit of Hegel* (New York: Oxford University Press, 1983), pp. 328–329, n. 15.

7. Jameson, *Late Marxism*, p. 16.

8. Bernstein, *Adorno: Disenchantment and Ethics*, p. 30.

9. Ibid.

10. Ibid., p. 35.

11. Jean-Paul Sartre, *Critique of Dialectical Reason: Theory of Practical Ensembles* (vol. 1), tr. Alan Sheridan-Smith (London: Verso, 1991), p. 45.

12. Susan Buck-Morss, *The Origin of Negative Dialectics: Theodor W. Adorno, Walter Benjamin, and the Frankfurt Institute* (New York: The Free Press, 1977), pp. 113–114.

13. In framing the movement of the various segments that comprise the freedom section in this way, I was basically guided by Jameson, although I have somewhat revised his rendition of it. See Jameson, *Late Marxism*, pp. 79–84 *passim.*

14. Theodor W. Adorno, "The Actuality of Philosophy," *Telos* no. 31 (Spring 1977): p. 128.

15. Buck-Morss, *The Origin of Negative Dialectics*, p. 112.

16. In the "Morality, Science, and Art" section of the previous chapter, we saw a perfect example of how this takes place. In applying the categorical imperative, it will be recalled, the social context is tacitly presupposed in the way that the maxim is formulated.

17. Bernstein, *Adorno: Disenchantment and Ethics*, p. 251.

18. Accordingly, Adorno states: "It would be a surrender to heteronomy to admit that autonomy is beyond realization. By stripping those socially substantive terms of their plain meaning, by sublimating them into ideas for the sake of a systematic accord, one would not only be ignoring the text. It is the true source of moral categories which those terms herald with a force too great to be controlled by Kant's intention" (ND, p. 257).

19. Theodor W. Adorno, "On the Historical Adequacy of Consciousness" (interview with Peter von Haselberg), *Telos* no. 56 (Summer 1983), pp. 100–101.

20. Marjorie Grene, *Sartre* (Lanham, Md.: University Press, of America 1983), p. 22.

21. Karl Marx, "The Eighteenth Brumaire of Louis Bonaparte," *The Marx-Engels Reader* (2nd ed.), ed. Robert C. Tucker (New York: W. W. Norton and Co. 1978), p. 595.

22. So, too, in "Aspects of Hegel's Philosophy," Adorno asserts: "If the formation of the concept of the transcendental subject or the absolute spirit sets itself completely outside individual consciousness as something spatiotemporal, when in fact the concept is achieved through individual consciousness, then the concept itself can no longer be made good." Adorno, *Hegel: Three Studies*, p. 15.

23. This quote, which is cited in *Negative Dialectics*, is from Marx and Engel's *The Holy Family*.

24. Adorno, *Hegel: Three Studies*, p. 29.

25. Theodor W. Adorno, "Education for Autonomy" (an interview by Hellmut Becker), *Telos* no. 156 (Summer 1983), p. 108.

26. Although Jameson wrongly compares Adorno's constellations with "Althusserian structural causality," in this limited sense there is an unwitting grain of truth in the comparison. In other words, unlike Althusser, Adorno presupposes the subject, but when Adorno speaks as if the subject that he presupposes is all but overrun by the overarching structures of a bad historical dialectic, as he occasionally does, he could begin to sound a bit like Althusser. In other words, Adorno has history do what Althusser does by theoretical fiat. Jameson, *Late Marxism*, p. 60.

27. Ronald Aronson, *Sartre's Second Critique* (Chicago: The University of Chicago Press, 1987), pp. 236–237.

28. Along these same lines, Adorno declares: "The object's residue as that which remains given after subjective appendages have been subtracted is a delusion of *prima philosophia*. . . . The object is more than pure factuality" (ND, pp. 187–188).

29. So, too, as is the case with Adorno, and in contrast to Kant, who also informs the thought of both (see in this regard, Sartre's "Existentialism is a Humanism"), Sartre refuses to carve out "the third." Thus, he would agree with Adorno's claim that "the Kantian answer—withdrawing the third, as infinite, from positive, finite cognition and using its unattainability to spur cognition to untiring effort—falls short" (ND, p. 175).

Bibliography

Adorno, Theodor W. *Against Epistemology: A Metacritique: Studies in Husserl and the Phenomenological Antinomies*, tr. Willis Domingo (Oxford: Blackwell, 1982).

———. *Dialectic of Enlightenment* (with Max Horkheimer), tr. John Cumming (New York: Continuum, 1991).

———. *Hegel: Three Studies*, tr. Shierry Weber Nicholsen (Cambridge, Mass.: MIT Press, 1993).

———. *Jargon of Authenticity*, tr. Knut Tarnowski and Frederic Will (Evanston: Northwestern University Press, 1973).

———. *Kierkegaard: Construction of the Aesthetic*, tr. Robert Hullot-Kentor (Minneapolis: University of Minnesota Press, 1989).

———. *Minima Moralia*, tr. E. F. N. Jephcott (London: Verso, 1974).

———. *Negative Dialectics*, tr. E. B. Ashton (New York: Continuum, 1992).

———. *Prisms*, tr. Samuel and Shierry Weber (Cambridge, Mass: MIT Press, 1994).

———. *The Authoritarian Personality* (with Else Frenkel-Brunswik, Daniel J. Levinson, and R. Nevitt Sanford), (abridged ed.) (New York: W. W. Norton & Co., 1982).

———. *The Positivist Dispute in German Sociology* (with others), tr. Glyn Adley and David Frisby (London: Heinemann, 1976).

———. "Commitment," in *The Essential Franfurt School Reader*, ed. Andrew Arato and Eike Gebhardt (New York: Continuum, 1993).

———. "Education for Autonomy" (an interview by Hellmut Becker), *Telos* no. 156 (Summer, 1983).

———. "Freudian Theory and the Pattern of Fascist Propaganda," in *The Culture Industry*, ed. J. M. Bernstein (London: Routledge, 1991).

———. "Husserl and the Problem of Idealism," *The Journal of Philosophy* no. 37 (1940).

———. "On the Historical Adequacy of Consciousness" (interview by Peter von Haselberg), *Telos* no. 56 (Summer 1983).

———. "Philosophy and Teachers," in *Critical Models: Interventions and Catchwords*, tr. Henry W. Pickford (New York: Columbia University Press, 1998).

———. "Progress," in *Critical Models: Interventions and Catchwords*, tr. Henry W. Pickford (New York: Columbia University Press, 1998).

———. "Society," in *Critical Theory and Society: A Reader*, ed. Stephen Bronner and Douglas Kellner (New York: Routledge, 1989).

———. "Sociology and Psychology," *New Left Review* 47 (1968).

———. "Subject and Object," in *The Essential Frankfurt School Reader*, ed. Andrew Arato and Eike Gebhardt (New York: Continuum, 1993).

———. "The Actuality of Philosophy," *Telos* no. 31 (Spring 1977).

———. "The Idea of Natural History," *Telos* no. 60 (Summer 1984).

Anderson, Thomas C. *Sartre's Two Ethics* (Chicago: Open Court, 1993).

Aronson, Ronald. *Sartre's Second Critique* (Chicago: The University of Chicago Press, 1987).

Benhabib, Seyla. *Critique, Norm, and Utopia: A Study of the Foundations of Critical Theory* (New York: Columbia University Press, 1986).

Benjamin, Jessica. "The End of Internalization: Adorno's Social Psychology," *Telos* no. 32 (1977).

Bernstein, J. M. *Adorno: Disenchantment and Ethics* (Cambridge: Cambridge University Press, 2001).

———. *Recovering Ethical Life: Jürgen Habermas and the Future of Critical Theory* (London: Routledge, 1995).

Bernstein, Richard J. *The New Constellation* (Cambridge: MIT Press, 1995).

Buck-Morss, Susan. *The Origin of Negative Dialectics: Theodor W. Adorno, Walter Benjamin, and the Frankfurt Institute* (New York: The Free Press, 1977).

Clark, Michael. "Adorno, Derrida, and the *Odyssey*: A Critique of Center and Periphery," *Boundary 2*: 16 (winter/spring 1989).

Dallmayr, Fred. *Between Freiburg and Frankfurt: Toward a Critical Ontology* (Amherst: University of Massachusetts Press, 1991).

Danto, Arthur C. *Sartre* (London: Fontana, 1991).

Deleuze, Gilles and Guattari, Félix. *A Thousand Plateaus*, tr. Brian Massumi (Minneapolis: University of Minnesota Press, 1987).

Derrida, Jacques. "Force of Law: The 'Mystical Foundation of Authority,'" in *Deconstruction and the Possibility of Justice*, eds., Drucilla Cornell, Michel Rosenfeld, and David Gray Carlson (New York: Routledge, 1992).

———. "The Ends Of Man," in *Margins of Philosophy*, tr. Alan Bass (Chicago: The University of Chicago Press, 1982).

Detmer, David. *Freedom as a Value* (La Salle, Illinois: Open Court, 1986).

Dews, Peter. *Logics of Disintegration: Poststructuralist Thought and the Claims of Critical Theory* (London: Verso, 1987).

———. *The Limits of Disenchantment: Essays on Contemporary European Philosophy* (New York: Verso, 1995).

Dreyfus, Hubert C. *Being-in-the-World: A Commentary on Heidegger's Being and Time, Division 1* (Cambridge, Mass: MIT Press, 1994).

Fingarette, Herbert. *Self-Deception* (London: Routledge & Kegan Paul, 1969).

Flynn, Thomas. *Sartre and Marxist Existentialism* (Chicago: University of Chicago Press, 1984).

———. "Praxis and Vision: Elements of a Sartrean Epistemology," *Philosophical Forum* 8 (1976–1977).

Fretz, Leo. "An Interview with Jean-Paul Sartre," in *Jean-Paul Sartre: Contemporary Approaches to His Philosophy*, ed. Hugh Silverman and Frederick Elliston (Pittsburgh: Duquesne University Press, 1980).

Frie, Roger. *Subjectivity and Intersubjectivity in Modern Philosophy and Psychoanalysis: A Study of Sartre, Binswanger, Lacan, and Habermas* (Lanham, Md.: Rowman and Littlefield, 1997).

Grene, Marjorie. *Sartre* (Lanham, Md.: University Press of America, 1983).

Habermas, Jürgen. *The Philosophical Discourse of Modernity*, tr. Frederick G. Lawrence (Cambridge, Mass: MIT Press, 1987).

———. *The Theory of Communicative Action, Volume 1: Reason and the Rationalization of Society*, tr. Thomas McCarthy (Boston: Beacon Press, 1984).

———. "Labor and Interaction: Remarks on Hegel's Jena Philosophy of Mind," in *Theory and Practice*, tr. John Viertel (Boston: Beacon Press, 1973).

Hegel, G. W. F. *Phenomenology of Spirit*, tr. A. V. Miller (Oxford: Oxford University Press, 1977).

———. *Philosophy of Right*, tr. T. M. Knox (Oxford: Oxford University Press, 1967).

Heidegger, Martin. *Being and Time*, tr. John Macquarrie and Edward Robinson (New York: Harper and Row, 1962).

———. "Letter on Humanism," in *Martin Heidegger: Basic Writings*, ed. David Farrell Krell (New York: HarperCollins 1993).

Hohehdahl, Peter. *Prismatic Thought: Theodor W. Adorno* (Lincoln, Nebraska: University of Nebraska Press, 1995).

Horkheimer, Max. *Critical Theory: Selected Essays* (New York: Continuum, 1992).

Hullot-Kentor, Robert. "Back to Adorno," *Telos* no. 81 (Fall 1989).

Jameson, Fredric. *Late Marxism: Adorno, or, The Persistence of the Dialectic* (London: Verso, 1990).

Jarvis, Simon. *Adorno: A Critical Introduction* (New York: Routledge, 1998).

Jay, Martin. *Adorno* (Cambridge, Mass.: Harvard University Press, 1984).

———. *The Dialectical Imagination* (Boston: Little, Brown and Company, 1973).

Jeanson, Francis. *Sartre and the Problem of Morality*, tr. Robert V. Stone (Bloomington, Indiana: Indiana University Press, 1980).

Kant, Immanuel. *Foundations of the Metaphysics of Morals* (2nd ed.), tr. Lewis White Beck (Upper Saddle River, N.J.: Prentice Hall, 1997).

Kellner, Douglas M. *Critical Theory, Marxism, and Modernity* (Baltimore: The Johns Hopkins University Press, 1989).

Kenevan, Phyllis Berdt. "Self-Consciousness and the Ego in the Philosophy of Sartre," in *The Philosophy of Jean-Paul Sartre*, ed. Paul Arthur Schilpp (La Salle, Ill.: Open Court, 1981).

Kierkegaard, Soren. *Concluding Unscientific Postscript to Philosophical Fragments*, tr. and ed. Howard V. Hong and Edna H. Hong (N.J.: Princeton University Press, 1992).

———. *Fear and Trembling* and *Repetition*, ed. and tr. Howard V. Hong and Edna H. Hong (N.J.: Princeton University Press, 1971).

———. *Philosophical Fragments*, tr. and ed. Howard V. Hong and Edna H. Hong (N.J.: Princeton University Press, 1985).

———. *The Concept of Irony*, tr. and ed. Howard V. Hong and Edna H. Hong (N.J.: Princeton University Press, 1989).

Kristeva, Julia. *Revolution in Poetic Language*, tr. Margaret Waller (New York: Columbia University Press, 1984).

Lowenthal, Leo. "Recollections of Adorno," *Telos* no. 61 (Fall 1984).

Lukács, Georg. *History and Class Consciousness: Studies in Marxist Dialectics*, tr. Rodney Livingstone (Cambridge, Mass.: MIT Press, 1971).

Lyotard, Jean-Francois. *Libidinal Economy*, tr. Iain Hamilton Grant (Indianapolis: Indiana University Press, 1993).

Mackey, Louis. "The Loss of the World in Kierkegaard's Ethics," *The Review of Metaphysics*, Vol. XV, no. 4 (June 1962).

Marcuse, Herbert. *Hegel's Ontology and the Theory of Historicity*, tr. Seyla Benhabib (Cambridge, Mass.: MIT Press, 1987).

———. *One-Dimensional Man* (Boston: Beacon Paperback, 1964).

———. *Studies in Critical Philosophy*, tr. Joris De Bres (Boston: Beacon Press, 1972).

Marx, Karl. *The Communist Manifesto* (With Friedrich Engels), tr. Paul M. Sweezy (New York: Monthly Review Press, 1954).

———. *The Economic and Philosophic Manuscripts of 1844*, ed. Dirk J. Struik, tr. Martin Milligan (New York: International Publishers, 1964).

———. *The German Ideology*, ed. C. J. Arthur (New York: International Publishers, 1993).

———. "The Eighteenth Brumaire of Louis Bonaparte," in *The Marx-Engels Reader* (2nd ed.), ed. Robert C. Tucker (New York: W. W. Norton and Co., 1978).

McBride, William L. *Sartre's Political Theory* (Bloomington: Indiana University Press, 1991).

McCulloch, Gregory. *Using Sartre* (London: Routledge, 1994).

Natanson, Maurice. *Edmund Husserl: Philosopher of Infinite Tasks* (Evanston, Ill.: Northwestern University, 1973).

Pippin, Robert. *Modernism as a Philosophical Problem* (Oxford: Blackwell, 1999).

Rauch, Leo and Sherman, David. *Hegel's Phenomenology of Self-Consciousness* (New York: SUNY Press, 1999).

Rose, Gillian. *Mourning Becomes the Law: Philosophy and Representation* (New York: Cambridge University Press, 1996).

Rybalka, Michel et al. "An Interview with Jean-Paul Sartre," in *The Philosophy of Jean-Paul Sartre*, ed. Paul Arthur Schilpp (La Salle, Ill.: Open Court, 1981).

Santoni, Ronald E. *Bad Faith, Good Faith, and Authenticity in Sartre's Early Philosophy* (Philadelphia: Temple University, 1995).

Sartre, Jean-Paul. *Anti-Semite and Jew*, tr. George J. Becker (New York: Schocken Books, 1974).

———. *Being and Nothingness: An Essay in Phenomenological Ontology*, tr. Hazel E. Barnes (New York: Washington Square Press, 1956).

———. *Critique of Dialectical Reason: Theory of Practical Ensembles* (vol. 1), tr. Alan Sheridan-Smith (London: Verso, 1991).

———. *Nausea*, tr. Lloyd Alexander (NewYork: New Directions, 1964).

———. *Notebook for an Ethics*, tr. David Pellauer (Chicago: University of Chicago Press, 1992).

———. *Search for a Method*, tr. Hazel E. Barnes (New York: Random House, 1968).

———. *The Emotions: Outline of a Theory*, tr. Bernard Frechtman (New York: Citadel, 1975).

———. *Transcendence of the Ego*, tr. Forest Williams and Robert Kirkpatrick (New York: Hill and Wang, 1990).

———. *Truth and Existence*, tr. Adrian van den Hoven, ed. Ronald Aronson (Chicago: The University of Chicago Press, 1992).

———. "Consciousness of Self and Knowledge of Self," tr. N. Lawrence and L. Lawrence, in *Readings in Existential Phenomenology*, ed. N. Lawrence and D. O'Connor (Englewood Cliffs, N.J.: Prentice-Hall, 1967).

———. "Existentialism Is a Humanism," in *Existentialism and Human Emotions*, tr. Bernard Frechtman (New York: Philosophical Library, 1957).

———. "Kierkegaard: The Singular Universal," in *Between Existentialism and Marxism*, tr. John Mathews (New York: Morrow Quill Paperbacks, 1974).

———. "Materialism and Revolution," in *Literary and Philosophical Essays*, tr. Annette Michelson (New York: Criterion Books, 1955).

———. "The Itinerary of a Thought," in *Between Existentialism and Marxism*, tr. John Mathews (New York: William Morrow and Co., 1979).

———. "The Wall," in *The Wall and Other Short Stories*, tr. Lloyd Alexander (New York: New Directions, 1975).

Sherman, David. "Adorno's Kierkegaardian Debt," *Philosophy & Social Criticism*, 27(1): 77–106 (2001).

———. "Camus's Meursault and Sartrian Irresponsibility," *Philosophy and Literature* 19(1): 60–77 (April 1995).

———. "The Ontological Need: Positing Subjectivity and Resistance in Hardt and Negri's Empire," *Telos* no. 128 (Summer 2004).

Solomon, Robert C. *Dark Feelings, Grim Thoughts: Experience and Reflection in Camus and Sartre* (New York: Oxford University Press, 2006).

———. *In the Spirit of Hegel* (New York: Oxford University Press, 1983).

Theunissen, Michael. *The Other: Studies in the Social Ontology of Husserl, Heidegger, Sartre, and Buber*, tr. Christopher Macann (Cambridge, Mass.: MIT Press, 1986).

Visker, Rudi. *Michel Foucault: Genealogy as Critique*, tr. Chris Turner (London: Verso, 1995).

Wellmer, Albrecht. "The Dialectic of Modernism and Postmodernism: The Critique of Reason since Adorno," in *The Persistence of Modernity: Essays on Aesthetics, Ethics, and Postmodernism*, tr. David Midgley (Cambridge, Mass.: MIT Press, 1993).

Whitebook, Joel. *Perversion and Utopia: A Study in Psychoanalysis and Critical Theory* (Cambridge, Mass.: MIT Press, 1995).

Wiggershaus, Rolf. *The Frankfurt School: Its History, Theories and Political Significance*, tr. Michael Robertson (Cambridge, Mass: MIT Press, 1995).

Wilder, Kathleen V. *The Bodily Nature of Consciousness: Sartre and Contemporary Philosophy of Mind* (Ithaca, New York: Cornell University Press, 1997).

Zizek, Slavoj. *The Ticklish Subject: The Absent Centre of Political Ontology* (London: Verso, 1999).

Index